Double Science is no trouble with CGP!

This chunky CGP book explains everything you'll need to do brilliantly in WJEC Double Award GCSE Science — whether you're taking Higher or Foundation! All the Higher Level material is clearly marked, so it's easy to see exactly what you need to revise.

We've even included exam practice questions on every page (with answers at the back), so you can test yourself as you go along. There's no better way to master the whole course!

How to access your free Online Edition

This book includes a free Online Edition to read on your PC, Mac or tablet.
To access it, just go to **cgpbooks.co.uk/extras** and enter this code...

1749 9016 6012 8166

By the way, this code only works for one person. If somebody else has used
this book before you, they might have already claimed the Online Edition.

CGP — still the best! ☺

Our sole aim here at CGP is to produce the highest quality books —
carefully written, immaculately presented and dangerously close to being funny.

Then we work our socks off to get them out to you
— at the cheapest possible prices.

Contents

Higher

This book covers both Foundation and Higher material.
We've clearly marked Higher-only material in brackets like this one.

Published by CGP.
From original material by Richard Parsons.

Editors: Luke Bennett, Laura Collins, Katherine Faudemer, Daniel Fielding, Emily Garrett, Sharon Keeley-Holden, Duncan Lindsay, Caroline Purvis, Hannah Taylor, Hayley Thompson, Charlotte Whiteley

Contributors: Paddy Gannon, Ann Shires

ISBN: 978 1 78908 081 0

Graph to show atmospheric CO_2 concentration and global temperature on page 85 based on data by EPICA community members 2004 and Siegenthaler et al 2005.

Traffic signs on page 210 © Crown Copyright. Contains public sector information licensed under the Open Government Licence v3.0.
https://www.nationalarchives.gov.uk/doc/open-government-licence/version/3/

Page 223 contains public sector information licensed under the Open Government Licence v3.0.
http://www.nationalarchives.gov.uk/doc/open-government-licence/version/3/

With thanks to Barrie Crowther, Mark Edwards, Mary Falkner, Emily Forsberg, Glenn Rogers, Ann Shires, Karen Wells and Sarah Williams for the proofreading.

With thanks to Emily Smith for the copyright research.

Printed by Elanders Ltd, Newcastle upon Tyne.
Clipart from Corel®
Illustrations by: Sandy Gardner Artist, email sandy@sandygardner.co.uk

What to Expect in the Exams

Before you get cracking with your revision, here's a handy guide to what you'll have to face in the exams — and the special features of this book that we've included especially to help you. You're welcome.

① Topics are Covered in *Different Papers*

For WJEC GCSE Science Double Award, you'll sit six exam papers.

Paper	Time	No. of marks	Units covered
Unit 1	1 hr 15 mins	60	1a, 1b and 1c
Unit 2	1 hr 15 mins	60	2a, 2b, 2c and 2d
Unit 3	1 hr 15 mins	60	3a, 3b and 3c
Unit 4	1 hr 15 mins	60	4a, 4b, 4c and 4d
Unit 5	1 hr 15 mins	60	5a, 5b, 5c and 5d
Unit 6	1 hr 15 mins	60	6a and 6b

You're expected to know the basic concepts in each of the sciences for both exams. So, for example, in the Chemistry Unit 5 paper you could be expected to know some of the basics from Chemistry Unit 2.

② There are Different *Question Types*

In each exam, you'll be expected to answer a mixture of structured questions, questions that have short, closed answers as well as open response questions.

For some open response questions, you'll be marked on the overall quality of your answer, not just its scientific content. So, always make sure...

- You answer the question fully.
- You include detailed, relevant information.
- Your answer is clear and has a logical structure.
- You've checked your spelling, punctuation and grammar.

③ You'll be *Tested* on your *Maths...*

At least 20% of the total marks for GCSE Science Double Award will come from questions that test your maths skills. For these questions, always remember to:

EXAMPLE:

Look out for these worked examples in this book — they show you maths skills you'll need in the exam.

- Show your working — you could get marks for this, even if your final answer's wrong.
- Check that the units of your answer are the same as the ones they asked for in the question.
- Make sure your answer is given to an appropriate number of significant figures.

④ *...and on your Practical Skills*

Whenever one of the specified practicals crops up in this book, it's marked up like this...

...and there's a whole section on Practical Skills on pages 225-233.

- GCSE Science Double Award contains 21 specified practicals that you'll do during the course. You might be asked about these, and the practical skills involved in them, in the exams.

- At least 15% of the total marks will be for questions that test your understanding of practical skills.

- For example, you might be asked to comment on the design of an experiment (the apparatus and method), make predictions, analyse or interpret results... Pretty much anything to do with planning and carrying out the investigations.

You'll also do two practical assessments in school. In each assessment you'll have to carry out an experiment to collect some results and then analyse and evaluate your results.

⑤ You'll need to know about *Working Scientifically*

Working Scientifically is all about how science is applied in the outside world by real scientists.

For example, you might be asked about ways that scientists communicate an idea to get their point across without being biased, or about the limitations of a scientific theory.

Working Scientifically is covered on pages 2-11.

You need to think about the situation that you've been given and use all your scientific savvy to answer the question. Always read the question and any data you've been given really carefully before you start writing your answer.

The Scientific Method

This section <u>isn't</u> about how to 'do' science — but it does show you the way <u>most scientists</u> work.

Scientists Come Up With Hypotheses — Then Test Them

1) Scientists try to <u>explain</u> things. They start by <u>observing</u> something they don't understand.

2) They then come up with a <u>hypothesis</u> — a possible <u>explanation</u> for what they've observed.

3) The next step is to <u>test</u> whether the hypothesis might be <u>right or not</u>. This involves making a <u>prediction</u> based on the hypothesis and testing it by <u>gathering evidence</u> (i.e. <u>data</u>) from <u>investigations</u>. If <u>evidence</u> from <u>experiments</u> backs up a prediction, you're a step closer to figuring out if the hypothesis is true.

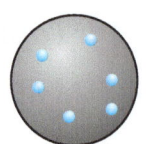

About 100 years ago, scientists hypothesised that atoms looked like this.

Several Scientists Will Test a Hypothesis

1) Normally, scientists <u>share</u> their <u>findings</u> in <u>peer-reviewed journals</u>, or at <u>conferences</u>.

2) <u>Peer review</u> is where <u>other scientists</u> check results and scientific explanations to make sure they're 'scientific' (e.g. that experiments have been done in a sensible way) <u>before</u> they're published. It helps to <u>detect false claims</u>, but it doesn't mean that findings are <u>correct</u> — just that they're not wrong in any <u>obvious</u> way.

3) Once other scientists have found out about a hypothesis, they'll start basing their <u>own predictions</u> on it and carry out their <u>own experiments</u>. They'll also try to <u>reproduce</u> the original experiments to <u>check the results</u> — and if all the experiments in the world <u>back up</u> the <u>hypothesis</u>, then scientists start to think the hypothesis is <u>true</u>.

4) However, if a scientist does an experiment that <u>doesn't fit</u> with the hypothesis (and other scientists can reproduce the results) then the hypothesis may need to be <u>modified</u> or <u>scrapped</u> altogether.

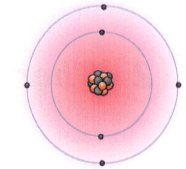

After more evidence was gathered, scientists changed their hypothesis to this.

If All the Evidence Supports a Hypothesis, It's Accepted — For Now

1) <u>Accepted hypotheses</u> are often referred to as <u>theories</u>. Our <u>currently accepted</u> theories are the ones that have survived this 'trial by evidence' — they've been <u>tested many times</u> over the years and <u>survived</u>.

2) However, theories <u>never</u> become totally indisputable <u>fact</u>. If <u>new evidence</u> comes along that <u>can't be explained</u> using the existing theory, then the hypothesising and testing is likely to <u>start all over again</u>.

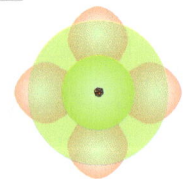

Now we think it's more like this.

Theories Can Involve Different Types of Models

1) A <u>representational model</u> is a <u>simplified description</u> or <u>picture</u> of what's going on in real life. Like all models, it can be used to <u>explain observations</u> and <u>make predictions</u>. E.g. we can use a simplified model to show the arrangement of the nucleus and electrons in an atom (see p.63). It can be used to explain trends down groups in the periodic table.

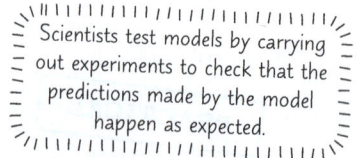

Scientists test models by carrying out experiments to check that the predictions made by the model happen as expected.

2) <u>Computational models</u> use computers to make <u>simulations</u> of complex real-life processes, such as climate change. They're used when there are a <u>lot</u> of different <u>variables</u> (factors that change) to consider, and because you can easily <u>change their design</u> to take into account <u>new data</u>.

3) All models have <u>limitations</u> on what they can <u>explain</u> or <u>predict</u>. E.g. <u>ball and stick models</u> (a type of spatial model) can be used to show how ions are arranged in an ionic compound. One of their limitations is that they <u>don't show</u> the <u>relative sizes</u> of the ions (see p.165).

I'm off to the zoo to test my hippo-thesis...

The scientific method has developed over time, and many people have helped to develop it. From Aristotle to modern day scientists, lots of people have contributed. And many more are likely to contribute in the future.

Communication & Issues Created by Science

Scientific developments can be great, but they can sometimes <u>raise more questions</u> than they answer...

It's Important to *Communicate* Scientific Discoveries to the *General Public*

Some scientific discoveries show that people should <u>change their habits</u>, or they might provide ideas that could be <u>developed</u> into new <u>technology</u>. So scientists need to <u>tell the world</u> about their discoveries.

<u>Gene technologies</u> are used in <u>genetic engineering</u> to produce <u>genetically modified crops</u>. Information about these crops needs to be communicated to <u>farmers</u> who might <u>benefit</u> from growing them and to the <u>general public</u>, so they can make <u>informed decisions</u> about the food they buy and eat.

Scientific *Evidence* can be *Presented* in a *Biased Way*

1) Reports about scientific discoveries in the <u>media</u> (e.g. newspapers or television) <u>aren't</u> peer-reviewed.

2) This means that, even though news stories are often <u>based</u> on data that has been peer-reviewed, the data might be <u>presented</u> in a way that is <u>over-simplified</u> or <u>inaccurate</u>, making it open to <u>misinterpretation</u>.

3) People who want to make a point can sometimes <u>present data</u> in a <u>biased way</u>. (Sometimes <u>without knowing</u> they're doing it.) For example, a scientist might overemphasise a relationship in the data, or a newspaper article might describe details of data <u>supporting</u> an idea without giving any evidence <u>against</u> it.

Scientific *Developments* are *Great*, but they can *Raise Issues*

Scientific <u>knowledge is increased</u> by doing experiments. And this knowledge leads to <u>scientific developments</u>, e.g. new technologies or new advice. These developments can create <u>issues</u> though. For example:

<u>Economic issues:</u> Society <u>can't</u> always <u>afford</u> to do things scientists recommend (e.g. investing in alternative energy sources) without <u>cutting back elsewhere</u>.

<u>Personal issues:</u> Some decisions will affect <u>individuals</u>. For example, someone might support <u>alternative energy</u>, but object if a <u>wind farm</u> is built next to their house.

<u>Social issues:</u> Decisions based on scientific evidence affect <u>people</u> — e.g. should fossil fuels be taxed more highly? <u>Would the effect on people's lifestyles be acceptable...</u>

<u>Environmental issues:</u> <u>Human activity</u> often affects the <u>natural environment</u>. For example, building a <u>dam</u> to generate electricity will change the <u>local habitat</u> so some species might be displaced. But it will also reduce our need for <u>fossil fuels</u>, so will help to reduce <u>climate change</u>.

Science *Can't Answer Every Question* — Especially *Ethical* Ones

1) We don't <u>understand everything</u>. We're always finding out <u>more</u>, but we'll never know <u>all</u> the answers.

2) In order to answer scientific questions, scientists need <u>data</u> to provide <u>evidence</u> for their hypotheses.

3) Some questions can't be answered <u>yet</u> because the data <u>can't</u> currently be <u>collected</u>, or because there's <u>not enough</u> data to <u>support</u> a theory.

4) <u>Eventually</u>, as we get <u>more evidence</u>, we'll answer some of the questions that <u>currently</u> can't be answered, e.g. what the impact of global warming on sea levels will be. But there will always be the "<u>Should we be doing this at all?</u>"-type questions that experiments <u>can't</u> help us to answer...

Think about <u>new drugs which can be taken to boost your 'brain power'</u>.

- Some people think they're <u>good</u> as they could improve concentration or memory. New drugs could let people think in ways beyond the powers of normal brains.

- Other people say they're <u>bad</u> — they could give you an <u>unfair advantage</u> in exams. And people might be <u>pressured</u> into taking them so that they could work more <u>effectively</u>, and for <u>longer hours</u>.

THE GAZETTE
BRAIN-BOOSTING DRUGS MAKE A MOCKERY OF EXAMS

THE POST
GENIUS PILLS TO BECOME THE NEW COFFEE

Tea to milk or milk to tea? — Totally unanswerable by science...

Science can't tell you whether or not you should do something. That's for you and society to decide. But there are tons of questions science might be able to answer, like where life came from and where my superhero socks are.

Risk

By reading this page you are agreeing to the risk of a paper cut or severe drowsiness...

Nothing is Completely Risk-Free

1) A hazard is something that could potentially cause harm.

2) All hazards have a risk attached to them — this is the chance that the hazard will cause harm.

3) The risks of some things seem pretty obvious, or we've known about them for a while, like the risk of causing acid rain by polluting the atmosphere, or of having a car accident when you're travelling in a car.

4) New technology arising from scientific advances can bring new risks, e.g. scientists are unsure whether nanoparticles that are being used in cosmetics and suncream might be harming the cells in our bodies. These risks need to be considered alongside the benefits of the technology, e.g. improved sun protection.

5) You can estimate the size of a risk based on how many times something happens in a big sample (e.g. 100 000 people) over a given period (e.g. a year). For example, you could assess the risk of a driver crashing by recording how many people in a group of 100 000 drivers crashed their cars over a year.

6) To make decisions about activities that involve hazards, we need to take into account the chance of the hazard causing harm, and how serious the consequences would be if it did. If an activity involves a hazard that's very likely to cause harm, with serious consequences if it does, it's considered high risk.

People Make Their Own Decisions About Risk

1) Not all risks have the same consequences, e.g. if you chop veg with a sharp knife you risk cutting your finger, but if you go scuba-diving you risk death. You're much more likely to cut your finger during half an hour of chopping than to die during half an hour of scuba-diving. But most people are happier to accept a higher probability of an accident if the consequences are short-lived and fairly minor.

2) People tend to be more willing to accept a risk if they choose to do something (e.g. go scuba diving), compared to having the risk imposed on them (e.g. having a nuclear power station built next door).

3) People's perception of risk (how risky they think something is) isn't always accurate. They tend to view familiar activities as low-risk and unfamiliar activities as high-risk — even if that's not the case. For example, cycling on roads is often high-risk, but many people are happy to do it because it's a familiar activity. Air travel is actually pretty safe, but a lot of people perceive it as high-risk.

4) People may underestimate the risk of things with long-term or invisible effects, e.g. using tanning beds.

Investigations Can be Hazardous

1) Hazards from science experiments might include:

- Microorganisms, e.g. some bacteria can make you ill.
- Chemicals, e.g. sulfuric acid can burn your skin and alcohols catch fire easily.
- Fire, e.g. an unattended Bunsen burner is a fire hazard.
- Electricity, e.g. faulty electrical equipment could give you a shock.

Hmm... Where did my bacteria sample go?

2) Part of planning an investigation is making sure that it's safe.

3) You should always make sure that you identify all the hazards that you might encounter. Then you should think of ways of reducing the risks from the hazards you've identified. For example:

- If you're working with sulfuric acid, always wear gloves and safety goggles. This will reduce the risk of the acid coming into contact with your skin and eyes.
- If you're using a Bunsen burner, stand it on a heatproof mat. This will reduce the risk of starting a fire.

You can find out about potential hazards by looking in textbooks, doing some Internet research, or asking your teacher.

Not revising — an unacceptable exam hazard...

The world's a dangerous place, but if you can recognise hazards, decide how to reduce their risks, and be happy to accept some risks, you can still have fun. Just maybe don't go skydiving with a great white shark on Friday 13th.

Designing Investigations

Dig out your lab coat and dust down your badly-scratched safety goggles... it's <u>investigation time</u>.

Investigations Produce Evidence to Support or Disprove a Hypothesis

1) Scientists <u>observe</u> things and come up with <u>hypotheses</u> to explain them (see p.2).
   You need to be able to do the same. For example:

   > <u>Observation</u>: People have big feet and spots. <u>Hypothesis</u>: Having big feet causes spots.

2) To <u>determine</u> whether or not a hypothesis is <u>right</u>, you need to do an <u>investigation</u> to gather evidence. To do this, you need to use your hypothesis to make a <u>prediction</u> — something you think <u>will happen</u> that you can test. E.g. people who have bigger feet will have more spots.

3) Investigations are used to see if there are <u>patterns</u> or <u>relationships</u> between <u>two variables</u>, e.g. to see if there's a pattern or relationship between the variables 'number of spots' and 'size of feet'.

Evidence Needs to be Repeatable, Reproducible and Valid

1) <u>Repeatable</u> means that if the <u>same person</u> does an experiment again using the <u>same methods</u> and equipment, they'll get <u>similar results</u>.

Investigations include experiments and studies.

2) <u>Reproducible</u> means that if <u>someone else</u> does the experiment, or a <u>different</u> method or piece of equipment is used, the results will still be <u>similar</u>.

3) If data is <u>repeatable</u> and <u>reproducible</u>, it's <u>reliable</u> and scientists are more likely to <u>have confidence</u> in it.

4) <u>Valid results</u> are both repeatable and reproducible AND they <u>answer the original question</u>. They come from experiments that were designed to be a **FAIR TEST**...

To Make an Investigation a Fair Test You Have to Control the Variables

1) In a lab experiment you usually <u>change one variable</u> and <u>measure</u> how it affects <u>another variable</u>.

2) To make it a fair test, <u>everything else</u> that could affect the results should <u>stay the same</u> — otherwise you can't tell if the thing you're changing is causing the results or not.

3) The variable you **CHANGE** is called the **INDEPENDENT** variable.

4) The variable you **MEASURE** when you change the independent variable is the **DEPENDENT** variable.

5) The variables that you **KEEP THE SAME** are called **CONTROL** variables.

   > You could find how <u>temperature</u> affects the rate of an <u>enzyme-controlled reaction</u>. The <u>independent variable</u> is the <u>temperature</u>. The <u>dependent variable</u> is the <u>rate of reaction</u>. <u>Control variables</u> include the <u>concentration</u> and <u>volume</u> of reactants, <u>pH</u>, the <u>time period</u> you measure, etc.

6) Because you can't always control all the variables, you often need to use a <u>control experiment</u>. This is an experiment that's kept under the <u>same conditions</u> as the rest of the investigation, but <u>doesn't</u> have anything <u>done</u> to it. This is so that you can see what happens when you don't change anything at all.

The Bigger the Sample Size the Better

1) Data based on <u>small samples</u> isn't as good as data based on large samples. A sample should <u>represent</u> the <u>whole population</u> (i.e. it should share as many of the characteristics in the population as possible) — a small sample can't do that as well. It's also harder to spot <u>anomalies</u> if your sample size is too small.

2) The <u>bigger</u> the sample size the <u>better</u>, but scientists have to be <u>realistic</u> when choosing how big. For example, if you were studying the effects of <u>living</u> near a <u>nuclear power plant</u>, it'd be great to study <u>everyone</u> who lived near a nuclear power plant (a huge sample), but it'd take ages and cost a bomb. It's more realistic to study a thousand people, with a range of ages, gender, and race.

This is no high street survey — it's a designer investigation...

Not only do you need to be able to plan your own investigations, you should also be able to look at someone else's plan and decide whether or not it needs improving. Those examiners aren't half demanding.

Collecting Data

You've designed the perfect investigation — now it's time to get your hands mucky and <u>collect some data</u>.

Your Data Should be Repeatable, Reproducible, Accurate and Precise

1) To <u>check repeatability</u> you need to <u>repeat</u> the readings and check that the results are similar. You need to repeat each reading at least <u>three times</u>.

2) To make sure your results are <u>reproducible</u> you can cross check them by taking a <u>second set of readings</u> with <u>another instrument</u> (or a <u>different observer</u>).

3) Your data also needs to be ACCURATE. Really accurate results are those that are <u>really close</u> to the <u>true answer</u>. The accuracy of your results usually depends on your <u>method</u> — you need to make sure you're measuring the right thing and that you don't <u>miss anything</u> that should be included in the measurements. E.g. estimating the <u>amount of gas</u> released from a reaction by <u>counting the bubbles</u> isn't very accurate because you might <u>miss</u> some of the bubbles and they might have different <u>volumes</u>. It's <u>more accurate</u> to measure the volume of gas released using a <u>gas syringe</u> (see p.88).

4) Your data also needs to be PRECISE. Precise results are ones where the data is <u>all really close</u> to the <u>mean</u> (average) of your repeated results (i.e. not spread out).

Brian's result was a curate.

Repeat	Data set 1	Data set 2
1	12	11
2	14	17
3	13	14
Mean	13	14

Data set 1 is more precise than data set 2.

Your Equipment has to be Right for the Job

1) The measuring equipment you use has to be <u>sensitive enough</u> to measure the changes you're looking for. For example, if you need to measure changes of 1 cm³ you need to use a measuring cylinder or burette that can measure in 1 cm³ steps — it'd be no good trying with one that only measures 10 cm³ steps.

2) The <u>smallest change</u> a measuring instrument can <u>detect</u> is called its RESOLUTION. E.g. some mass balances have a resolution of 1 g, some have a resolution of 0.1 g, and some are even more sensitive.

3) Also, equipment needs to be <u>calibrated</u> by measuring a known value. If there's a <u>difference</u> between the <u>measured</u> and <u>known value</u>, you can use this to correct the inaccuracy of the equipment.

You Need to Look out for Errors and Anomalous Results

1) The results of your experiment will always <u>vary a bit</u> because of RANDOM ERRORS — unpredictable differences caused by things like <u>human errors</u> in <u>measuring</u>. The errors when you make a reading from a ruler are random. You have to estimate or round the distance when it's between two marks — so sometimes your figure will be a bit above the real one, and sometimes it will be a bit below.

2) You can <u>reduce</u> the effect of random errors by taking <u>repeat readings</u> and finding the <u>mean</u>. This will make your results <u>more precise</u>.

3) If a measurement is wrong by the <u>same amount every time</u>, it's called a SYSTEMATIC ERROR. For example, if you measured from the very end of your ruler instead of from the 0 cm mark every time, all your measurements would be a bit small. Repeating the experiment in the exact same way and calculating a mean <u>won't</u> correct a systematic error.

If there's no systematic error, then doing repeats and calculating a mean can make your results more accurate.

4) Just to make things more complicated, if a systematic error is caused by using <u>equipment</u> that <u>isn't zeroed properly</u>, it's called a ZERO ERROR. For example, if a mass balance always reads 1 gram before you put anything on it, all your measurements will be 1 gram too heavy.

5) You can <u>compensate</u> for some systematic errors if you know about them though, e.g. if your mass balance always reads 1 gram before you put anything on it you can subtract 1 gram from all your results.

6) Sometimes you get a result that <u>doesn't fit in</u> with the rest at all. This is called an ANOMALOUS RESULT. You should investigate it and try to <u>work out what happened</u>. If you can work out what happened (e.g. you measured something totally wrong) you can <u>ignore</u> it when processing your results.

Watch what you say to that mass balance — it's very sensitive...

Weirdly, data can be really precise but not very accurate. For example, a fancy piece of lab equipment might give results that are really precise, but if it's not been calibrated properly those results won't be accurate.

Working Scientifically

Processing and Presenting Data

Processing your data means doing some calculations with it to make it more useful. Once you've done that, you can present your results in a nice chart or graph to help you spot any patterns in your data.

Data Needs to be Organised

Tables are dead useful for organising data. When you draw a table use a ruler and make sure each column has a heading (including the units).

You Might Have to Process Your Data

1) When you've done repeats of an experiment you should always calculate the mean (a type of average). To do this add together all the data values and divide by the total number of values in the sample.

2) You might also need to calculate the range (how spread out the data is). To do this find the largest number and subtract the smallest number from it.

Ignore anomalous results when calculating these.

EXAMPLE: The results of an experiment to find the volume of gas produced in an enzyme-controlled reaction are shown below. Calculate the mean volume and the range.

Repeat 1 (cm³)	Repeat 2 (cm³)	Repeat 3 (cm³)	Mean (cm³)	Range (cm³)
28	37	32	(28 + 37 + 32) ÷ 3 = 32	37 − 28 = 9

3) You might also need to calculate the median or mode (two more types of average). To calculate the median, put all your data in numerical order — the median is the middle value. The number that appears most often in a data set is the mode.

If you have an even number of values, the median is halfway between the middle two values.

> E.g. If you have the data set: 1 2 1 1 3 4 2
> The median is: 1 1 1 **2** 2 3 4. The mode is **1** because 1 appears most often.

Higher

Round to the Lowest Number of Significant Figures

The first significant figure of a number is the first digit that's not zero. The second and third significant figures come straight after (even if they're zeros). You should be aware of significant figures in calculations.

1) In any calculation, you should round the answer to the lowest number of significant figures (s.f.) given.

2) Remember to write down how many significant figures you've rounded to after your answer.

3) If your calculation has multiple steps, only round the final answer, or it won't be as accurate.

EXAMPLE: The mass of a solid is 0.24 g and its volume is 0.715 cm³. Calculate the density of the solid.

Density = 0.24 g ÷ 0.715 cm³ = 0.33566... = 0.34 g/cm³ (2 s.f.) — *Final answer should be rounded to 2 s.f.*

2 s.f.   3 s.f.

If Your Data Comes in Categories, Present It in a Bar Chart

1) If the independent variable is categoric (comes in distinct categories, e.g. flower colour, blood group) you should use a bar chart to display the data.

2) You also use them if the independent variable is discrete (the data can be counted in chunks, where there's no in-between value, e.g. number of protons is discrete because you can't have half a proton).

3) There are some golden rules you need to follow for drawing bar charts:

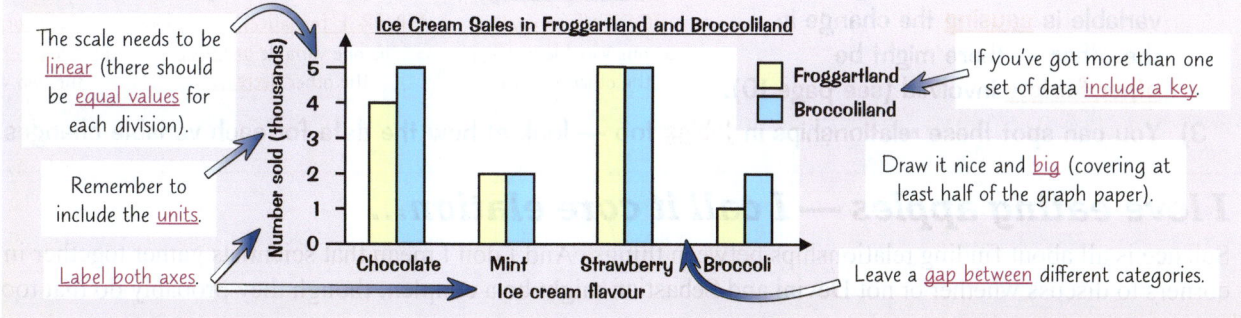

The scale needs to be linear (there should be equal values for each division).

Remember to include the units.

Label both axes.

If you've got more than one set of data include a key.

Draw it nice and big (covering at least half of the graph paper).

Leave a gap between different categories.

If Your Data is Continuous, Plot a Graph

If both variables are continuous (numerical data that can have any value within a range, e.g. length, volume, temperature) you should use a graph to display the data.

Here are the rules for plotting points on a graph:

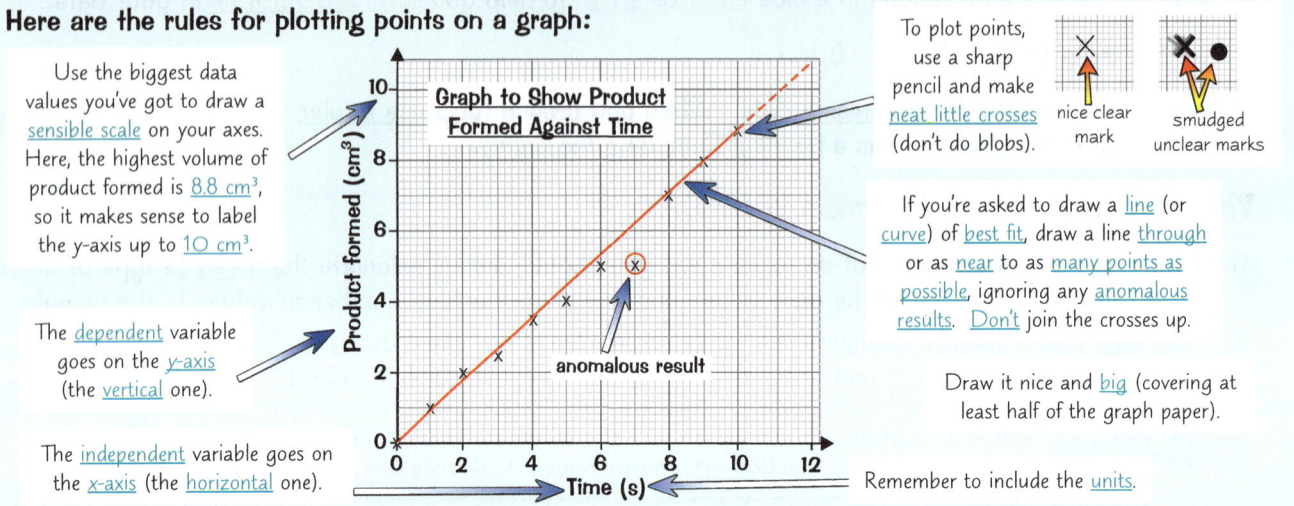

Use the biggest data values you've got to draw a sensible scale on your axes. Here, the highest volume of product formed is 8.8 cm³, so it makes sense to label the y-axis up to 10 cm³.

The dependent variable goes on the y-axis (the vertical one).

The independent variable goes on the x-axis (the horizontal one).

To plot points, use a sharp pencil and make neat little crosses (don't do blobs). nice clear mark / smudged unclear marks

If you're asked to draw a line (or curve) of best fit, draw a line through or as near to as many points as possible, ignoring any anomalous results. Don't join the crosses up.

Draw it nice and big (covering at least half of the graph paper).

Remember to include the units.

Graphs Can Give You Information About Your Data

1) The gradient (slope) of a graph tells you how quickly the dependent variable changes if you change the independent variable.

$$\text{gradient} = \frac{\text{change in } y}{\text{change in } x}$$

This graph shows the volume of gas produced in a reaction against time. The graph is linear (it's a straight line graph), so you can simply calculate the gradient of the line to find out the rate of reaction.

1) To calculate the gradient, pick two points on the line that are easy to read and a good distance apart.

2) Draw a line down from one of the points and a line across from the other to make a triangle. The line drawn down the side of the triangle is the change in y and the line across the bottom is the change in x.

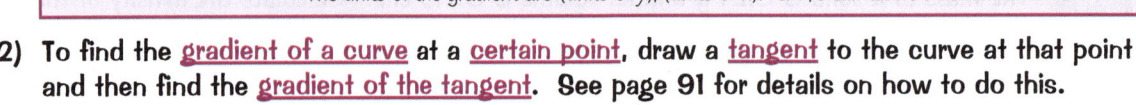

Change in y = 6.8 − 2.0 = 4.8 cm³   Change in x = 5.2 − 1.6 = 3.6 s

$$\text{Rate} = \text{gradient} = \frac{\text{change in } y}{\text{change in } x} = \frac{4.8 \text{ cm}^3}{3.6 \text{ s}} = 1.3 \text{ cm}^3/\text{s}$$

You can use this method to calculate other rates from a graph, not just the rate of a reaction. Just remember that a rate is how much something changes over time, so x needs to be the time.

The units of the gradient are (units of y)/(units of x). cm³/s can also be written as cm³s⁻¹.

2) To find the gradient of a curve at a certain point, draw a tangent to the curve at that point and then find the gradient of the tangent. See page 91 for details on how to do this.

3) The intercept of a graph is where the line of best fit crosses one of the axes. The x-intercept is where the line of best fit crosses the x-axis and the y-intercept is where it crosses the y-axis.

Graphs Show the Relationship Between Two Variables

1) You can get three types of correlation (relationship) between variables:

2) Just because there's correlation, it doesn't mean the change in one variable is causing the change in the other — there might be other factors involved (see page 10).

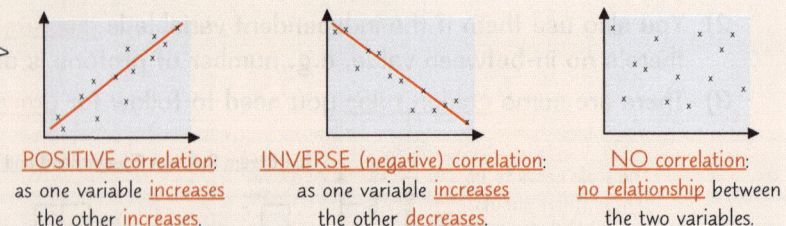

POSITIVE correlation: as one variable increases the other increases.

INVERSE (negative) correlation: as one variable increases the other decreases.

NO correlation: no relationship between the two variables.

3) You can spot these relationships in tables too — look at how the data for each variable changes.

I love eating apples — I call it core elation...

Science is all about finding relationships between things. And I don't mean that scientists gather together in corners to discuss whether or not Devini and Sebastian might be a couple... though they probably do that too.

Units and Equations

Graphs and maths skills are all very well, but the numbers don't mean much if you can't get the units right.

S.I. Units Are Used All Round the World

1) It wouldn't be all that useful if I defined volume in terms of bath tubs, you defined it in terms of egg-cups and my pal Sarwat defined it in terms of balloons — we'd never be able to compare our data.

2) To stop this happening, scientists have come up with a set of standard units, called S.I. units, that all scientists use to measure their data. Here are some S.I. units you'll see in GCSE Science:

Quantity	S.I. Base Unit
mass	kilogram, kg
length	metre, m
time	second, s
amount of a substance	mole, mol
temperature	kelvin, K

Scaling Prefixes Can Be Used for *Large* and *Small* Quantities

1) Quantities come in a huge range of sizes. For example, the volume of a swimming pool might be around 2 000 000 000 cm³, while the volume of a cup is around 250 cm³.

2) To make the size of numbers more manageable, larger or smaller units are used. These are the S.I. base unit (e.g. metres) with a prefix in front:

prefix	tera (T)	giga (G)	mega (M)	kilo (k)	deci (d)	centi (c)	milli (m)	micro (μ)	nano (n)
multiple of unit	10^{12}	10^{9}	1 000 000 (10^{6})	1000	0.1	0.01	0.001	0.000001 (10^{-6})	10^{-9}

3) These prefixes tell you how much bigger or smaller a unit is than the base unit. So one kilometre is one thousand metres.

The conversion factor is the number of times the smaller unit goes into the larger unit.

4) To swap from one unit to another, all you need to know is what number you have to divide or multiply by to get from the original unit to the new unit — this is called the conversion factor.

- To go from a bigger unit (like m) to a smaller unit (like cm), you multiply by the conversion factor.
- To go from a smaller unit (like g) to a bigger unit (like kg), you divide by the conversion factor.

5) Here are some conversions that'll be useful for GCSE Science:

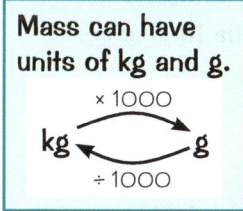

Mass can have units of kg and g.

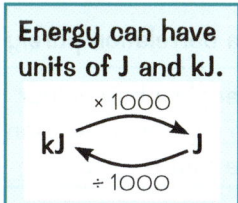

Energy can have units of J and kJ.

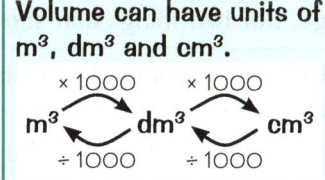

Volume can have units of m³, dm³ and cm³.

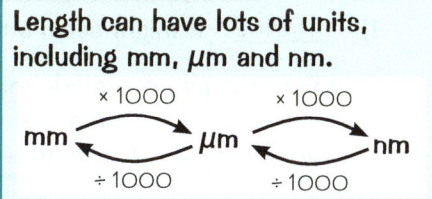

Length can have lots of units, including mm, μm and nm.

Always Check The Values Used in *Equations* Have the *Right Units*

1) Formulas and equations show relationships between variables.

2) To rearrange an equation, make sure that whatever you do to one side of the equation you also do to the other side.

You can find the speed of a wave using the equation: wave speed = frequency × wavelength. You can rearrange this equation to find the frequency by dividing each side by wavelength to give: frequency = wave speed ÷ wavelength.

3) To use a formula, you need to know the values of all but one of the variables. Substitute the values you do know into the formula, and do the calculation to work out the final variable.

4) Always make sure the values you put into an equation or formula have the right units. For example, you might have done an experiment to find the speed of a trolley. The distance the trolley travels will probably have been measured in cm, but the equation to find speed uses distance in m. So you'll have to convert your distance from cm to m before you put it into the equation.

5) To make sure your units are correct, it can help to write down the units on each line of your calculation.

I wasn't sure I liked units, but now I'm converted...

It's easy to get in a muddle when converting between units, but there's a handy way to check you've done it right. If you're moving from a smaller unit to a larger unit (e.g. g to kg) the number should get smaller, and vice versa.

Drawing Conclusions

Congratulations — you're nearly at the end of a gruelling investigation, time to <u>draw conclusions</u>.

You Can *Only Conclude* What the Data Shows and *NO MORE*

1) Drawing conclusions might seem pretty straightforward — you just <u>look at your data</u> and <u>say what pattern or relationship you see</u> between the dependent and independent variables.

The table on the right shows the rate of a reaction in the presence of two <u>different</u> catalysts:

Catalyst	Rate of reaction (cm³/s)
A	13.5
B	19.5
No catalyst	5.5

<u>CONCLUSION</u>:
Catalyst <u>B</u> makes <u>this reaction</u> go faster than catalyst A.

2) But you've got to be really careful that your conclusion <u>matches the data</u> you've got and <u>doesn't go any further</u>.

You <u>can't</u> conclude that catalyst B increases the rate of <u>any other reaction</u> more than catalyst A — the results might be completely different.

3) You also need to be able to <u>use your results</u> to <u>justify your conclusion</u> (i.e. back up your conclusion with some specific data).

The rate of this reaction was <u>6 cm³/s faster</u> using catalyst B compared with catalyst A.

4) When writing a conclusion you need to <u>refer back</u> to the original hypothesis and say whether the data <u>supports it</u> or not:

The hypothesis for this experiment might have been that catalyst B would make the reaction go <u>quicker</u> than catalyst A. If so, the data <u>supports</u> the hypothesis.

Correlation *DOES NOT* Mean *Cause*

If two things are correlated (i.e. there's a relationship between them) it <u>doesn't</u> necessarily mean a change in one variable is <u>causing</u> the change in the other — this is <u>REALLY IMPORTANT</u> — <u>DON'T FORGET IT</u>. There are <u>three possible reasons</u> for a correlation:

1) <u>CHANCE</u>: It might seem strange, but two things can show a correlation purely due to <u>chance</u>.

For example, one study might find a correlation between people's hair colour and how good they are at frisbee. But other scientists <u>don't</u> get a correlation when they investigate it — the results of the first study are just a <u>fluke</u>.

2) <u>LINKED BY A 3RD VARIABLE</u>: A lot of the time it may <u>look</u> as if a change in one variable is causing a change in the other, but it <u>isn't</u> — a <u>third variable links</u> the two things.

For example, there's a correlation between <u>water temperature</u> and <u>shark attacks</u>. This isn't because warmer water makes sharks crazy. Instead, they're linked by a third variable — the <u>number of people swimming</u> (more people swim when the water's hotter, and with more people in the water you get more shark attacks).

3) <u>CAUSE</u>: Sometimes a change in one variable does <u>cause</u> a change in the other. You can only conclude that a correlation is due to cause when you've <u>controlled all the variables</u> that could, just could, be affecting the result.

For example, there's a correlation between <u>smoking</u> and <u>lung cancer</u>. This is because chemicals in tobacco smoke cause lung cancer. This conclusion was only made once <u>other variables</u> (such as age and exposure to other things that cause cancer) had been <u>controlled</u> and shown <u>not</u> to affect people's risk of getting lung cancer.

I conclude that this page is a bit dull...

...although, just because I find it dull doesn't mean that I can conclude it's dull (you might think it's the most interesting thing since that kid got his head stuck in the railings near school). In the exams you could be given a conclusion and asked whether some data supports it — so make sure you understand how far conclusions can go.

Uncertainties and Evaluations

Hurrah! The end of another investigation. Well, now you have to work out all the things you did wrong.

Uncertainty *is the Amount of Error Your Measurements Might Have*

1) When you repeat a measurement, you often get a slightly different figure each time you do it due to random error. This means that each result has some uncertainty to it.

2) The measurements you make will also have some uncertainty in them due to limits in the resolution of the equipment you use (see page 6).

3) This all means that the mean of a set of results will also have some uncertainty to it. You can calculate the uncertainty of a mean result using the equation:

4) The larger the range, the less precise your results are and the more uncertainty there will be in your results. Uncertainties are shown using the '±' symbol.

The range is the largest value minus the smallest value (p.7).

$$\text{uncertainty} = \frac{\text{range}}{2}$$

 **EXAMPLE:** The table below shows the results of a respiration experiment to determine the volume of carbon dioxide produced. Calculate the uncertainty of the mean.

Repeat	1	2	3	mean
Volume of CO_2 produced (cm^3)	20.1	19.8	20.0	20.0

1) First work out the range:
Range = 20.1 − 19.8
= 0.300 cm^3

2) Use the range to find the uncertainty:
Uncertainty = range ÷ 2 = 0.300 ÷ 2 = 0.150 cm^3. So the uncertainty of the mean = 20.0 ± 0.150 cm^3

5) Measuring a greater amount of something helps to reduce uncertainty. For example, in a rate of reaction experiment, measuring the amount of product formed over a longer period compared to a shorter period will reduce the percentage uncertainty in your results.

Evaluations — *Describe How it Could be Improved*

An evaluation is a critical analysis of the whole investigation.

1) You should comment on the method — was it valid? Did you control all the other variables to make it a fair test?

2) Comment on the quality of the results — was there enough evidence to reach a valid conclusion? Were the results repeatable, reproducible, accurate and precise?

3) Were there any anomalous results? If there were none then say so. If there were any, try to explain them — were they caused by errors in measurement? Were there any other variables that could have affected the results? You should comment on the level of uncertainty in your results too.

4) All this analysis will allow you to say how confident you are that your conclusion is right.

5) Then you can suggest any changes to the method that would improve the quality of the results, so that you could have more confidence in your conclusion. For example, you might suggest changing the way you controlled a variable, or increasing the number of measurements you took. Taking more measurements at narrower intervals could give you a more accurate result. For example:

Enzymes have an optimum temperature (a temperature at which they work best). Say you do an experiment to find an enzyme's optimum temperature and take measurements at 10 °C, 20 °C, 30 °C, 40 °C and 50 °C. The results of this experiment tell you the optimum is 40 °C. You could then repeat the experiment, taking more measurements around 40 °C to a get a more accurate value for the optimum.

6) You could also make more predictions based on your conclusion, then further experiments could be carried out to test them.

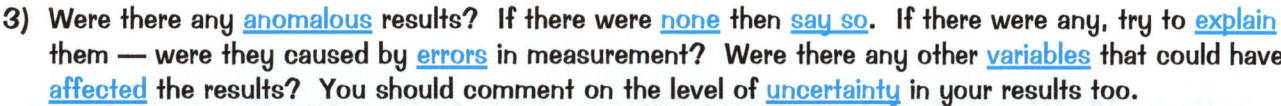
When suggesting improvements to the investigation, always make sure that you say why you think this would make the results better.

Evaluation — next time, I'll make sure I don't burn the lab down...

So there you have it — Working Scientifically. Make sure you know this stuff like the back of your hand. It's not just in the lab that you'll need to know how to work scientifically. You can be asked about it in the exams as well.

Cells

Biology is all about <u>living stuff</u>. And living stuff contains <u>cells</u>. So let's make a <u>start</u> with cells...

All Living Things are Made of Cells

1) <u>Cells</u> are the <u>basic structures</u> that make up <u>living organisms</u> — they're like the <u>building blocks of life</u>.
2) Complex organisms like <u>plants</u> and <u>animals</u> are <u>multicellular</u> — they're made up of <u>lots and lots</u> of cells.

Plant and Animal Cells have Similarities and Differences

The different parts of a cell are called <u>subcellular structures</u>.
Most <u>animal</u> cells have the following subcellular structures — make sure you know them all:

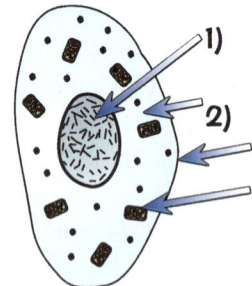

1) <u>Nucleus</u> — contains <u>chromosomes</u> (see p.132). These carry the <u>genetic information</u> that controls the activities of the cell.
2) <u>Cytoplasm</u> — gel-like substance where most of the <u>chemical reactions</u> happen.
3) <u>Cell membrane</u> — holds the cell together and controls what goes <u>in</u> and <u>out</u> of it.
4) <u>Mitochondria</u> — these are where most of the reactions for <u>aerobic respiration</u> take place (see page 21). Respiration transfers <u>energy</u> that the cell needs to work.

Plant cells usually have <u>all the bits</u> that <u>animal</u> cells have, plus a few <u>extra</u> things that animal cells <u>don't</u> have:

Nucleus

1) Rigid <u>cell wall</u> — made of <u>cellulose</u>. It <u>supports</u> the cell and strengthens it.
2) A large <u>vacuole</u> — contains <u>cell sap</u>, a watery solution of sugar and salts. The vacuole <u>swells up</u> as water enters the cell — this <u>pushes</u> the cell contents against the <u>cell wall</u>, making the cell <u>firm</u>.
3) Cytoplasm containing <u>chloroplasts</u> — <u>photosynthesis</u> occurs in the chloroplasts, which makes food for the plant (see page 39). They contain a <u>green</u> substance called <u>chlorophyll</u>, which absorbs the <u>light</u> needed for photosynthesis.

Cells in Multicellular Organisms Differentiate to Become Specialised

1) <u>Differentiation</u> is the process by which a cell <u>changes</u> to become <u>specialised</u> for its job.
2) As cells change, they develop <u>different subcellular structures</u> and turn into <u>different types of cells</u>. This allows them to carry out <u>specific functions</u> more efficiently than if they remained unspecialised.

For example, <u>sperm cells</u> are specialised for <u>reproduction</u>. The function of a sperm cell is to get the <u>male DNA</u> to the <u>female DNA</u> in an egg. So...
- It has a <u>long tail</u> and a <u>streamlined head</u> to help it <u>swim</u> to the egg.
- It has a lot of <u>mitochondria</u> to provide it with enough <u>energy</u> for swimming.
- It carries <u>enzymes</u> in its head to digest through the egg cell membrane.

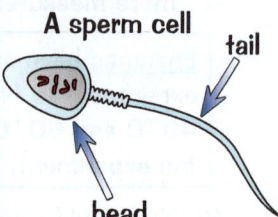

A sperm cell

tail

head

Cell structures — become an estate agent...

Cells were first seen way back in 1665 by looking at cork (which is made from tree bark) under a microscope.

Q1   Name three subcellular structures found in plant cells but not animal cells.   [3 marks]

Microscopy

Microscopes are pretty important for biology. So here are a couple of pages all about them...

Cells are *Studied* Using *Microscopes*

1) Microscopes let us see things that we can't see with the naked eye. The microscopy techniques we can use have developed over the years as technology and knowledge have improved.

2) Light microscopes were invented in the 1590s. They use light and lenses to form an image of a specimen and magnify it (make it look bigger). They let us see individual cells and large subcellular structures, like nuclei. However, there's a limit to how much they can magnify an image (it's about 1500 times).

3) Electron microscopes were invented in the 1930s. They use electrons instead of light to form an image. They have a much higher magnification than light microscopes (it can be 10 000 times higher). They also have a higher resolution, which produces a sharper image. Electron microscopes let us see smaller things in more detail, like the internal structure of mitochondria. However they can only be used to view dead tissue.

You Need to be Able to Use the *Formulae* for *Magnification*

What are you looking at?

1) If you know the power of the lenses used by a light microscope to view an image, you can work out the total magnification of the image using this simple formula:

> **total magnification = power of eyepiece lens × power of objective lens**

2) If you don't know which lenses were used, you can still work out the magnification of an image as long as you can measure the image and know the real size of the specimen. This is the formula you need:

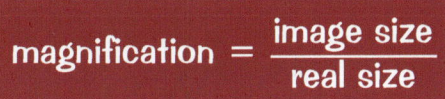

$$\text{magnification} = \frac{\text{image size}}{\text{real size}}$$

Image size and real size should have the same units. If they don't, you'll need to convert them first (see page 9).

If you want to work out the image size or the real size of the object, you can rearrange the formula using this formula triangle:

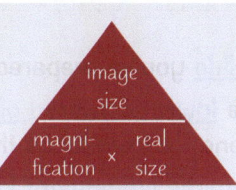

Cover up the thing you're trying to find. The parts you can still see are the formula you need to use.

EXAMPLE:
A specimen is 50 μm wide. Calculate the width of the image of the specimen under a magnification of × 100. Give your answer in mm.

1) Rearrange the formula.
2) Fill in the values you know.
3) Remember the units in your answer.

image size = magnification × real size
image size = 100 × 50
          = 5000 μm = 5 mm

Remember, to convert from micrometres (μm) to millimetres (mm), you need to divide by 1000 (see p.9). E.g. 5000 μm ÷ 1000 = 5 mm

You Need to Know How to Work With Numbers in *Standard Form*

1) Because microscopes can see such tiny objects, sometimes it's useful to write numbers in standard form.

2) This is where you change very big or small numbers with lots of zeros into something more manageable, e.g. 0.017 can be written 1.7×10^{-2}.

3) To do this, you need to move the decimal point left or right to produce a number between 1 and 10.

4) The number of places the decimal point moves is then represented by a power of 10 — this is positive if the decimal point's moved to the left, and negative if it's moved to the right. So 0.0025 in standard form is 2.5×10^{-3} because the decimal point's been moved 3 places to the right.

Your resolution to revise should be increasing right now...

Keep an eye on the units for image size and real size — if they're not the same, it just won't work.

Q1   An onion cell is viewed under a microscope with × 100 magnification. The image of the cell is 7.5 mm wide. What is the real width of the onion cell? Give your answer in μm.   [2 marks]

More Microscopy

It's all very well knowing what microscopes <u>do</u> — you also have to know how to actually <u>use</u> one.

You Need to **Prepare** Your *Slide*

If you want to look at a specimen (e.g. plant or animal cells) under a light microscope, you need to put it on a <u>microscope slide</u> first. A slide is a strip of clear <u>glass</u> or <u>plastic</u> onto which the specimen is <u>mounted</u>.

Here's how to prepare a slide to view <u>onion cells</u>:

1) Add a <u>drop of water</u> to the middle of a clean slide.

2) Cut up an onion and separate it out into <u>layers</u>. Use <u>tweezers</u> to peel off some <u>epidermal tissue</u> from the bottom of one of the layers.

3) Using the tweezers, place the epidermal tissue into the <u>water</u> on the slide.

4) Add a drop of <u>iodine solution</u>. Iodine solution is a <u>stain</u>. Stains are used to highlight objects in a cell by adding <u>colour</u> to them. This allows more <u>detail</u> to be seen.

5) Place a <u>cover slip</u> (a square of thin, transparent plastic or glass) on top. To do this, stand the cover slip <u>upright</u> on the slide, <u>next to</u> the water droplet. Then carefully <u>tilt</u> and <u>lower</u> it so it covers the specimen. Try <u>not</u> to get any <u>air bubbles</u> under there — they'll <u>obstruct</u> your view of the specimen. If you do get air bubbles, <u>gently tap</u> the cover slip. Use <u>tissue paper</u> to <u>soak up</u> any excess iodine solution.

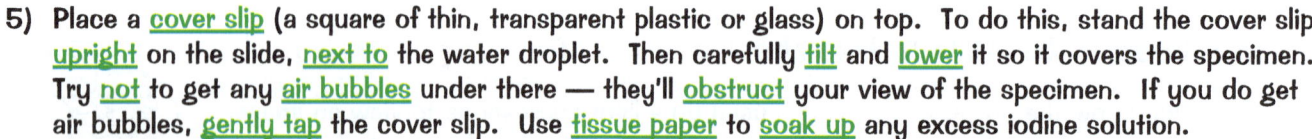

You can also look at your <u>cheek cells</u> under a microscope. To do this, rub a cotton bud over the inside of your cheek and then wipe the bud on a slide. <u>Methylene blue</u> is the stain used. You must dispose of the bud and slide in <u>disinfectant</u> afterwards to prevent virus transmission.

Use a *Light Microscope* to Look at Your *Slide*

1) Clip the <u>slide</u> you've prepared onto the <u>stage</u>.

2) Select the <u>lowest-powered objective lens</u> (i.e. the one that produces the lowest magnification).

3) Use the <u>coarse adjustment knob</u> to move the stage up to just below the objective lens.

4) Look down the <u>eyepiece</u>. Use the coarse adjustment knob to move the stage downwards until the image is <u>roughly in focus</u>.

5) Adjust the <u>focus</u> with the <u>fine adjustment knob</u>, until you get a <u>clear image</u> of what's on the slide.

6) If you need to see the slide with <u>greater magnification</u>, swap to a <u>higher-powered objective lens</u> and refocus.

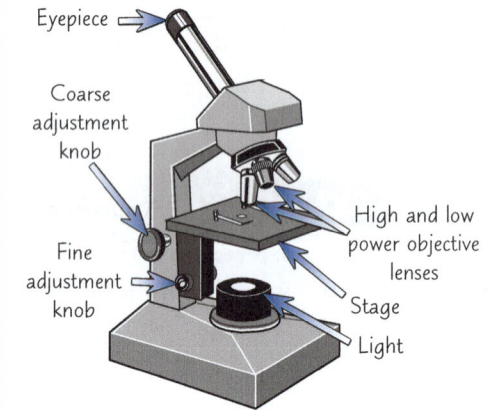

Draw Your Observations **Neatly** with a *Pencil*

1) Draw what you see under the microscope using a <u>pencil</u> with a <u>sharp point</u>.

2) Make sure your drawing takes up <u>at least half</u> of the space available and that it is drawn with <u>clear, unbroken lines</u>.

3) Your drawing should not include any <u>colouring</u> or <u>shading</u>.

4) If you are drawing <u>cells</u>, the <u>subcellular structures</u> should be drawn in <u>proportion</u>.

5) Remember to include a <u>title</u> and write down the <u>magnification</u> of your <u>drawing</u>. (If you know the real size of the cell, you can work out the magnification of your drawing using the formula: magnification = image size ÷ real size — see page 13.)

6) <u>Label</u> the <u>important features</u> of your drawing (e.g. nucleus, chloroplasts), using <u>straight, uncrossed lines</u>.

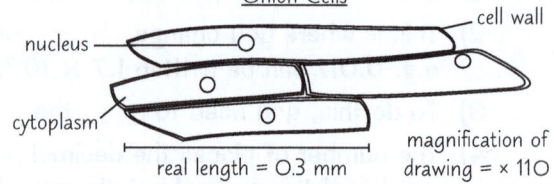

A light microscope is better than a heavy one...

If you can use a microscope, you're halfway to ruling the world. That's what I like to think, anyway.

Q1   Why might you add stain to the sample on a microscope slide?   [1 mark]

Cell Organisation

Some organisms contain loads of <u>cells</u>, but how, you might wonder, do all these cells end up making a working human or squirrel... the answer's <u>organisation</u>. Without it, they'd just make a big splodge.

Large Multicellular Organisms are Made Up of Organ Systems

1) During the <u>development</u> of a multicellular organism, cells become <u>specialised</u> to carry out a particular function (see page 12).
2) These specialised cells form <u>tissues</u>, which form <u>organs</u>, which form <u>organ systems</u> (see below).
3) <u>Large multicellular organisms</u> (e.g. squirrels) have different <u>organ systems</u> inside them for <u>exchanging</u> and <u>transporting</u> materials.

Similar Cells are Organised into Tissues

A <u>tissue</u> is a <u>group</u> of <u>similar cells</u> that work together to carry out a particular <u>function</u>. It can include <u>more than one type</u> of cell.

In <u>mammals</u> (like humans), examples of tissues include:
1) <u>Muscular tissue</u>, which <u>contracts</u> (shortens) to <u>move</u> whatever it's attached to.
2) <u>Glandular tissue</u>, which <u>makes</u> and <u>secretes</u> chemicals like <u>enzymes</u> and <u>hormones</u>.
3) <u>Epithelial tissue</u>, which <u>covers</u> some parts of the body, e.g. the <u>inside</u> of the <u>gut</u>.

Epithelial cell

less than 0.1 mm

Epithelial tissue

Tissues are Organised into Organs

An <u>organ</u> is a group of <u>different tissues</u> that work together to perform a certain <u>function</u>.

For example, the <u>stomach</u> is an organ made of these tissues:
1) <u>Muscular tissue</u>, which moves the stomach wall to <u>churn up the food</u>.
2) <u>Glandular tissue</u>, which makes <u>digestive juices</u> to digest food.
3) <u>Epithelial tissue</u>, which covers the <u>outside</u> and <u>inside</u> of the stomach.

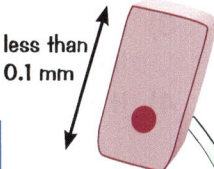

Stomach

about 10 cm (over 1000 times longer than an epithelial cell)

Organs are Organised into Organ Systems

An <u>organ system</u> is a <u>group of organs</u> working together to perform a particular <u>function</u>.

For example, the <u>digestive system</u> (found in humans and other mammals) <u>breaks down</u> and <u>absorbs</u> food. It's made up of these organs:
1) <u>Glands</u> (e.g. the <u>pancreas</u> and <u>salivary glands</u>), which produce <u>digestive juices</u>.
2) The <u>stomach</u> and <u>small intestine</u>, which <u>digest</u> food.
3) The <u>liver</u>, which produces <u>bile</u>.
4) The <u>small intestine</u>, which <u>absorbs</u> soluble <u>food</u> molecules.
5) The <u>large intestine</u>, which <u>absorbs water</u> from undigested food, leaving <u>faeces</u>.

Organ systems work together to make entire <u>organisms</u>.

Salivary glands

Liver

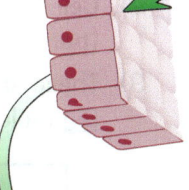

Digestive system

Stomach
Pancreas
Small intestine
Large intestine

Soft and quilted — the best kind of tissues...

So in summary, an organism consists of organ systems, which are groups of organs, which are made of tissues, which are groups of cells working together. Now just for the thrill of it, here's a practice question.

Q1   The bladder is an organ. Explain what this means.   [2 marks]

Cell Membranes and Diffusion

Substances need to move <u>in</u> and <u>out</u> of cells, through the <u>cell membrane</u>. One way this happens is by <u>diffusion</u>.

Diffusion is the *Movement* of Particles from *Higher* to *Lower Concentration*

1) <u>Diffusion</u> is simple. It's just the <u>movement</u> of particles from places where there are <u>lots</u> of them to places where there are <u>fewer</u> of them. That's all it is — just the <u>natural tendency</u> for stuff to <u>spread out</u>. Here's the fancy <u>definition</u>:

> <u>Diffusion</u> is the <u>net (overall) movement</u> of <u>particles</u> from an area of <u>higher concentration</u> to an area of <u>lower concentration</u>.

2) If something moves from an area of <u>higher concentration</u> to an area of <u>lower concentration</u>, it is said to have moved <u>down</u> its <u>concentration gradient</u>.

3) Diffusion happens in both <u>liquids</u> and <u>gases</u> — that's because the particles in these substances are free to <u>move about</u> randomly.

4) It's also a <u>passive process</u> — this means it doesn't need any energy to make it happen.

Cell Membranes are *Pretty Clever*

1) They're clever because they <u>hold</u> the cell together <u>but</u> they let stuff <u>in and out</u> as well. Substances can move in and out of cells by <u>diffusion</u>, <u>osmosis</u> and <u>active transport</u> (see next page).

2) Cell membranes are <u>selectively permeable</u>. This means they have very <u>small holes</u> (pores) in them, which only <u>very small molecules</u> can pass through.

3) These small molecules include things like <u>glucose</u>, <u>amino acids</u>, <u>water</u>, <u>oxygen</u> and <u>carbon dioxide</u>. <u>Big</u> molecules like <u>starch</u> and <u>proteins</u> can't fit through.

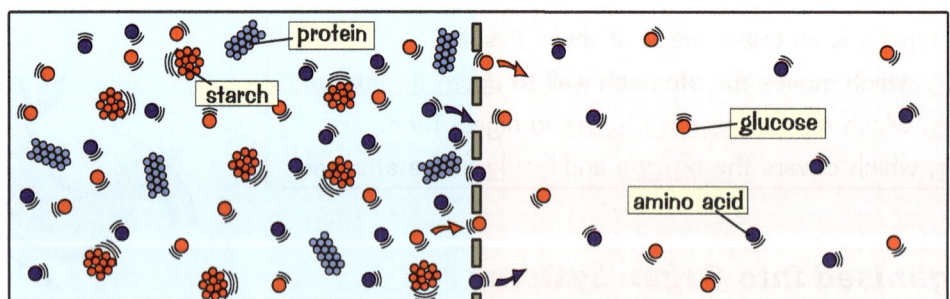

protein

starch

glucose

amino acid

The diffusion of oxygen and carbon dioxide is important for aerobic respiration — see p.21.

You Can *Investigate Diffusion* in a *Non-Living System*

1) Just like cell membranes, <u>Visking tubing</u> is <u>selectively permeable</u>. This means it can be used as a <u>model</u> of living material. For example, you can use it to demonstrate that <u>large molecules</u> can't diffuse through cell membranes, but <u>smaller ones</u> can.

2) Start by tying up one end of a length of Visking tubing. Fill the tube you make with <u>glucose solution</u>, tie up the other end to seal it, and place the tube in a beaker of <u>pure water</u> overnight. The next day, <u>test for glucose</u> in the water <u>outside</u> the tube using the <u>Benedict's test</u> (see p.28).

3) Repeat the experiment again using <u>starch solution</u> instead of glucose solution and test for the presence of starch in the water using the <u>iodine test</u> (see p.28).

4) You should find that the <u>glucose</u> is able to <u>pass through</u> the tubing into the water, but the <u>starch</u> molecules <u>cannot</u>. This is because the sugar molecules are <u>small enough</u> to pass through the <u>pores</u> in the Visking tubing but the starch molecules are <u>too big</u>.

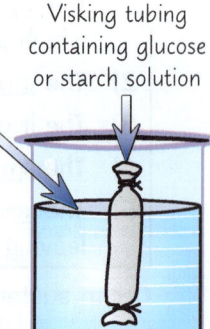

Visking tubing containing glucose or starch solution

Pure water

Revision by diffusion — you wish...

Hopefully there'll have been a net movement of information from this page into your brain...

Q1   What is diffusion?   [1 mark]

Osmosis and Active Transport

Some substances can move in and out of cells by osmosis and active transport...

Osmosis *is a* Special Case *of Diffusion,* That's All

> Osmosis is the net movement of water molecules across a selectively permeable membrane from a region of higher water concentration to a region of lower water concentration.

You could also describe osmosis as the net movement of water molecules across a selectively permeable membrane from a region of lower solute concentration to a region of higher solute concentration.

1) The water molecules actually pass both ways through the membrane during osmosis. This happens because water molecules move about randomly all the time.

2) But because there are more water molecules on one side than on the other, there's a steady net flow of water into the region with fewer water molecules, i.e. into the more concentrated solute solution.

3) This means the solute solution gets more dilute. The water acts like it's trying to "even up" the concentration either side of the membrane.

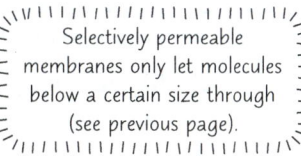
Selectively permeable membranes only let molecules below a certain size through (see previous page).

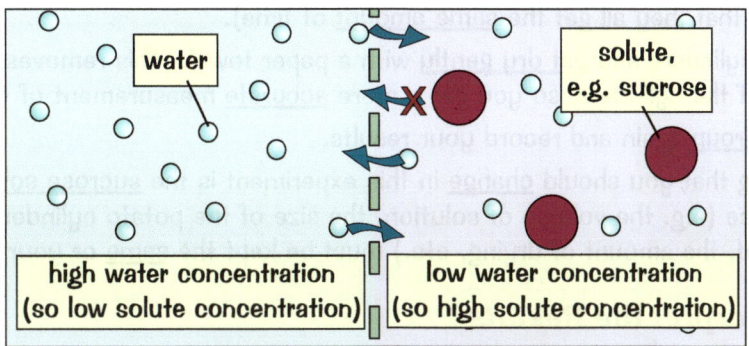

water

solute, e.g. sucrose

high water concentration (so low solute concentration)

low water concentration (so high solute concentration)

Net movement of water molecules

Active Transport *is the* Opposite *of Diffusion*

> Active transport is the movement of particles across a membrane against a concentration gradient (i.e. from an area of lower to an area of higher concentration) using energy released during respiration.

1) Active transport is a bit different from diffusion because particles are moved up a concentration gradient rather than down. Active transport is also an active process, so it requires energy (unlike diffusion, which is a passive process).

2) The energy required is released during respiration in the form of ATP (see p.21).

3) Here's an example of active transport at work in the digestive system:

> 1) When there's a higher concentration of nutrients in the gut than in the blood they diffuse naturally into the blood.
>
> 2) BUT — sometimes there's a lower concentration of nutrients in the gut than in the blood.
>
> 3) Active transport allows nutrients to be taken into the blood, despite the fact that the concentration gradient is the wrong way. This is essential to stop us starving.

Plants use active transport to obtain the minerals they need from the soil.

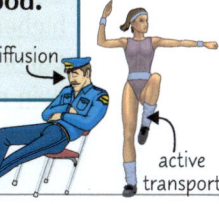
diffusion

active transport

Higher

Active transport — buses that are just always on the go...

Revision tip #1: draw yourself a table to show the similarities and differences between diffusion, active transport and osmosis. It should help you get all three processes straight in your head before the exam.

Q1   Give two ways in which active transport differs from diffusion.   [2 marks]

Unit 1a — Cells and Respiration

Investigating Osmosis

For all you non-believers — here's an <u>experiment</u> you can do to see <u>osmosis in action</u>.

You Can Do an *Experiment* to *Investigate Osmosis*

This experiment involves putting <u>potato cylinders</u> into <u>different concentrations</u> of <u>sucrose solution</u> to see what effect different <u>water concentrations</u> have on them.

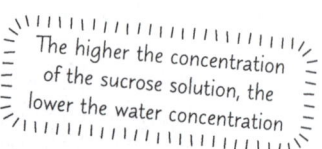
The higher the concentration of the sucrose solution, the lower the water concentration

First You Do the Experiment...

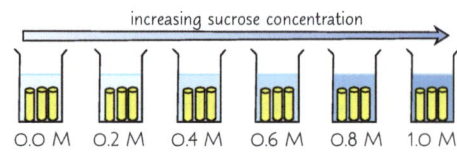
increasing sucrose concentration

0.0 M   0.2 M   0.4 M   0.6 M   0.8 M   1.0 M

1) Prepare <u>sucrose solutions</u> of different concentrations ranging from <u>pure water</u> to a <u>very concentrated sucrose solution</u>.

2) Use a cork borer to cut a <u>potato</u> into the <u>same sized pieces</u> (The pieces should preferably be from the <u>same potato</u>.)

3) Divide the cylinders into <u>groups of three</u> and use a <u>mass balance</u> to measure the <u>mass</u> of each <u>group</u>.

'M' is a unit of concentration (you might also see it written as mol dm^{-3}). The solution with a concentration of 0.0 M is pure water.

4) Place <u>one group</u> in each solution.

5) <u>Leave</u> the cylinders in the solution for <u>at least 40 minutes</u> (making sure that they all get the <u>same amount</u> of time).

6) <u>Remove</u> the cylinders and <u>pat dry gently</u> with a paper towel. This removes <u>excess water</u> from the surface of the cylinders, so you get a more <u>accurate</u> measurement of their <u>final masses</u>.

7) <u>Weigh</u> each <u>group</u> again and record your results.

8) The <u>only</u> thing that you should <u>change</u> in this experiment is the <u>sucrose solution concentration</u>. Everything else (e.g. the volume of solution, the size of the potato cylinders, the type of potatoes used, the amount of drying, etc.) must be kept the <u>same</u> or your results <u>won't be valid</u>.

...Then You *Interpret* the *Results*

1) Once you've got all your results, you need to <u>calculate</u> the <u>percentage change in mass</u> for each group of cylinders <u>before</u> and <u>after</u> their time in the sucrose.

Calculating the percentage change allows you to compare the effect of sucrose concentration on cylinders that didn't have the same initial mass.

EXAMPLE: A group of cylinders weighed 13.2 g at the start of the experiment. At the end they weighed 15.1 g. Calculate the percentage change in mass.

To find the <u>percentage change in mass</u>, use the following <u>formula</u>:

$$\text{percentage change} = \frac{\text{final mass} - \text{initial mass}}{\text{initial mass}} \times 100$$

$$\text{percentage change} = \frac{15.1 - 13.2}{13.2} \times 100 = 14.4\%$$

The positive result tells you the potato cylinders gained mass. If the answer was negative then the potato cylinders lost mass.

2) Then you can plot a <u>graph</u> and <u>analyse your results</u>:

At the points <u>above</u> <u>the x-axis</u>, the water concentration of the <u>sucrose solutions</u> is <u>higher</u> than in the <u>cylinders</u>. The cylinders <u>gain mass</u> as water is <u>drawn in</u> by osmosis.

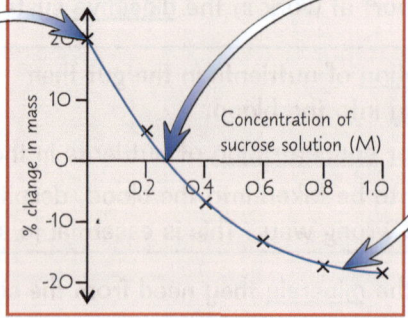
Concentration of sucrose solution (M)
% change in mass

Where there is <u>no change</u> in mass (where the curve <u>crosses the x-axis</u>) the fluid <u>inside</u> the cylinders and the <u>sucrose solution</u> are <u>isotonic</u> — they have the <u>same water concentration</u>.

At the points <u>below the x-axis</u>, the water concentration of the <u>sucrose solutions</u> is <u>lower</u> than in the <u>cylinders</u>. This causes the cylinders to <u>lose water</u> so their mass <u>decreases</u>.

So that's how they make skinny fries...

This experiment used sucrose as a solute, but you could do the experiment with different solutes (e.g. salt).

Q1   A group of potato cubes were placed in a sucrose solution and left for one hour. The cubes weighed 13.3 g at the start of the experiment and 11.4 g at the end. Calculate the percentage change in mass.   [2 marks]

Enzymes

<u>Chemical reactions</u> are what make you work. And <u>enzymes</u> are what make them work.

Enzymes *Are* Proteins *That Act As* Catalysts

> A catalyst is a substance which increases the speed of a reaction, without being changed or used up in the reaction.

1) Living things have thousands of different <u>chemical reactions</u> going on inside them all the time. These reactions need to be <u>carefully controlled</u> — to get the <u>right amounts</u> of substances.

2) You can usually make a reaction happen more quickly by <u>raising the temperature</u>. This would speed up the <u>useful</u> reactions but also the <u>unwanted</u> ones too... not good.

3) So... <u>living cells</u> produce <u>enzymes</u> which act as <u>biological catalysts</u>. Enzymes reduce the need for <u>high temperatures</u> and we only have enzymes to speed up the <u>useful reactions</u> in the body. These useful reactions include <u>metabolic reactions</u>, which involve <u>breaking down</u> large molecules into smaller molecules or <u>building up</u> large molecules from small molecules.

4) Like all proteins, enzymes are made up of <u>chains</u> of <u>amino acids</u> (see p.135). These chains are folded into <u>unique shapes</u>, which enzymes need to do their jobs (see below).

Enzymes Have *Special Shapes* So They Can *Catalyse Reactions*

1) Chemical reactions usually involve chemicals either being <u>split apart</u> or <u>joined together</u>.

2) The <u>substrate</u> is the molecule <u>changed</u> in the reaction.

3) Every enzyme has an <u>active site</u> — the part where it joins on to its substrate to <u>catalyse</u> the reaction.

4) Enzymes usually only work with <u>one substrate</u>. They are said to have a <u>high specificity</u> for their substrate.

5) This is because, for the enzyme to work, the substrate has to <u>fit</u> into the active site.

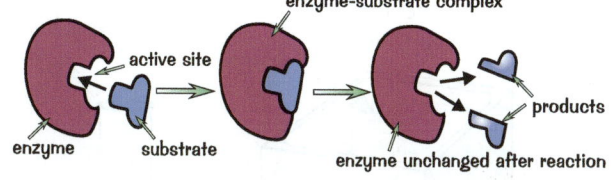

enzyme-substrate complex

active site

enzyme   substrate

products

enzyme unchanged after reaction

6) When a substrate molecule <u>collides</u> with an enzyme molecule, the substrate's <u>shape</u> must <u>match</u> the active site's shape or the reaction <u>won't be catalysed</u>. This is called the <u>'lock and key' model</u>, because the <u>substrate</u> fits into the <u>enzyme</u> just like a <u>key</u> fits into a <u>lock</u>.

7) When a substrate molecule and enzyme molecule collide, an <u>enzyme-substrate complex</u> is formed.

8) It's the <u>specific sequence</u> of <u>amino acids</u> that determines any protein's <u>structure</u> and therefore its <u>function</u>. In an <u>enzyme</u>, the specific sequence of amino acids determines the <u>shape</u> of the enzyme's <u>active site</u>, which allows it to <u>catalyse</u> a specific reaction.

Enzymes *Need the* Right Temperature *and pH*

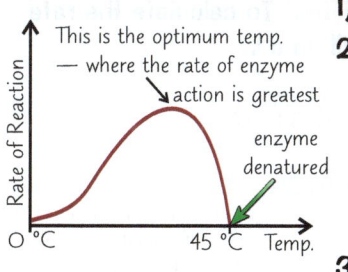

This is the optimum temp. — where the rate of enzyme action is greatest

enzyme denatured

Rate of Reaction

O °C   45 °C   Temp.

1) Changing the <u>temperature</u> changes the <u>rate</u> of an enzyme-catalysed reaction.

2) Like with any reaction, a higher temperature <u>increases</u> the rate at first. The enzymes and substrate have <u>more energy</u>, so they <u>move about more</u> and are <u>more likely</u> to <u>collide</u> and form <u>enzyme-substrate complexes</u>. But if it gets <u>too hot</u>, some of the <u>bonds</u> holding the enzyme together <u>break</u>. This changes the shape of the enzyme's <u>active site</u>, so the substrate <u>won't fit</u>. The enzyme is said to be <u>denatured</u>. Boiling denatures most enzymes.

3) All enzymes have an <u>optimum temperature</u> that they work best at.

4) The <u>pH</u> also affects enzymes. If it's too high or too low, the pH interferes with the <u>bonds</u> holding the enzyme together. This changes the <u>shape</u> of the <u>active site</u> and <u>denatures</u> the enzyme.

5) All enzymes have an <u>optimum pH</u> that they work best at. It's often <u>neutral pH 7</u>, but <u>not always</u>.

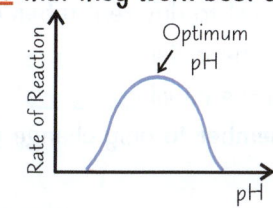

Optimum pH

Rate of Reaction

pH

If the lock and key mechanism fails, get in through a window...

Make sure you use the special terms like 'active site' and 'denatured' — the examiners will love it.

Q1   Describe what happens to enzymes above their optimum pH.   [2 marks]

PRACTICAL Investigating Enzyme Activity

You'll soon know how to investigate the effect of a variable on the rate of enzyme activity... I bet you're thrilled.

You Can Investigate How Temperature Affects Enzyme Activity

One way to investigate how temperature affects enzyme activity is to test how fast a substrate disappears. Here's an example:

The enzyme amylase catalyses the breakdown of starch to maltose. It's easy to detect starch using iodine solution — if starch is present, the iodine solution will change from browny-orange to blue-black.

1) Start by measuring out a set volume of starch solution into a test tube
    and a set volume of amylase into another test tube.

2) Put a drop of iodine solution into each well on the spotting tile.

3) Put both of the test tubes into the water bath at 20 °C. After five minutes pour the
    amylase into the starch solution and mix well. Start the stopwatch.

4) Use continuous sampling to record how long it takes for the amylase to break down all of the starch.
    To do this, take a fresh sample of the mixture every thirty seconds and put a drop into a new well.
    Wash out the pipette between each sample. Once the iodine solution does not turn blue-black,
    it means all the starch has been converted to maltose.

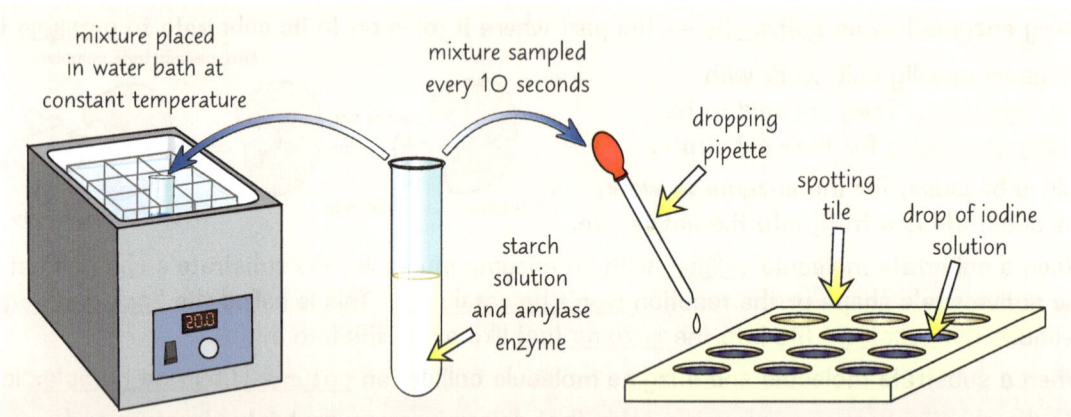

mixture placed in water bath at constant temperature

mixture sampled every 10 seconds

dropping pipette

spotting tile

drop of iodine solution

starch solution and amylase enzyme

5) Repeat steps 1-4 three times and calculate the mean. Then repeat the experiment with the water bath at
    30 °C, 40 °C, 50 °C and 60 °C to see how it affects the time taken for the starch to be broken down.

6) Remember to control any variables (e.g. the volume of amylase) each time to make it a fair test.

7) After the experiment you can calculate the mean rate of reaction at each temperature to analyse
    your results. Rate is a measure of how much something changes over time. To calculate the rate
    for this experiment, use the formula: 1 ÷ time taken (in s). The units will be s^{-1}.

You Can Investigate Other Factors That Affect Enzyme Activity

You can adapt the experiment above to measure variables other than temperature.
For example:

1) To investigate the effect of pH, add a buffer solution with a different
    pH level to different tubes containing the starch-amylase mixture.

> A buffer solution is able to resist changes to pH.

2) Vary the initial concentration of the starch to investigate the effect of substrate concentration.

3) Vary the initial concentration of the amylase to investigate the effect of enzyme concentration.

Just remember to only change one variable at a time and keep the rest the same.

If only enzymes could speed up revision...

You need to use your knowledge of how enzymes work to form a conclusion from the results of your experiment.

Q1   An enzyme-controlled reaction took 65 seconds to complete.
      Calculate the rate of reaction in s^{-1}. Give your answer to 1 significant figure.   [2 marks]

Respiration

You need energy to keep your body going. Energy comes from food, and it's released by respiration.

Respiration is NOT "Breathing In and Out"

1) Respiration is the process of releasing energy from the breakdown of glucose (a sugar). Some energy is released to the environment as heat.

2) Respiration goes on in every cell in all living organisms, all the time — it's a universal chemical process.

3) The energy released by respiration can't be used directly by cells — so it's used to make a substance called ATP. ATP acts as an energy store.

You only need to know about ATP if you're taking the Higher papers.

4) The energy released by respiration is needed for many cellular processes, such as:
   • metabolic processes — e.g. making larger molecules from smaller ones,
   • contracting muscles (in animals),
   • maintaining a steady body temperature (in mammals and birds).

5) Respiration actually involves a series of different chemical reactions. They are all controlled by enzymes, so the rate of respiration is affected by both temperature and pH (see p.19).

6) There are two types of respiration, aerobic and anaerobic.

Aerobic Respiration Needs Plenty of Oxygen

1) "Aerobic" means "with oxygen", so aerobic respiration is what happens when there's plenty of oxygen.

2) This is the type of respiration that you're using most of the time.

3) Here is the overall equation for aerobic respiration:

glucose + oxygen ⟶ carbon dioxide + water

In plant and animal cells, aerobic respiration takes place in the mitochondria.

4) Aerobic respiration is the most efficient way to release energy from glucose. It produces lots of ATP (32 molecules per molecule of glucose).

Anaerobic Respiration Doesn't Use Oxygen At All

1) "Anaerobic" just means "without oxygen".

2) In anaerobic respiration, the glucose is only partially broken down. This limits the number of ATP molecules that can be produced (to 2 molecules per molecule of glucose), making anaerobic respiration less efficient than aerobic respiration.

Animals Produce Lactic Acid

1) When you do really vigorous exercise your body can't supply enough oxygen to your muscles for aerobic respiration — even though your heart rate and breathing rate increase as much as they can. Your muscles have to start respiring anaerobically as well.

2) In animals (including humans) anaerobic respiration produces lactic acid. This is the word equation for anaerobic respiration in animals:

glucose ⟶ lactic acid

4) Lactic acid is harmful to the body. It has to be removed from cells and broken down. The advantage is that at least you can keep on using your muscles.

5) After resorting to anaerobic respiration, when you stop exercising you'll have an oxygen debt. Basically you need extra oxygen to break down the lactic acid that's built up and to allow aerobic respiration to begin again. So you need to keep breathing hard for a while to repay the debt.

Respiration releases energy — but this page has worn me out...

Thank goodness for respiration — releasing the energy stored in my tea and biscuits to my brain cells. Great.

Q1   Give the word equation for aerobic respiration.   [2 marks]

Investigating Respiration

Ready to boil over with excitement as you see energy is released as heat during respiration? Good.

The Energy Released as Heat During Respiration can be Measured

On the previous page, I said that respiration releases energy to the environment as heat
— well here's an experiment to measure that released energy. You'll just need some humble peas.

1) Firstly, prepare two sets of peas. Put the first set of peas in between two
wet paper towels in an airtight container. They will start to germinate (you
should see little sprouts coming out of them). Germinating peas will respire.

2) Boil a similar-sized, second set of peas. This will kill the peas and
make sure they can't respire. The dead peas will act as your control.

3) You also need to put both sets of peas in a solution of weak disinfectant. This will kill
any bacteria or fungi on the surface of the peas. If you don't do this, you could end
up measuring heat released from respiring bacteria or fungi as well as from the peas.

4) Then add each set of peas to a vacuum flask, making sure there's some air left in the flasks
(so the peas can respire aerobically). The vacuum flasks are well-insulated, meaning that
energy transferred by heat from the respiring peas is not lost to the surrounding environment.
This means more of the energy will go into increasing the temperature of the flask.

5) Place a thermometer into each flask and seal the top with cotton wool.

6) Record the temperature of each flask daily for a week.

7) When the germinating peas respire and transfer energy to their surroundings as heat,
the test flask's temperature will increase compared to the control flask.

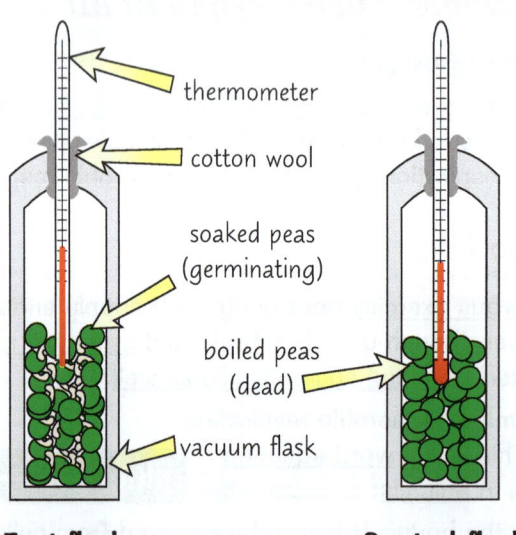

thermometer

cotton wool

soaked peas
(germinating)

boiled peas
(dead)

vacuum flask

Test flask   **Control flask**

What did one flask say to the other? I've found my inner peas...

Controls are important in experiments — they're used to check the thing you're changing (the independent variable)
is what's affecting the results. So don't lose control in the exams — make sure you understand what they're all about.

Q1   A student carried out an experiment to measure the energy released by respiration using
germinating beans in a vacuum flask.
   a) What should the student have used as a control?   [1 mark]
   b) Explain why the student used a vacuum flask for her experiment rather than a plastic bottle.   [2 marks]

The Respiratory System

This page is all about getting <u>air into</u> and <u>out of</u> your <u>lungs</u>. Take a <u>deep breath</u> and dive in...

Large Organisms *Need a* Complex Respiratory System

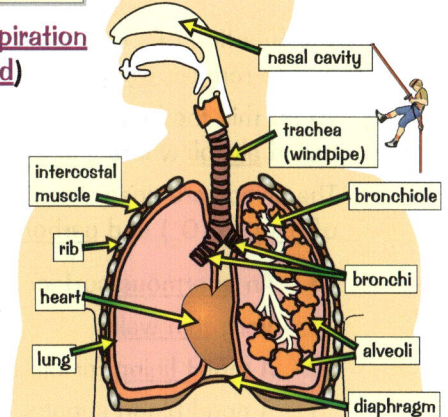

1) In order to supply all their cells with enough <u>oxygen</u> for <u>aerobic respiration</u> (and so that an <u>equivalent volume</u> of <u>carbon dioxide</u> can be <u>removed</u>) large organisms require a <u>complex respiratory system</u>.

2) A respiratory system contains <u>specialised organs</u> for the <u>exchange</u> of oxygen and carbon dioxide.

3) In the <u>human</u> respiratory system, these organs are the <u>lungs</u>. The lungs are like pink <u>sponges</u> and are protected by the <u>ribcage</u>.

4) The air that you breathe in goes through the <u>trachea</u> into two tubes (called <u>bronchi</u>), which split into progressively smaller tubes (called <u>bronchioles</u>). Finally it reaches small elastic sacs called <u>alveoli</u> where the gas exchange takes place (see next page).

Inspiration *is Breathing* In *and* Expiration *is Breathing* Out

Inspiration

1) The intercostal and diaphragm <u>muscles contract</u>.

2) This causes the <u>ribcage</u> to move <u>up</u> and <u>out</u> and the diaphragm to <u>flatten</u>, <u>increasing</u> the <u>volume</u> of the <u>thorax</u> (the space between the neck and abdomen).

3) As the thoracic volume increases, the lung <u>pressure</u> <u>decreases</u> (to below <u>atmospheric pressure</u>).

4) This causes air to <u>flow into</u> the lungs.

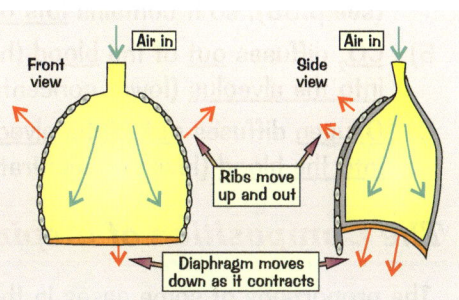

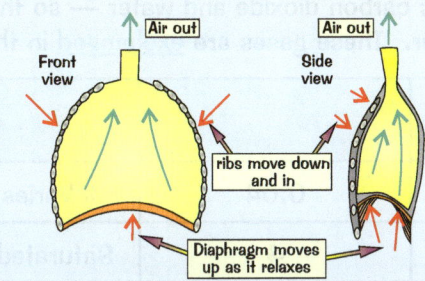

Expiration

1) The intercostal and diaphragm <u>muscles relax</u>.

2) The <u>ribcage</u> moves <u>down</u> and <u>in</u> and the diaphragm becomes <u>curved again</u>, <u>decreasing</u> the <u>volume</u> of the <u>thorax</u>.

3) The thoracic volume decreases, causing the <u>air pressure</u> to <u>increase</u> (to above atmospheric pressure).

4) Air is <u>forced out</u> of the lungs.

The <u>Bell Jar</u> model shows us what's <u>going on</u> when you <u>breathe</u>:

- The <u>bell jar</u> represents your <u>thorax</u>.
- The <u>glass tube</u> going into the jar represents your <u>trachea</u>.
- The <u>rubber sheet</u> works like your <u>diaphragm</u>. As you pull it down, air rushes in and the <u>balloons</u> (which represent your <u>lungs</u>) <u>inflate</u>. If you let the sheet <u>relax</u> back up, the balloons <u>deflate</u> again.

However the bell jar <u>isn't</u> an <u>exact model</u>: Its main limitations are:

- The <u>glass</u> the jar is made from is <u>rigid</u> and <u>can't move</u> up and out to increase the <u>volume</u> of the jar like your <u>ribcage</u> can.
- The <u>balloons</u> are <u>empty</u>, but your lungs are made up of <u>lots of alveoli</u>, which <u>individually</u> inflate and deflate.

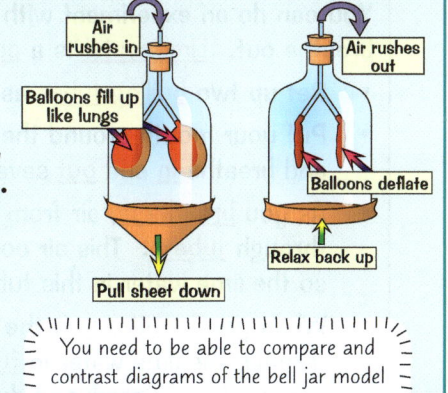

You need to be able to compare and contrast diagrams of the bell jar model and the human respiratory system.

When you breathe you inspire, when you don't breathe you expire...

You need to know how a bell jar can model your respiratory systems, but make sure you also know its limitations.

Q1 Explain why large multicellular organisms need complex respiratory systems. [2 marks]

Gas Exchange

Gas exchange <u>isn't too tricky</u> — it's just a simple <u>trade</u> of <u>gases</u> between the <u>air</u> and your <u>blood</u>.

Gas Exchange *Happens in the Lungs*

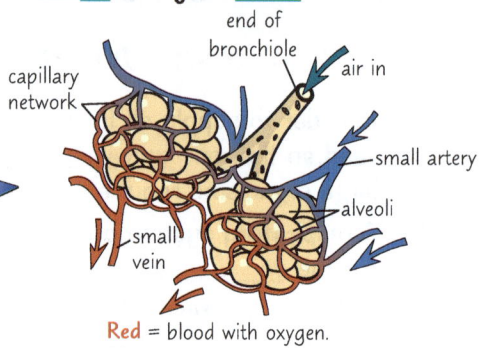

1) The function of the lungs is to transfer <u>oxygen</u> to the <u>blood</u> and to remove <u>waste carbon dioxide</u> from it.

2) To do this the lungs contain millions of little air sacs called <u>alveoli</u> where <u>gas exchange</u> takes place.

3) The alveoli are specialised to maximise the <u>rate of diffusion</u> of <u>oxygen</u> (O_2) and <u>carbon dioxide</u> (CO_2). They have:

- An <u>enormous</u> surface area (about 75 m² in humans).
- Very <u>thin walls</u>.
- A <u>moist lining</u> for dissolving gases.
- A <u>good blood supply</u>.

Red = blood with oxygen.
Blue = blood with carbon dioxide.

4) The <u>blood</u> passing next to the alveoli has just <u>returned</u> to the <u>lungs</u> from the rest of the body via the heart (see p.35), so it contains <u>lots of CO_2</u> and <u>very little O_2</u>.

5) <u>CO_2</u> diffuses <u>out</u> of the <u>blood</u> (higher concentration) <u>into the alveolus</u> (lower concentration) to be breathed out.

6) <u>Oxygen</u> diffuses <u>out</u> of the <u>alveolus</u> (higher concentration) <u>into the blood</u> (lower concentration).

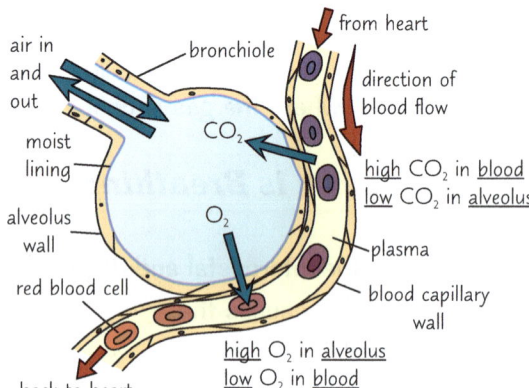

The Composition *of Inspired and* Expired *Air is Different*

The <u>proportions</u> of some <u>gases</u> in the air you <u>breathe in</u> are <u>different</u> from the proportions you <u>breathe out</u>. This is because <u>aerobic respiration</u> uses up oxygen and produces carbon dioxide and water — so there's <u>less O_2</u> and <u>more CO_2</u> and <u>water vapour</u> in <u>expired air</u> than inspired air. These gases are <u>exchanged</u> in the <u>lungs</u>.

> None of the chemical reactions in the body use nitrogen from the air or produce nitrogen gas, so the % of nitrogen doesn't change.

	Nitrogen (%)	Oxygen (%)	Carbon Dioxide (%)	Water Vapour
Inspired Air	79	21	0.04	% Varies
Expired Air	79	16	4	Saturated

You can do an experiment with <u>lime water</u> to show that <u>carbon dioxide</u> is <u>released</u> when we breathe out. <u>Lime water</u> is a <u>colourless</u> solution which turns <u>cloudy</u> in the presence of <u>carbon dioxide</u>.

- Set up two <u>boiling tubes</u> as shown on the right. Put the same volume of lime water in each.
- Put your mouth around the <u>mouthpiece</u> and breathe <u>in</u> and <u>out</u> several times.
- As you <u>breathe in</u>, air from the room is drawn in through <u>tube A</u>. This air contains <u>little</u> carbon dioxide so the lime water in this tube <u>remains colourless</u>.
- When you <u>breathe out</u>, the air you <u>exhale</u> bubbles through the lime water in <u>tube B</u>. This air <u>contains carbon dioxide</u> produced during <u>respiration</u>, so the lime water in this tube turns <u>cloudy</u>.

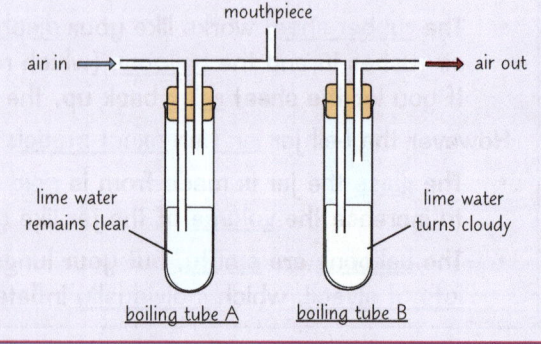

Well if you ask me, the composition of this page is inspired...

Remembering the direction of CO_2 and O_2 concentration gradients is the key to nailing gas exchange.

Q1   Give three ways in which the alveoli are specialised to maximise the diffusion of gases.   [3 marks]

Smoking

Be warned: your <u>lifestyle</u> can muck your lungs up good and proper...

Ciliated Epithelial Cells Are Specialised for Moving Materials

1) Your airways are lined with <u>ciliated epithelial cells</u>.
These cells have <u>cilia</u> (hair-like structures) along their <u>upper surfaces</u>.

2) Other cells in the airways produce a sticky substance called <u>mucus</u>.
A function of mucus is to <u>trap particles</u> and <u>bacteria</u> present in the air.

3) The cilia <u>beat</u> to help to <u>move mucus</u> (and everything trapped in it)
up to the <u>throat</u> so it can be <u>swallowed</u> and <u>doesn't reach</u> the lungs.

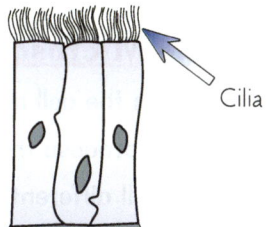
Cilia

Smoking Affects Cilia

1) <u>Cigarette smoke</u> contains <u>particles</u> which <u>clog</u> the <u>mucus</u> in the airways.

2) Cigarette smoke also contains <u>chemicals</u> which <u>paralyse</u> cilia (prevent them
from moving). This means they <u>can't</u> move <u>mucus</u> up to the throat effectively.

3) This can increase the risk of <u>respiratory infections</u> developing because <u>bacteria</u> that are
<u>normally removed</u> by cilia and mucus are more likely to enter the respiratory system.

4) It also <u>restricts</u> a smoker's ability to <u>expel</u> air from the lungs,
as the airways are <u>partially blocked</u> by mucus.

> Cigarettes also contain nicotine, which is an addictive substance, so
> it can be difficult to quit smoking, despite knowing the health risks.

Smoking is Linked to Lung Cancer

1) Cigarette smoke contains <u>tar</u>, which is full of toxic chemicals.
Some of the chemicals are <u>carcinogens</u>, which means they can cause <u>cancer</u>.

2) Lung cancer can cause <u>blockages of the airways</u> and <u>fluid</u> can build up in the lungs.
This makes it very <u>difficult</u> for the person to <u>breathe</u> properly and can be <u>painful</u>.
Lung cancer can <u>spread</u> to other areas of the body and eventually cause <u>death</u>.

Smoking Can Lead to Emphysema

1) <u>Emphysema</u> is a <u>lung disease</u> in which <u>foreign particles</u> become trapped in the alveoli.
It is often caused by <u>smoking</u> but can also be caused by long-term exposure to <u>air pollution</u>.

2) The trapped particles cause <u>inflammation</u>,
which attracts a type of <u>white blood cell</u> called a
<u>phagocyte</u> to the area. The phagocytes produce
an <u>enzyme</u> that <u>breaks down</u> the <u>alveoli walls</u>.

> See p.158
> for more on
> phagocytes.

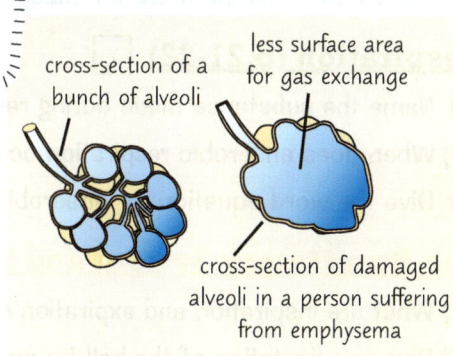
cross-section of a bunch of alveoli
less surface area for gas exchange
cross-section of damaged alveoli in a person suffering from emphysema

3) The destruction of the alveoli walls <u>reduces</u> the <u>surface
area</u> of the alveoli, so the <u>rate of gas exchange decreases</u>.
It also makes it <u>harder</u> for the alveoli to <u>recoil</u> and expel air.

4) The narrowing of airways leads to <u>symptoms</u>
such as <u>shortness of breath</u> and <u>wheezing</u>.
People with emphysema have an increased <u>breathing
rate</u> as they try to increase the amount of air
(containing oxygen) reaching their lungs.

The jokes in this book are just getting cilia and cilia...

Smoking can cause many different problems in your lungs. Make sure you know how smoking can cause the
diseases on this page and also familiarise yourself with the consequences of developing these diseases.

Q1 Explain one way in which smoking increases the risk of developing a respiratory infection. [3 marks]

Revision Questions for Unit 1a

Well, that wraps up Unit 1a — I think you'll agree it's been a breath-taking ride. Anyway, time to test yourself.
- Try these questions and tick off each one when you get it right.
- When you've done all the questions for a topic and are completely happy with it, tick off the topic.

Cells and Microscopy (p.12-14) ☑

1) What does the cell nucleus contain?
2) Name the process that occurs in chloroplasts.
3) What is cell differentiation?
4) Give one advantage and one disadvantage of using an electron microscope over a light microscope.
5) How can you work out the total magnification of a microscope using the power of the eyepiece lens and the power of the objective lenses?
6) True or false? Scientific drawings should be accurately coloured in.

Cell Organisation, Cell Membranes and Diffusion (p.15-16) ☐

7) What is a tissue?
8) What is an organ system?
9) What is a selectively permeable membrane?
10) True or False? Proteins can diffuse across cell membranes.

Osmosis and Active Transport (p.17-18) ☐

11) Give the definition of osmosis.
12) What is active transport?
13) How can you use potato cylinders to show osmosis in action?

Enzymes (p.19-20) ☐

14) What function do enzymes have in biological reactions?
15) What are enzymes made up of?
16) Why is the shape of an enzyme important for its function?
17) What will happen to the rate of an enzyme-catalysed reaction if it gets too hot?
18) Give one variable you'd need to control when investigating the effect of temperature on enzyme activity.

Respiration (p.21-22) ☑

19) Name the substance made during respiration that releases energy to an organism's cells.
20) When does anaerobic respiration occur in animals?
21) Give the word equation for anaerobic respiration.

The Respiratory System and Smoking (p.23-25) ☐

22) What are inspiration and expiration?
23) Give one limitation of the bell jar model.
24) True or False? Blood passing next to the alveoli has lots of CO_2.
25) Why is the composition of expired air different from the composition of inspired air?
26) How does smoking affect cilia?
27) How can smoking lead to emphysema?

Digestion

The whole point of <u>digestion</u> is to <u>break down</u> the <u>food</u> you eat into <u>small molecules</u> that your cells can absorb and use. As you might imagine, this involves lots of different chemical reactions and our old friends, <u>enzymes</u>.

Digestive Enzymes **Break Down** *Big Molecules*

1) BIG insoluble molecules (e.g. starch, proteins and fats) in food are <u>too big</u> to <u>cross cell membranes</u>. This means they <u>can't be absorbed</u> from the gut <u>into the blood</u>, so <u>digestive enzymes</u> break these BIG molecules down into smaller ones like <u>sugars</u> (e.g. glucose), <u>amino acids</u>, <u>glycerol</u> and <u>fatty acids</u>.

2) These smaller, <u>soluble</u> molecules can <u>easily</u> cross cell membranes, meaning they can be <u>easily absorbed</u> from the gut into the blood, to be <u>transported</u> around the body for <u>use</u> by the <u>body cells</u>, e.g in respiration (see page 21).

Carbohydrases **Convert** *Carbohydrates* **into** *Simple Sugars*

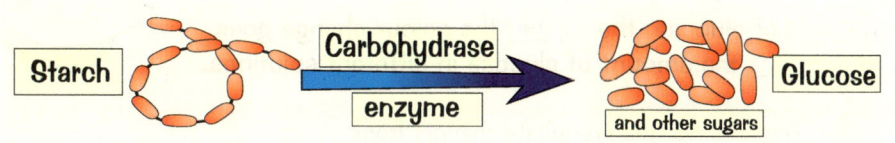

Starch is a carbohydrate made up of a chain of glucose molecules.

Proteases **Convert** *Proteins* **into** *Amino Acids*

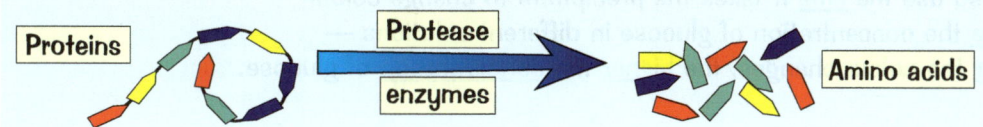

Lipases **Convert** *Lipids* **into** *Glycerol* **and** *Fatty Acids*

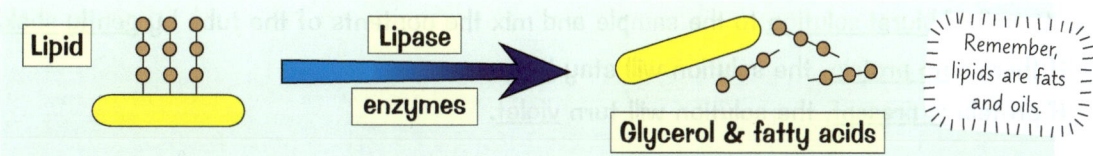

Remember, lipids are fats and oils.

Bile Neutralises **the** *Stomach Acid* **and** *Emulsifies* **Fats**

1) Bile is <u>secreted by</u> the <u>liver</u>. It's <u>stored</u> in the <u>gall bladder</u> before it's released into the <u>small intestine</u>.

2) Bile <u>emulsifies</u> fats. In other words it breaks the fat into <u>tiny droplets</u>. This gives a much <u>bigger surface area</u> of fat for the enzyme lipase to work on — which makes its digestion <u>faster</u>.

3) The <u>hydrochloric acid</u> in the stomach makes the pH <u>too acidic</u> for enzymes (e.g. lipase) in the small intestine to work properly. Bile is <u>alkaline</u> — it <u>neutralises</u> the acid and makes conditions <u>alkaline</u>. The enzymes in the small intestine <u>work best</u> in these alkaline conditions.

What do you call an acid that's eaten all the pies...

Make sure you know the examples of carbohydrase, protease and lipase, and the reactions that they catalyse.

Q1   Bile is a product of the liver. Describe and explain its role in digestion.   [4 marks]

Testing for Biological Molecules

Starch, glucose and proteins are all <u>biological molecules</u> (molecules found in living organisms). You need to know how you can <u>test for them</u> using different <u>chemicals</u>.

Starch *is Tested for with* Iodine Solution

Iodine solution is iodine dissolved in potassium iodide solution.

1) Just add <u>iodine solution</u> to the test sample.
2) If starch <u>is present</u>, the sample changes from <u>brown</u> to a dark, <u>blue-black</u> colour.
3) If there's <u>no starch</u>, it stays brown.

You Can Test for Glucose *Using* Benedict's Reagent

1) Add <u>Benedict's reagent</u> (which is <u>blue</u>) to a sample in a <u>boiling tube</u> and <u>heat</u> it in a water bath that's set to <u>75 °C</u>. If the test's <u>positive</u> it will form a <u>coloured precipitate</u> (solid particles suspended in the solution).

2) The <u>higher</u> the <u>concentration</u> of glucose, the <u>further</u> the colour change goes — you can use this to <u>compare</u> the amount of glucose in different solutions.

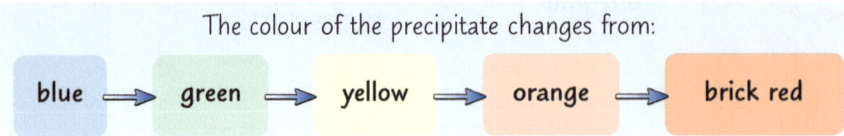

The colour of the precipitate changes from:

blue → green → yellow → orange → brick red

3) You can also use the <u>time</u> it takes the precipitate to change colour to <u>compare</u> the concentration of glucose in different solutions — the <u>quicker</u> the colour changes, the <u>higher</u> the <u>concentration</u> of glucose.

The Biuret Test *is Used for* Proteins

1) If you needed to find out if a substance contained <u>protein</u> you'd use the <u>biuret test</u>.
2) Prepare a sample and transfer 2 cm³ of your sample to a <u>test tube</u>.
3) Add 2 cm³ of <u>biuret solution</u> to the sample and mix the contents of the tube by <u>gently shaking it</u>.
   - If there's <u>no protein</u>, the solution will stay <u>blue</u>.
   - If protein <u>is present</u>, the solution will turn <u>violet</u>.

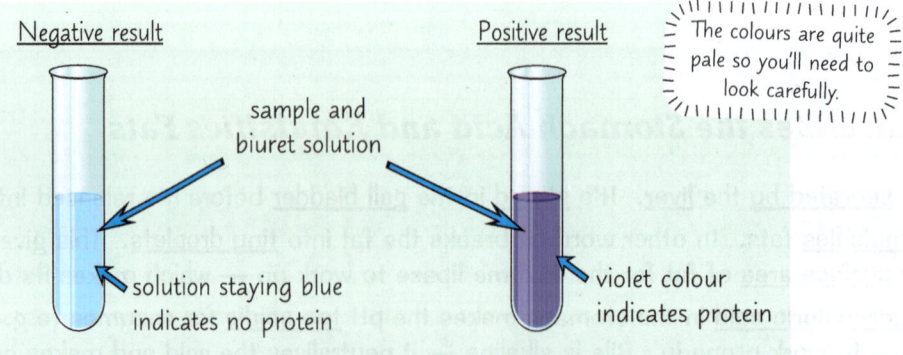

Negative result   Positive result

The colours are quite pale so you'll need to look carefully.

sample and biuret solution

solution staying blue indicates no protein

violet colour indicates protein

The Anger Test — annoy test subject. Red face = anger present...

OK, so this stuff isn't thrilling but learning it is better than being dropped into a 75 °C water bath. Yowch.

Q1   A solution that has been mixed with biuret solution turns violet.
      What conclusion would you draw from this test?   [1 mark]

The Digestive System

Here's a nice big picture of the whole of the <u>digestive system</u> — I know its what you've always wanted...

Organs in the Digestive System Have a Specific Role

1) Enzymes used in the digestive system are produced by specialised cells in <u>glands</u> and in the <u>gut lining</u>.

2) Different enzymes catalyse the <u>breakdown</u> of different food molecules.

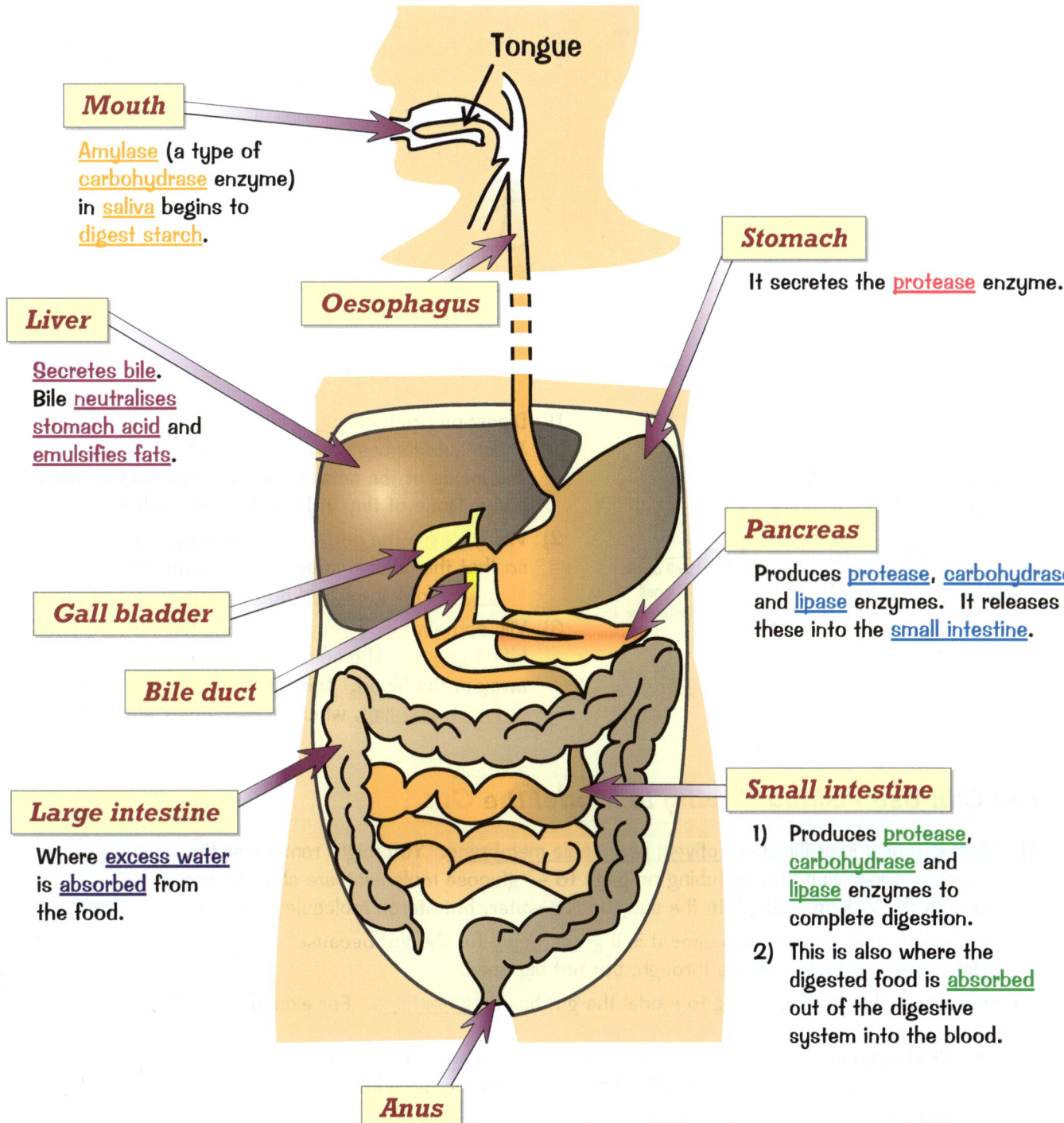

Tongue

Mouth

<u>Amylase</u> (a type of <u>carbohydrase</u> enzyme) in <u>saliva</u> begins to <u>digest starch</u>.

Stomach

It secretes the <u>protease</u> enzyme.

Oesophagus

Liver

<u>Secretes bile</u>. Bile <u>neutralises</u> <u>stomach acid</u> and <u>emulsifies fats</u>.

Pancreas

Produces <u>protease</u>, <u>carbohydrase</u> and <u>lipase</u> enzymes. It releases these into the <u>small intestine</u>.

Gall bladder

Bile duct

Small intestine

1) Produces <u>protease</u>, <u>carbohydrase</u> and <u>lipase</u> enzymes to complete digestion.

2) This is also where the digested food is <u>absorbed</u> out of the digestive system into the blood.

Large intestine

Where <u>excess water</u> is <u>absorbed</u> from the food.

Anus

Mmmm — so who's for a chocolate digestive...

Did you know that the whole of your digestive system is actually a hole that goes right through your body. Think about it. It just gets loads of food, digestive juices and enzymes piled into it. Most of it's then absorbed into the body and the rest is politely stored for removal.

Q1   Name two parts of the digestive system that produce protease enzymes.   [2 marks]

More on the Digestive System

There's a bit more you need to know about how food <u>moves through</u> and is <u>absorbed</u> in the digestive system.

Food is Moved Through The Gut by Peristalsis

1) There's <u>muscular</u> tissue all the way along the <u>passage</u> that food passes through during digestion.

2) Its job is to <u>squeeze</u> balls of food (called boluses) through your gut — <u>otherwise</u> it would get <u>clogged up</u> with bits of old food. Mmm.

3) This squeezing action, which is <u>waves</u> of <u>circular muscle contraction</u> and <u>relaxation</u>, is called <u>peristalsis</u>.

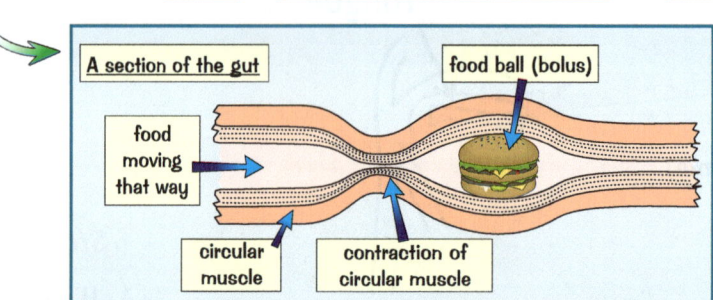

A section of the gut

food ball (bolus)

food moving that way

circular muscle

contraction of circular muscle

Dissolved Food and Water are Absorbed in the Digestive System

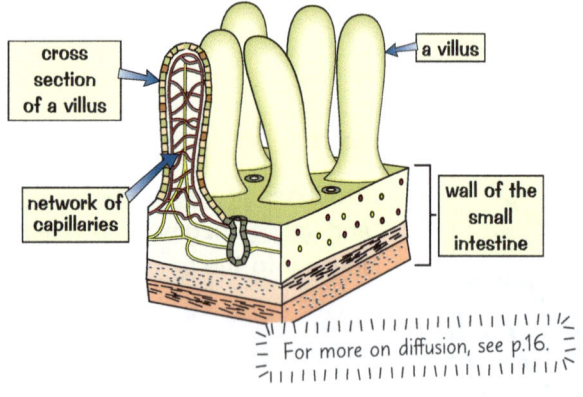

cross section of a villus

a villus

network of capillaries

wall of the small intestine

For more on diffusion, see p.16.

1) Digestion produces <u>soluble substances</u> such as <u>glucose</u>. These substances are absorbed in the <u>small intestine</u>. The inside of the small intestine is covered in millions and millions of tiny little projections called <u>villi</u>.

2) Villi <u>increase</u> the <u>surface area</u> in a big way so that the soluble substances are quickly <u>absorbed</u> into the <u>blood</u> by <u>diffusion</u>.

3) Villi contain <u>blood vessels</u> so they have a very good <u>blood supply</u>. The soluble substances are taken away in the blood. This helps to <u>maintain</u> a steep <u>diffusion gradient</u>, which assists quick absorption.

You Can Use Visking Tubing to Model the Gut

1) <u>Visking tubing</u> is artificial <u>selectively permeable membrane</u>. You might remember the <u>experiment</u> involving Visking tubing on page 16 — glucose molecules are able to pass through the Visking tubing into the surrounding water, but starch molecules are not.

2) The Visking tubing in this experiment is a <u>good model</u> for the <u>gut</u> because it lets <u>small molecules</u> diffuse through, but not big ones.

3) However, using Visking tubing to model the gut has its <u>limitations</u>. For example:

- Visking tubing has <u>no blood supply</u>, so it <u>can't maintain</u> a <u>diffusion gradient</u> from the inside of the tubing to the outside.
- Visking tubing <u>doesn't have</u> any <u>villi</u>, so the <u>surface area</u> is <u>smaller</u>.

So Visking tubing is not an <u>exact</u> model, but it's <u>good enough</u> to show how diffusion in the gut works.

Sadly, this information won't just diffuse into your head...

Make sure you get to grips with how digested food is absorbed through the wall of the small intestine.

Q1 Give two ways that villi in the small intestine aid quick absorption of glucose into the blood. [2 marks]

Diet

Your body needs the right fuel or it won't work properly — that means cutting down on the lard.

The Products of Digestion Are Used in The Body

Our body needs the digested products of the food we eat (that's why we eat it).
The digested products of different food molecules each have different functions in the body. For example:

Food Molecule	Digested Product	Function(s) of Digested Product
Carbohydrates	Glucose	Provides energy or is stored as glycogen so it can be used as a source of glucose later.
Fats and oils (lipids)	Fatty acids and glycerol	Provides energy.
Proteins	Amino acids	Needed to build proteins in the body which is important for the growth and repair of tissue.

A Balanced Diet Keeps Your Body Healthy

1) A balanced diet gives you all the essential nutrients you need in the right proportions (see below).

2) The nutrient groups are carbohydrates, proteins, fats (see above) vitamins, minerals, fibre and water.

3) Each of these nutrients have different functions in the body, which is why you need all of them in the right proportions to stay healthy.

Nutrient	Function
Minerals	E.g. iron is needed so that your body can make haemoglobin — the protein in red blood cells that carries oxygen.
Vitamins	E.g. vitamin C is needed in the growth, repair and maintenance of body tissue.
Fibre	Fibre provides bulk and helps the movement of material through your digestive system, keeping your digestive system healthy.
Water	Water helps to prevent dehydration and is used in lots of important body functions and processes.

Energy and Nutrient Needs Vary Between People

A balanced diet isn't a set thing — it's different for everyone. The balance of the different nutrients a person needs depends on things like their age and activity level.

Age ⟹ Children and teenagers need more protein for growth.

Physical activity ⟹ Active people need more protein for muscle development, and more carbohydrate for energy. While they're active, they're also likely to sweat more, so they'll need to drink more water too.

A plate of protein and carbohydrates, ta — easy on the vitamin C...

Take the time to understand the role of each nutrient group so you know why they are needed for a balanced diet.

Q1   Why might a person increase their protein intake after starting an intense exercise programme?   [1 mark]

Food and Health

The food you eat has a big effect on your health — keeping healthy can be a bit of a balancing act...

Different Foods Contain Different Amounts of Energy

1) Some foods contain small amounts of energy while others are very high in energy. For example:

Low energy foods:	High energy foods:
• Vegetables (e.g. celery)	• Confectionery (e.g. chocolate)
• Fruits (e.g. grapefruit)	• Dairy (e.g. butter)

2) To help stay healthy, the amount of energy you take in from the food you eat must be balanced with how much energy your body actually needs. For example, running a marathon uses a lot of energy so you'd need to take in more energy than normal to balance the energy used.

3) However, if you take in more energy from your diet than you use, your body will store the extra energy as fat — so you will put on weight.

4) If a person weighs over 20% more than the recommended weight for their height, then they are classed as obese.

Having an Unbalanced Diet Can Affect Your Health

Eating an excess of certain dietary nutrients can have pretty bad consequences on your health.

Too much sugar can lead to:	Too much fat can lead to:	Too much salt (sodium) can lead to:
• Type 2 diabetes (page 154)	• Heart disease (see p.37)	• High blood pressure (see p.37)
• Obesity	• Obesity	
• Tooth decay	• Circulatory disease	

Thrombosis is the formation of a blood clot in a blood vessel.

Being overweight can cause mobility issues because the extra weight makes it harder to move around.

Food Labels Give Nutritional Information

You can analyse the information given in food labels to see how food might affect your health — take a look at this example comparing two food labels:

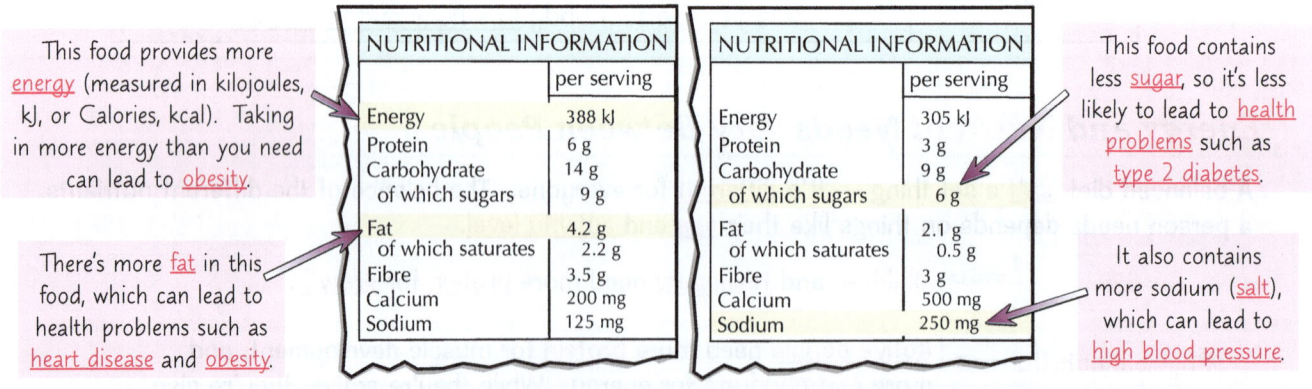

This food provides more energy (measured in kilojoules, kJ, or Calories, kcal). Taking in more energy than you need can lead to obesity.

There's more fat in this food, which can lead to health problems such as heart disease and obesity.

NUTRITIONAL INFORMATION	
	per serving
Energy	388 kJ
Protein	6 g
Carbohydrate	14 g
of which sugars	9 g
Fat	4.2 g
of which saturates	2.2 g
Fibre	3.5 g
Calcium	200 mg
Sodium	125 mg

NUTRITIONAL INFORMATION	
	per serving
Energy	305 kJ
Protein	3 g
Carbohydrate	9 g
of which sugars	6 g
Fat	2.1 g
of which saturates	0.5 g
Fibre	3 g
Calcium	500 mg
Sodium	250 mg

This food contains less sugar, so it's less likely to lead to health problems such as type 2 diabetes.

It also contains more sodium (salt), which can lead to high blood pressure.

So that's why celery is tired all the time...

Knowing exactly what's in the food you're eating and how it can affect your health is the key to having a balanced diet. That's why food producers have to put the nutritional information of their products on the packet.

Q1   Give three health risks associated with having an unbalanced diet with too much sugar.   [3 marks]

Energy in Food

I bet you've always been told not to play with your <u>food</u> — well on this page I'm going to <u>encourage</u> you to...

Food Can be Burnt to See How Much Energy it Contains

The posh name for this is <u>calorimetry</u>. You need to know how to do it with a <u>simple experiment</u>:

First You Need a Dry Food, Water and a Flame...

1) You need a <u>food</u> that'll <u>burn easily</u> — something that's dry, e.g. dried beans or pasta, will work best.

2) <u>Weigh</u> a small amount of the food and then <u>skewer</u> it on a <u>mounted needle</u>.

3) Next, add <u>a set volume</u> of water to a <u>boiling tube</u> (held with a clamp) — this will be used to <u>measure</u> the amount of <u>energy</u> that's transferred when the food is <u>burnt</u>.

4) Measure the <u>temperature</u> of the <u>water</u>, then <u>set fire</u> to the food using a <u>Bunsen burner flame</u>. Make sure the Bunsen isn't near the water or your results might be a bit wonky.

5) Immediately <u>hold</u> the burning food <u>under</u> the boiling tube until it <u>goes out</u>. Then <u>relight</u> the food and <u>hold</u> it under the tube — <u>keep doing this</u> until the food <u>won't</u> catch fire again.

6) The last thing to do is measure the <u>temperature</u> of the <u>water</u> again. Then you're ready for a bit of <u>maths</u>...

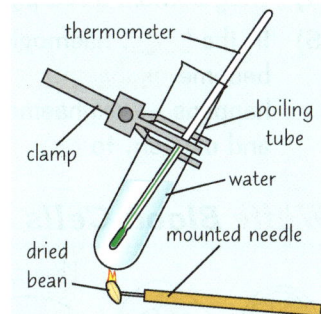

thermometer

boiling tube

clamp

water

dried bean

mounted needle

...Then You Can Calculate the Amount of Energy in the Food

1) First work out how many <u>joules</u> (J) of energy the food contains using this formula:

$$\text{Energy in Food (in J)} = \text{Mass of water (in g)} \times \text{Temperature change of water (in °C)} \times 4.2$$

1 cm³ of water is the same as 1 g of water.

2) Then work out how many joules are in <u>each gram</u> of the food. You need to do this calculation so you can <u>compare</u> the energy values of different foods <u>fairly</u>.

$$\text{Energy per gram of food (in J/g)} = \frac{\text{Energy in food (in J)}}{\text{Mass of food (in g)}}$$

EXAMPLE: A student burned 0.2 g of popcorn and 0.5 g of bread separately under 20 cm³ of water. During the experiment, the temperature of the water increased by 28.6 °C when the popcorn was burnt and 38.7 °C when the bread was burnt. Which food has more energy per unit mass?

1) First find the amount of energy in each type of food:

Energy in the popcorn = 20 g × 28.6 °C × 4.2
= 2402.4 J

Energy in the bread = 20 g × 38.7 °C × 4.2
= 3250.8 J

2) Then convert this into joules per gram:

Popcorn: 2402.4 ÷ 0.2
= 12 012.0 J/g

Bread: 3250.8 ÷ 0.5
= 6501.6 J/g

Answer: the popcorn has more energy per unit mass.

3) The experiment <u>isn't perfect</u> — quite a bit of the <u>energy</u> released from burning is <u>lost</u> to the surroundings. It's why the energy value on the <u>packet</u> of the food you used is likely to be <u>much higher</u> than your own.

4) There are measures you can take to <u>increase</u> the <u>accuracy</u> of the experiment. For example, <u>insulating</u> the boiling tube, e.g. with foil, would minimise heat loss and keep <u>more energy</u> in the water.

I think I accidentally measured the energy in my thumb...

Food scientists use fancy machines called calorimeters to measure the energy content of our food — they're insulated and sealed so produce much more accurate results than the experiment on this page. (But they're not as fun.)

Q1   A student performed a calorimetry experiment on a small piece of bread. Why is it important to record the increase in temperature as soon as possible after the bread is burnt in this experiment? [1 mark]

Circulatory System — Blood

Blood is a tissue. One of its jobs is to act as a huge transport system. There are four main things in blood...

Red Blood Cells Carry Oxygen

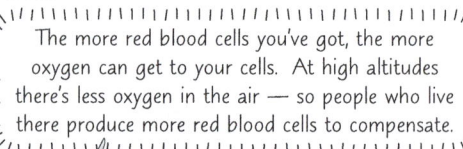

cell membrane

1) The job of red blood cells is to carry oxygen from the lungs to all the cells in the body.

2) They have a biconcave disc shape (in other words, they look a bit like a jam doughnut that's being pressed in at the top and bottom) to give a large surface area for absorbing oxygen.

3) They don't have a nucleus — this allows more room to carry oxygen.

4) They contain a red pigment called haemoglobin, which contains iron.

5) In the lungs, haemoglobin binds to oxygen to become oxyhaemoglobin. In body tissues, the reverse happens — oxyhaemoglobin splits up into haemoglobin and oxygen, to release oxygen to the cells.

The more red blood cells you've got, the more oxygen can get to your cells. At high altitudes there's less oxygen in the air — so people who live there produce more red blood cells to compensate.

White Blood Cells Defend Against Infectious Disease

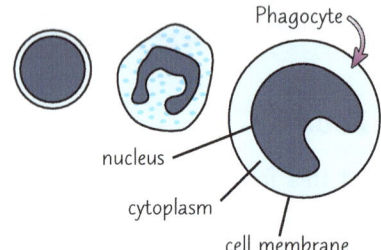

Phagocyte

nucleus

cytoplasm

cell membrane

1) Phagocytes are white blood cells that can change shape to engulf (gobble up) unwelcome microorganisms — this is called phagocytosis.

2) Lymphocytes are white blood cells that produce antibodies against microorganisms (see p.158). Some also produce antitoxins to neutralise any toxins produced by the microorganisms.

3) When you have an infection, your white blood cells multiply to fight it off — so a blood test will show a high white blood cell count.

Platelets Help Blood Clot

1) These are small fragments of cells. They have no nucleus.

2) They help the blood to clot at a wound — to stop all your blood pouring out and to stop microorganisms getting in. (So platelets kinda float about waiting for accidents to happen.)

3) Lack of platelets can cause excessive bleeding and bruising.

Plasma is the Liquid That Carries Everything in Blood

This is a pale straw-coloured liquid which carries just about everything:

1) Red and white blood cells and platelets.

2) Nutrients like glucose and amino acids. These are the soluble products of digestion, which are absorbed from the gut and taken to the cells of the body.

3) Carbon dioxide from the organs to the lungs.

4) Urea from the liver to the kidneys.

5) Hormones.

6) Plasma also distributes heat around the body to keep your body's internal temperature stable.

Platelets — ideal for small dinners...

When you're ill the doctor often takes a blood sample for analysis. Blood tests can be used to diagnose loads of things — not just disorders of the blood. This is because the blood transports so many chemicals produced by so many organs... and it's easier to take blood than, say, a piece of muscle.

Q1 Describe the purpose of platelets in blood. [1 mark]

Q2 Name the pigment in red blood cells that is responsible for the transport of oxygen. [1 mark]

Circulatory System — Heart

The circulatory system carries <u>food</u> and <u>oxygen</u> to every cell in the body. As well as being a delivery service, it's also a waste collection service — it carries <u>waste products</u> to where they can be removed from the body.

The DOUBLE Circulatory System, Actually

1) The circulatory system is made up of the <u>heart</u>, <u>blood vessels</u> and <u>blood</u>. Humans have a <u>double circulatory system</u> — <u>two circuits</u> joined together:

2) In the first one (the <u>pulmonary</u> circuit), the <u>right ventricle</u> (see below) pumps <u>deoxygenated</u> blood (blood with low oxygen) to the <u>lungs</u> to take in <u>oxygen</u>. The blood then <u>returns</u> to the heart.

3) In the second one (the <u>systemic</u> circuit), the <u>left ventricle</u> (see below) pumps <u>oxygenated</u> blood around all the <u>other organs</u> of the <u>body</u>. The blood <u>gives up</u> its oxygen at the body cells and the <u>deoxygenated</u> blood <u>returns</u> to the heart to be pumped out to the <u>lungs</u> again.

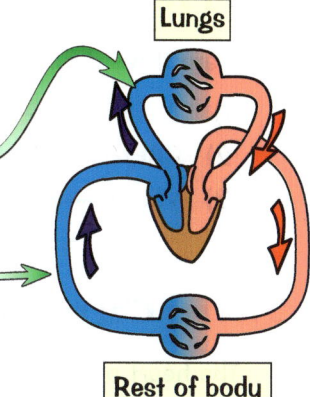

Lungs

Rest of body

The Heart is a Muscle That Contracts to Pump Blood Around The Body

1) The <u>heart</u> uses its <u>four chambers</u> (right and left atria and ventricles) to pump blood around.

2) The heart has <u>valves</u> to make sure that blood flows in the right direction. When the ventricles <u>contract</u>, the valves to the <u>atria close</u> and the valves to the <u>blood vessels open</u>. This prevents <u>backflow</u> — when the blood flows <u>backwards</u>.

1) <u>Blood flows into</u> the two <u>atria</u> from the <u>vena cava</u> and the <u>pulmonary vein</u>.

2) The <u>atria contract</u>, pushing the blood into the <u>ventricles</u>.

3) The <u>ventricles contract</u>, forcing the blood into the <u>pulmonary artery</u> and the <u>aorta</u>, and <u>out</u> of the <u>heart</u>.

4) The blood then flows to the <u>organs</u>, including the <u>lungs</u>, through <u>arteries</u>, and <u>returns</u> through <u>veins</u> (see next page).

5) The atria fill again and the whole cycle <u>starts over</u>.

- The <u>left</u> ventricle has a much <u>thicker wall</u> than the <u>right</u> ventricle. It needs the <u>greater pressure</u> generated by the thicker <u>muscle</u> because it has to pump blood around the <u>whole body</u>, whereas the right ventricle only has to pump it to the <u>lungs</u>.

- The heart is made up of <u>cardiac muscle</u>.

- Blood is supplied to the cardiac muscle by the <u>coronary arteries</u>, which branch from the base of the <u>aorta</u>. They allow the <u>oxygen</u> and <u>glucose</u> needed for respiration to <u>diffuse</u> into the cardiac muscle cells of the <u>thick heart wall</u>. Muscle contraction needs <u>energy</u>, so if the cardiac muscle cells <u>can't</u> respire, they <u>can't contract</u>.

- When your <u>heart rate increases</u> (e.g. during exercising) your heart muscle is <u>contracting</u> at a <u>faster rate</u>.

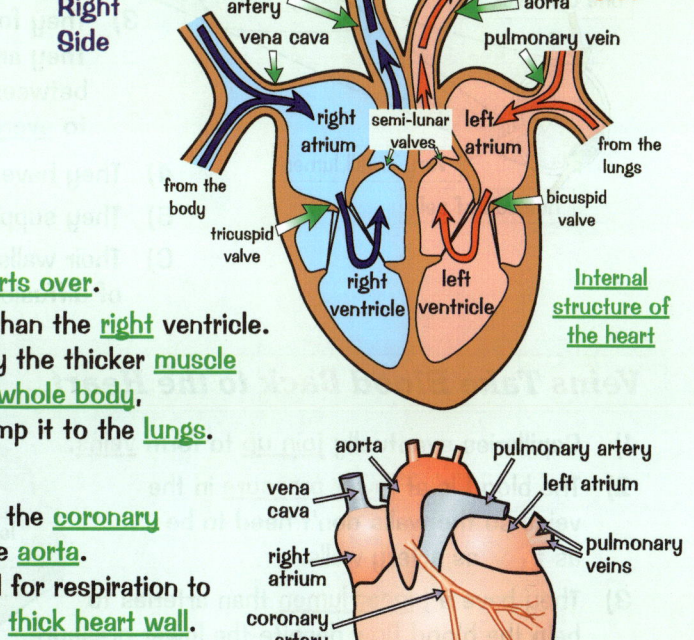

Atria is plural. Atrium is when there is just one.

blue = deoxygenated blood
red = oxygenated blood

Right Side

Left Side

pulmonary artery

vena cava

to the lungs

to the body

aorta

pulmonary vein

right atrium

semi-lunar valves

left atrium

from the body

from the lungs

bicuspid valve

tricuspid valve

right ventricle

left ventricle

Internal structure of the heart

aorta

vena cava

right atrium

coronary artery

right ventricle

vena cava

pulmonary artery

left atrium

pulmonary veins

left ventricle

External structure of the heart

3) You may get to carry out a <u>heart dissection</u> or you may get to watch one being carried out. <u>Dissection</u> is a good way to show how the <u>heart's structure</u> relates to its <u>function</u>.

Okay — let's get to the heart of the matter...

Interesting fact — when doctors use a stethoscope to listen to your heart, it's the valves closing that they hear.

Q1   What is the function of the coronary arteries?   [1 mark]

Circulatory System — Blood Vessels

Want to know more about the <u>circulatory system</u>... Good. Because here's another page.

Blood Vessels are Designed for Their Function

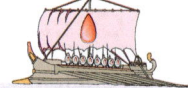

There are three different types of blood vessel:

1) ARTERIES — these carry the blood from the <u>heart</u> to the <u>organs</u>.

2) CAPILLARIES — these are involved in the <u>exchange of materials</u> at the tissues.

3) VEINS — these carry the blood from the <u>organs</u> to the <u>heart</u>.

Arteries Carry Blood Under Pressure

1) The heart pumps the blood out at <u>high pressure</u> so the artery walls are <u>strong</u> and <u>elastic</u>.

2) The walls are <u>thick</u> compared to the size of the hole down the middle (the "<u>lumen</u>" — silly name).

3) They contain thick layers of <u>muscle</u> to make them <u>strong</u>, and <u>elastic fibres</u> to allow them to stretch and <u>spring back</u>.

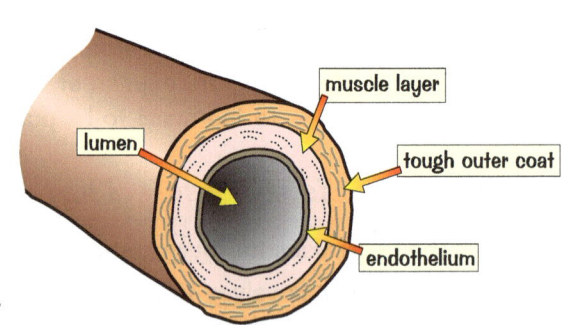

Capillaries are Really Small

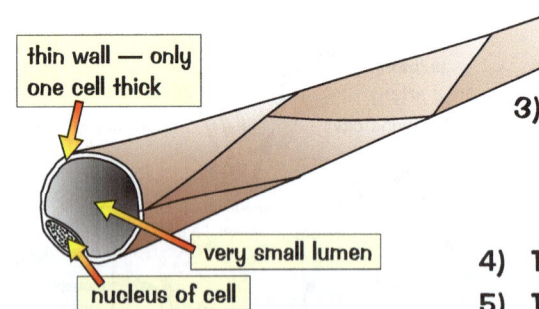

1) In the organs, <u>arteries</u> branch into <u>capillaries</u>.

2) Capillaries are really <u>tiny</u> — too small to see.

3) They form <u>extensive</u> networks that spread throughout the body. They are also very <u>narrow</u>, so they can squeeze into the gaps between cells. This means they can carry the blood <u>really close</u> to <u>every cell</u> in the body to <u>exchange substances</u> with them.

4) They have <u>permeable walls</u>, so substances can <u>diffuse in</u> and <u>out</u>.

5) They supply <u>food</u> and <u>oxygen</u>, and take away <u>waste</u> like <u>CO_2</u>.

6) Their walls are usually <u>only one cell thick</u>. This <u>increases</u> the rate of diffusion by <u>decreasing</u> the <u>distance</u> over which it occurs.

Veins Take Blood Back to the Heart

1) Capillaries eventually <u>join up</u> to form <u>veins</u>.

2) The blood is at <u>lower pressure</u> in the veins so the walls don't need to be as <u>thick</u> as artery walls.

3) They have a <u>bigger lumen</u> than arteries to help the blood <u>flow</u> despite the lower pressure.

4) They also have <u>valves</u> to help keep the blood flowing in the <u>right direction</u>.

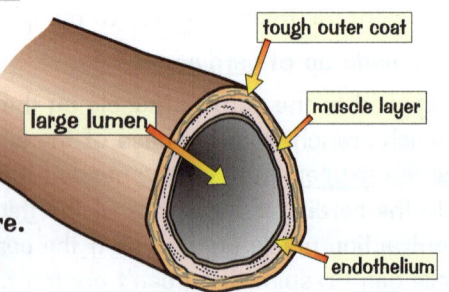

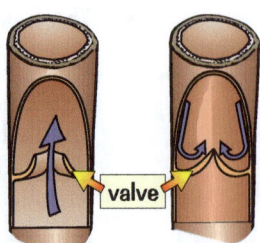

Learn this page — don't struggle in vein...

Here's an interesting fact for you — your body contains about 60 000 miles of blood vessels. That's about six times the distance from London to Sydney in Australia. Of course, capillaries are really tiny, which is how they can be such a big length — they can only be seen with a microscope.

Q1   Explain why veins have valves.   [1 mark]

Q2   Explain the advantage of capillary walls being only one cell thick.   [1 mark]

Cardiovascular Disease

Cardiovascular disease is a big, big problem in the UK. The good news is that knowing about and avoiding some of the risk factors related to cardiovascular disease can help to reduce your chance of getting it.

Cardiovascular Disease Affects The Heart and Blood Vessels

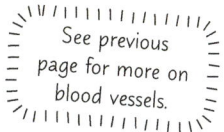

See previous page for more on blood vessels.

1) Cardiovascular disease (CVD) is any disease associated with your heart and blood vessels. E.g. coronary heart disease, heart attacks and strokes.

2) Cholesterol is a fatty substance that the body needs to make things like cell membranes. But too much cholesterol in the blood can cause fatty deposits to build up in arteries.

3) Deposits occur in areas where the artery wall has been damaged, e.g. by high blood pressure.

4) These deposits narrow the arteries, restricting blood flow. Over time the fatty deposits harden, forming atheromas. Coronary heart disease is when the coronary arteries have lots of atheromas in them, which restricts blood flow to the heart.

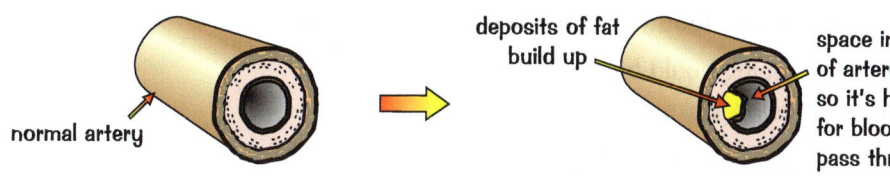

normal artery

deposits of fat build up

space in centre of artery shrinks, so it's harder for blood to pass through

5) Sometimes bits of atheromas can break off or damage the blood vessel, causing a blood clot. Complete blockage of an artery by atheromas or blood clots can lead to a heart attack, where part of the cardiac muscle is deprived of oxygen. If the blockage occurs in the brain, it can cause a stroke.

Lifestyle Factors May Increase the Risk of Cardiovascular Disease

1) Risk factors are things that are linked to an increase in the likelihood that a person will develop a certain disease during their lifetime. They don't guarantee that someone will get the disease.

2) Some risk factors are lifestyle factors that people can change. For example:

> Smoking is a major risk factor associated with cardiovascular disease. This is because:
> - Nicotine in cigarette smoke increases heart rate, which increases blood pressure.
> - Increased blood pressure increases the risk of atheromas forming in arteries.

> High levels of salt and fat in your diet are linked to cardiovascular disease because:
> - Too much fat in your diet can increase your blood cholesterol level.
> - Too much salt in your diet can increase your blood pressure.

> Exercise can lower both blood pressure and blood cholesterol, so a lack of exercise can increase the risk of high blood pressure and high cholesterol, which increases the risk of CVD.

3) Other risk factors are unavoidable. For example, a person's age or gender may make them more likely to get a disease. Genetic factors can also be risk factors:

> Inheriting particular genes from your parents may increase your risk of developing coronary heart disease.

Look after yerselves me hearties...

Risk factors won't always cause CVD directly. For example, a high fat diet and a lack of exercise lead to problems such as high blood pressure and high cholesterol levels, and it's these problems which actually cause CVD.

Q1   Explain how atheromas in the arteries can lead to a heart attack.   [2 marks]

Q2   What is a risk factor for disease?   [1 mark]

Revision Questions for Unit 1b

Well, that wraps up <u>Unit 1b</u> — now for some questions to see if you've been paying attention...
- Try these questions and <u>tick off each one</u> when you <u>get it right</u>.
- When you've done <u>all the questions</u> for a topic and are <u>completely happy</u> with it, tick off the topic.

The Digestive System and Testing for Biological Molecules (p.27-30) ☐

1) Why do large molecules in food, such as starch, need to be broken down into smaller molecules?
2) Name the enzyme that digests starch.
3) What type of enzyme converts proteins into amino acids?
4) State the colour change that occurs when iodine solution is added to a sample containing starch.
5) What chemical reagent is used to test for the presence of glucose?
6) Where in the digestive system does starch digestion begin?
7) Name the process which moves food through the digestive system.
8) a) Describe how Visking tubing could be used to model the gut.
   b) Give one limitation of using Visking tubing to model the gut.

Diet, Food and Health (p.31-33) ☐

9) Name the product of protein digestion and give its function in the body.
10) What is a balanced diet?
11) List all of the nutrient groups needed for a balanced diet.
12) Name three health risks associated with having an unbalanced diet with too much fat.
13) True or False? A diet low in salt can lead to high blood pressure.
14) Describe an experiment you could carry out to find the energy content of a piece of pasta.

The Circulatory System and Cardiovascular Disease (p.34-37) ☐

15) Describe the shape of a red blood cell.
16) True or False? Red blood cells have a nucleus.
17) What is the function of white blood cells?
18) What effect would a lack of platelets have on the body?
19) Name five substances carried by blood plasma.
20) Which circuit of the double circulatory system pumps deoxygenated blood to the lungs?
21) Where in the heart is the tricuspid valve located?
22) Where does blood in the left ventricle flow to when the left ventricle contracts?
23) Why does the left ventricle have a thicker wall than the right ventricle?
24) Which type of blood vessel carries blood back to the heart?
25) Why do capillaries form extensive networks in the body?
26) What is an atheroma?
27) Give three risk factors that increase a person's risk of developing cardiovascular disease.

Photosynthesis

You don't know photosynthesis 'til you know its equation. It's in a nice green box so you can't possibly miss it.

Plants are Able to Make Their Own Food by Photosynthesis

1) During photosynthesis, photosynthetic organisms, such as green plants and algae, use energy from the Sun to make glucose.

2) Photosynthesis happens inside subcellular structures called chloroplasts. These contain enzymes that catalyse the reactions of photosynthesis. They also contain chlorophyll, which absorbs light energy.

3) During photosynthesis, carbon dioxide and water are converted into glucose. Oxygen is also produced as a by-product. This is the word equation for photosynthesis:

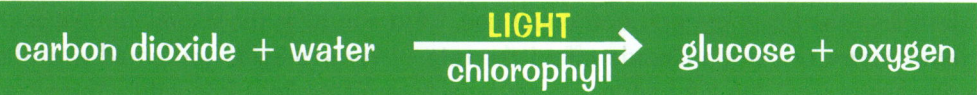

$$\text{carbon dioxide} + \text{water} \xrightarrow[\text{chlorophyll}]{\text{LIGHT}} \text{glucose} + \text{oxygen}$$

4) Plants use glucose in five main ways:

- For respiration — this releases energy from glucose which enables the plants to convert the rest of the glucose into various other useful substances.
- Making cellulose — glucose is converted into cellulose for making strong plant cell walls.
- Making proteins — glucose is combined with nitrate ions (absorbed from the soil) to make amino acids, which are then made into proteins.
- Stored as oils or fats — glucose is turned into lipids (fats and oils) for storing in seeds.
- Stored as starch — glucose is turned into starch and stored in roots, stems and leaves, ready for use when photosynthesis isn't happening, like in the winter.

The Starch Test Shows Whether Photosynthesis is Taking Place

Glucose is stored by plants as starch. If a plant can't photosynthesise, it can't make starch — you can use this to show what factors are needed for photosynthesis.

First, you need to know how to test a leaf for starch. Start by dunking the leaf in boiling water (hold it with tweezers or forceps). This kills the leaf, so stops any chemical reactions happening inside it. Now put the leaf in a boiling tube with some ethanol and heat it gently in an electric water bath — this gets rid of any chlorophyll and makes the leaf a white-ish colour. Finally, rinse the leaf in cold water (to soften it) and add a few drops of iodine solution — if starch is present the leaf will turn blue-black. Now for the experiment — this example demonstrates how you can show that carbon dioxide is needed for photosynthesis:

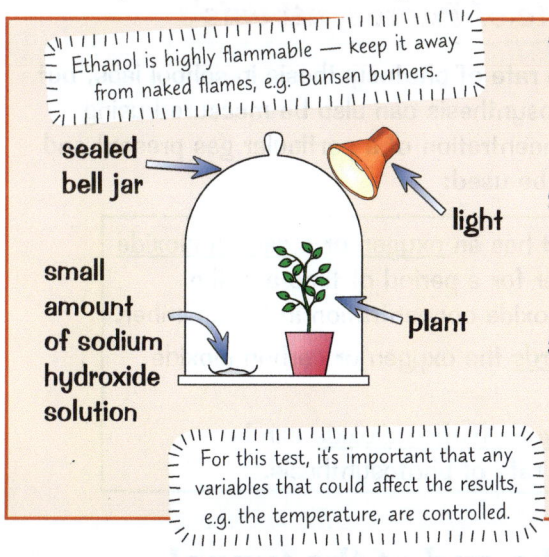

Ethanol is highly flammable — keep it away from naked flames, e.g. Bunsen burners.

sealed bell jar

light

small amount of sodium hydroxide solution

plant

For this test, it's important that any variables that could affect the results, e.g. the temperature, are controlled.

1) Start by destarching some plants (i.e. leave them in the dark for 48 hours so that they use up their starch stores). This means that the starch test will only show a colour change if new starch has been produced.

2) Keep one plant in a sealed jar with dilute sodium hydroxide solution, which absorbs CO_2 out of the air, and leave another plant out in the open for a while — then perform the starch test on a leaf from each plant.

3) The leaf from the plant left in the open should turn blue-black, but the leaf from the plant in the sealed jar won't. This shows that no starch has been made in the leaf grown without CO_2, which means that CO_2 is needed for photosynthesis to happen.

The end of unit test — shows whether revision has taken place...

You must learn the photosynthesis equation. Learn it so well that you'll still remember it when you're 109.

Q1 Explain how the starch test can be used to show that plants need CO_2 to photosynthesise.   [4 marks]

Investigating the Rate of Photosynthesis

If you've always wanted to investigate how different factors affect the rate of photosynthesis, you're in luck...

Oxygen Production Shows the Rate of Photosynthesis   [PRACTICAL]

H

1) The rate of photosynthesis can be affected by light intensity, CO_2 concentration and temperature. Any of these can become limiting factors — they can stop photosynthesis from happening any faster.

2) You can investigate how each of the different factors affect the rate of photosynthesis. A classic way to do this is to use pondweed and to measure oxygen production over time.

3) The rate at which the pondweed produces oxygen corresponds to the rate at which it's photosynthesising — the faster the rate of oxygen production, the faster the rate of photosynthesis.

4) The box below describes the basic method you could use. You can alter the experiment to test how light intensity, temperature or carbon dioxide affect the rate — for example, you could vary the distance of the pondweed from the light source in order to investigate light intensity. There's more on how to alter the experiment over the next two pages.

1) The apparatus is set up according to the diagram.

2) A set amount of sodium hydrogencarbonate (which gives off CO_2) may be added to the water to control the amount of CO_2 the pondweed receives.

3) The pondweed is left to photosynthesise for a set amount of time.

4) As it photosynthesises, oxygen bubbles will be released. The number of oxygen bubbles produced in one minute are counted and used as a measurement of the rate of photosynthesis.

5) The results are recorded in a table, and the experiment is then repeated to test a range of values for the factor being investigated, e.g. a range of different distances from the light source.

6) Variables other than the one being investigated should be kept the same, e.g. if light intensity is being investigated, keep the temperature and carbon dioxide concentration the same, leave the pondweed for the same amount of time.

7) Once the experiment is completed, a graph of the results can be produced to help to identify any patterns, e.g. you could plot the number of bubbles produced against the distance from the light source.

For more accurate results, you could replace the boiling tube with a measuring cylinder and use this to record the volume of gas given off.

There are Other Ways of Measuring the Rate of Photosynthesis

The experiment above is a common way of investigating the rate of photosynthesis in school labs, but it isn't the only method that can be used. The rate of photosynthesis can also be measured using gas sensors and data loggers — gas sensors detect the concentration of a particular gas present and data loggers record the data for you. This is how they can be used:

1) Leaves from a plant can be put into a chamber that has an oxygen or a carbon dioxide sensor attached. The leaves are left in the chamber for a period of time and the sensor regularly measures the oxygen or carbon dioxide concentration in the chamber.

2) The sensor is attached to a data logger which records the oxygen or carbon dioxide concentration detected by the sensor.

3) The rate at which the leaves produce oxygen or use up carbon dioxide can be determined by the data logger, which indicates the rate of photosynthesis.

That was intense — but I see light at the end of the tunnel...

The investigation at the top of the page can be varied to see how different factors affect the rate of photosynthesis. The next two pages have more on this but it's best to understand what's happening here before moving on.

Q1   Explain how the rate of oxygen production corresponds to the rate of photosynthesis.   [2 marks]

Limiting Factors of Photosynthesis

Now that you know light, CO_2 and temperature all <u>affect</u> the <u>rate of photosynthesis</u>, you also need to know <u>how</u> they affect the rate, so you can take a gander at a load of lovely pictures... well, graphs. I've also thrown an <u>equation</u> in for good measure. I can tell these pages are going to be your favourites...

Here Are Three Important *Graphs* for *Rate of Photosynthesis*

1) Not Enough LIGHT Slows Down the Rate of Photosynthesis

1) <u>Light energy</u> is needed for photosynthesis.

2) As the <u>light level</u> is raised, the rate of photosynthesis <u>increases steadily</u> — but only up to a <u>certain point</u>.

3) Beyond that, it <u>won't</u> make any difference — it'll be either the <u>temperature</u> or the <u>CO_2 level</u> which is the limiting factor.

4) In the lab you can investigate light intensity by <u>moving</u> a <u>lamp</u> closer to or further away from your plant.

5) But if you just plot the rate of photosynthesis against "distance of lamp from the plant", you get a <u>weird-shaped graph</u>. To get a graph like the one above you either need to <u>measure</u> the light intensity at the plant using a <u>light meter</u> or do a bit of nifty maths with your results. Here's why:

The distance from the lamp and light intensity are <u>inversely proportional</u> to each other — this means that as the <u>distance increases</u>, the <u>light intensity decreases</u>. However, light intensity decreases in proportion to the <u>square</u> of the distance. This is called the <u>inverse square law</u> and is written like this:

Putting one over the distance shows the <u>inverse</u>.

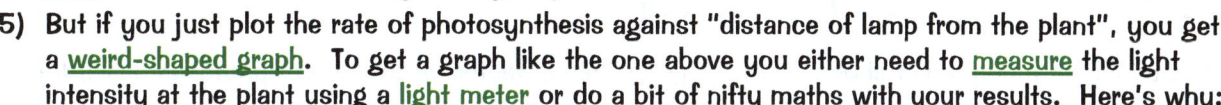

$$\text{light intensity (i)} \propto \frac{1}{\text{distance (d)}^2}$$

<u>Halving</u> the distance → intensity is $2 \times 2 = \underline{4}$ times <u>greater</u>
<u>Tripling</u> the distance → intensity is $3 \times 3 = \underline{9}$ times <u>smaller</u>

EXAMPLE: Use the inverse square law to calculate the light intensity when the lamp is 10 cm from the pondweed.

1) <u>Use the formula</u> $\frac{1}{d^2}$.

   $\text{light intensity} = \frac{1}{d^2}$

2) Fill in the <u>values</u> you know — you're given the distance, so put that in.

   $\text{light intensity} = \frac{1}{10^2}$

3) Calculate the <u>answer</u>.

   $= 0.01$ a.u.

'a.u.' stands for 'arbitrary units'.

2) Too Little CARBON DIOXIDE Also Slows it Down

1) <u>CO_2</u> is needed for photosynthesis.

2) This means that <u>increasing the concentration</u> of <u>CO_2</u> will increase the rate of photosynthesis — but only up to a point. After this the graph <u>flattens out</u> — CO_2 is no longer the <u>limiting factor</u>.

3) If <u>CO_2</u> is in plentiful supply, then the factor limiting photosynthesis must be <u>light</u> or <u>temperature</u>.

4) In the experiment on the previous page, dissolving different amounts of <u>sodium hydrogencarbonate</u> in the same volume of water will vary the CO_2 concentration.

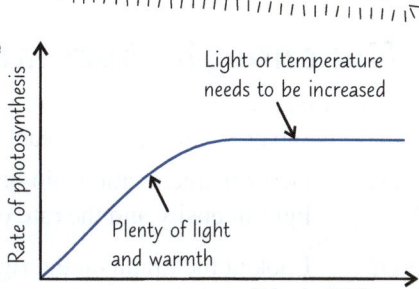

On a warm, sunny day, the limiting factor is often CO_2 concentration.

Light or temperature needs to be increased

Plenty of light and warmth

Higher

Limiting Factors of Photosynthesis

3) The TEMPERATURE has to be Just Right

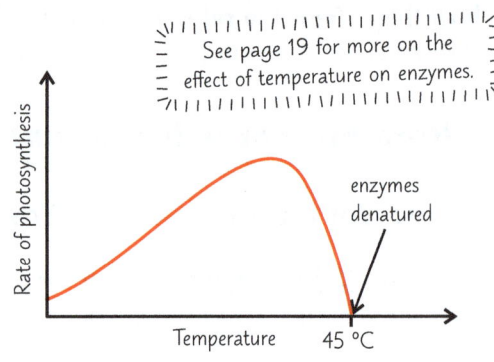

See page 19 for more on the effect of temperature on enzymes.

1) Usually, if the temperature is the limiting factor it's because it's too low — the enzymes needed for photosynthesis work more slowly at low temperatures.

2) But if the plant gets too hot, the enzymes it needs for photosynthesis and its other reactions will be denatured — the rate of reaction decreases dramatically.

3) This happens at about 45 °C (pretty hot for outdoors, but greenhouses can get that hot if you're not careful).

4) In the experiment on page 40, you can vary the temperature of the beaker using a water bath.

One Graph May Show the Effect of Many Limiting Factors

You could get a graph that shows more than one limiting factor on the rate of photosynthesis, for example:

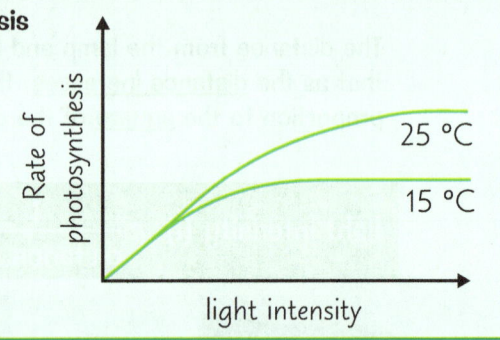

1) The graph on the right shows how the rate of photosynthesis is affected by light intensity and temperature.

2) At the start, both of the lines show that as the light intensity increases, the rate of photosynthesis increases steadily.

3) But the lines level off when light is no longer the limiting factor. The line at 25 °C levels off at a higher point than the one at 15 °C, showing that temperature must have been a limiting factor at 15 °C.

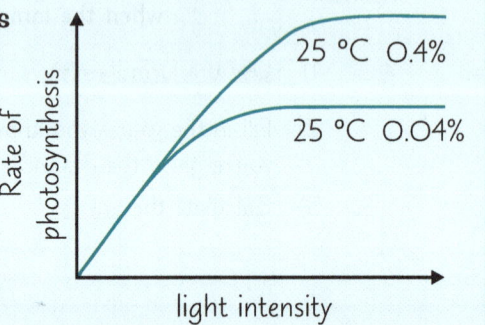

1) The graph on the right shows how the rate of photosynthesis is affected by light intensity and CO_2 concentration.

2) Again, both the lines level off when light is no longer the limiting factor.

3) The line at the higher CO_2 concentration of 0.4% levels off at a higher point than the one at 0.04%. This means CO_2 concentration must have been a limiting factor at 0.04% CO_2. The limiting factor here isn't temperature because it's the same for both lines (25 °C).

Not enough chocolate — that's my limiting factor...

...don't blame it on the temperature, blame it on the plant. Make sure you understand what each of the graphs on these two pages show and how each of the three limiting factors affects the rate of photosynthesis.

Q1 Describe the relationship between increasing light intensity and the rate of photosynthesis. [2 marks]

Q2 Look at the graph on the right.
   a) What is limiting the rate of photosynthesis at point **A**? [1 mark]
   b) What is limiting the rate of photosynthesis at point **B**? [1 mark]

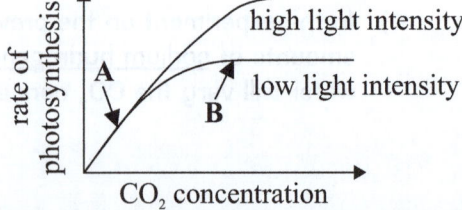

Food Chains and Food Webs

Organisms within an ecosystem <u>eat each other</u> — what eats what can be beautifully presented in a <u>food chain</u> or <u>food web</u>. But before we get into that, it's helpful to know how an <u>ecosystem</u> is <u>structured</u>...

Ecosystems are Organised into Different Levels

Ecosystems have <u>different levels</u> of <u>organisation</u>:
1) <u>Population</u> — <u>All</u> the organisms of <u>one species</u> in a <u>habitat</u>.
2) <u>Community</u> — <u>All</u> the organisms (<u>different species</u>) living in a habitat.
3) <u>Ecosystem</u> — A community of <u>organisms</u> along with all the <u>non-living conditions</u>.

A species is a group of similar organisms that can reproduce to give fertile offspring.

Food Chains Show What's Eaten by What in an Ecosystem

1) <u>Food chains</u> always start with a <u>producer</u> — an organism that <u>makes its own food</u>, usually using energy from the Sun's radiation. Producers are usually <u>green plants</u>, which make <u>glucose</u> via photosynthesis (see p.39). Green plants only capture <u>a small percentage</u> of the Sun's energy that reaches them.
2) Some of the glucose made by a plant is used to make <u>other biological molecules</u>. These molecules are the plant's <u>biomass</u> — the <u>mass</u> of <u>living material</u>. Biomass can be thought of as <u>energy stored</u> in a plant.
3) <u>Biomass</u> is <u>transferred</u> through living organisms in an ecosystem when organisms <u>eat</u> other organisms — this means that <u>light energy</u> from the Sun <u>supports nearly all life on Earth</u>.
4) Producers are eaten by <u>first stage (primary) consumers</u>. First stage consumers are then eaten by <u>second stage (secondary) consumers</u> and second stage consumers are eaten by <u>third stage (tertiary) consumers</u>.
5) First stage consumers are <u>herbivores</u> (animals that eat plants), and animals at other stages are <u>carnivores</u> (animals that eat other animals).
6) Each <u>stage</u> (e.g. producers, first stage consumers) is called a <u>trophic level</u>.
7) <u>Uneaten remains</u> and organisms' <u>waste products</u> are <u>broken down</u> by <u>decomposers</u>. Decomposers are usually <u>microorganisms</u>, such as bacteria and fungi.

Here's an <u>example</u> of a food chain — the <u>arrows</u> show you the <u>direction</u> of <u>energy transfer</u>:

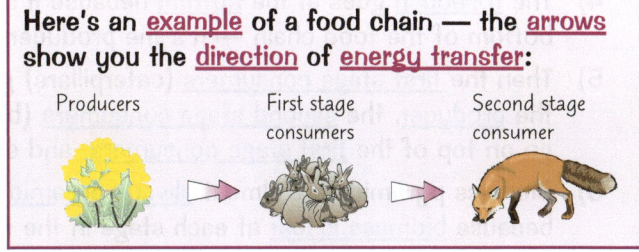

Producers — First stage consumers — Second stage consumer

Food Webs Show How Food Chains are Linked

1) There are many different species within an environment — which means <u>lots of different</u> possible <u>food chains</u>. You can draw a <u>food web</u> to show them.
2) All the species in a food web are <u>interdependent</u>, which means if one species changes, it <u>affects all the others</u>.

For example, in the food web on the right, if lots of water spiders died, then:
- There would be <u>less food</u> for the <u>frogs</u>, so their numbers might <u>decrease</u>.
- The number of <u>mayfly larvae</u> might <u>increase</u> since the water spiders wouldn't be eating them.
- The <u>diving beetles</u> wouldn't be <u>competing</u> with water spiders for food, so their numbers might <u>increase</u>.

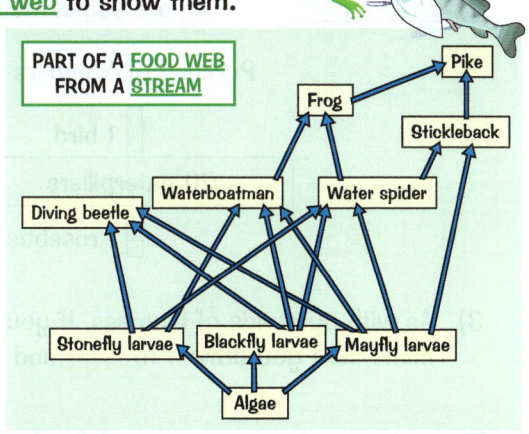

PART OF A <u>FOOD WEB</u> FROM A <u>STREAM</u>

Food webs — nothing to do with ordering pizza online, I'm afraid...

Food webs are handy for looking at relationships between individual species. Unfortunately, you hardly ever see simple food webs in the real world — they're normally as tangled together and interlinked as a bowl of spaghetti.

Q1 Describe the role of decomposers in an ecosystem. [1 mark]

Pyramids of Biomass and Numbers

The amount of biomass decreases as you move up a trophic level. Pyramids of biomass are used as models to show how the biomass changes. And pyramids of numbers are similar, but they show how the number of organisms at each trophic level. Trust me, you're going to like this page.

You Need to be Able to Understand and Draw Pyramids of Biomass

1) You can draw a pyramid of biomass from a food chain.
   Let's start with this food chain as an example:

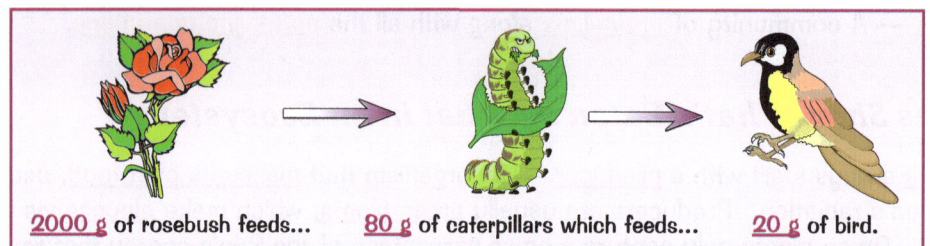

2000 g of rosebush feeds...   80 g of caterpillars which feeds...   20 g of bird.

2) Each bar on a pyramid of biomass shows the mass of living material at that stage of the food chain — basically how much all the organisms at each level would 'weigh' if you put them all together.

3) So the 'rosebush' bar on this pyramid would need to be longer than the 'caterpillars' bar, which in turn should be longer than the 'bird' bar... and so on.

4) The rosebush goes at the bottom because it's at the bottom of the food chain — it's the producer.

5) Then the first stage consumers (caterpillars) go on top of the producer, the second stage consumers (birds) go on top of the first stage consumers, and so on.

20 g	bird
80 g	caterpillars
2000 g	rosebush

(not drawn to scale)

6) Biomass pyramids are almost always pyramid-shaped because biomass is lost at each stage in the food chain (see next page).

7) If you're given data and asked to draw a pyramid of biomass in the exam, make sure that your bars are drawn to a sensible scale (e.g. 5 small squares on a grid = 1 kg), and that each bar is clearly labelled with the name of the organism that the bar represents and the biomass of that stage in the food chain.

Pyramids of Numbers can be Different Shapes

1) Pyramids of numbers are similar to pyramids of biomass, but each bar on a pyramid of numbers shows the number of organisms at that stage of the food chain — not their mass.

2) Pyramids of numbers are sometimes other shapes (not just pyramids):

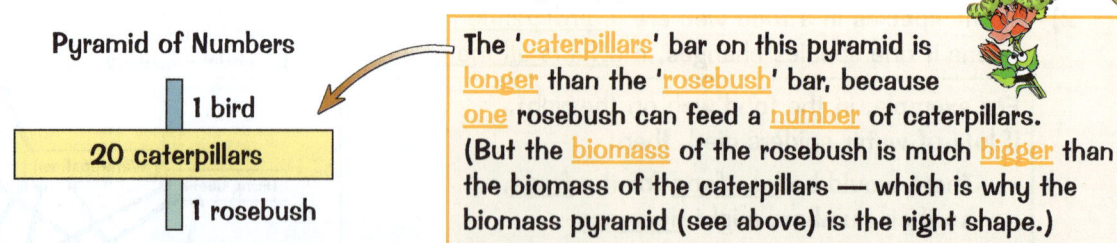

Pyramid of Numbers

	1 bird
20 caterpillars	
	1 rosebush

The 'caterpillars' bar on this pyramid is longer than the 'rosebush' bar, because one rosebush can feed a number of caterpillars. (But the biomass of the rosebush is much bigger than the biomass of the caterpillars — which is why the biomass pyramid (see above) is the right shape.)

3) As with pyramids of biomass, if you're asked to draw a pyramid of numbers in the exam, make sure you draw it to scale and clearly label each bar.

Constructing pyramids is a breeze — just ask the Egyptians...

Pyramids of numbers could also have a big bar across the top if, for example, there were loads of fleas feeding on one fox. But the tiny fleas would still have less biomass than the fox, so the biomass pyramid would look normal.

Q1   Look at the two diagrams on the right. One is a pyramid of biomass and one is a pyramid of numbers. Which one is the pyramid of numbers? Explain your answer.

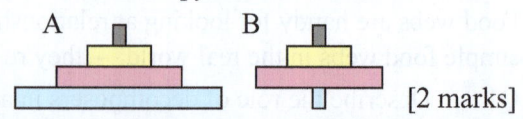

[2 marks]

Energy Transfer

Great, steak for dinner — some <u>energy</u> from a cow to help you <u>grow</u>. But not all of the energy will be <u>stored</u> in your body — you'll need to <u>use</u> some of that energy, e.g. for <u>moving about</u>. This is how energy is <u>lost</u>...

Energy is Lost Between Each Trophic Level

1) <u>Energy</u> (stored as <u>biomass</u>) is <u>transferred</u> through the living organisms of an ecosystem when organisms <u>eat</u> other organisms. However, <u>not much energy</u> gets transferred from one <u>trophic level</u> to the <u>next</u>.

2) Some of the <u>energy</u> taken in by organisms is used for <u>repairing</u> and <u>maintaining cells</u>, and for <u>growing</u>. This energy is <u>stored as biomass</u>. Energy that does not become biomass is lost from the food chain.

3) Some of the <u>glucose</u> produced by plants is used <u>immediately</u> as the plant <u>respires</u> (see page 39). It doesn't become biomass and isn't transferred to the animals eating the plant.

4) <u>Animals</u> use some of the <u>energy</u> they consume for <u>respiration</u> (to release energy for <u>movement</u>, <u>keeping warm</u>, etc.). This energy doesn't become biomass either, so it <u>doesn't get passed on</u> to the next trophic level — it's <u>lost</u> from the food chain.

Energy lost as HEAT
MOVEMENT
WASTE

5) <u>More energy</u> is lost from the food chain through <u>waste materials</u> (e.g. in an animal's <u>urine</u> and <u>faeces</u>) and in <u>uneaten</u> parts of organisms.

6) This all explains why you hardly ever get <u>food chains</u> with more than about <u>five trophic levels</u>. So much <u>energy</u> is <u>lost</u> at each stage that there's <u>not enough left</u> to support organisms after that many stages. You also tend to get <u>fewer organisms</u> at each <u>trophic level</u> (although this isn't always the case — see pyramids of number on the previous page).

You Need to be Able to Interpret Data on Energy Transfer

Higher

kJ (kilojoules) is a unit of energy.

1) The numbers in the diagram, show the <u>amount of energy</u> available to the <u>next level</u>. So <u>80 000 kJ</u> is the amount of energy available to the <u>greenflies</u>, and <u>10 000 kJ</u> is the amount available to the <u>ladybirds</u>.

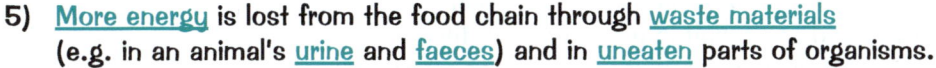
rosebush: 80 000 kJ | greenflies: 10 000 kJ | ladybirds: 900 kJ | bird: 40 kJ

2) You can work out how much energy has been <u>lost</u> at each level by taking away the energy that is available to the <u>next</u> level from the energy that was available from the <u>previous</u> level.

3) You can also calculate the <u>efficiency of energy transfer</u> between levels using this formula:

$$\text{efficiency} = \frac{\text{energy available to the next level}}{\text{energy that was available to the previous level}} \times 100$$

The 'efficiency of energy transfer' is usually pretty low (around 10%).

EXAMPLE: Using the food chain above, calculate the energy lost between the first and second trophic levels.

80 000 kJ – 10 000 kJ = 70 000 kJ lost

Biomass at 1st trophic level.   Biomass at 2nd trophic level.

EXAMPLE: Using the food chain above, Calculate the efficiency of energy transfer between the first and second trophic levels.

10 000 ÷ 80 000 x 100 = 12.5% efficient

Put the values into the equation shown above.

4) You can also calculate the <u>biomass</u> lost between trophic levels or the efficiency of <u>biomass transfer</u> using the formulae above — just substitute the word 'biomass' for 'energy'.

I could do with an extra energy transfer today...

Staying alive is important, but it sure does require a lot of energy. Organisms really aren't very efficient at transferring energy to the next trophic level — they lose loads through respiration and so on. Chew on that...

Q1   Give two ways that energy is lost between trophic levels.   [2 marks]

Humans and Wildlife

In case you haven't realised, there are loads of humans on the planet, and by the time you've finished reading this page there'll be even more. Unfortunately, a growing number of humans can be bad news for wildlife...

Human Activities can have a Negative Impact on Wildlife

1) The world's population is rising very quickly.

2) As the population continues to grow, we need to produce more food so that everyone has enough to eat.

3) We also need to supply all the other things that the increasing population needs, e.g. more houses, clothes, technology, transport, etc. This leads to economic development — where governments try to improve the standard of living for people (e.g. by providing the goods and services they need).

4) Producing more food and economic development is good for the human population, but it can be very damaging for wildlife. Here are two reasons why:

- Habitat destruction — human activities (e.g. farming, building, quarrying) reduce the amount of land and resources available to other animals and plants. For example, woodland may be cleared for farmland and can result in a reduction in the number of tree species. It also destroys the habitats of other organisms — species will die or be forced to migrate elsewhere.

- Waste — the increasing population means we're producing more waste, which can damage ecosystems in many ways. For example, sewage and toxic chemicals from industry and agriculture can pollute lakes, rivers and oceans, affecting the plants and animals that rely on them for survival.

There are Many Organisations That Try to Protect Wildlife

1) We need to make sure that humans have everything they need to survive, but the needs of wildlife have to be considered too. There are measures in place to help ensure that we get the balance right.

2) In the UK, when a new development is proposed, planning authorities have to decide whether it could have a significant effect on the environment. If they decide it could, then an Environmental Impact Assessment must be carried out. This assessment could involve biologists, who may help to determine what impact the development could have on local wildlife. The data that's collected is used to decide whether the development should be allowed, refused or altered to reduce its effect on wildlife. This decision can be particularly important for endangered species, e.g. newts and bats.

For example, a property developer wants to build several houses on an old golf course, which contains lots of small ponds and is surrounded by woodland. An Environmental Impact Assessment is carried out by a biologist to determine whether the development would cause any disruption to bat flight paths, or to any newts living in the ponds. If these species are present, the development plans may be refused or modified to prevent or reduce disruption to these species.

3) And it's not just when new developments are being proposed that wildlife is considered — there are many organisations set up which regularly monitor human activities that could negatively impact wildlife, and help to protect or improve ecosystems. Some of these organisations are government agencies — for example, the Environment Agency monitors the disposal of waste.

I wish I'd done an impact assessment before I ran into that wall...

Humans have to be really careful when it comes to using the Earth's resources to support the growing population. Without careful planning and monitoring we could end up causing irreparable harm to wildlife.

Q1   Explain one way that the rising human population may have a negative impact on wildlife.   [2 marks]

Intensive Farming

The aim of intensive farming is to be as <u>efficient</u> as possible. There are <u>two sides</u> to the story though...

Intensive Farming is Used to Produce More Food

1) <u>Intensive farming</u> is all about <u>maximising</u> the <u>amount</u> of food that can be produced, in the <u>quickest</u> and most <u>cost effective</u> way.

2) This generally includes using <u>chemicals</u> and <u>carefully controlling growing conditions</u> for plants and animals.

3) These practices greatly <u>increase livestock</u> (animal) and <u>plant yields</u>.

The yield just means how much food is produced.

There are Advantages and Disadvantages of Intensive Farming

Farming Method	Why is it advantageous to use?	What are the disadvantages?
<u>Fertilisers</u>	Plants need <u>certain nutrients</u>, e.g. <u>nitrates</u>, <u>potassium</u>, <u>phosphates</u> and <u>magnesium</u>, to help them grow. If plants don't get enough of these nutrients, their <u>growth</u> and <u>health</u> are affected. Sometimes these nutrients are <u>missing</u> from the soil because they've been used up by a <u>previous crop</u>. Farmers use artificial fertilisers to <u>replace</u> these missing nutrients or provide <u>more</u> of them.	<u>Excess fertilisers</u> may run into water (e.g. lakes) and have a <u>negative effect</u> on <u>wildlife</u> there — see next page.
<u>Pesticides</u>	These are <u>chemicals</u> that kill <u>farm pests</u>, e.g. insects, rats and mice. Pesticides that kill insects are called <u>insecticides</u>. Killing pests that would otherwise <u>eat</u> or <u>damage</u> crops means there are more crops left for us.	<u>Excess pesticides</u> can be washed into <u>water</u> and pollute the freshwater environment. This has a <u>negative</u> effect on the <u>wildlife</u> there. Pesticides can also <u>build up</u> in food chains (see next page).
<u>Disease Control</u>	<u>Antibiotics</u> are drugs that kill bacteria — they can be given to animals to <u>prevent</u> them from becoming <u>ill</u>. This means <u>fewer</u> animals are lost to <u>disease</u>. Giving antibiotics can also <u>increase</u> animals' <u>growth</u>. The more animals that survive and the <u>bigger</u> they grow, the more food there is for us.	Antibiotic use can lead to the development of <u>antibiotic-resistant bacteria</u> in the animals, which can then spread to humans, e.g. during meat preparation and consumption. Antibiotic-resistant bacteria are <u>bad news</u> for <u>humans</u> because they could mean that the antibiotics we use to cure some <u>human illnesses</u> no longer work (see p.147 for more on antibiotic resistance).
<u>Battery (factory) farming</u>	Battery farming involves <u>limiting</u> the <u>movement</u> of animals (e.g. pigs and chickens) and keeping them in a <u>temperature-controlled environment</u>. This means the animals use less energy <u>moving</u> around and <u>controlling</u> their own <u>body temperature</u>, so <u>more energy</u> is available for <u>growth</u> and <u>more meat</u> can be produced. Fish can also be <u>factory farmed</u> in <u>cages</u> where their movement is restricted.	Keeping the animals so close together, means that <u>diseases</u> can <u>spread</u> easily. If this happens, the farmer might have to <u>destroy</u> all the <u>infected animals</u>, which can be <u>costly</u>. There are also <u>ethical objections</u> to this farming method, as some people think that making animals live in <u>unnatural</u> and <u>uncomfortable</u> conditions is <u>cruel</u> and that we have a duty to treat animals <u>humanely</u>.

With any luck, this topic won't be too intensive in the exam...

Intensive farming helps us to feed the growing human population, but it has its disadvantages too.

Q1   Explain how battery farming increases livestock yields.   [3 marks]

Pollution

Humans produce lots of pollution, which can damage the environment and negatively affect wildlife.

Fertilisers and Untreated Sewage can Cause Water Pollution

1) Nutrients are put onto fields as fertilisers. If too much fertiliser is applied and it rains, nutrients find their way into rivers and lakes. This results in an excess of nutrients in the water.

2) Sewage contains all of the waste matter that goes down our toilets and drains. Sewage is usually treated so that the nutrient-rich matter and other pollutants are removed. The treated wastewater is then released into water. If untreated sewage is released it results in an excess of nutrients in the water.

3) The excess of nutrients in water from fertilisers and untreated sewage can lead to the death of many of the species that live in the water. Here's how it works:

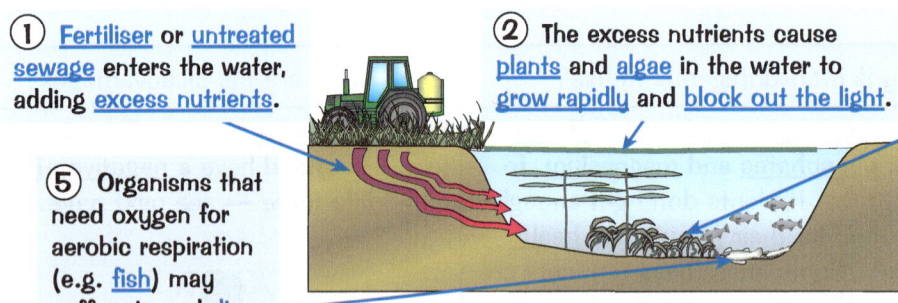

① Fertiliser or untreated sewage enters the water, adding excess nutrients.

② The excess nutrients cause plants and algae in the water to grow rapidly and block out the light.

③ Plants can't photosynthesise due to lack of light and start to die and decompose.

⑤ Organisms that need oxygen for aerobic respiration (e.g. fish) may suffocate and die.

④ With more food available, the microorganisms that break down the decomposing plants increase in number and use up the dissolved oxygen in the water.

Toxic Chemicals can Build Up in a Food Chain

1) Pesticides and industrial waste can contain harmful chemicals, such as heavy metals, e.g. lead and arsenic.

2) If pesticides and industrial waste enter water (e.g. by being washed into soils and rivers), the chemicals they contain can get into food chains.

3) Some of the chemicals can't be broken down in animal tissues, so when they enter a food chain, they are passed along it.

4) This means that more and more of the chemicals accumulate at each level in the food chain, so animals high up the food chain can receive a toxic dose. This can result in reduced fertility or death of animals high up the food chain.

5) When harmful chemicals build up in a food chain like this it's called bioaccumulation. Here is a well-known example:

Otters were almost wiped out over much of crop-dominated southern England by a pesticide called DDT in the early 1960s. The diagram shows the food chain which ends with the otter. DDT (like most pesticides) can't be broken down by animals — so it accumulates along the food chain and the otter ends up with most of the DDT collected by all the other animals.

① Pesticide seeps into the river
② Small water plants take up a little pesticide
③ Each little tiny animal eats lots of small plants
④ Each small fish eats lots of tiny animals
⑤ Each eel eats lots of small fish
⑥ Each otter eats lots of eels and ends up with lots of pesticide

Hopefully by now you've accumulated lots of biology knowledge...

Unfortunately not everyone thinks about wildlife when using pesticides and fertilisers, and disposing of waste. Our actions can have severe consequences for wildlife, particularly in aquatic ecosystems.

Q1 Explain how excess fertilisers in a pond could reduce the oxygen concentration of the water. [4 marks]

Indicator Species

The presence or absence of certain organisms in an area can be monitored and used as an indicator of pollution.

Indicator Species *Are Used to Show the Level of Pollution*

Some organisms are very sensitive to changes in their environment and so can be studied to monitor pollution — these organisms are known as indicator species.

1) Water Pollution

1) If untreated sewage or fertilisers are released into a river, the microorganisms in the water increase in number and use up the oxygen (see previous page).

2) Some invertebrate animals, like stonefly larvae and freshwater shrimps are good indicators for water pollution because they're very sensitive to the concentration of dissolved oxygen in the water. If you find stonefly larvae in a stream, it indicates that the water is clean.

3) Other invertebrate species are adapted to live in polluted conditions — so if you see a lot of them you know there's a problem. E.g. blood worms and sludgeworms indicate a very high level of water pollution.

2) Air Pollution

1) Air pollution can be monitored by looking at particular types of lichen that are very sensitive to the concentration of sulfur dioxide in the atmosphere. (Sulfur dioxide is a pollutant released from car exhausts, power stations, etc.)

2) The number and type of lichen at a particular location will indicate how clean the air is. E.g. the air is clean if there are lots of lichen — especially bushy lichen, which need cleaner air than crusty lichen.

Bushy lichen   Crusty lichen

3) You might get some data on indicator species in the exam, e.g. data showing there are more lichen species further away from a city centre. This is probably because outside the city centre, there is less pollution and the air contains less sulfur dioxide and other pollutants.

The Use of Indicator Species *Isn't Without Flaws*

1) There are a couple of ways of using indicator species to measure pollution:
   - You could do a simple survey to see if a species is present or absent from an area. This is a quick way of telling whether an area is polluted or not, but it's no good for telling how polluted an area is.
   - Counting the number of times an indicator species occurs in an area will give you a numerical value, allowing you to see roughly how polluted one area is in comparison with another.

Finding a numerical value allows you to investigate the abundance and distribution of species — there's more about this on pages 128-129.

2) Using indicator species is a simple and cost-effective way of saying whether or not an area is polluted. But indicator species can't give accurate figures for exactly how much pollution is present. There may be factors other than pollution playing a role in the presence or absence of a species in an environment.

3) Sometimes, it's better to use non-living indicators. For example, you can monitor the level of pollution in a stream by looking for changes in the dissolved oxygen concentration or the pH of the water over time. You can measure the oxygen concentration of water using a dissolved oxygen meter or a chemical test and you can measure the pH using an electronic pH meter or a pH indicator.

Teenagers are an indicator species — not found in clean rooms...

Don't forget that the absence of an indicator species could mean the opposite of what they indicate. E.g. the absence of stonefly larvae could indicate polluted water. Nice and simple, innit?

Q1   Lichen grows on trees in the local park. Explain what this indicates about the air quality.   [2 marks]

Revision Questions for Unit 1c

Phew, Unit 1c sure was a lengthy one — now here's a full page of questions to test your knowledge.

- Try these questions and tick off each one when you get it right.
- When you've done all the questions for a topic and are completely happy with it, tick off the topic.

Photosynthesis (p.39-42) ☐

1) Where in a plant cell does photosynthesis take place?
2) What is the word equation for photosynthesis?
3) Give five ways in which plants use the glucose they make during photosynthesis.
4) Describe how you would test a leaf for the presence of starch.
5) Why might you use sodium hydroxide in an experiment to investigate photosynthesis?
6) What is meant by a 'limiting factor' of photosynthesis?
7) Describe a method that you could use to measure the effect of light intensity on the rate of photosynthesis.
8) Describe how gas sensors and data loggers can be used to measure the rate of photosynthesis.
9) What effect would a low carbon dioxide concentration have on the rate of photosynthesis?
10) What effect would a temperature above 45 °C have on the rate of photosynthesis?

Food Webs, Ecological Pyramids and Energy Transfer (p.43-45) ☐

11) What do food chains always start with?
12) What is a 'herbivore'?
13) Which trophic level would you find a herbivore in?
14) True or false? The bottom bar on a pyramid of biomass represents the producer.
15) What do the bars in a pyramid of numbers represent?
16) Why are you unlikely to see a food chain with 10 trophic levels?
17) What is the formula for calculating the efficiency of energy transfer between trophic levels?

The Impact of Humans on Ecosystems (p.46-49) ☐

18) Explain why the negative impacts that humans have on wildlife may increase as the human population size increases.
19) Explain how Environmental Impact Assessments help to protect wildlife.
20) Describe what is meant by 'intensive farming'.
21) Give four methods of intensive farming.
22) Other than fertilisers, give one source of pollution that can result in excess nutrients in water sources.
23) Give two sources of heavy metals found in soils and rivers.
24) What is meant by 'bioaccumulation'?
25) Which animals in a food chain are impacted most by bioaccumulation?
26) What is an 'indicator species'?
27) How can indicator species be used to find out if water is polluted?
28) Other than using indicator species, give two ways that water pollution can be monitored.

Elements, Compounds and Mixtures

Elements make up <u>everything</u> that we use and see in our everyday lives...

Elements *Consist of* One Type *of Atom* Only

1) Quite a lot of everyday substances are <u>elements</u>:

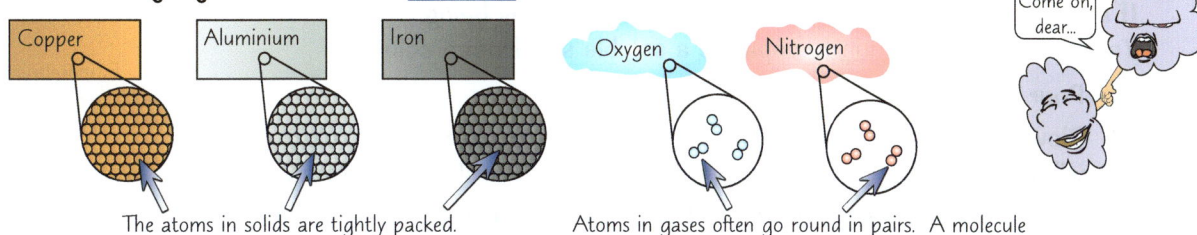

The atoms in solids are tightly packed.

Atoms in gases often go round in pairs. A molecule with two atoms in it is called a diatomic molecule.

Come on, dear...

2) It's <u>impossible</u> to break down an element into a simpler substance.

3) For example, if iron is <u>heated</u>, it produces <u>molten iron</u>. The iron doesn't break down into any other substance.

4) Elements are the <u>building blocks</u> of all other substances, such as <u>compounds</u>.

The melting point of iron is around 1500 °C.

Compounds *are* Chemically Bonded

1) A <u>compound</u> is a substance that is made of <u>two or more</u> different types of <u>atom</u> which are <u>chemically joined</u> (<u>bonded</u>).

2) For example, <u>carbon dioxide</u> is a <u>compound</u> formed from a <u>chemical reaction</u>. One carbon atom reacts with two oxygen atoms to form a <u>molecule</u> of carbon dioxide, with the <u>formula</u> CO_2.

carbon + oxygen → carbon dioxide

3) It's <u>very difficult</u> to <u>separate</u> the two original elements out again.

4) The <u>properties</u> of a compound are often <u>totally different</u> from the properties of the <u>original elements</u>.

5) For example, if a mixture of iron and sulfur is <u>heated</u>, the iron and sulfur atoms react to form the compound <u>iron sulfide</u> (FeS).

6) Iron sulfide is not much like iron (e.g. it's not attracted to a magnet), nor is it much like sulfur (e.g. it's not yellow in colour).

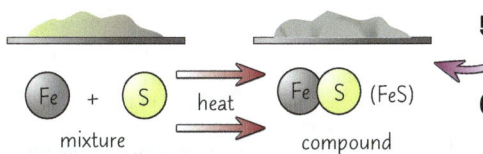

Fe + S —heat→ Fe S (FeS)

mixture   compound

Mixtures *are* Easily Separated *— Not Like Compounds*

1) Unlike in a compound, there's <u>no chemical bond</u> between the different parts of a mixture. The parts can be separated out by <u>physical methods</u> such as distillation (see page 52).

2) The <u>properties</u> of a mixture are just a <u>combination</u> of the properties of the <u>separate parts</u>. E.g. a <u>mixture</u> of <u>iron filings</u> and <u>sulfur powder</u> will show the properties of <u>both iron and sulfur</u>. It will contain grey magnetic bits of iron and bright yellow bits of sulfur.

Iron and sulfur mixed together, but unreacted

Not learning this stuff will only compound your problems...

Sometimes it's easiest to explain things in chemistry using examples. If you understand the difference between the mixture of iron powder and sulfur powder, and the compound iron sulfide, it'll make this stuff easier to remember.

Q1   State whether each of the following is an element, a compound or a mixture:
      a) carbon dioxide gas   b) chlorine gas   c) air   [3 marks]

Separating Mixtures

Separating mixtures is really easy. All you need is some special scientific equipment and the instructions. Luckily all the instructions you need are here... (Equipment sold separately.)

Evaporation Can Separate Soluble Solids from Solutions

If a solid can be dissolved in a liquid it's described as being soluble.
You can use evaporation to separate a soluble salt from a solution:

1) Pour the solution into an evaporating dish.

2) Slowly heat the solution. The solvent will evaporate and the solution will get more concentrated. Eventually, crystals will start to form.

3) Keep heating the evaporating dish until all you have left is a dry solid.

4) Evaporation is a quick way of separating a soluble salt from a solution, but only if the salt doesn't decompose (break down) when heated.

Evaporating dish

You don't have to use a Bunsen burner — you could use an electric heater (p.230).

Filtration is Used to Separate an Insoluble Solid from a Liquid

1) To separate an insoluble solid from a liquid, you can use filtration.

2) This means it can be used in purification. For example, solid impurities can be separated out from a reaction mixture using filtration.

3) All you do is pop some filter paper into a funnel and pour your mixture into it. The liquid part of the mixture runs through the paper, leaving behind a solid residue.

Filter paper folded into a cone shape.

The solid is left in the filter paper.

Simple Distillation is Used to Separate Out Solutions

1) Simple distillation is used for separating out a liquid from a solution.

2) The solution is heated. The part of the solution that has the lowest boiling point evaporates first.

3) The vapour is then cooled, condenses (turns back into a liquid) and is collected.

4) The rest of the solution is left behind in the flask.

5) Distillation can be used to separate a mixture of liquids as well.

6) The problem with simple distillation is that you can only use it to separate things with very different boiling points.

7) If the two boiling points are close together, it's hard to keep the solution (or mixture) at the right temperature to evaporate one but not the other.

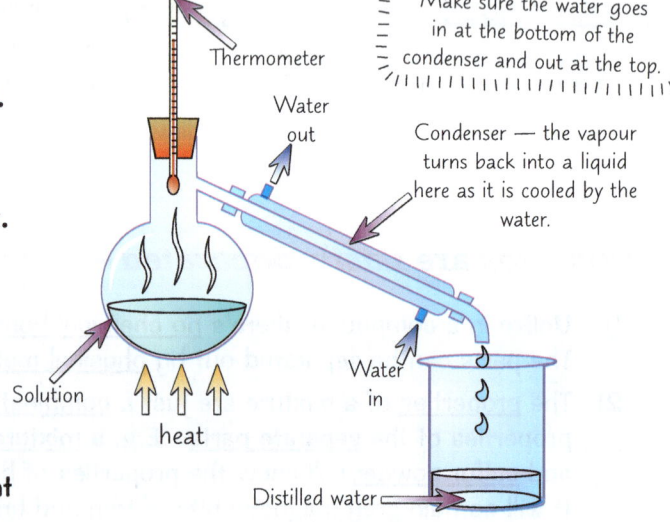

Make sure the water goes in at the bottom of the condenser and out at the top.

Thermometer

Water out

Condenser — the vapour turns back into a liquid here as it is cooled by the water.

Solution

heat

Water in

Distilled water

There's more on distillation on page 76.

It's impossible to filter the boredom out from revision — sadly...

There is one thing you shouldn't separate from revision, though — practice questions. Oh look, here's some now.

Q1   Which technique could be used to separate a soluble solid from a solution?   [1 mark]

Q2   Describe the process of simple distillation.   [3 marks]

Unit 2a — The Nature of Substances and Chemical Reactions

Chromatography

Last page on separation, I promise. This one's even got a nice equation for you to learn too — how exciting...

You Need to Know How to Do Paper Chromatography

1) Draw a line near the bottom of a sheet of filter paper — this is the baseline.
(Use a pencil to do this — pencil marks are insoluble so won't dissolve in the solvent.)

2) Add spots of different inks to the line at regular intervals.

3) Loosely roll the sheet up and put it in a beaker of solvent, e.g. water.

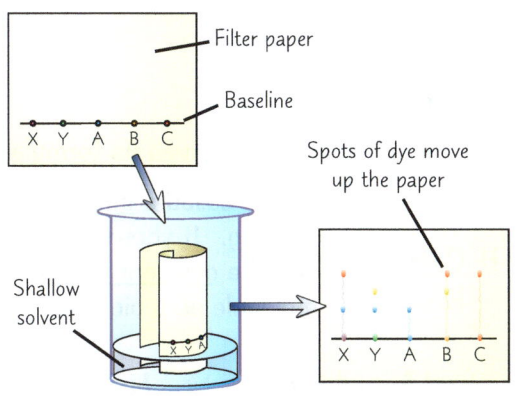

Filter paper

Baseline

X Y A B C

Spots of dye move up the paper

Shallow solvent

X Y A

X Y A B C

Chromotography isn't just used to separate dyes in inks. It can be used to separate other coloured mixtures of soluble substances.

4) The solvent used depends on what's being tested. Some compounds dissolve well in water, but sometimes other solvents, like ethanol, are needed.

5) Make sure the level of solvent is below the baseline — you don't want the inks to dissolve into the solvent.

6) Place a lid on top of the container to stop the solvent evaporating.

7) The solvent seeps up the paper, carrying the inks with it.

8) Each different dye in the inks will move up the paper at a different rate and form a spot in a different place.

9) When the solvent has nearly reached the top of the paper, take the paper out of the beaker and leave it to dry.

10) The end result is a pattern of spots called a chromatogram.

How Chromatography Separates Mixtures...

1) Chromatography works because different dyes will move up the paper at different rates.

2) Some dyes will be more attracted to the paper so spend more time stuck to it and not travel as far, whilst others will be more soluble in the solvent so will travel further up the paper.

3) The distance the dyes travel up the paper depends on the solvent and the paper you use.

You can Calculate an R_f Value for Each Chemical

1) An R_f value is the ratio between the distance travelled by the dissolved substance and the distance travelled by the solvent (the solvent front). You can find R_f values using the formula:

$$R_f = \frac{\text{distance moved by substance}}{\text{distance moved by solvent front}}$$

Distance moved by solvent

Spot of chemical

Baseline

A

B

R_f value of this chemical = B ÷ A

2) To find the distance travelled by the solute, measure from the baseline to the centre of the spot.

3) Chromatography is often carried out to see if a certain substance is present in a mixture. You run a pure sample of a substance that you think may be in your mixture alongside a sample of the mixture itself. If the sample has the same R_f value as one of the spots, they're likely the same.

I tried dyeing my hair once — it ended up fluorescent green...

… not a good look. You'd look amazing if you could remember this page on chromatography, though.
That equation is pretty important, so make sure you know how to use that — examiners really like R_f values.

Q1   A student carries out an investigation using paper chromatography. A spot of dye has moved 2 cm up the paper and the solvent has travelled 6 cm. Calculate the R_f value for this spot.   [1 mark]

Chemical Formulae

I bet you've been dying to know how to write out chemical formulae — you're welcome...

Atoms Can be Represented by Symbols

1) Atoms of each element can be represented by a one or two letter symbol — it's a type of shorthand that saves you the bother of having to write the full name of the element.

2) Some make perfect sense, e.g. C = carbon, O = oxygen, Mg = magnesium

3) Others less so, e.g. Na = sodium, Fe = iron, Pb = lead

4) You'll see these symbols on the periodic table (see page 65).

Most of these odd symbols actually come from the Latin names of the elements.

The Formula of a Molecule Shows the Numbers of Atoms

You can work out how many atoms of each type there are in a substance when you're given its formula.

This is called a molecular formula. It shows the number and type of atoms in a molecule.

$$CH_4$$

Methane contains 1 carbon atom and 4 hydrogen atoms.

This is called a structural formula. It shows the atoms and the covalent bonds in a molecule as a picture.

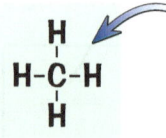

Don't panic if a formula has brackets in it — they're easy to deal with.

$$CH_3(CH_2)_2CH_3$$

For example, the 2 after the bracket here means that there are 2 lots of CH_2. So altogether there are 4 carbon atoms and 10 hydrogen atoms.

If you have the structural formula of a molecule, you can use it to write the molecular formula — just count up and write down how many atoms of each element there are in the structural formula.

Here, each carbon in the formula matches up with one carbon in the structural formula.

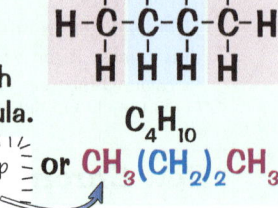

$$C_4H_{10}$$ or $$CH_3(CH_2)_2CH_3$$

You Need to Learn the Formulae of Some Molecules

It's a good idea to learn the chemical formulae of these common molecules. They crop up all the time.

- Water — H_2O
- Ammonia — NH_3
- Carbon dioxide — CO_2
- Hydrogen — H_2
- Chlorine — Cl_2
- Oxygen — O_2

You Can Work Out the Formula of an Ionic Compound

1) Ionic compounds are made up of a positively charged part and a negatively charged part.

2) The overall charge of any compound is zero. So all the negative charges in the compound must balance all the positive charges.

3) You can use the charges on the individual ions present to work out the formula for the ionic compound.

4) You need to be able to write formulae using chemical symbols.

EXAMPLE: What is the chemical formula of calcium nitrate?

1) Write out the formulae for the calcium and nitrate ions. Ca^{2+}, NO_3^-

2) The overall charge on the formula must be zero, so work out the ratio of Ca : NO_3 that gives an overall neutral charge.

To balance the 2+ charge on Ca^{2+}, you need two NO_3^- ions. So formula = $Ca(NO_3)_2$

The brackets show you need two of the whole nitrate ion.

$(+2) + (2 \times -1) = 0$

My phone is like an ionic compound — it has zero overall charge...

Make sure you can understand formulae, whether they're written as a molecular or a structural formula.

Q1   The formula of the compound pentanol can be written $CH_3(CH_2)_4OH$.
How many hydrogen atoms are there in one molecule of pentanol?   [1 mark]

Chemical Equations

If you thought ~~maths equations~~ were a drag then I'm here to tell you it gets much, much ~~worse~~ better...

Equations *Show the Reactants and Products of a Reaction*

A chemical reaction can be described as the process of going from reactants to products.
You can write word equations or symbol equations to show any chemical reaction.

> E.g. magnesium reacts with oxygen to produce magnesium oxide:
>
> Word equation: magnesium + oxygen   →   magnesium oxide
>
> Symbol equation: $2Mg$ + O_2 → $2MgO$
>
> Mg Mg   O O   Mg O   Mg O

The substances on the left are reactants and those on the right are products.

Look out for state symbols in equations — they tell you the physical states of reactants and products:

  (s) — Solid   (l) — Liquid   (g) — Gas   (aq) — Aqueous (dissolved in water)

Here's the example including state symbols: $2Mg(s) + O_2(g) \rightarrow 2MgO(s)$

Solid magnesium reacts with oxygen gas to make solid magnesium oxide.

Symbol Equations *Need to be Balanced*

1) There must always be the <u>same</u> number of atoms of each element on <u>both sides</u> of the equation — atoms can't just <u>disappear</u>.

2) You <u>balance</u> the equation by putting numbers <u>in front</u> of the formulae where needed. Take this equation for reacting sulfuric acid with sodium hydroxide:

$$H_2SO_4 + NaOH \rightarrow Na_2SO_4 + H_2O$$

3) The <u>formulae</u> are all correct but the numbers of some atoms <u>don't match up</u> on both sides.

4) You <u>can't change formulae</u> like H_2SO_4 to H_2SO_5. You can only put numbers <u>in front of them</u>.

5) The more you <u>practise</u>, the <u>quicker</u> you get, but all you do is this:

  • Find an element that <u>doesn't balance</u> and <u>pencil in a number</u> to try and sort it out.

  • <u>See where it gets you</u>. It may create <u>another imbalance</u>, but if so, pencil in <u>another number</u> and see where that gets you.

  • Carry on chasing <u>unbalanced</u> elements and it'll <u>sort itself out</u> pretty quickly.

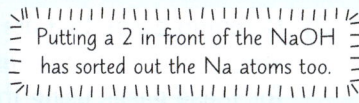
$E=mc^2$

> **EXAMPLE:**   In the equation above you'll notice you're short of <u>H atoms</u> on the RHS (Right-Hand Side).
>
> 1) The only thing you can do about that is make it <u>$2H_2O$</u> instead of just H_2O:
>
> $$H_2SO_4   +   NaOH   \rightarrow   Na_2SO_4 + 2H_2O$$
>
> 2) But that now gives <u>too many</u> H atoms and O atoms on the RHS, so to balance that up you could try putting a <u>2</u> in front of the <u>NaOH</u> on the LHS (Left-Hand Side):
>
> $$H_2SO_4   +   2NaOH   \rightarrow   Na_2SO_4 + 2H_2O$$
>
> *Putting a 2 in front of the NaOH has sorted out the Na atoms too.*
>
> 3) And suddenly there it is — <u>everything balances</u>.

Balanced Equation — the hardest yoga pose...

There's not much to balancing equations — it's just trial and error, really. It'll get a lot easier with practice...

Q1   Balance the equation: $Fe + Cl_2 \rightarrow FeCl_3$ [1 mark]

Q2   Hydrogen and oxygen molecules are formed in a reaction where water splits apart.
For this reaction: a) State the word equation.   b) Give a balanced symbol equation.   [3 marks]

Chemical Reactions

Chemical reactions often give a change in appearance, or some <u>indication</u> that a reaction is going on.

Atoms are *Rearranged* During *Chemical Reactions*

1) Chemical changes happen during <u>chemical reactions</u>, when bonds between atoms break and the atoms <u>change places</u>. The atoms from the substances you <u>start off</u> with (the <u>reactants</u>) are rearranged to form one or more <u>different substances</u> (the <u>products</u>).

2) The number of <u>atoms</u> in the reactants <u>equals</u> the number of atoms in the products (see previous page).

3) Chemical changes are often <u>hard to reverse</u>.

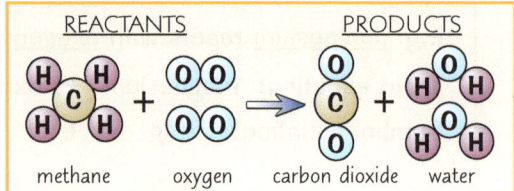

REACTANTS   PRODUCTS

methane   oxygen   carbon dioxide   water

There are *Observations* that Show a *Reaction* is Happening

It's normally obvious that <u>chemical reactions</u> are happening — they are often seen by a change in <u>colour</u> or <u>temperature</u>, or by <u>effervescence</u> (bubbles).

Colour Changes

1) Colour changes in chemical reactions can show <u>pH changes</u> (p.227), <u>displacement reactions</u> (p.71), <u>redox reactions</u> (p.178) etc.

2) For example, if you add <u>chlorine water</u> (an <u>aqueous solution</u> of <u>Cl_2</u>) to <u>potassium bromide</u> solution, the solution changes colour from <u>colourless</u> to <u>orange</u> — this shows that a reaction has taken place.

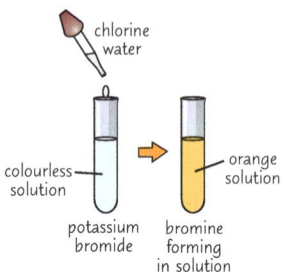

chlorine water

colourless solution

orange solution

potassium bromide   bromine forming in solution

Temperature Changes

1) When a chemical reaction happens, <u>energy</u> is either <u>taken in</u> or <u>given out</u> — this is shown by a <u>temperature change</u>.

2) Energy is <u>transferred</u> from the reactants to the surroundings in an <u>exothermic</u> reaction.

3) Energy is <u>transferred</u> from the surroundings to the reactants in an <u>endothermic</u> reaction. (There's more on exothermic and endothermic reactions on page 183).

4) An example of this is the reaction between <u>sodium</u> and <u>water</u>. When sodium is added to water, the heat from the reaction causes sodium to <u>melt</u> and form a ball. This shows that there has been a <u>reaction</u> because there has been a <u>temperature increase</u> — it's an <u>exothermic</u> reaction.

Sodium

Sodium melts to form a ball that moves quickly around the surface (floating) whilst fizzing and hissing rapidly.

5) This reaction also <u>effervesces</u>...

Effervescence

1) Sometimes <u>gases</u> are formed when a <u>chemical reaction</u> takes place. When these gases <u>escape</u> from the <u>solution</u> you'll see <u>bubbles</u> or <u>fizzing</u> — the fancy word for this is <u>effervescence</u>.

2) Common gases that are released during chemical reactions are <u>hydrogen</u>, <u>oxygen</u> and <u>carbon dioxide</u> — you can <u>test</u> for these gases using the tests on page 73 and page 86.

3) For example, when an <u>acid</u> reacts with a <u>carbonate</u>, <u>carbon dioxide</u> is formed and the solution <u>effervesces</u> (p.173).

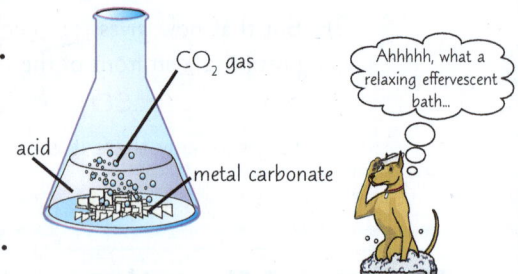

CO_2 gas

acid

metal carbonate

Ahhhhh, what a relaxing effervescent bath...

I can relate to chemical changes, I also find it hard to reverse...

Don't get mixed up between a 'clear' solution and a 'colourless' solution. Clear solutions can still have a colour, it just means they are see-through (or transparent) — they aren't cloudy.

Q1   Give one observation that indicates a reaction is taking place.   [1 mark]

Relative Formula Mass

Calculating relative formula mass is straightforward enough, but things can get a bit more confusing when you start working out the percentage compositions of compounds. Best get cracking, I suppose...

Compounds *Have a* Relative Formula Mass, M_r

The relative atomic mass, A_r, of an element is a measure of the average mass of one atom of that element. You can use the A_r to calculate the masses of reactants and formulae of reactions — see pages 59-60.

If you have a compound like $MgCl_2$ then it has a relative formula mass, M_r, which is just the relative atomic masses of all the atoms in the molecular formula added together.

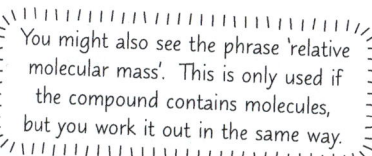

> You might also see the phrase 'relative molecular mass'. This is only used if the compound contains molecules, but you work it out in the same way.

EXAMPLE: Find the relative formula mass of $MgCl_2$.
A_r of Mg = 24 and A_r of Cl = 35.5

Add up all the relative atomic masses of the atoms in the compound.

$Mg + (2 \times Cl) = 24 + (2 \times 35.5) = 95$ So M_r of $MgCl_2$ = 95

There are two chlorine atoms in $MgCl_2$, so the relative atomic mass of chlorine needs to be multiplied by 2.

You Can Calculate the % Mass *of an* Element *in a* Compound

Keep up.

This is actually dead easy — so long as you've learnt this formula:

$$\text{Percentage mass of an element in a compound} = \frac{A_r \times \text{number of atoms of that element}}{M_r \text{ of the compound}} \times 100$$

EXAMPLE: Find the percentage mass of sodium in sodium carbonate, Na_2CO_3.
A_r of sodium = 23, A_r of carbon = 12, A_r of oxygen = 16

M_r of Na_2CO_3 = $(2 \times 23) + 12 + (3 \times 16) = 106$

Percentage mass of sodium = $\dfrac{A_r \times \text{number of atoms of that element}}{M_r \text{ of the compound}} \times 100 = \dfrac{23 \times 2}{106} \times 100 = 43\%$ (2 s.f.)

You might also come across more complicated questions where you need to work out the percentage mass.

EXAMPLE: A mixture contains 20% iron ions by mass. What mass of iron chloride ($FeCl_2$) would you need to provide the iron ions in 50 g of the mixture? A_r of Fe = 56, A_r of Cl = 35.5.

1) Find the mass of iron in the mixture.

The mixture contains 20% iron by mass, so in 50 g there will be $50 \times \dfrac{20}{100} = 10$ g of iron.

2) Calculate the percentage mass of iron in iron chloride.

Percentage mass of iron = $\dfrac{A_r \times \text{number of atoms of that element}}{M_r \text{ of the compound}} \times 100 = \dfrac{56}{56 + (2 \times 35.5)} \times 100 = 44.09...\%$

3) Calculate the mass of iron chloride that contains 10 g of iron.

Iron chloride contains 44.09% iron by mass, so there will be 10 g of iron in $10 \div \dfrac{44.09...}{100} = 23$ g (2 s.f.)

So you need 23 g of iron chloride to provide the iron in 50 g of the mixture.

Relative mass — when you go to church with your parents...

Get to grips with all this stuff by practising.

You'll need these for the questions below: $A_r(H) = 1$, $A_r(O) = 16$, $A_r(Li) = 7$, $A_r(S) = 32$.

Q1 Calculate the relative formula mass (M_r) of: a) H_2O b) LiOH   c) H_2SO_4 [3 marks]

Q2 Calculate the percentage composition by mass of potassium in potassium hydroxide (KOH).   [2 marks]

The Mole

<u>Moles</u> can be pretty confusing. It's probably the word that puts people off. It's difficult to see the relevance of the word "mole" to anything but a small burrowing animal.

"The Mole" is Simply the Name Given to an Amount of a Substance

1) Just like "a million" is this many: 1 000 000; or "a billion" is this many: 1 000 000 000, so "<u>the Avogadro constant</u>" is this many: <u>600 000 000 000 000 000 000 000</u> or <u>6×10^{23}</u>. And that's <u>all</u> it is. Just a <u>number</u>.

2) <u>One mole</u> of any substance is just an <u>amount</u> of that substance that contains an <u>Avogadro number of particles</u> — so 6×10^{23} particles. The particles could be atoms, molecules, ions or electrons.

3) The burning question, of course, is why is it such a silly long number like that, and with a 6 at the front?

4) The answer is that the mass of that number of <u>atoms</u> or <u>molecules</u> of any substance is exactly the same number of grams as the <u>relative atomic mass</u> (A_r) or <u>relative formula mass</u> (M_r) of the element or compound.

5) In other words, <u>one mole</u> of atoms or molecules of any substance will have <u>a mass in grams</u> equal to the <u>relative formula mass</u> (A_r or M_r) for that substance. Here are some examples:

> <u>Carbon</u> has an A_r of **12**.   So <u>one mole</u> of carbon weighs exactly **12 g**.
> <u>Nitrogen gas</u>, N_2, has an M_r of **28** (2×14).   So <u>one mole</u> of N_2 weighs exactly **28 g**.
> <u>Carbon dioxide</u>, CO_2, has an M_r of **44** ($12 + [2 \times 16]$).   So <u>one mole</u> of CO_2 weighs exactly **44 g**.

6) This means that 12 g of carbon, or 28 g of N_2, or 44 g of CO_2, all contain the <u>same number of particles</u>, namely <u>one mole</u> or 6×10^{23} atoms or molecules.

Higher

Nice Formula to Find the Number of Moles in a Given Mass:

$$\text{number of moles} = \frac{\text{mass in g (of an element or compound)}}{M_r \text{ (of the element or compound)}}$$

EXAMPLE: How many moles are there in 66 g of carbon dioxide (CO_2)?
A_r of C = 12 and A_r of O = 16.

1) Calculate the M_r of carbon dioxide. M_r of CO_2 = 12 + (16 × 2) = 44
2) Use the formula above to find out how many moles there are.   No. of moles = Mass (g) ÷ M_r = 66 ÷ 44 = 1.5 mol
   Easy Peasy.

'mol' is the symbol for the unit 'moles'.

You can <u>rearrange</u> the equation above using this handy <u>formula triangle</u>. You could use it to find the <u>mass</u> of a known number of moles of a substance, or to find the M_r of a substance from a known mass and number of moles. Just <u>cover up</u> the thing you want to find with your finger and write down what's left showing.

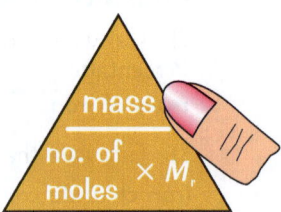

EXAMPLE: What mass of carbon is there in 4 moles of carbon dioxide?
There are 4 moles of carbon in 4 moles of CO_2.
Cover up 'mass' in the <u>formula triangle</u>. That leaves you with 'no. of moles × M_r'.
So the mass of 4 moles of carbon = 4 × 12 = **48 g**

What do moles have for pudding? Jam moly-poly...

Calculations involving moles can send some people into a spin. Don't be one of those people — there's really no need to freak out about moles. Go back over this page until you've got your head round it all.

Q1   Calculate the number of moles in 90 g of water (H_2O). $A_r(O)$ = 16, $A_r(H)$ = 1.   [2 marks]
Q2   Calculate the mass of 0.20 mol of sodium sulfate (Na_2SO_4). $A_r(Na)$ = 23, $A_r(S)$ = 32, $A_r(O)$ = 16. [2 marks]

Calculating Masses in Reactions

These can be kinda scary too, but no need to fear — just grab a brew, relax and enjoy.

You can Calculate the Amount of *Product* from a *Mass* of *Reactant*

You can use a balanced chemical equation to work out the mass of product formed from a given mass of a reactant (and vice versa). Here's how...

> The total relative mass of the reactants must be equal to the total relative mass of the products.

1) Write out the balanced equation.

2) Work out relative formula masses (M_r) of the reactant and product you're interested in.

3) Find out how many moles there are of the substance you know the mass of.

4) Use the balanced equation to work out how many moles there'll be of the other substance (i.e. how many moles of product will be made by this many moles of reactant).

5) Use the number of moles to calculate the mass.

What mass of magnesium oxide (MgO) is produced when 60 g of magnesium is burnt in air?
$A_r(Mg) = 24$, $A_r(O) = 16$.

1) Write out the balanced equation: $2Mg + O_2 \rightarrow 2MgO$

2) Work out the relative formula masses of the reactants and products you're interested in:
Mg: 24   MgO: 24 + 16 = 40

In this reaction, O_2 is in excess. This means that there is more O_2 available to react than there is Mg. So, it's the amount of Mg that determines how much MgO is made.

3) Calculate the number of moles of magnesium in 60 g:
moles = mass ÷ M_r = 60 ÷ 24 = 2.5

4) Look at the ratio of moles in the equation — 2 moles of Mg react to produce 2 moles of MgO. So 2.5 moles of Mg will react to produce 2.5 moles of MgO.

5) Calculate the mass of 2.5 moles of magnesium oxide:
mass = moles × M_r = 2.5 × 40 = 100 g

This tells us that 60 g of magnesium will produce 100 g of magnesium oxide. If the question had said, "Find how much magnesium gives 500 g of magnesium oxide", you'd calculate the number of moles of magnesium oxide first, because that's the one you'd have the information about. Got it? Good-O!

The mass of product (in this case magnesium oxide) is called the yield of a reaction. Masses you calculate in this way are called theoretical yields. In practice you never get 100% of the yield, so the amount of product you get will be less than you calculated.

Percentage Yield Compares Actual and Theoretical Yield

The more reactant you start with, the higher the yield will be — that's pretty obvious.
But the percentage yield doesn't depend on the amount of reactants you started with — it's a percentage.

1) The theoretical yield of a reaction can be calculated from the balanced equation (see above).

2) Percentage yield is given by the formula:

$$\text{percentage yield} = \frac{\text{actual yield (grams)}}{\text{theoretical yield (grams)}} \times 100$$

3) Percentage yield is always somewhere between 0 and 100%.

4) A 100% yield means that you got all the product you expected to get.

5) A 0% yield means that no reactants were converted into product, i.e. no product at all was made.

These pages — masses and masses of fun...

A specially organically grown, hand-picked question for you, my dear. $A_r(Cl) = 35.5$, $A_r(K) = 39$, $A_r(Br) = 80$.

Q1   Chlorine (Cl_2) and potassium bromide (KBr) react according to this equation: $Cl_2 + 2KBr \rightarrow Br_2 + 2KCl$
    a) Calculate the mass of Br_2 formed when 23.8 g of KBr reacts with an excess of Cl_2.   [4 marks]
    b) When carried out, the reaction gives a yield of 12.4 g of Br_2. What is the percentage yield?   [2 marks]

Calculating Formulae from Reacting Masses

This sounds a lot worse than it really is. Just follow the same <u>method</u> every time and you'll be laughing.

Finding the **Formula** of a Compound (from Masses or Percentages)

1) The <u>smallest whole number ratio</u> of atoms in a compound is used to find the molecular formula.

2) Try this for an easy peasy <u>stepwise method</u> for calculating a molecular formula:

> 1) <u>List all the elements</u> in the compound (there are usually only two or three).
> 2) <u>Underneath them</u>, write their <u>experimental masses</u>.
> 3) Find the number of <u>moles</u> of each element by <u>dividing</u> each mass by the <u>relative atomic mass</u> (A_r) for that particular element.
> 4) Turn the numbers you get into <u>a nice simple ratio</u> by dividing by the <u>smallest</u> number of moles.
> 5) Get the ratio in its <u>simplest whole number form</u>. This is the <u>simplest</u> formula that tells you the <u>ratio</u> of atoms of different elements in the compound.
> 6) This is different to the <u>molecular formula</u> of a compound, which tells you the <u>actual number</u> of atoms of each element in a single molecule.
> 7) The <u>molecular formula</u> is found by <u>comparing</u> the <u>relative molecular mass</u> to the relative molecular mass of the <u>simplest formula</u> (empirical formula).

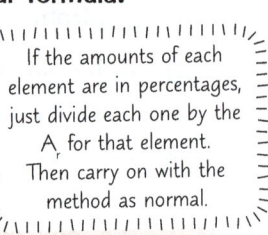

If the amounts of each element are in percentages, just divide each one by the A_r for that element. Then carry on with the method as normal.

The simplest formula is sometimes called the empirical formula.

EXAMPLE:

In an experiment, 9.3 g of phosphorus combined with oxygen to form 21.3 g of a phosphorus oxide. Find the molecular formula of the phosphorus oxide.
M_r of phosphorus oxide = 284, A_r(P) = 31, A_r(O) = 16.

1) The <u>mass of oxygen gained</u> is the difference between the mass of the phosphorus oxide and the mass of the phosphorus.

$$21.3 \text{ g} - 9.3 \text{ g} = 12.0 \text{ g}$$

Start by finding the simplest formula:

2) Divide the experimental masses by the relative atomic masses, to find the number of <u>moles</u> of each element.

P	O
$9.3 \div 31 = 0.3$	$12.0 \div 16 = 0.75$

3) <u>Divide</u> by the <u>smallest</u> number of moles.

$0.3 \div 0.3 = 1$ $0.75 \div 0.3 = 2.5$

4) Multiply to get <u>whole numbers</u>.

$1 \times 2 = 2$ $2.5 \times 2 = 5$

So the simplest formula is 2 atoms of P to 5 atoms of O — P_2O_5.

You don't have to multiply if you get whole numbers in step 4.

Find the molecular formula from the relative molecular mass:

5) Find the <u>mass</u> of the <u>simplest formula</u>.

$(2 \times 31) + (5 \times 16) = 142 \text{ g}$

6) Divide the relative molecular mass by the mass of the simplest formula.

$284 \div 142 = 2$

7) Multiply the simplest formula by this value to work out the <u>molecular formula</u>.

$P_2O_5 \times 2 = P_4O_{10}$

MY simplest ratio of work to rest is 0:1...

Make sure you read through the example thoroughly, until you're sure you can follow what's going on.

Q1 A sample of a sulfur oxide is made up of 40.0 % sulfur and 60.0% oxygen. Calculate the simplest formula of this sulfur oxide. A_r(S) = 32, A_r(O) = 16. [2 marks]

Q2 A 45.6 g sample of an oxide of nitrogen contains 13.9 g of nitrogen. A_r(N) = 14, A_r(O) = 16. What is the simplest formula of the nitrogen oxide? [3 marks]

Higher

Calculating Formulae from Reacting Masses

Ever wanted to know how to carry out <u>experiments</u> to determine the <u>molecular formula</u> of a compound?
No? Can't say I have either. Unfortunately you need to know how to anyway...

You can find *Empirical Formulae* using *Combustion...*

<u>Combustion</u> happens when a substance <u>reacts</u> with <u>oxygen</u> when it's burned in air. Here's how you could use <u>combustion</u> to calculate the <u>simplest formula</u> of a metal oxide, e.g. magnesium oxide:

1) Get a <u>crucible</u> and heat it until it's red hot. (This will make sure it's <u>clean</u> and there are no traces of <u>oil or water</u> lying around from a previous experiment.)

2) Leave the crucible to <u>cool</u>, then <u>weigh</u> it, along with its lid.

3) Add some clean <u>magnesium ribbon</u> to the crucible. <u>Reweigh</u> the crucible, lid and magnesium ribbon. The <u>mass of magnesium</u> you're using is this reading minus the initial reading for the mass of the crucible and lid.

4) <u>Heat</u> the crucible containing the magnesium. Put the lid on the crucible so as to <u>stop</u> any bits of solid from <u>escaping</u>, but leave a <u>small gap</u> to allow <u>air</u> to enter the crucible.

5) Heat the crucible strongly for around <u>10 minutes</u>, or until all the magnesium ribbon has turned <u>white</u>.

6) Allow the crucible to <u>cool</u> and <u>reweigh</u> the crucible with the lid and its contents. The <u>mass</u> of <u>magnesium oxide</u> you have is this reading, minus the initial reading for the mass of the crucible and lid.

lid — *crucible containing magnesium ribbon* — *gauze* — *tripod* — **HEAT**

Once you've done the experiment, you should have all the <u>data</u> you need to work out the <u>simplest formula</u> of the <u>magnesium oxide</u> using the <u>method</u> on the <u>previous page</u>. If you know the <u>relative molecular mass</u>, you could use the simplest formula to work out the <u>molecular formula</u> (again, the method's on the previous page).

If the data collected gives a molecular formula that you know is wrong, there might have been an incomplete reaction.

... or using *Reduction*

<u>Reduction</u> is the <u>loss</u> of <u>oxygen</u> from a substance (see page 178 for more on reduction). When you reduce a <u>metal oxide</u>, you're left with the <u>pure metal</u> — e.g. the product from reducing <u>copper(II) oxide</u> is <u>copper</u>. You can reduce a <u>metal oxide</u> to find out its <u>simplest formula</u>. Here's how you'd do it for copper(II) oxide:

1) Place a rubber <u>bung</u> (with a hole through the middle) into a <u>test tube</u> with a small hole in the end, and <u>weigh</u> them.

2) Take the bung out of the test tube and spread out a small amount of <u>copper(II) oxide</u> in the <u>middle</u> of the tube.

3) Re-insert the bung and <u>weigh</u> the test tube again. Set up the equipment as shown in the diagram.

4) Expel the air from the test tube by gently turning on the <u>gas</u>. After about <u>5 seconds</u>, light the gas by holding a burning splint next to the hole in the end of the test tube. You can control the size of the flame by changing the <u>amount of gas</u> that's flowing through the test tube.

5) Use a Bunsen burner to heat the copper(II) oxide for about <u>10 minutes</u> (or until the solid changes colour from <u>black</u> to a <u>brownish-pink colour</u>). You should be left with <u>copper</u> as all the oxygen has now been lost.

6) Turn off the Bunsen burner and leave the test tube to <u>cool</u>.

7) Once the tube has cooled, <u>turn off</u> the gas and <u>weigh</u> the test tube with the bung and its contents.

burning gas — *clamp* — *copper(II) oxide* — *gas* — *Bunsen burner*

As above, you can use the data to calculate the simplest formula of <u>copper(II) oxide</u>.

A red hot crucible — the scene of hotly contested snooker matches...

In both of these practicals, you weigh the container three times — before and after adding the solid, and after heating.

Q1   Describe how combustion could be used to find the information needed to calculate the empirical formula of a metal oxide.

[4 marks]

Revision Questions for Unit 2a

That's about it for Unit 2a — there's just these few revision questions to go and then you're all done.

- Try these questions and tick off each one when you get it right.
- When you've done all the questions for a topic and are completely happy with it, tick off the topic.

Elements, Compounds and Separating Mixtures (p.51-53) ☐

1) How many different types of atom make up an element? ☐
2) Explain the difference between a compound and a mixture. ☑
3) What could you separate using evaporation? ☑
4) Describe the process of filtration. ☑
5) Explain how simple distillation can separate two liquids. ☑
6) Explain why some solutes travel further than others in paper chromatography. ☑
7) How do you calculate an R_f value in chromatography? ☑

Chemical Formulae, Equations and Reactions (p.54-56) ☐

8) What is represented by the lines in a structural formula? ☐
9) How many atoms of hydrogen are in a molecule of $CH_3(CH_2)_2CH_3$? ☑
10) What is the molecular formula for carbon dioxide? ☑
11) What is the overall charge of an ionic compound? ☑
12) State what is shown on the right-hand side of a chemical equation. ☑
13) What observation can indicate that a displacement reaction has happened? ☑
14) What type of observable change occurs in an endothermic reaction? ☑
15) What is the name given to the release of bubbles during a chemical reaction? ☑

Relative Mass and The Mole (p.57-58) ☐

16) How do you calculate the relative formula mass, M_r, of a substance? ☐
17) How can you calculate the percentage mass of an element in a compound? ☑
18) How is the Avogadro constant related to the definition of a mole? ☑
19) What is the formula that relates the number of moles of a substance to its mass and M_r? ☑

Calculating Masses and Formulae (p.59-61) ☐

20) What is the equation for calculating percentage yield? ☐
21) What is the percentage yield of a reaction where no products are made? ☑
22) How does the molecular formula of a compound relate to its simplest formula? ☑

The Atom

All substances are made of <u>atoms</u>. They're really <u>tiny</u> — too small to see, even with a microscope.

Atoms Contain Protons, Neutrons and Electrons

The atom is made up of three <u>subatomic particles</u> — protons, neutrons and electrons.

- <u>Protons</u> are <u>heavy</u> and <u>positively charged</u>.
- <u>Neutrons</u> are <u>heavy</u> and <u>neutral</u>.
- <u>Electrons</u> have <u>hardly any mass</u> and are <u>negatively charged</u>.

Particle	Relative mass	Relative charge
Proton	1	+1
Neutron	1	0
Electron	0.0005	−1

Relative mass (measured in atomic mass units) measures mass on a scale where the mass of a proton or neutron is 1.

Protons and neutrons are still teeny tiny — they're just heavy compared to electrons.

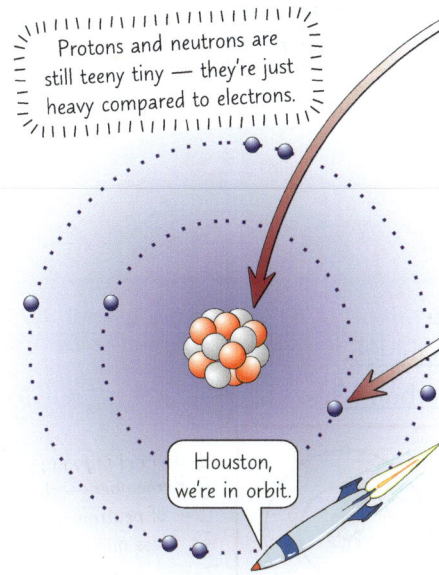

Houston, we're in orbit.

The Nucleus

1) It's in the <u>middle</u> of the atom.
2) It contains <u>protons</u> and <u>neutrons</u>.
3) It has a <u>positive charge</u> because of the protons.
4) Almost the <u>whole</u> mass of the atom is <u>concentrated</u> in the nucleus.
5) Compared to the overall size of the atom, the nucleus is <u>tiny</u>. Its radius is 10^{-14} m (around <u>1/10 000</u> of the radius of an atom).

The Electrons

1) Electrons orbit <u>around</u> the nucleus in electron <u>shells</u>.
2) They're <u>negatively charged</u>.
3) They're <u>tiny</u>, but they cover <u>a lot of space</u>.
4) The orbit of the <u>outer electron(s)</u> determines the size of the atom. Atoms have a radius (known as the atomic radius) of about 10^{-10} m.
5) Electrons have a <u>tiny</u> mass (so small that it's sometimes given as zero).

In an Atom the Number of Protons Equals the Number of Electrons

1) Atoms are <u>neutral</u> — they have <u>no charge</u> overall (unlike ions).
2) This is because they have the <u>same number</u> of <u>protons</u> as <u>electrons</u>.
3) The <u>charge</u> on the electrons is the <u>same</u> size as the charge on the <u>protons</u>, but <u>opposite</u> — so the charges <u>cancel out</u>.

There's more on ions on the next page.

Atomic Number and Mass Number Describe an Atom

1) The <u>nuclear symbol</u> of an atom tells you its <u>atomic number</u> and <u>mass number</u>.
2) The <u>atomic number</u> tells you how many <u>protons</u> an atom has. Every atom of an element has the <u>same number of protons</u>.
3) For a <u>neutral</u> atom, the number of protons equals the number of electrons, so the number of electrons equals the <u>atomic number</u>.
4) The <u>mass number</u> tells you the <u>total number</u> of <u>protons and neutrons</u> in the atom.
5) To work out the number of <u>neutrons</u> in an atom, just subtract the <u>atomic number</u> from the <u>mass number</u>.

Nuclear symbol for sodium.
Mass number → 23
Atomic number → 11
$^{23}_{11}\text{Na}$
Element symbol

Think like a proton — stay positive...

You need to learn what's in that table with the relative masses and relative charges of the different parts of the atom.

Q1   A certain neutral atom of potassium has an atomic number of 19 and a mass number of 39. Give the number of electrons, protons and neutrons in the atom.   [3 marks]

Ions, Isotopes and Relative Atomic Mass

Atoms were reasonably straightforward weren't they? Think again. Here come isotopes to spice things up.

Ions have Different Numbers of Protons and Electrons

1) Ions form when atoms (or groups of atoms) gain or lose electrons.

2) Negative ions form when atoms gain electrons — they have more electrons than protons.
    Positive ions form when atoms lose electrons — they have more protons than electrons.

> • F⁻ — there's a single negative charge, so there must be one more electron than protons.
>   F has an atomic number of 9, so has 9 protons. So F⁻ must have 9 + 1 = 10 electrons.
> • Fe^{2+} — there's a 2+ charge, so there must be two more protons than electrons.
>   Fe has an atomic number of 26, so has 26 protons. So Fe^{2+} must have 26 – 2 = 24 electrons.

Isotopes are the Same Except for Extra Neutrons

1) Isotopes are different forms of the same element, which have
    the same number of protons but a different number of neutrons.

2) So isotopes have the same atomic number but different mass numbers.

3) A very popular example of a pair of isotopes is carbon-12 and carbon-13.

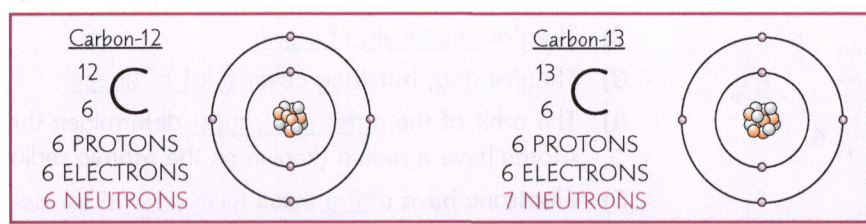

Remember — the number of neutrons is just the mass number minus the atomic number.

Relative Atomic Mass Takes Isotopes Into Account

1) In the periodic table, the elements all have two numbers next to them.
    The bigger one is the relative atomic mass (A_r) of the element.

2) Because many elements can exist as a number of different isotopes,
    relative atomic mass (A_r) is used instead of mass number when
    referring to an element as a whole.

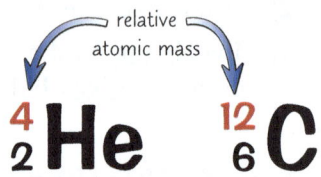

3) If an element has more than one isotope, its A_r is the average of the mass numbers of all the different
    isotopes, taking into account how much there is of each one. So, it might not be a whole number.

> For example, chlorine has two stable isotopes, chlorine-35 and chlorine-37. There's quite a
> lot of chlorine-35 around and not so much chlorine-37 — so chlorine's A_r works out as 35.5.

4) If an element only has one isotope, its A_r will be the same as its mass number.

Don't trust atoms — they make up everything...

Atoms, ions and isotopes — make sure you know what they are and the differences between them.

Q1 a) Bromine has an atomic number of 35. It exists naturally with 2 isotopes, bromine-79 and
        bromine-81. Work out how many neutrons, protons and electrons are in each isotope.   [2 marks]
    b) Bromine tends to react by forming Br⁻ ions. How many electrons are in a Br⁻ ion?   [1 mark]

The Periodic Table

The periodic table gives you information about all the elements. I present to you a chemist's best friend...

The Periodic Table Helps you to See Patterns in Properties

1) There are 100ish elements, which all materials are made of.

2) In the periodic table the elements are laid out in order of increasing atomic number. Arranging the elements like this means there are repeating patterns in the properties of the elements. (The properties are said to occur periodically, hence the name periodic table.)

3) If it wasn't for the periodic table organising everything, you'd have a heck of a job remembering all those properties. It's ace.

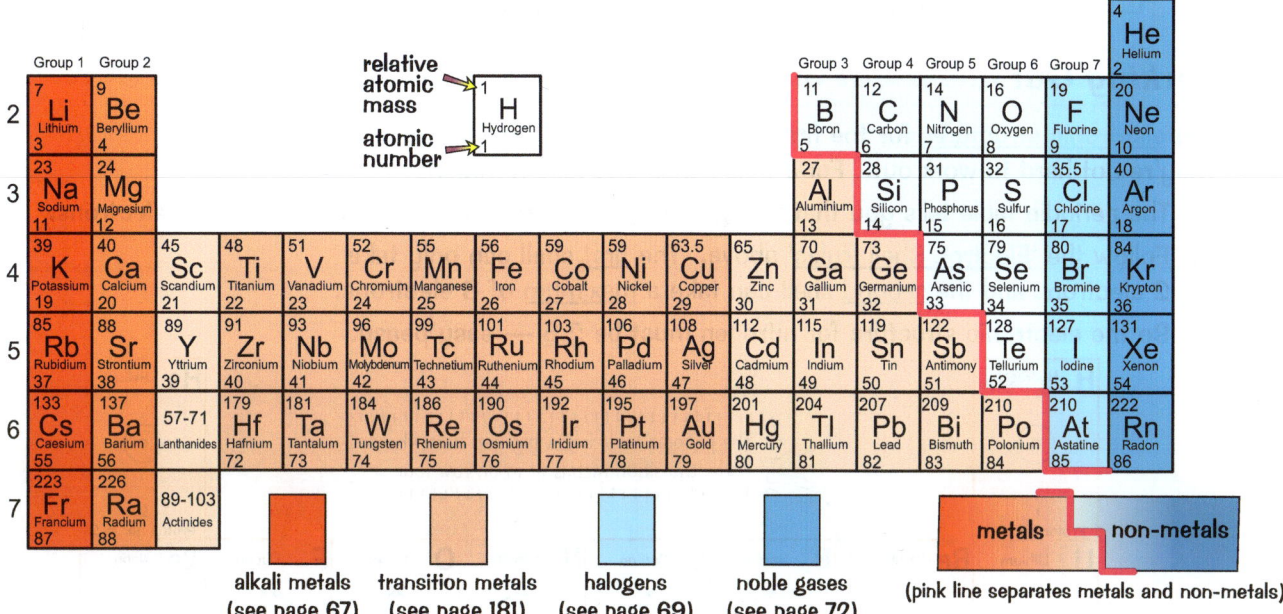

alkali metals (see page 67)   transition metals (see page 181)   halogens (see page 69)   noble gases (see page 72)   metals   non-metals (pink line separates metals and non-metals)

4) Elements with similar properties form columns.

5) These vertical columns are called groups.

6) The group number tells you how many electrons there are in the outer shell. For example, Group 1 elements all have one electron in their outer shell and Group 7 all have seven electrons in their outer shell. The exception to the rule is Group 0, for example helium has two electrons in its outer shell. This is useful as the way atoms react depends upon the number of electrons in their outer shell. So all elements in the same group are likely to react in a similar way.

7) If you know the properties of one element, you can predict properties of other elements in that group — and in the exam, you might be asked to do this. For example the Group 1 elements are Li, Na, K, Rb, Cs and Fr. They're all alkali metals and they react in a similar way (see pages 67-68).

8) You can also make predictions using trends in reactivity. E.g. in Group 1, the elements react more vigorously as you go down the group. And in Group 7, reactivity decreases as you go down the group.

9) The rows are called periods. Each new period represents another full shell of electrons

10) The properties of elements change as you move across a period. Elements on the left and in the centre of a period have metallic properties, whilst elements on the right are non-metals. Many elements between the metals and non-metals (in Groups 3, 4 and 5) show both metallic and non-metallic properties.

I'm in a chemistry band — I play the symbols...

Because the periodic table is organised into groups and periods, it allows us to see trends in both reactivity and properties. And this means we can make predictions about how reactions will occur. How neat is that?

Q1   Using a periodic table, state how many electrons beryllium has in its outer shell.   [1 mark]

Q2   Chlorine reacts in a similar way to bromine. Suggest a reason why.   [1 mark]

Q3   Sodium readily forms 1+ ions. Suggest what ions potassium forms and explain your answer.   [1 mark]

Electron Shells

Like snails, electrons live in shells. Unlike snails, electrons won't nibble on your petunias...

Electron Shell Rules:

1) Electrons occupy shells (sometimes called energy levels).
2) The lowest energy levels are always filled first.
3) Only a certain number of electrons are allowed in each shell:

1st shell	2nd shell	3rd shell
2 electrons	8 electrons	8 electrons

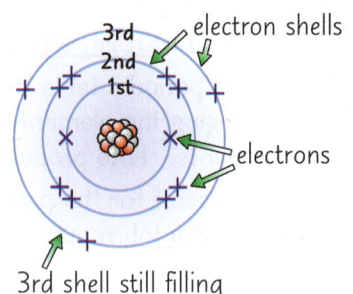

3rd shell still filling

Working Out Electronic Structures

The electronic structures for the first 20 elements are shown in the diagram below.
They're not hard to work out. For a quick example, take nitrogen:

1) The periodic table tells you that nitrogen has seven protons, so it must have seven electrons.
2) Follow the 'Electron Shell Rules' above. The first shell can only take 2 electrons and the second shell can take a maximum of 8 electrons.
3) So the electronic structure for nitrogen must be 2.5 — easy peasy.

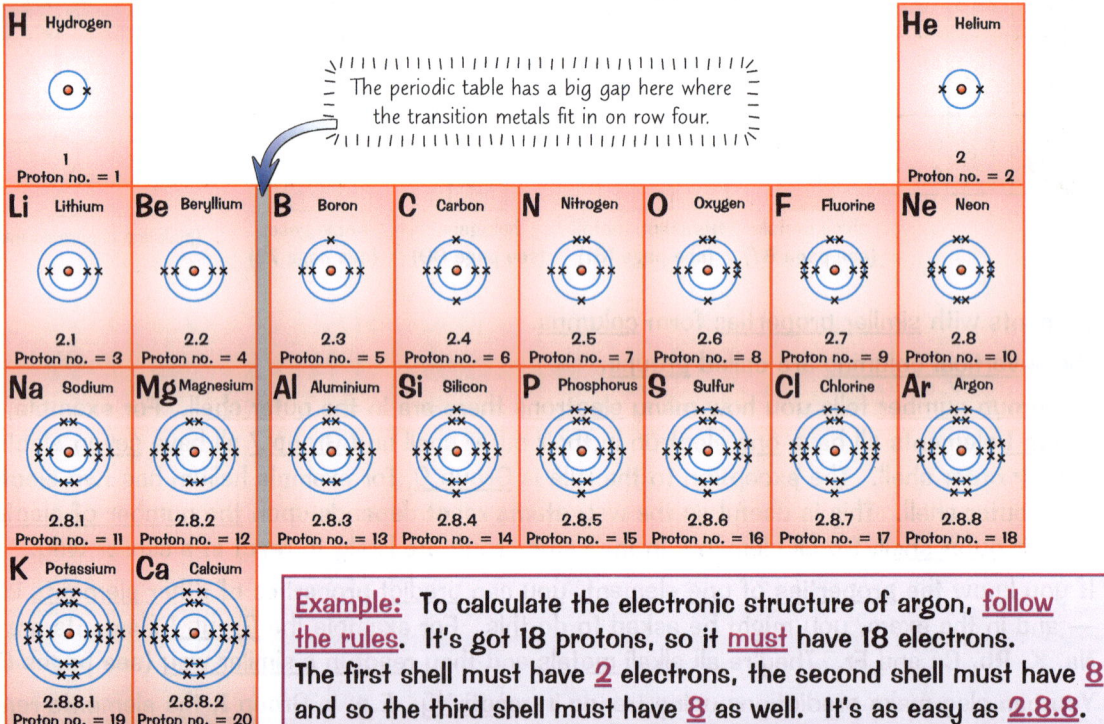

The periodic table has a big gap here where the transition metals fit in on row four.

Example: To calculate the electronic structure of argon, follow the rules. It's got 18 protons, so it must have 18 electrons. The first shell must have 2 electrons, the second shell must have 8, and so the third shell must have 8 as well. It's as easy as 2.8.8.

You can also work out the electronic structure of an element from its period and group.

- The number of shells which contain electrons is the same as the period of the element.
- The group number tells you how many electrons occupy the outer shell of the element.

Example: Sodium is in period 3, so it has 3 shells occupied — so the first two shells must be full (2.8). It's in Group 1, so it has 1 electron in its outer shell. So its electronic structure is 2.8.1.

The electronic structure of the fifth element — it's a bit boron...

Electronic structures may seem a bit complicated at first but once you learn the rules, they're a piece of cake.

Q1   Give the electronic structure of aluminium (atomic number = 13).   [1 mark]

Q2   In which group and period of the periodic table would you expect to find the element with electronic structure 2.8.8.2?   [2 marks]

Unit 2b — Atomic Structure and the Periodic Table

Group 1 — The Alkali Metals

Group 1 elements are known as the alkali metals — these are silvery solids that have to be stored in oil (and handled with forceps) as they react vigorously with water. As elements go, they're pretty demanding...

The Group 1 Elements are Reactive, Soft Metals

1) The alkali metals are lithium, sodium, potassium, rubidium, caesium and francium.
2) They all have one electron in their outer shell which makes them very reactive and gives them similar properties.
3) The alkali metals are all soft and have low density. The first three in the group are less dense than water.

Melting and Boiling Points Decrease Down Group 1

1) Group 1 metals form regular structures held together with metallic bonds (see page 163). In these bonds, the outer electron of each atom is free to move around (delocalised). There are strong attractions between these electrons and the positively charged nuclei.
2) As you go down Group 1, the atoms get bigger — the nucleus is further away from the free electrons, so the attractions get weaker.
3) This means that less energy is needed to break the metallic bonds and turn the solid metal into a liquid and then to a gas — so melting and boiling points decrease down the group.

In the exam, you could be given the property of one Group 1 metal and asked to predict the property of a different Group 1 metal. So make sure you know these trends.

Group 1 Metals are Very Reactive

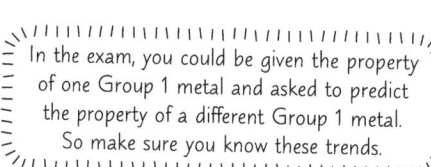

Higher

1) The Group 1 metals want to have a full outer shell so that they have a stable electronic structure. The easiest way to achieve this is by losing their single outer electron to form a 1+ ion.
2) The more readily a metal loses its outer electrons, the more reactive it is — so the Group 1 metals are very reactive.
3) As you go down Group 1, the alkali metals get more reactive. The negatively charged outer electron is less strongly attracted to the positively charged nucleus. This is because it's further away (there are more electron shells) — so it's more easily lost, as less energy is needed to remove it.
4) Group 2 elements are less reactive than Group 1 elements because they have to lose 2 electrons to get a full outer shell — this is harder than losing just 1 electron.

Group 1 Elements React in Similar Ways

1) Group 1 elements can take part in different reactions, e.g. with water and chlorine gas.
2) Because Group 1 elements all have a single outer electron, they will react with a particular reactant to produce the same type of product. E.g. the reactions of Group 1 metals with chlorine gas produce metal chlorides. This means that the balanced symbol equations will follow the same pattern — make sure you know how to write them.
3) Although the reactions are similar, the reactions become more vigorous as atomic number increases. This is because the elements become more reactive down the group.
4) So, if you know how one Group 1 metal reacts, you can use the pattern of reactivity to predict how other Group 1 metals will react and the products that will form.

Wanna know more about Group 1 metals? K. Really? Na...

Well, I'm afraid we still have another page to go about Group 1. It's a good one though — I'm not even Li-ing...

Q1   State and explain the trend in reactivity as you go down Group 1.   [3 marks]

Unit 2b — Atomic Structure and the Periodic Table

Reactions of the Alkali Metals

Now you've learnt the basics about the Group 1 elements it's time to learn some cool reactions.

Group 1 Metals React with Oxygen in the Air

1) The Group 1 metals are shiny when freshly cut, but quickly react with oxygen and water in air and tarnish as a metal oxide is formed. Different oxides will form depending on the Group 1 metal.

2) As you go down Group 1, the elements tarnish much more quickly.

3) Lithium, sodium and potassium are stored in oil to prevent the reaction with air.

4) Rubidium and caesium are much more reactive, so are sealed in glass tubes under special conditions.

5) Group 1 metals will also burn in air to produce white metal oxides. You can identify the metal from the colour of the flame — see page 73 for more.

Reaction with Cold Water Produces a Hydroxide and Hydrogen Gas

1) When the alkali metals are put in water, they react to produce hydrogen gas and a metal hydroxide (an alkali). For example, here are the overall equations for the reactions of the first three alkali metals with water:

$$2Li_{(s)} + 2H_2O_{(l)} \rightarrow 2LiOH_{(aq)} + H_{2(g)}$$
lithium + water → lithium hydroxide + hydrogen

$$2Na_{(s)} + 2H_2O_{(l)} \rightarrow 2NaOH_{(aq)} + H_{2(g)}$$
sodium + water → sodium hydroxide + hydrogen

$$2K_{(s)} + 2H_2O_{(l)} \rightarrow 2KOH_{(aq)} + H_{2(g)}$$
potassium + water → potassium hydroxide + hydrogen

universal indicator — Lithium — The lump of lithium moves slowly around the surface, floating on top of the water, fizzing and hissing, until it disappears.

Water (neutral) — The water has become alkaline so the indicator solution turns purple. — time of reaction

Sodium — Sodium melts to form a ball that floats and moves quickly around the surface whilst fizzing and hissing rapidly.

Potassium — Potassium melts and floats when added to water. It reacts vigorously, burns with a lilac flame — and sometimes explodes.

2) As you go down Group 1, the elements become more reactive (in fact, rubidium and caesium actually explode).

3) You can see this in the rate of reaction with water (i.e. the time taken for a lump of the same size of each element to react completely with the water and disappear).

4) Lithium takes longer than sodium or potassium to react, so it's the least reactive. Potassium takes the shortest time to react of these three elements, so it's the most reactive.

5) The reaction between water and potassium produces enough heat to melt the metal. Similarly, the reaction between sodium and water produces enough heat to melt the sodium until it forms a ball. Lithium reacts more slowly, and has a higher melting point, so it doesn't melt during the reaction.

Reactions with Group 7 Elements Produce a Salt

1) The Group 1 metals react vigorously when heated in a Group 7 gas (see next page) to form white crystalline salts called 'metal halides'. The colour of the flame produced depends on the metal used.

2) As you go down Group 1, reactivity increases so the reaction with Group 7 elements gets more vigorous.

$$2Na_{(s)} + Cl_{2(g)} \rightarrow 2NaCl_{(s)}$$
sodium + chlorine → sodium chloride

$$2K_{(s)} + Br_{2(l)} \rightarrow 2KBr_{(s)}$$
potassium + bromine → potassium bromide

Back to the drawing board with my lithium swim shorts design...

The reactions of alkali metals with water need safety precautions because they fizz and might explode. Cool stuff.

Q1   Which Group 1 element has the least vigorous reaction with chlorine gas?   [1 mark]

Q2   Give the balanced symbol equation for the reaction between sodium and water.   [2 marks]

Group 7 — The Halogens

Here's a page on another periodic table group that you need to be familiar with — <u>the halogens</u>.

Group 7 *Elements are Known as the Halogens*

Group 7 is made up of the elements fluorine, chlorine, bromine, iodine and astatine.

Group 7	Group 0
	He
9 **F** Fluorine 19	Ne
17 **Cl** Chlorine 35.5	Ar
35 **Br** Bromine 80	Kr
53 **I** Iodine 127	Xe
85 **At** Astatine 210	Rn

1) All Group 7 elements have <u>7 electrons in their outer shell</u>
   — so they all have <u>similar chemical properties</u>.

2) The halogens exist as <u>diatomic molecules</u> (e.g. Cl_2, Br_2, I_2).
   Sharing one pair of electrons in a <u>covalent bond</u>
   (see page 166) gives both atoms a <u>full outer shell</u>.

3) As you go <u>down Group 7</u>, the <u>melting points</u>
   and <u>boiling points</u> of the halogens <u>increase</u>.

4) This means that at <u>room temperature</u>:
   - <u>Chlorine</u> (Cl_2) is a poisonous (toxic),
     green gas (it has a low boiling point).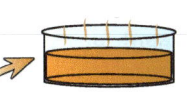
   - <u>Bromine</u> (Br_2) is a poisonous, <u>red-brown liquid</u>,
     which gives off an <u>orange vapour</u> at room temperature.
   - <u>Iodine</u> (I_2) is a <u>dark grey crystalline solid</u>
     which gives off a <u>purple vapour</u> when heated.

Reactivity Decreases *Going Down* Group 7

$$Cl \quad + \; e^- \rightarrow \quad Cl^-$$

Higher

1) A halogen atom only needs to <u>gain one electron</u>
   to form a <u>1– ion</u> with a <u>stable electronic structure</u>.

2) The <u>easier</u> it is for a halogen atom to <u>attract</u> an
   electron, the <u>more reactive</u> the halogen will be.

3) As you go <u>DOWN</u> Group 7, the halogens become <u>less reactive</u> — it gets <u>harder</u> to attract the <u>extra</u>
   <u>electron</u> to fill the outer shell when it's <u>further away</u> from the nucleus (the <u>atomic radius</u> is <u>larger</u>).

4) Group 6 elements are <u>less reactive</u> than Group 7 elements because they have to gain
   <u>two electrons</u> to get a <u>full outer shell</u> — this is <u>harder</u> than gaining just one electron.

Chlorine and *Iodine* have *Lots of Uses*

1) Chlorine is <u>toxic</u> — it <u>kills</u> disease-causing <u>microorganisms</u>, such as <u>bacteria</u>.

2) It's an important part of <u>water treatment</u>. Adding chlorine to
   water <u>sterilises</u> it, making it <u>safe</u> to <u>drink</u> or <u>swim in</u>. The amount
   of chlorine used is <u>carefully monitored</u> so it is sufficient to kill
   <u>harmful bacteria</u> without making the water <u>toxic to people</u>.

3) If we didn't treat our <u>drinking water</u> with <u>chlorine</u> in this way, we'd be at
   risk of getting all sorts of <u>nasty</u> and potentially <u>dangerous infections</u>.

4) Chlorine is also used to make <u>cleaning products</u>.

1) Iodine is also <u>toxic</u> — it is used as an <u>antiseptic</u> in hospitals
   to <u>sterilise skin</u> before operations, because it kills bacteria.

2) <u>Radioactive</u> forms of iodine are used in <u>nuclear medicine</u>.

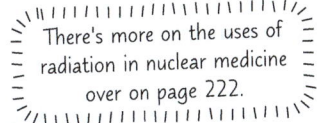
There's more on the uses of radiation in nuclear medicine over on page 222.

Halogens — one electron short of a full shell...

Another page, another periodic table group to learn the properties and the trends of. When you're pretty confident
that you've got all the stuff from this page in your head, have a go at the question below, just to check.

Q1   The melting point of chlorine (Cl_2) is –101.5 °C. Predict whether bromine (Br_2)
      would be a solid, a liquid or a gas at –101.5 °C. Explain your answer.   [2 marks]

Reactions of the Halogens

There are a few reactions that the Group 7 elements take part in that you need to learn about.

The Halogens React With Alkali Metals to Form Salts

1) The halogens will react vigorously with alkali metals (Group 1 elements) to form white salts called 'metal halides'.

2) On the right is an example of this reaction. There are some more on page 68.

$$2K_{(s)} \quad + \quad I_{2(s)} \quad \rightarrow \quad 2KI_{(s)}$$
$$\text{potassium} \quad + \quad \text{iodine} \quad \rightarrow \quad \text{potassium iodide}$$

The Halogens React With Iron to Form Iron Halides

1) When iron reacts with a Group 7 element an exothermic reaction occurs (page 183) and an iron halide (iron salt) is produced.

2) The salts formed are iron(III) salts. They are coloured solids.

3) Chlorine reacts the most vigorously with iron. Bromine and iodine react less vigorously — they have to be heated for a reaction to happen.

Iron(III) salts are ionic compounds that contain Fe^{3+} ions.

$$2Fe \quad + \quad 3Cl_2 \quad \rightarrow \quad 2FeCl_3$$
$$\text{iron} \quad + \quad \text{chlorine} \quad \rightarrow \quad \text{iron(III) chloride}$$

$$2Fe \quad + \quad 3Br_2 \quad \rightarrow \quad 2FeBr_3$$
$$\text{iron} \quad + \quad \text{bromine} \quad \rightarrow \quad \text{iron(III) bromide}$$

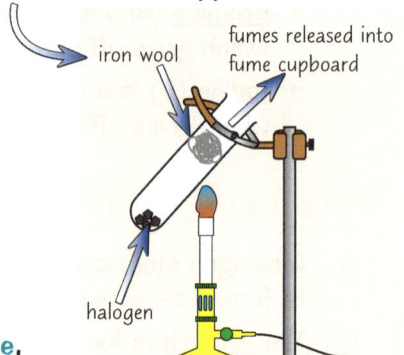

fumes released into fume cupboard

iron wool

halogen

Higher

4) The reaction with iron becomes less vigorous down Group 7. Although this follows the general trend in Group 7 reactivity, it isn't actually a very fair comparison of the reactivities of the halogens.

5) This is because the halogens are in different states at room temperature, which affects how reactive they are.

6) A better way to compare their reactivities is through displacement reactions...

A More Reactive Halogen Will Displace a Less Reactive One

1) A displacement reaction is a good way to compare the reactivities of two halogens as they compete directly against each other.

2) A displacement reaction is where a more reactive element 'pushes out' (displaces) a less reactive element from a compound.

3) For example, chlorine is more reactive than bromine (it's higher up Group 7). If you add chlorine water (an aqueous solution of Cl_2) to potassium bromide solution, the chlorine will displace the bromine from the salt solution.

4) The chlorine is reduced to chloride ions, so the salt solution becomes potassium chloride. The bromide ions are oxidised to bromine, which turns the solution orange.

All equations for halogen displacement reactions follow this pattern.

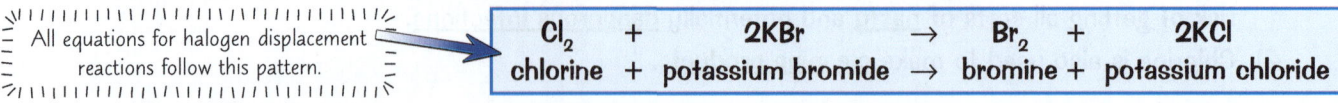

$$Cl_2 \quad + \quad 2KBr \quad \rightarrow \quad Br_2 \quad + \quad 2KCl$$
$$\text{chlorine} \quad + \quad \text{potassium bromide} \quad \rightarrow \quad \text{bromine} \quad + \quad \text{potassium chloride}$$

5) The halogens always gain electrons whilst the halide ions lose electrons.

You can see the loss and gain of electrons by looking at the ionic equation. Check out more about ionic equations on page 73.

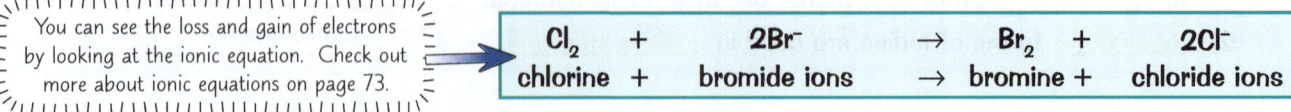

$$Cl_2 \quad + \quad 2Br^- \quad \rightarrow \quad Br_2 \quad + \quad 2Cl^-$$
$$\text{chlorine} \quad + \quad \text{bromide ions} \quad \rightarrow \quad \text{bromine} \quad + \quad \text{chloride ions}$$

Bro-mine — the coolest element...

Don't forget that iron(III) salts are formed in those halogen reactions, you can't just say 'iron salts' in the exam.

Q1 Write a balanced symbol equation for the reaction between sodium metal (Na) and iodine (I_2). [2 marks]

Q2 Write a balanced symbol equation for the reaction between iron (Fe) and chlorine (Cl_2). [2 marks]

Halogen Displacement Reactions

The halogens are a pretty competitive lot really. In fact the <u>more reactive</u> ones will push the <u>less reactive</u> ones out of a compound. How uncivilised — has nobody ever taught them that it's bad manners to push?

Displacement Reactions *Show Reactivity Trends*

<u>Displacement reactions</u> can be used to provide <u>evidence</u> for the reactivity trend of the halogens. Here's how they're done:

1) First, a small amount of a <u>halide salt solution</u> is measured out and added to a test tube. All halide salt solutions are <u>colourless</u>.

2) A few drops of a <u>halogen solution</u> are added to the test tube, and the tube is shaken gently.

3) If there is a <u>colour change</u>, then a reaction has happened — the halogen has displaced the halide ions from the salt.

4) If no reaction happens, there <u>won't</u> be a colour change — the halogen is <u>less reactive</u> than the halide and so can't displace it.

5) The process can be repeated using different combinations of halide salt and halogen.

6) The table below shows what should happen when different combinations of <u>chlorine</u>, <u>bromine</u> and <u>iodine</u> water are mixed with solutions of the salts <u>potassium chloride</u>, <u>potassium bromide</u> and <u>potassium iodide</u>.

Start with:	Potassium chloride solution $KCl_{(aq)}$ — colourless	Potassium bromide solution $KBr_{(aq)}$ — colourless	Potassium iodide solution $KI_{(aq)}$ — colourless
Add chlorine water $Cl_{2\,(aq)}$ — colourless	no reaction	orange solution ($Br_{2\,(aq)}$) formed	brown solution ($I_{2\,(aq)}$) formed
Add bromine water $Br_{2\,(aq)}$ — orange	no reaction	no reaction	brown solution ($I_{2\,(aq)}$) formed
Add iodine water $I_{2\,(aq)}$ — brown	no reaction	no reaction	no reaction

7) <u>Chlorine</u> displaces both bromine and iodine from salt solutions. E.g.:

$$Cl_2 \ + \ 2KI \ \rightarrow \ I_2 \ + \ 2KCl$$
chlorine + potassium iodide → iodine + potassium chloride

8) <u>Bromine</u> can't displace chlorine, but it does displace iodine.

$$Br_2 \ + \ 2KI \ \rightarrow \ I_2 \ + \ 2KBr$$
bromine + potassium iodide → iodine + potassium bromide

9) <u>Iodine</u> can't displace chlorine or bromine.

10) This provides evidence for the <u>reactivity trend</u> — the halogens can only displace halide ions of halogens that are below them in Group 7. So they get <u>less reactive</u> as you go <u>down</u> the group.

You can use the *Results* to make *Predictions*

1) For example, you can use the trend you've identified to <u>predict</u> how astatine might react.

2) Since astatine is even lower in Group 7 than iodine, you'd predict it to be the <u>least reactive halogen</u>. Therefore you'd predict it <u>wouldn't displace</u> any other halogens from their salt solutions.

New information displaces old information from my brain...

If you remember that the halogens get less reactive as you go down the group, you can work out what will happen when you mix any halogen with any halide salt. You need to know the colour changes that go with the reactions too.

Q1   A student added a few drops of a halogen solution to some potassium iodide solution. The solution turned brown. She added a few drops of the same halogen solution to some potassium bromide solution. No reaction occurred. Name the halogen solution that the student used.   [1 mark]

Higher

Group 0 — The Noble Gases

The elements in <u>Group 0</u> of the periodic table are known as the <u>noble gases</u>. 'Noble' here is just being used in the old chemistry sense of being <u>unreactive</u> — nothing to do with them being particularly honourable or good.

Group 0 Elements are All Inert, Colourless Gases

<u>Group 0</u> elements are called the <u>noble gases</u>. Group 0 is made up of the elements helium, neon, argon, krypton, xenon and radon.

1) All of the Group 0 elements are <u>colourless gases</u> at room temperature.

2) The noble gases are all <u>monatomic</u> — that just means that their gases are made up of <u>single atoms</u> (not molecules).

3) They're also more or less <u>inert</u> — this means they <u>don't react</u> with much at all. The reason for this is that they have a <u>full outer shell</u> of electrons. This means they <u>don't</u> easily <u>give up</u> or <u>gain</u> electrons.

4) As the noble gases are inert, they're <u>non-flammable</u> — they won't set on fire.

5) These properties make the gases pretty <u>hard to observe</u> — it took a long time for them to be discovered.

Group 0		
		4 **He** Helium 2
Group 7		20 **Ne** Neon 10
	F	
	Cl	40 **Ar** Argon 18
	Br	84 **Kr** Krypton 36
	I	131 **Xe** Xenon 54
	At	222 **Rn** Radon 86

The Noble Gases have Many Everyday Uses...

The properties of the noble gases make them suitable for a few different uses:

Helium

1) Helium has a very <u>low density</u> — lower than air.

2) <u>Helium</u> is used in <u>airships</u>, <u>weather balloons</u> and <u>party balloons</u> — its low density makes balloons <u>float</u> in air.

3) Helium is very unreactive and also <u>non-flammable</u>. This makes it <u>safe</u> to use in balloons.

The first gas balloons used in weather balloons and airships were filled with hydrogen, rather than helium. Although hydrogen does have a really low density, it's highly flammable and forms an explosive mixture with air, which was sometimes a recipe for disaster.

Neon

1) Neon emits a <u>bright light</u> when a <u>current</u> is passed through it.

2) It's mostly used in <u>bright signs</u> to produce a <u>red-orange</u> glow.

3) Neon is also used in <u>cryogenics</u> and <u>lasers</u>.

Argon

1) Argon is <u>very unreactive</u> and <u>non-flammable</u>.

2) <u>It's used</u> in <u>filament lamps</u> (light bulbs). Since it's <u>non-flammable</u>, it helps stop the very hot filament from becoming <u>damaged</u>.

3) <u>Argon</u> can also be used to protect metals that are being <u>welded</u>. The inert atmosphere stops the hot metal reacting with <u>oxygen</u>.

arrrrr

Noble gas jokes are rubbish — I never get a reaction from them...

The noble gases might seem a bit dull, given how unreactive they are, but they're not so bad. They'd be pretty good at hide and seek for a start. And what would helium balloon sellers be without them? Deflated — that's what.

Q1   Explain why Group 0 elements are unreactive.   [1 mark]

Tests for Ions and Hydrogen

Have you ever wondered how you could identify mystery <u>ions and gases</u>? Well you're in for a treat...

Ionic Equations *Show Just the Useful Bits of Reactions*

In an <u>ionic equation</u> only the particles that react and the products they form are shown. For example...

1) This ionic equation <u>just</u> shows the <u>displacement</u> of <u>zinc ions</u> by magnesium metal. ⟶ $Mg_{(s)} + Zn^{2+}_{(aq)} \rightarrow Mg^{2+}_{(aq)} + Zn_{(s)}$
2) Here's what the <u>full equation</u> would be if you'd started off with zinc chloride: ⟶ $Mg_{(s)} + ZnCl_{2(aq)} \rightarrow MgCl_{2(aq)} + Zn_{(s)}$
3) If you write out the equations showing all the ions, you'll see that the chloride ions <u>don't change</u> — they're <u>spectator ions</u>. They're of no interest here, so can be crossed out.
$$Mg_{(s)} + Zn^{2+}_{(aq)} + 2Cl^{-}_{(aq)} \rightarrow Mg^{2+}_{(aq)} + 2Cl^{-}_{(aq)} + Zn_{(s)}$$
4) Instead, the ionic equation for this displacement reaction just <u>concentrates</u> on the substances which are <u>actually reacting</u> (p.70).

Ionic equations should always include state symbols. You'll be told if there's a mark for doing this in the exam.

<u>Ionic equations</u> are handy for showing what happens in a test for an ion...

Test for *Halide Ions Using Silver Nitrate Solution*

To test for <u>chloride</u> ions (Cl^-), <u>bromide</u> ions (Br^-) or <u>iodide</u> ions (I^-), add some <u>dilute nitric acid</u> (HNO_3), followed by a few drops of <u>silver nitrate solution</u> ($AgNO_3$).

A <u>chloride</u> gives a white precipitate of <u>silver chloride</u>.
$$Ag^{+}_{(aq)} + Cl^{-}_{(aq)} \longrightarrow AgCl_{(s)}$$

A <u>bromide</u> gives a cream precipitate of <u>silver bromide</u>.
$$Ag^{+}_{(aq)} + Br^{-}_{(aq)} \longrightarrow AgBr_{(s)}$$

An <u>iodide</u> gives a yellow precipitate of <u>silver iodide</u>.
$$Ag^{+}_{(aq)} + I^{-}_{(aq)} \longrightarrow AgI_{(s)}$$

The nitric acid is added first to get rid of any carbonate ions — they produce a white precipitate with silver nitrate solution too, which would confuse the results. You can't use hydrochloric acid, because you'd be adding chloride ions.

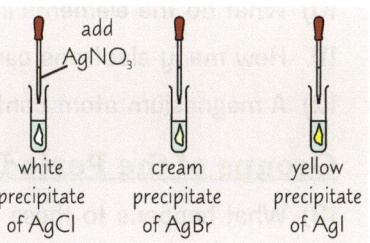

add $AgNO_3$

| white precipitate of AgCl | cream precipitate of AgBr | yellow precipitate of AgI |

There are also <u>spectator ions</u> in these reactions. E.g. if NaCl is tested, Na^+ and NO_3^- are spectator ions. They are unchanged in the reaction: $Na^{+}_{(aq)} + Cl^{-}_{(aq)} + Ag^{+}_{(aq)} + NO_{3}^{-}{}_{(aq)} \rightarrow AgCl_{(s)} + Na^{+}_{(aq)} + NO_{3}^{-}{}_{(aq)}$

You Can Use *Flame Tests to Identify Metal Ions*

Compounds of some metals produce a characteristic colour when heated in a flame.

1) You can test for <u>metal ions</u> by putting the substance in a <u>flame</u> and seeing what <u>colour</u> the flame goes.

- <u>Lithium</u>, Li^+, gives a red flame.
- <u>Sodium</u>, Na^+, gives a yellow-orange flame.
- <u>Potassium</u>, K^+, gives a lilac flame.
- <u>Calcium</u>, Ca^{2+}, gives a brick red flame.
- <u>Barium</u>, Ba^{2+}, gives an apple green flame.

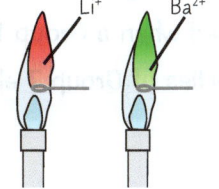

Remember — metals always form positive ions.

This test only works if the mystery compound contains just one type of metal ion — otherwise you'll get a confusing mixture of colours.

2) To carry out a flame test in the lab, first <u>clean</u> a <u>nichrome wire loop</u> by dipping it into <u>hydrochloric acid</u> and then rinsing it in <u>deionised water</u>.

3) Then dip the <u>wire loop</u> into a sample of the <u>metal compound</u> and put the loop in the blue part of a Bunsen flame (the hottest bit). Record what <u>colour</u> the flame goes.

Test for *Hydrogen Using a Lit Splint*

If you hold a <u>lit splint</u> at the open end of a test tube containing hydrogen, you'll get a "<u>squeaky pop</u>". (The noise comes from the hydrogen burning quickly with the oxygen in the air to form H_2O.)

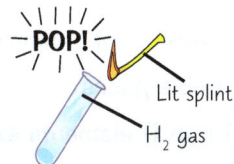

POP!
Lit splint
H_2 gas

Squeaky pop is all I hear on the radio nowadays...

Try to find an easy way to remember the flame test colours that works for you, purple potassium, Braeburn barium.

Q1 In a flame test, which element does an apple green flame indicate the presence of? [1 mark]

Revision Questions for Unit 2b

Well that's Unit 2b nearly finished — just this page and then it's time for a nice cup of tea and a biscuit. Try these questions and tick off each one when you get it right.

- When you've done all the questions for a topic and are completely happy with it, tick off the topic.

Atoms, Ions and Isotopes (p.63-64) ☐

1) Which subatomic particle is negatively charged?

2) Which subatomic particle has a relative mass of 1 and a relative charge of 0?

3) What two subatomic particles make up the nucleus of an atom?

4) What does the mass number tell you about an atom?

5) How can you calculate the number of neutrons in an atom?

6) How many electrons does a Mg^{2+} ion have?

7) What are isotopes?

8) True or false? The relative atomic mass of an element is the sum of the mass numbers of all its different isotopes.

The Periodic Table and Electronic Structure (p.65-66) ☐

9) What does the group number of an element in the periodic table tell you about its electronic structure?

10) What do the elements in each period have in common?

11) How many electrons can the first electron shell of an atom contain?

12) A magnesium atom contains 12 electrons. What is the electronic structure of magnesium?

Groups of the Periodic Table (p.67-73) ☐

13) What happens to these properties of Group 1 elements as you move down a group:
    a) melting / boiling point?
    b) reactivity?

14) Do Group 1 elements gain or lose electrons during reactions? How many?

15) What happens to a Group 1 element if it is left in air? What type of substance is formed?

16) Which Group 1 metal has the least vigorous reaction with water?

17) What type of product is formed when a Group 1 metal reacts with chlorine gas?

18) What happens to these properties of Group 7 elements as you move down a group:
    a) melting / boiling point?
    b) reactivity?

19) Give one use of chlorine and one use of iodine.

20) Which iron salt is produced when iron reacts with bromine?

21) Why do displacement reactions give stronger evidence for the Group 7 reactivity series than their reactions with iron?

22) What would you observe if chlorine water was added to potassium iodide solution?

23) Why does no reaction occur when iodine water is added to potassium bromide?

24) Name two noble gases.

25) Why are Group 0 elements extremely unreactive?

26) Give one use of neon.

27) What colour flame would you see if testing for calcium?

28) Describe the test used to identify hydrogen gas.

Water Treatment

Water treatment is <u>essential</u> for a healthy life — untreated water can make you very <u>poorly</u>.

There are a Variety of Water Resources

There are a number of <u>sources of water</u>, which can be <u>treated</u> to provide <u>drinking water</u>. These include:

1) <u>GROUNDWATER</u>: from rocks that trap water underground (aquifers). This contains <u>ions</u> such as Mg^{2+}, Ca^{2+}, Na^+ and K^+ — these ions come from <u>minerals</u> in the rocks.

2) <u>RAINWATER</u>: from rain — this contains <u>dissolved gases</u> such as CO_2 and O_2. When CO_2 dissolves in water it <u>lowers</u> the <u>pH</u> of the water.

Water sources contain <u>man-made pollutants</u> like <u>pesticides</u>, <u>fertilisers</u>, and household and industrial <u>waste</u>. As well as man-made pollutants, water can also contain <u>natural pollutants</u> like <u>bacteria</u> and <u>viruses</u>.

There is a Demand for Sustainable Water

1) Fresh water is <u>crucial</u> to humans — not just for <u>drinking</u>, but also for <u>farming</u> and <u>industry</u>.

2) The global population is <u>increasing</u>, so there is an even greater need for <u>water</u>.

3) Because of this, water is expected to become more <u>scarce</u> with <u>water shortages</u> being possible. <u>Climate change</u> also <u>increases</u> the risk of <u>droughts</u>, which makes water shortages more likely.

4) As the <u>demand</u> for water <u>goes up</u> so will the <u>price</u>, so to make our water supply <u>sustainable</u> and <u>affordable</u> we need to <u>reduce</u> our water consumption.

5) We also need to <u>collect</u> and <u>treat</u> our water in ways that <u>don't</u> damage the environment.

Water is Purified in Water Treatment Plants

The water that comes out of your taps doesn't come <u>straight from the source</u> — first it has to be <u>purified</u>. How much purification it needs depends on the source. But, wherever it comes from, most of our water is purified using the following processes:

1) <u>Sedimentation</u> — large solid particles in the water <u>settle</u> at the <u>bottom</u> of the water tank because of <u>gravity</u>.

2) <u>Filtration</u> — small <u>insoluble</u> particles are removed by <u>filtering</u> through layers of <u>sand and gravel</u>.

3) <u>Chlorination</u> — chlorine gas is bubbled through to kill <u>harmful bacteria</u> and other <u>microbes</u>.

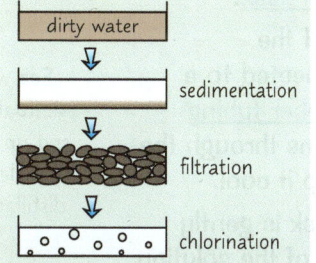

Some soluble impurities that are dissolved in the water are not removed as they can't be filtered out — these include the minerals which cause water hardness (p.79).

Adding Fluoride to Water Has Pros and Cons

Fluoride ions are found <u>naturally</u> in a lot of water sources. Adding <u>more fluoride</u> ions to water supplies is a <u>controversial</u> issue in the UK. There are some advantages and disadvantages that you should know:

1) There is <u>strong evidence</u> that <u>fluoride ions</u> prevent <u>tooth decay</u> in children — reliable surveys of school children support this claim.

2) Some studies however have linked <u>high doses</u> of fluoride to <u>bone</u> and <u>stomach cancer</u> and <u>infertility</u> in humans, so some people believe that fluoride <u>shouldn't be added</u> to drinking water. There is also concern about whether it's right to '<u>mass medicate</u>' — people can <u>choose</u> whether to use a <u>fluoride toothpaste</u> or <u>mouthwash</u>, but they can't choose whether their tap water has added fluoride.

There's more about ethics in science in the 'Working Scientifically' section on page 3.

3) <u>Levels of chemicals</u> added to drinking water need to be carefully <u>monitored</u>. For example, in some areas the water may already contain a lot of fluoride, so adding more could be harmful.

If water from the ground is ground water, why isn't rain sky water?

Ahhh... Every glass of tap water I drink tastes all the sweeter for knowing what it had to go through to get to me...

Q1   Outline how water is purified in a water treatment plant.   [3 marks]

Distillation and Desalination

Distillation means <u>separating</u> a pure liquid from a solution by <u>evaporation</u> and <u>condensation</u>.
You can <u>distil sea water</u> to get <u>fresh water</u> — this is called '<u>desalination</u>' (removing all of the salt).

You Can Get Safe Water by *Distilling Sea Water*

1) In some <u>dry</u> countries, sea water is <u>distilled</u> to produce drinking water — this is the <u>simplest</u> way of removing the salt.

2) On a small scale, sea water can be distilled using a <u>solar still</u>.

3) On a larger scale, traditional <u>distillation apparatus</u> is used, which usually involves <u>burning fossil fuels</u> to heat the water.

4) This needs <u>loads of energy</u> (and therefore loads of money) to heat such a large amount of water. This makes it <u>expensive</u> and <u>impractical</u> — it's not always a viable process in poorer countries.

5) Distillation is also only possible in countries that are <u>near the sea</u>.

6) There are other ways of removing salt from sea water. For example, the salt water can be forced through <u>membranes</u> which only allow the water molecules through, and not the salt.

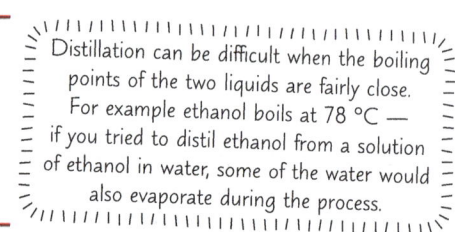

Simple Distillation *Separates Out Solutions*

All <u>pure liquids</u> boil at a <u>specific temperature</u> (known as the boiling point) — water boils at <u>100 °C</u>. If you have a <u>mixture</u> of two or more liquids with <u>different boiling points</u>, you can <u>separate</u> them out using <u>distillation</u>. Distillation can also be used to <u>desalinate</u> sea water. It works like this:

> **Higher** — Distillation can be difficult when the boiling points of the two liquids are fairly close. For example ethanol boils at 78 °C — if you tried to distil ethanol from a solution of ethanol in water, some of the water would also evaporate during the process.

1) The sample of sea water is poured into the <u>distillation flask</u>.

2) The bottom end of the <u>condenser</u> is connected to a cold tap using <u>rubber tubing</u> and <u>cold water</u> runs through the condenser to keep it cool.

3) The distillation flask is gently heated. The part of the solution that has the lowest boiling point will <u>evaporate</u> — in this case, that's the water.

4) The water <u>vapour</u> passes into the condenser where it <u>cools</u> and <u>condenses</u> (turns back into a liquid). It then flows into the beaker where it is <u>collected</u>.

5) Eventually you'll end up with just the <u>salt</u> left in the flask, and <u>pure water</u> in the beaker.

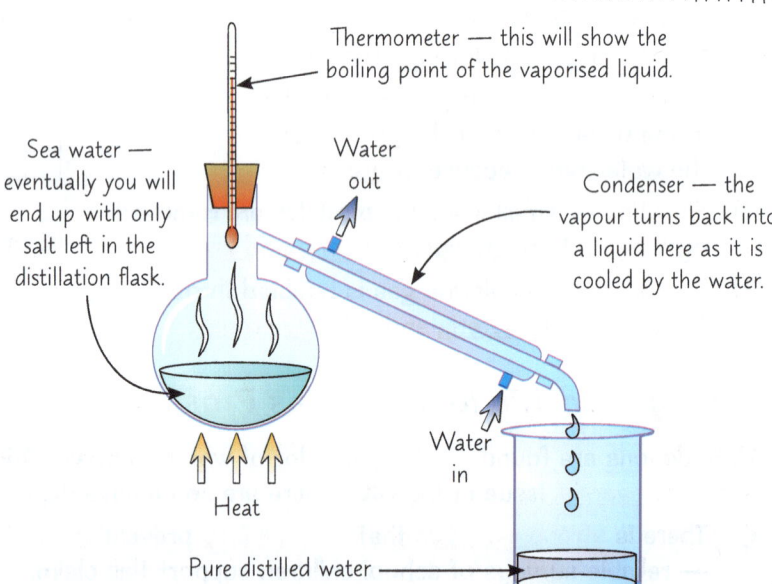

Thermometer — this will show the boiling point of the vaporised liquid.

Sea water — eventually you will end up with only salt left in the distillation flask.

Water out

Condenser — the vapour turns back into a liquid here as it is cooled by the water.

Heat

Water in

Pure distilled water

If you're not part of the solution you're part of the... pure liquid?

Distillation might be the easiest method of desalinating sea water, but that doesn't mean it's easy to remember — read over the method of distillation and then try scribbling it down until you know it off by heart.

Q1   Why is distillation an expensive method of desalinating sea water?   [1 mark]

Solubility Curves

This page is all about <u>solutions</u>. Study it carefully and you might even get some solutions to exam questions...

Solubility is a Measure of How Much Solute will Dissolve in a Solvent

1) A <u>solute</u> is a substance that dissolves in a liquid to make a solution.
The <u>solvent</u> is the liquid that the solute dissolves in.

2) The ability of a <u>solute</u> to <u>dissolve</u> in a solvent is known as its <u>solubility</u>.

3) When <u>no more</u> of the <u>solute</u> can dissolve in the <u>solvent</u>, the solution is <u>saturated</u>.

4) Solubility is often measured in <u>grams of solute</u> per <u>100 grams of solvent</u>.

> <u>For example</u>: If **23** grams of a substance can dissolve in 100 grams of water before the solution becomes <u>saturated</u>, that substance has a solubility of <u>23 g per 100 g of water</u>.

5) The <u>solubility</u> of most solid substances <u>increases</u> as you increase the <u>temperature</u>.

6) A graph of solubility versus temperature is known as a <u>solubility curve</u>:

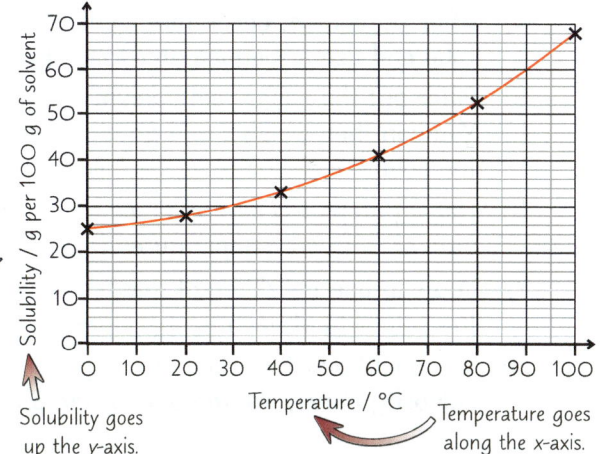

Solubility goes up the *y*-axis.

Temperature goes along the *x*-axis.

7) The <u>temperature scale</u> on a solubility curve usually ranges from <u>0 °C – 100 °C</u> because water <u>freezes</u> at 0 °C and <u>boils</u> at 100 °C.

8) You can use solubility curves to find the solubility of a substance at a <u>specific temperature</u>.

9) To do this, draw a <u>line</u> from the temperature that you're interested in (on the *x*-axis) up to the <u>curve</u>. Then, <u>read across</u> from the curve to the *y*-axis to find the <u>solubility</u> of the substance at that <u>particular temperature</u>. For example, on the graph on the right, the solubility at **25 °C** is **32 g** per 100 g of solvent.

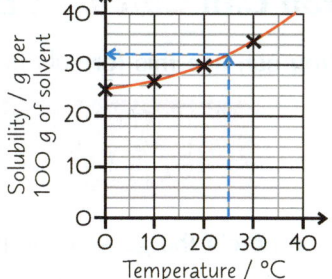

You Can Plot a Solubility Curve   Here's how you do it:

1) Measure out a set <u>volume</u> of <u>water</u>. Let it stand for a while until it reaches room temperature.

2) Weigh out a set <u>mass</u> of the <u>solute</u>. It must be <u>a bit greater</u> than the mass that will dissolve in that volume of water at room temperature.

> If you're not sure what mass to use, do a trial run, where you add the solute a bit at a time, to work it out.

3) Add the solute to the water and stir until <u>most</u> of the solute has dissolved.

4) Now <u>heat</u> the solution gently until <u>all</u> of the solute has dissolved.

5) Leave the solution to <u>cool</u>. Record the <u>temperature</u> at which <u>crystals</u> start to appear.

> You might need to use an ice bath to cool the solution.

6) Divide the mass of the <u>solute</u> by the mass of the <u>water</u> then <u>multiply by 100</u> to find the <u>solubility</u> (in g per 100 g of solvent) at this temperature.
(This is the formula for calculating solubility that's shown on the next page.)

7) Repeat the experiment several times. Use a <u>slightly greater</u> volume of <u>water</u> each time, but always add the <u>same mass</u> of solute that you used in the first experiment.

8) Find the <u>solubility</u> at each <u>temperature</u>. Plot these values on a graph to make a <u>solubility curve</u>.

How do dissolved soldiers greet their General? They give a solute...

Learning all the definitions in chemistry can be a right pain, but it's worth it for those juicy marks in the exam.

Q1   What is meant by the 'solubility' of a substance?   [1 mark]

Q2   Look at the first graph on this page. What is the solubility when the temperature is 70 °C?   [1 mark]

Investigating Solubility

You can measure solubility by making saturated solutions at different temperatures.

You Can Investigate how Temperature Affects Solubility

Here's how you could investigate how the solubility of solid ammonium chloride is affected by temperature:

1) Measure out a set volume of water and put it in a boiling tube.

2) Weigh out a mass of ammonium chloride that's greater than the amount that will dissolve in this much water. Add it to the water.

> Adding an excess of the solid means you can be sure that the solution you've made is saturated.

3) Give the solution a good stir and place the boiling tube in a water bath set to 25 °C.

4) After 5 minutes, check that all of the excess solid has sunk to the bottom of the tube and use a thermometer to check that the solution has reached 25 °C.

5) Filter out the excess ammonium chloride and allow it to dry. You can then weigh it and go on to work out how much of the solute is dissolved in the solution (see below).

6) Repeat steps 1-5 several times more, but with the water bath at different temperatures (e.g. 35 °C, 45 °C, etc.).

7) You can use the different masses to work out the solubility at each temperature (see below).

8) You could plot the results on a graph to give a solubility curve, like the one on the previous page.

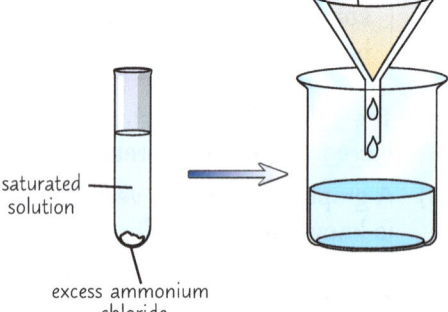

saturated solution

excess ammonium chloride

You Can Calculate the Solubility from the Masses of the Solid and Water

You can use this formula to find the mass of solute dissolved from the results of the experiment above:

$$\text{Mass of solute dissolved (g)} = \text{mass of solid added to solvent (g)} - \text{mass of dried excess solid (g)}$$

And here's the general formula for calculating the solubility of a solid:

$$\text{solubility (g per 100 g of solvent)} = \frac{\text{mass of solute dissolved (g)}}{\text{mass of water (g)}} \times 100$$

Example: Use the following experimental data to find the solubility of ammonium chloride at 35 °C.

Mass of ammonium chloride added	65.0 g
Mass of excess dried ammonium chloride	13.3 g
Mass of water	120.0 g

Method:

1) Find the mass of the solute dissolved in the solution:
mass of solute dissolved = mass of solid added – mass of dried excess solid
= 65.0 g – 13.3 g = 51.7 g

2) Use the equation above to calculate the solubility:
solubility = (mass of solute dissolved ÷ mass of water) × 100
= (51.7 ÷ 120.0) × 100 = 43.0833... = 43.1 g per 100 g of water (to 3 s.f.)

Adding some sugar to your morning beverage — solubilitea...

Who knows, you might be lucky enough to get to do this experiment in class. Wouldn't that be exciting...

Q1 Describe an experiment that could be used to determine the solubility of a solid at 40 °C. [5 marks]

Water Hardness

Water where you live might be <u>hard</u> or <u>soft</u>. It depends on the <u>rocks</u> your water meets on its way to you.

Hard Water Makes Scum and Scale

1) If you live in an area with <u>soft water</u>, you'll get a nice <u>lather</u> when you use soap. But with <u>hard water</u> you get a <u>nasty scum</u> instead. The problem is dissolved <u>ions</u> in the water (see below) reacting with the soap to make <u>scum</u> which is insoluble. So to get a decent lather you need to use <u>more soap</u>.

2) When <u>heated</u>, hard water also forms furring or <u>scale</u> (mostly calcium carbonate) on the insides of pipes, boilers and kettles. This makes them <u>less efficient</u> and can even completely block pipes.

Hardness is Caused by Ca^{2+} and Mg^{2+} Ions

1) Most hard water is hard because it contains lots of <u>calcium ions</u> (Ca^{2+}) and <u>magnesium ions</u> (Mg^{2+}).

2) Rain falling on some types of rocks (e.g. <u>limestone</u>, <u>chalk</u> and <u>gypsum</u>) can dissolve compounds like <u>magnesium sulfate</u> (which is soluble), and <u>calcium sulfate</u> (which is also soluble, though only a bit).

3) Ca^{2+} ions are good for healthy <u>teeth</u> and <u>bones</u>.

4) Studies found that people who live in <u>hard water</u> areas are at <u>less risk</u> of developing <u>heart disease</u> than people who live in soft water areas. This could be to do with the <u>minerals</u> in hard water.

Remove the Dissolved Ca^{2+} and Mg^{2+} Ions to Make Hard Water Soft

There are two kinds of hardness — <u>temporary</u> and <u>permanent</u>.

• <u>Temporary hardness</u> is caused by dissolved <u>calcium hydrogencarbonate</u> or <u>magnesium hydrogencarbonate</u>.

• <u>Permanent hardness</u> is caused by dissolved <u>calcium sulfate</u> or <u>magnesium sulfate</u> (amongst other things).

1) <u>Temporary hardness</u> can be removed by <u>boiling</u> water in an ordinary kettle. But this <u>won't</u> get rid of permanent hardness, and you can only use it to treat <u>small amounts</u> of water.

Higher

The metal hydrogencarbonate <u>decomposes</u> on heating to form an <u>insoluble</u> metal carbonate. This solid is the 'limescale' on your kettle.

> e.g. calcium hydrogencarbonate → calcium carbonate + water + carbon dioxide

2) <u>Both types of hardness</u> can be softened by adding <u>sodium carbonate</u>, Na_2CO_3 (washing soda). This causes <u>limescale</u> to form, which can <u>block</u> washing machine pipes.

Higher

The <u>carbonate ions</u> react with the Ca^{2+} and Mg^{2+} ions to make an <u>insoluble</u> <u>precipitate</u> of calcium carbonate or magnesium carbonate (limescale). Removing the Ca^{2+} and Mg^{2+} ions from the water makes it soft.

> e.g. $Ca^{2+}_{(aq)} + CO_3^{2-}_{(aq)} \rightarrow CaCO_{3(s)}$

3) <u>Both types of hardness</u> can be removed by running water through '<u>ion exchange columns</u>' which are sold in shops. They use concentrated <u>sodium chloride</u>, which is <u>low cost</u> and <u>widely available</u>. However, ion exchange columns are quite <u>expensive</u> to buy.

Higher

These columns have big resin molecules with lots of <u>sodium ions</u> (or <u>hydrogen ions</u>) attached to them. They '<u>exchange</u>' these for calcium or magnesium ions in the water that runs through them.

> e.g. $Na_2Resin_{(s)} + Ca^{2+}_{(aq)} \rightarrow CaResin_{(s)} + 2Na^{+}_{(aq)}$
>
> ('Resin' is a huge insoluble resin molecule.)

For every Ca^{2+} ion removed from the water, two Na^{+} ions are released from the resin.

All of the sodium ions will <u>eventually</u> be <u>used up</u> so no more calcium ions can be <u>removed</u>. The columns can be <u>regenerated</u> by being rinsed in a cheap <u>sodium chloride</u> solution so that they can be <u>used again</u>.

And if the water's really hard, you can chip your teeth...

Hard water provides minerals that are good for health, but it creates an awful lot of unnecessary expense.

Q1   Explain how ion exchange columns remove hardness from water.   [2 marks]

**PRACTICAL**

Measuring Water Hardness

If you live in an area of <u>hard water</u> you might already know about it because you sometimes get a grimy layer of <u>scale</u> floating on the top of your tea... Plus you get through more shampoo than you can shake a stick at...

Use *Titration* to *Compare* the *Hardness* of *Water Samples*

Method

1) Fill a burette with <u>50 cm³ of soap solution</u>.

2) Add <u>50 cm³</u> of the first <u>water</u> sample to a flask.

3) Use the burette to add <u>1 cm³ of soap solution</u> to the flask.

4) Put a <u>bung</u> in the flask and <u>shake</u> for 5 seconds.

5) <u>Repeat</u> steps 3 and 4 until a <u>good lasting lather</u> is formed. (A lasting lather is one where the <u>bubbles cover the surface</u> for <u>at least 30 seconds</u>.)

6) <u>Record</u> how much soap solution was needed to create a lasting lather.

7) <u>Repeat</u> steps 1-6 with the other water samples.

8) Next, <u>boil fresh samples</u> of each type of water for <u>ten minutes</u>, and <u>repeat</u> the experiment.

shake shake shake
Good lather

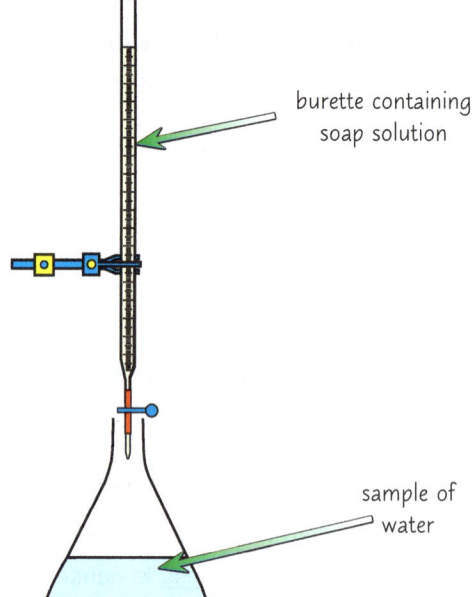
burette containing soap solution

sample of water

Results

This method was carried out on <u>3 samples of water</u> — <u>distilled</u> water, <u>local tap water</u> and <u>imported tap water</u>. Here's the <u>table of results</u>:

Sample	Volume of soap solution needed to give a good lather	
	using unboiled water (cm³)	using boiled water (cm³)
Distilled	1	1
Local water	7	1
Imported water	14	8

1) You can represent these results with a <u>bar chart</u>. The results tell you the following things about the water:

2) Distilled water contains little or no <u>hardness</u> — only the <u>minimum</u> volume of soap solution was needed.

3) The sample of <u>imported water</u> contains <u>more hardness</u> than <u>local water</u> — <u>more soap solution</u> was needed to produce a lather.

4) The local water contains <u>temporary hardness</u> — all the hardness is <u>removed by boiling</u>. You can tell because the same volume of soap solution was needed for <u>boiled local water</u> and <u>distilled water</u>.

5) The imported water contains both <u>temporary</u> and <u>permanent hardness</u>. 8 cm³ of soap solution is still needed to produce a lather after boiling.

6) If your brain's really switched on, you'll see that the local water and the imported water contain the <u>same amount</u> of <u>temporary hardness</u>. In both cases, the amount of soap solution needed in the <u>boiled</u> sample is <u>6 cm³ less</u> than in the <u>unboiled</u> sample.

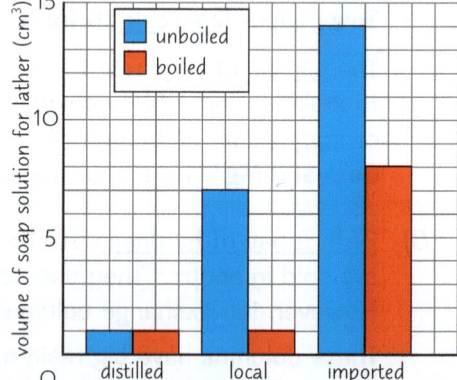
volume of soap solution for lather (cm³)
- unboiled
- boiled
distilled local imported

My water's harder than yours...

Read this page carefully to make sure you really understand this method. Once you're confident, try this question.

Q1 Describe an investigation that could be used to test which of three water solutions was temporary hard water, which was permanent hard water and which was soft water. [6 marks]

The Earth's Structure

This page is all about the <u>structure</u> of <u>the Earth</u> — what the planet's like inside, and how scientists study it...

The Earth has a *Crust*, a *Mantle* and a *Core*

1) The <u>crust</u> is Earth's thin outer layer of solid rock (its average depth is 20 km).

2) The <u>lithosphere</u> includes the crust and upper part of the <u>mantle</u>, and is made up of a <u>jigsaw</u> of 'tectonic plates'. The <u>lithosphere</u> is <u>relatively cold and rigid</u>, and is over 100 km thick in places.

3) The <u>mantle</u> is the <u>semi-solid</u> section between the crust and the core. Near the crust it's <u>fairly rigid</u>. As you go deeper into the mantle the <u>temperature increases</u> — here it becomes <u>less rigid</u> and can <u>flow slowly</u>.

4) At the centre of the Earth is the <u>core</u>, which is made mainly of <u>iron</u>.

5) The <u>core</u> is just over <u>half</u> the Earth's radius. The <u>inner core</u> is <u>solid</u>, while the <u>outer core</u> is molten <u>liquid</u>.

6) <u>Radioactive decay</u> is responsible for a lot of the <u>heat</u> inside the Earth. This heat creates <u>convection currents</u> in the mantle, which causes the <u>plates</u> of the lithosphere to <u>move</u>.

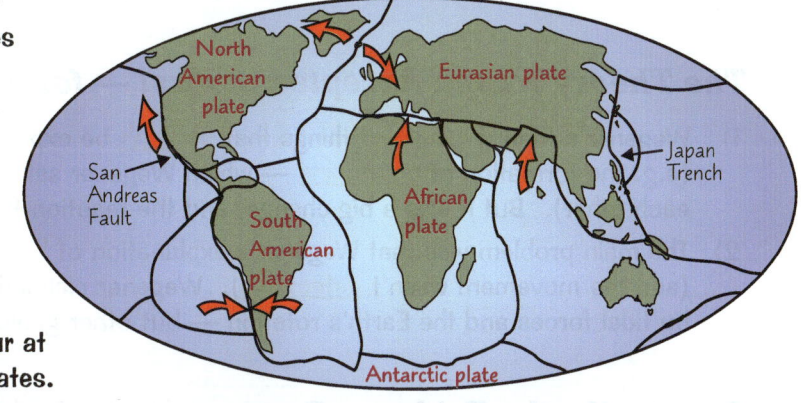

The *Earth's Surface* is Made Up of *Tectonic Plates*

1) The crust and the upper part of the mantle are cracked into about seven major pieces and lots of minor pieces called <u>tectonic plates</u>. These plates are a bit like <u>big rafts</u> that 'float' on the mantle.

2) The plates don't stay in one place though. That's because the <u>convection currents</u> in the mantle cause the plates to <u>drift</u>.

3) This map shows the <u>edges</u> of the plates as they are now, and the <u>directions</u> they're moving in (red arrows).

4) Most of the plates are moving at speeds of <u>a few cm per year</u> relative to each other.

5) Occasionally, the plates move very <u>suddenly</u>, causing an <u>earthquake</u>.

6) <u>Volcanoes</u> and <u>earthquakes</u> often occur at the boundary between two tectonic plates.

Earthquakes and *Volcanoes* Show Tectonic Plates

If you plot active volcanoes and earthquakes on a map of the world, you can see that the markers tend to sit along the same lines as the <u>plate boundaries</u>.

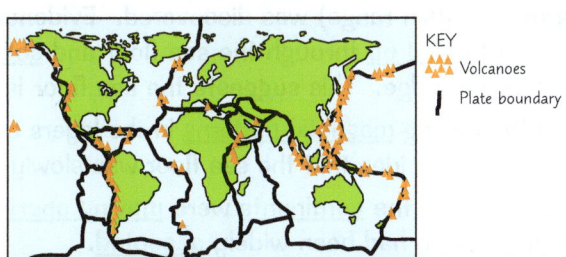

KEY
- ▲▲ Volcanoes
- | Plate boundary

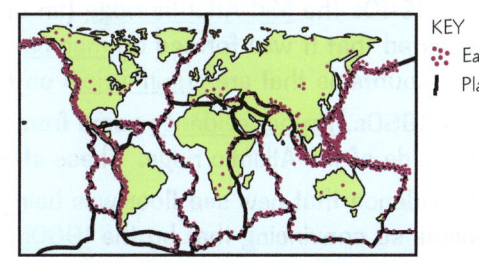

KEY
- ⁘ Earthquakes
- | Plate boundary

Wash tectonic plates by hand — they won't fit in the dishwasher...

So everyone standing on the surface of our little blue-green planet is actually floating round very slowly on a sea of semi-liquid rock. Make sure you understand the stuff about tectonic plates — there's more coming up...

Q1   Which metal mostly makes up the Earth's core?   [1 mark]

Plate Tectonics

The idea that the Earth's surface is made up of moving plates of rock took a while to catch on.

Observations About the Earth Hadn't Been Explained

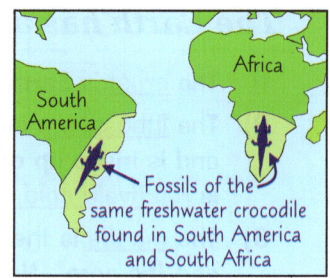

Fossils of the same freshwater crocodile found in South America and South Africa

1) For years, fossils of very similar plants and animals had been found on opposite sides of the Atlantic Ocean. Most people thought this was because the continents had been linked by 'land bridges', which had sunk or been covered by water as the Earth cooled. But not everyone was convinced.

2) Other things about the Earth puzzled people too — like why the coastlines of Africa and South America look like they could fit together.

Explaining These Observations Needed a Leap of Imagination

What was needed was a scientist with a bit of insight... a smidgeon of creativity... a touch of genius...

1) In 1914 Alfred Wegener hypothesised that Africa and South America had previously been one continent which had then split. He started to look for more evidence to back up his hypothesis. He found it...

2) For example there were matching layers of the same age and type of rocks on different continents, and fossils of similar plants and animals found on opposite sides of huge oceans.

3) Wegener's theory of 'continental drift' supposed that about 300 million years ago there had been just one 'supercontinent' — which he called Pangaea. According to Wegener, Pangaea broke into smaller chunks, and these chunks (our modern-day continents) are still slowly 'drifting' apart. This idea is the basis behind the modern theory of plate tectonics.

The Theory Wasn't Accepted at First — for a Variety of Reasons

1) Wegener's theory explained things that couldn't be explained by the 'land bridge' theory (e.g. the formation of mountains — which Wegener said happened as continents smashed into each other). But it was a big change, and the reaction from other scientists was hostile.

2) The main problem was that Wegener's explanation of how the 'drifting' happened wasn't convincing (and the movement wasn't detectable). Wegener claimed the continents' movement could be caused by tidal forces and the Earth's rotation — but other geologists showed that this was impossible.

Eventually, the Evidence Became Overwhelming

1) As far back as the 1930s, scientists began to suggest that it could be convection currents in the mantle that caused the plates to move. But at that time many people still weren't convinced by the theory of continental drift, because there wasn't much evidence to show that the plates actually were moving.

2) In the 1940s the Mid-Atlantic ridge (an underwater mountain range) was discovered. Evidence suggested that it was formed by magma (molten rock) rising up through the sea floor and solidifying, to form mountains that are symmetrical on each side of the ridge. This suggests the sea floor is spreading.

3) In the 1950s, further evidence came from studies of matching magnetic patterns in the layers of rocks on either side of the Atlantic ridge. These studies backed up the idea that the sea floor was slowly spreading.

4) The evidence that new sea floor was being created and that the continents were moving apart became so convincing that by the 1960s, Wegener's theory had been widely accepted.

I told you so — but no one ever believes me...

Wegener wasn't right about everything, but his main idea was correct. The scientific community was a bit slow to accept it, but once there was more evidence to support it, they got on board. That's science for you...

Q1   Give one piece of evidence that Wegener gave for his theory of continental drift.   [1 mark]

Plate Boundaries

The Earth's surface is made of huge floating plates that are constantly moving... Rock on.

There are Three Types of Plate Boundary

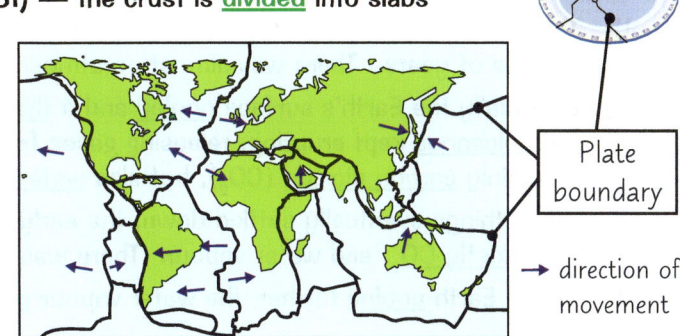

1) The outer layer of the Earth is the crust (page 81) — the crust is divided into slabs called tectonic plates that float on the mantle.

2) Plates are made of two types of crust — continental (thick crust beneath the land) and oceanic (thinner crust beneath the sea).

3) The plates move slowly because of convection currents in the mantle underneath the crust.

4) The places where plates meet are called plate boundaries.

Plate boundary

→ direction of movement

Constructive Boundaries

1) Constructive boundaries are where two plates are moving away from each other. This usually happens at a mid-ocean ridge, e.g. at the mid-Atlantic ridge.

2) Magma (molten rock) rises from the mantle to fill the gap and cools, creating new crust made from igneous rock.

3) You get lots of volcanic activity and earthquakes at constructive boundaries.

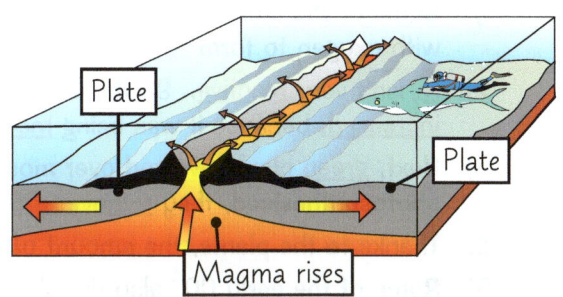

Plate

Plate

Magma rises

Destructive Boundaries

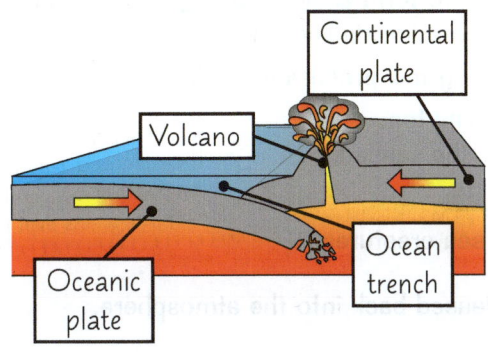

Continental plate

Volcano

Ocean trench

Oceanic plate

1) Destructive boundaries are where two plates are moving towards each other, e.g. along the west coast of South America.

2) Where an oceanic plate meets a continental plate, the denser oceanic plate is forced down into the mantle and melted to give magma. This creates volcanoes and ocean trenches (very deep sections of the ocean floor where the oceanic plate goes down).

3) Earthquakes also often occur at destructive boundaries.

Where two continental plates collide, the ground folds and creates mountain ranges.

Conservative Boundaries

1) Conservative boundaries are where two plates are moving sideways past each other, or are moving in the same direction but at different speeds, e.g. along the west coast of the USA.

2) Crust isn't created or destroyed.

3) This type of movement creates powerful earthquakes.

4) No volcanoes are created since neither plate is melted.

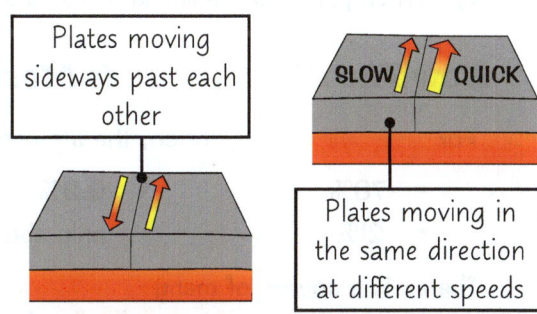

Plates moving sideways past each other

SLOW QUICK

Plates moving in the same direction at different speeds

Giant plates whacking into each other — smashing stuff...

That's it for all this Earth structure and plate tectonics stuff. Make sure you understand the Earth's structure and what tectonic plates are — try writing out a quick description of each type of plate boundary to see what you know.

Q1   Describe how constructive boundaries create new crust.   [2 marks]

The Atmosphere

Scientists have looked at evidence from rocks, air bubbles in ice and fossils to see how our atmosphere has changed over millions of years. Here's the most widely accepted theory about how our atmosphere evolved...

Volcanoes *Gave Out* Carbon Dioxide *and* Water Vapour

1) The Earth's surface was originally molten for many millions of years. There was almost no atmosphere.

2) Eventually the Earth's surface cooled and a thin crust formed, but volcanoes kept erupting, releasing gases from inside the Earth — mainly carbon dioxide (CO_2), but also water vapour and ammonia.

3) When things eventually settled down, the early atmosphere was mostly CO_2, and water vapour. There was very little oxygen.

4) As the Earth cooled further, the water vapour condensed to form the oceans.

This change happened fairly quickly compared to the changes below, which took billions of years.

Green Plants *Evolved and Produced* Oxygen

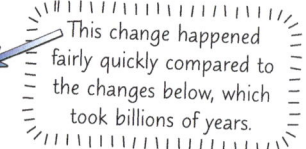

1) Some of the ammonia in the early atmosphere reacted with oxygen to form nitrogen gas (N_2).

2) N_2 isn't very reactive. So the amount of N_2 in the atmosphere increased, because it was being made but not broken down.

3) Next, green plants evolved over most of the Earth. As they photosynthesised, they removed CO_2 and produced O_2.

4) Thanks to the plants, the amount of O_2 in the air gradually built up and the level of CO_2 fell.

5) Some of the early CO_2 also dissolved into the oceans. And much of the remaining CO_2 eventually got locked up in fossil fuels and sedimentary rocks:

- When ancient marine plants and animals died, they fell to the seabed and were buried by sediment. Over millions of years, they were compressed to form sedimentary rocks, oil and gas — locking the carbon within them and reducing carbon dioxide levels in the atmosphere.

- Things like coal, crude oil and natural gas that are made by this process are called 'fossil fuels'.

- Crude oil and natural gas are formed from deposits of plankton. Pockets of these fossil fuels get trapped in rocks under the seabed.

- Coal is a sedimentary rock made from thick plant deposits.

- Limestone and chalk formed from the shells of ancient sea creatures.

These processes reduced the amount of CO_2 in the atmosphere to less than 1%.

6) As we burn fossil fuels, more of this 'locked up' CO_2 gets released back into the atmosphere. O_2 is used up too.

7) When plants and animals respire they also release CO_2 into the atmosphere (and take in O_2).

Now The Atmosphere *is Mostly* Nitrogen *and* Oxygen

For 200 million years or so, the atmosphere has been about how it is now:

- 78% nitrogen
- 0.9% argon (and other noble gasses)
- 21% oxygen
- only about 0.04% carbon dioxide

Air also contains a variable amount of water vapour.

The air is a source of many useful gases such as nitrogen, oxygen, neon and argon. These gases can be separated using fractional distillation (see page 186) because they all have different boiling points.

I went to a restaurant on the moon — nice view, no atmosphere...

We can breathe easy knowing that our atmosphere has developed into a lovely oxygen-rich one. Aaaahh.

Q1   The atmosphere of Earth was originally composed mostly of carbon dioxide.
     Explain how the proportion of carbon dioxide in the atmosphere decreased over time.   [3 marks]

Greenhouse Gases and Climate Change

Greenhouse gases are important but can also cause <u>problems</u> — it's all about keeping a delicate <u>balance</u>.

Carbon Dioxide is a Greenhouse Gas

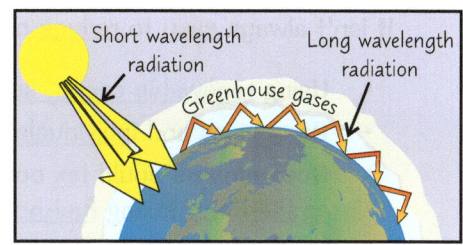

1) Greenhouse gases like <u>carbon dioxide</u>, <u>methane</u> and <u>water vapour</u> act like an insulating layer in the Earth's atmosphere — this helps the Earth to stay <u>warm</u> enough to support <u>life</u>.

2) All particles <u>absorb</u> certain frequencies of radiation. Greenhouse gases <u>don't</u> absorb the <u>incoming short wavelength</u> radiation from the sun — but they <u>do</u> absorb the <u>long wavelength radiation</u> that gets radiated back from the Earth. Then they <u>re-radiate</u> it in all directions — including <u>back towards the Earth</u>. The long wavelength radiation is <u>thermal radiation</u>, so it results in <u>warming</u> of the surface of the Earth. This is the <u>greenhouse effect</u>.

3) Some forms of <u>human activity</u> affect the amount of greenhouse gases in the atmosphere. For example carbon that is '<u>locked up</u>' in fossil fuels is released as carbon dioxide when fossil fuels are burned.

Increasing Carbon Dioxide is Linked to Climate Change

1) Over the last 200 years, the percentage of carbon dioxide in the atmosphere has <u>increased</u> — this correlates with an <u>increased use of fossil fuels</u> by people as well as an increase in <u>global temperature</u> (global warming).

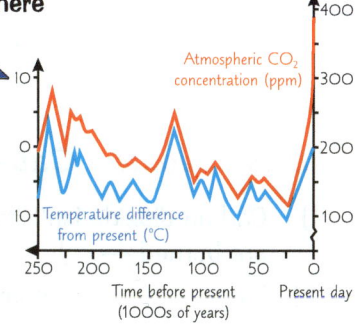

2) The Earth's temperature varies naturally, but recently the average temperature of the Earth's surface has been <u>increasing</u>. Most scientists agree that extra CO_2 and other greenhouse gases from <u>human activity</u> are causing this increase and this will lead to further <u>climate change</u>.

3) <u>Many studies</u> looking at rising CO_2 levels and climate change have produced <u>similar findings</u> — increasing our <u>confidence</u> in the evidence.

Historical Data is Much Less Accurate Than Current Records

1) <u>Current global temperature</u> and <u>carbon dioxide levels</u> can be worked out pretty accurately as they're based on measurements taken all over the world.

2) Historical data is <u>less accurate</u> — less data was taken over fewer locations and the methods used to collect the data were less accurate. If you go back far enough, there are <u>no records</u> of global temperature and carbon dioxide levels at all...

3) But there are ways to <u>estimate past data</u>. For example, you can analyse <u>fossils</u>, <u>tree rings</u> or <u>gas bubbles</u> trapped in <u>ice sheets</u> to estimate past levels of atmospheric carbon dioxide.

4) The problem with using these kinds of measurements is that they're <u>less precise</u> than current measurements made using <u>instrumental sampling</u>. They're also <u>less representative</u> of global levels.

Climate Change Could Have Dangerous Consequences

The Earth's climate is <u>complex</u>, but it's still important to make <u>predictions</u> about the possible <u>consequences</u> of climate change so that policy-makers can make decisions <u>now</u>. For example:

1) An increase in global temperature could lead to <u>increased melting</u> of polar ice caps, sea ice and glaciers — causing a further <u>rise</u> in <u>sea levels</u>.

2) Changes in <u>climate</u> and <u>rainfall patterns</u> could cause some areas to get <u>hotter and drier</u>, leading to <u>droughts</u>, while others get <u>more rain</u>, leading to <u>flooding</u>.

Give the climate some privacy — it's changing...

It's not all depressing news. There are steps we can take to cut our carbon dioxide emissions coming up, so chin up.

Q1   Give an example of an environmental problem that could be caused by global warming.   [1 mark]

Reducing Pollution and Tests for Gases

When you burn fossil fuels you release lots of carbon dioxide — and some other nasties like sulfur dioxide too.

There are Ways of Reducing Greenhouse Gas Emissions

It isn't always easy to reduce our greenhouse gas emissions — here are a few ways that it can be done:

- Using renewable energy sources (like solar or wind energy) or nuclear energy instead of fossil fuels.
- Companies and individuals can reduce their energy use whenever possible.
- Governments could tax companies or individuals based on the amount of greenhouse gases they emit — e.g. taxing fuel-hungry cars could mean that people choose to buy more fuel-efficient ones.

Large-scale greenhouse gas producers can also take steps to deal with the gases they do produce:

- Companies can offset the CO_2 they emit by buying carbon credits — this means that they invest in a scheme that removes it from the atmosphere. For example, if a company emits a certain amount of CO_2, they can pay for trees to be planted that will remove an equivalent amount of CO_2 by photosynthesis. If a business offsets all its greenhouse gas emissions, it's said to be carbon neutral.
- There's also technology that captures the CO_2 produced by burning fossil fuels before it's released into the atmosphere. The CO_2 can then be stored deep underground in gaps in the rocks. This is called carbon capture and storage.

Sulfur Dioxide Causes Acid Rain

1) Carbon dioxide isn't the only gas produced when fossil fuels are burned — sulfur dioxide (SO_2) is a problem too.
2) The sulfur dioxide comes from compounds containing sulfur in the fossil fuels.
3) When sulfur dioxide mixes with water in clouds, it forms dilute sulfuric acid. This falls as acid rain — normal rain has a pH of about 5.5 but acid rain has a lower pH of 2-4.
4) Acid rain causes lakes to become acidic and many plants and animals die as a result.
5) Acid rain kills trees and other plants, damages limestone buildings and stone statues and can also make metal statues and buildings (like bridges) corrode faster.
6) Soil and lakes that have been affected by acid rain can be treated with a weak alkali to neutralise them.
7) A technique called sulfur scrubbing is used in power stations to remove the sulfur dioxide before gases escape from the power stations.

You Can Test for Carbon Dioxide and Oxygen Gas

Carbon Dioxide:
Bubbling carbon dioxide through an aqueous solution of calcium hydroxide (also known as limewater) makes the solution turn milky.

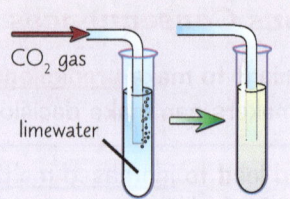

Oxygen:
If you put a glowing splint inside a test tube containing oxygen, the oxygen will relight the glowing splint.

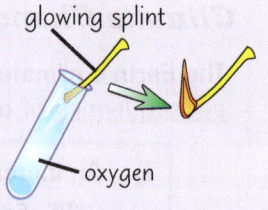

Cutting greenhouse gas production — emission possible...?

If you're wondering why the gas tests are on this page, it's not just because I had to fit them in *somewhere*. Honest...

Q1 Suggest one thing a company could do to reduce the harmful effect of the carbon dioxide it emits.   [1 mark]

Q2 Give two examples of problems caused by acid rain.   [2 marks]

Revision Questions for Unit 2c

<u>Unit 2c</u> is finally finished — time to see what you've actually remembered with some lovely questions.

- Try these questions and <u>tick off each one</u> when you <u>get it right</u>.
- When you've done <u>all the questions</u> for a topic and are <u>completely happy</u> with it, tick off the topic.

Water Treatment (p.75-76) ☑

1) Name two man-made pollutants that may be present in water sources. ☐
2) Give one advantage and one disadvantage of adding fluoride ions to drinking water. ☐
3) Give one reason why distilling sea water isn't always a viable option for producing drinking water. ☑
4) Draw the apparatus you would use to carry out a simple distillation. ☐

Solubility (p.77-78) ☐

5) Define the term 'saturated solution'. ☑
6) What variables go on the *x*-axis and *y*-axis of a solubility curve? ☑
7) Write down the formula that you would use to calculate
   the solubility of a substance in units of g/100g of solvent. ☑

Hard Water (p.79-80) ☐

8) What are the two main ions that cause water hardness? ☑
9) Give two possible health benefits of drinking hard water. ☑
10) Give two methods of removing permanent hardness from water. ☑

The Earth's Structure and Tectonics (p.81-83) ☐

11) Describe the inner structure of the Earth. ☑
12) Give the name of Wegener's 'supercontinent'. ☑
13) Briefly explain why some scientists didn't accept Wegener's theory of continental drift at first. ☑
14) Describe what happens to the plates at each of these types of plate boundary:
    a) Constructive
    b) Destructive
    c) Conservative ☑

The Atmosphere (p.84-86) ☐

15) Name two of the gases given out by volcanoes millions of years ago
    that formed the Earth's early atmosphere. ☑
16) How was nitrogen gas originally put into the atmosphere? ☐
17) What are the current % proportions of oxygen, nitrogen,
    argon and carbon dioxide in the atmosphere? ☑
18) Explain how the greenhouse effect works to keep the Earth warm. ☑
19) How is human activity leading to an increase in carbon dioxide in the atmosphere? ☑
20) Explain how acid rain is formed. ☑
21) What is the chemical test for oxygen? ☑

Reaction Rates

Reactions can be <u>fast</u> or <u>slow</u> — you've probably already realised that. It's exciting stuff. Honest.

The *Rate of Reaction* is a Measure of *How Fast* the *Reaction Happens*

The <u>rate of a reaction</u> is how quickly a reaction happens. It can be observed <u>either</u> by measuring how quickly the reactants are used up or how quickly the products are formed. The <u>rate of a reaction</u> can be calculated using the following formula:

$$\text{Rate of Reaction} = \frac{\text{amount of reactant used or amount of product formed}}{\text{time}}$$

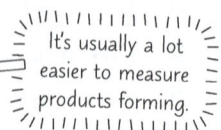 It's usually a lot easier to measure products forming.

You Can Do *Experiments* to Follow *Reaction Rates*

There are different ways that the rate of a reaction can be <u>measured</u>. Here are three examples:

Precipitation

1) This method works for any reaction where mixing <u>two see-through solutions</u> produces a <u>precipitate</u>, which <u>clouds</u> the solution.

2) You <u>mix</u> the two reactant solutions and put the flask on a piece of paper that has a <u>mark</u> on it.

3) <u>Observe</u> the mark through the mixture and measure how long it takes for the mark to be <u>obscured</u>. The <u>faster</u> it disappears, the <u>faster</u> the reaction.

4) The result is <u>subjective</u> — <u>different people</u> might not agree on <u>exactly</u> when the mark 'disappears'.

You can use this method to investigate how temperature affects the rate of the reaction between sodium thiosulfate and dilute hydrochloric acid. See page 90.

5) Using <u>data-logging apparatus</u> (e.g. a <u>light sensor</u> connected to a computer) can help you decide <u>more accurately</u> when the mixture reaches a certain level of cloudiness.

Change in Mass (Usually Gas Given Off)

1) You can measure the rate of a reaction that <u>produces a gas</u> (e.g. the reaction of an acid with a metal or a carbonate) using a <u>mass balance</u>.

2) As the gas is released, the <u>lost mass</u> is easily measured on the balance. The <u>quicker</u> the reading on the balance <u>drops</u>, the <u>faster</u> the reaction.

3) You know the reaction has <u>finished</u> when the reading on the balance <u>stops changing</u>.

4) You can use your results to plot a <u>graph</u> of <u>change in mass</u> against <u>time</u>.

5) This method does release the gas produced straight into the room — so if the gas is <u>harmful</u>, you must take <u>safety precautions</u>, e.g. do the experiment in a <u>fume cupboard</u>.

The cotton wool lets gases through but stops any solid, liquid or aqueous reactants flying out during the reaction.

The *Volume* of Gas Given Off

1) You can use a <u>gas syringe</u> to measure the <u>volume</u> of gas given off.

2) The <u>more</u> gas given off during a set <u>time interval</u>, the <u>faster</u> the reaction.

3) You can tell the reaction has <u>finished</u> when <u>no more gas</u> is produced.

4) You can use your results to plot a graph of <u>gas volume</u> against <u>time elapsed</u>.

5) You need to be careful that you're using the <u>right size</u> gas syringe for your experiment though — if the reaction is too <u>vigorous</u>, you can blow the plunger out of the end of the syringe.

You could also collect the gas using an upside down measuring cylinder in a water bath. See page 229.

Retraction rate — how fast my mates disappear when I tell a joke...

Lots of different ways to follow reaction rates here — well... three. Precipitation, mass loss and gas formation.

Q1   Outline how you could use a mass balance to measure the rate of a reaction where a gas is formed. [3 marks]

Q2   Give one advantage of using data-logging apparatus in reaction rate investigations.   [1 mark]

Rate Experiments Involving Gases

You'll probably have to <u>measure</u> the <u>rate of a reaction</u> in class at some point. Time to learn how to do it...

You can Measure how Surface Area Affects Rate

Here's how you can carry out an experiment to measure the effect of <u>surface area</u> on <u>rate</u>, using marble chips and hydrochloric acid.

1) Set the apparatus up as shown in the diagram on the right.

2) Measure the <u>volume</u> of gas produced using a <u>gas syringe</u> (or a measuring cylinder in a water bath — see page 229). Take readings at <u>regular time intervals</u> and record the results in a table.

3) You can plot a <u>graph</u> of your results — <u>time</u> goes on the <u>x-axis</u> and <u>volume</u> goes on the <u>y-axis</u>.

4) <u>Repeat</u> the experiment with <u>exactly the same volume</u> and <u>concentration</u> of acid, and <u>exactly the same mass</u> of marble chips, but with the marble <u>more crunched up</u>.

5) Then <u>repeat</u> with the same mass of <u>powdered chalk</u>.

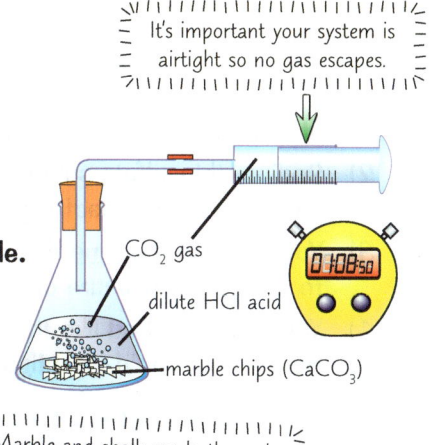

It's important your system is airtight so no gas escapes.

CO_2 gas

dilute HCl acid

marble chips ($CaCO_3$)

Marble and chalk are both made of calcium carbonate ($CaCO_3$).

Finer Particles of Solid Mean a Higher Rate

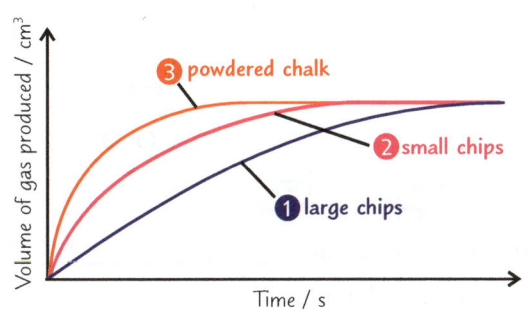

1) The <u>sooner</u> a reaction finishes, the <u>faster</u> the reaction.

2) The <u>steeper</u> the gradient of the graph, the <u>faster</u> the rate of reaction. When the line becomes flat, <u>no more gas</u> is being produced and the reaction has <u>finished</u>.

3) Using <u>finer particles</u> means that the marble has a <u>larger surface area</u>.

4) <u>Lines 1 to 3</u> on the graph on the left show that the <u>finer</u> the particles are (and the <u>greater</u> the surface area of the solid reactants), the <u>faster</u> the reaction and the <u>sooner</u> the reaction finishes.

Changing the Concentration of Acid Affects the Rate too

The reaction between marble chips and hydrochloric acid is good for measuring how <u>changing the reactant concentration</u> affects reaction rate. You could replace the marble chips with a strip of magnesium here too though.

You could also measure the rates of these reactions by measuring the loss of mass as the gas is produced.

More Concentrated Solutions Mean a Higher Rate

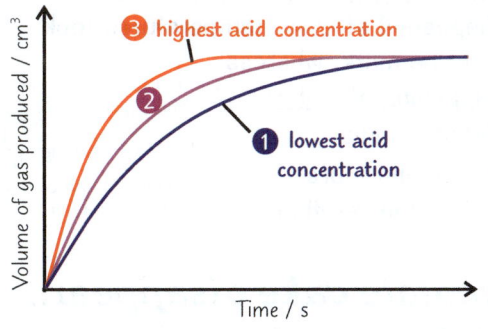

1) You can measure the effect of <u>concentration</u> on rate by following the <u>same method</u> described above. However, this time you repeat the experiment with exactly the same mass and surface area of marble chips and exactly the same volume of acid, but using <u>different concentrations</u> of acid.

2) <u>Lines 1 to 3</u> on the graph show that a <u>higher</u> concentration gives a <u>faster reaction</u>, with the reaction <u>finishing</u> sooner.

I prefer chalk to marble chips — I like the finer things in life...

Doing rate experiments lets you collect data. Collecting data lets you plot graphs, and you can use graphs to find reaction rates. But that's all still to come. I bet you're just itching to read on...

Q1 Describe how you could investigate how the surface area of calcium carbonate affects the rate of reaction between calcium carbonate and hydrochloric acid.

[3 marks]

Rate Experiments Involving Precipitation

That's right — another page, another reaction rate experiment to learn. But this one involves a pretty precipitation reaction. Beautiful stuff, don't say I don't spoil you...

Reaction Rate *is Also Affected by* Temperature

1) You can see how temperature or concentration affects reaction rate by looking at the reaction between sodium thiosulfate and hydrochloric acid.

2) Sodium thiosulfate solution and hydrochloric acid are both clear, colourless solutions. They react together to form a yellow precipitate of sulfur.

3) You can use the time that it takes for the coloured precipitate to form as a measure of the rate of this reaction.

> How temperature, concentration and pressure affect the rate of a reaction can be explained using particle theory (pages 92-93).

4) You use a method like the one on page 88 to carry out this experiment. Here's how you'd investigate the effect of temperature on the rate of reaction:

- Measure out fixed volumes of sodium thiosulfate solution (warmed to 60°C in a water bath) and hydrochloric acid, using a measuring cylinder.

- Mix the solutions in a conical flask. Place the flask over a black mark on a piece of paper which can be seen through the solution. Watch the black mark disappear through the cloudy, yellow sulfur and time how long it takes to go.

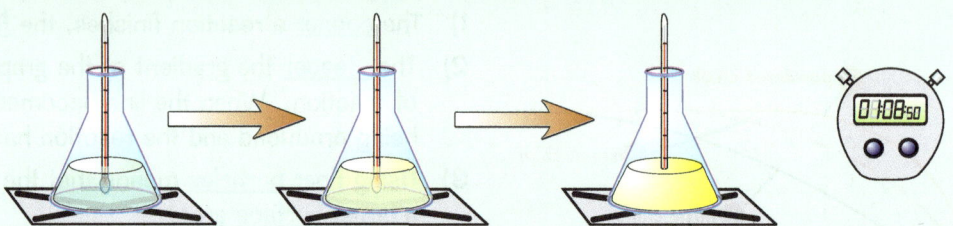

- The reaction can be repeated for sodium thiosulfate solutions at different temperatures.

- The depth and volumes of liquid must be kept the same each time. The concentrations of the solutions must also be kept the same.

- You can use your results to measure what effect changing the temperature has on the rate of the reaction. The shorter the length of time taken for the mark to be obscured, the faster the rate.

> You'll need one lot of sodium thiosulfate solution that's been cooled to 5 °C and another lot that's been heated to 60 °C in a water bath. Then you just mix different proportions of these together to produce sodium thiosulfate solutions at a whole range of temperatures.

Higher Temperatures *Mean a* Higher Rate

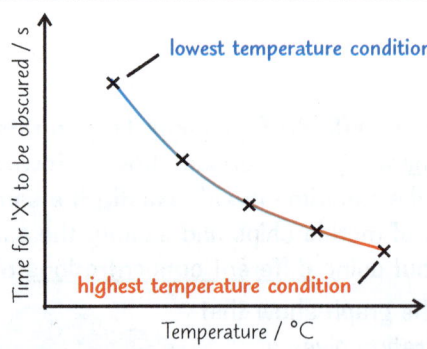

lowest temperature condition

highest temperature condition

Time for 'X' to be obscured / s

Temperature / °C

1) You can plot the time taken for the mark to disappear against the temperature of the reacting solutions.

2) If you look at the graph, you can see that the reactions that happened at lower temperatures took longer to obscure the mark, whereas the reactions happening at higher temperatures did so sooner.

> You can calculate the rate of the reaction using $\frac{1}{time}$, and plot a graph of that too.

3) So increasing the temperature increases the rate of the reaction

---

And for my next trick, I'll make this chocolate cake disappear...

When repeating this experiment, you need to keep everything exactly the same apart from the temperature — then you can sleep easy knowing that it was the temperature change that affected the reaction rate and not anything else.

Q1 Azim carries out an experiment to measure how temperature affects the rate of reaction between sodium thiosulfate and hydrochloric acid. He uses the time taken for a mark underneath the reaction vessel to be obscured as a measure of rate. How would you expect the time taken for the mark to disappear to change as the temperature of the reacting sodium thiosulfate was increased?

[1 mark]

Calculating Rates

You can work out rates of reaction using graphs. I bet you can't wait to find out how...

Faster Rates of Reaction are Shown by Steeper Gradients

1) If you have a graph of amount of product formed (or reactant used up) against time, then the gradient (slope) of the graph will be equal to the rate of the reaction.

2) The steeper the slope, the more product that is being formed (or reactant used up) per second, and so the faster the rate.

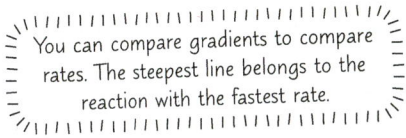
You can compare gradients to compare rates. The steepest line belongs to the reaction with the fastest rate.

Draw a Tangent to Find the Gradient of a Curve

1) If your graph (or part of it) is a curve, the gradient, and therefore rate, is different at different points along the curve.

2) To find the gradient of the graph at a certain point, you'll have to draw a tangent at that point.

3) A tangent is just a line that touches the curve and has the same gradient as the line at that point.

4) To draw a tangent, place a ruler on the line of best fit at the point you're interested in, so you can see the whole curve. Adjust the ruler so the space between the ruler and the curve is the same on both sides of the point. Draw a line along the ruler to make the tangent.

5) The rate at that point is then just the gradient of the tangent.

6) The gradient of a straight line is given by the equation:

> gradient = change in y ÷ change in x

EXAMPLE:

The graph below shows the concentration of product formed, measured at regular intervals during a chemical reaction. What is the rate of reaction at 3 minutes?

1) Position a ruler on the graph at the point where you want to know the rate — here it's 3 minutes.

2) Adjust the ruler until the space between the ruler and the curve is equal on both sides of the point.

3) Draw a line along the ruler to make the tangent. Extend the line right across the graph.

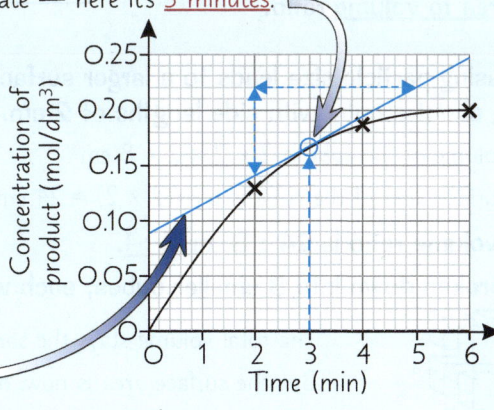

4) Pick two points on the line that are easy to read. Use them to calculate the gradient of the tangent in order to find the rate:

gradient = change in y ÷ change in x
= (0.22 − 0.14) ÷ (5.0 − 2.0)
= 0.08 ÷ 3.0
= 0.027

So, the rate of reaction at 3 minutes was 0.027 mol/dm^3/min.

...and that's why I love cows — oh sorry, I went off on a tangent ...

Lots of nifty graph skills here. Gradients aren't too hard, but make sure those tangents don't trip you up.

Use the graph at the top of the page to answer the following question:

Q1   Work out the rate of reaction at 20 seconds.   [2 marks]

Factors Affecting Rate of Reaction

The rate of a reaction depends on these things — temperature, concentration (or pressure for gases) and the size of the particles (for solids). The next couple of pages explain why these things affect the reaction rate.

Particles *Must Collide* with *Enough Energy* in *Order to React*

Reaction rates can be explained using particle theory. It's simple really.

The rate of a chemical reaction depends on:

- The collision frequency of reacting particles (how often they collide). The more successful collisions there are, the faster the reaction is.

- The energy transferred during a collision. There is a minimum amount of energy that particles need in order to react when they collide. Particles must collide with at least this minimum energy for the collision to be successful.

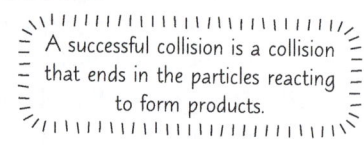
A successful collision is a collision that ends in the particles reacting to form products.

The *More Collisions*, the *Higher* the *Rate of Reaction*

Reactions happen if particles collide with enough energy to react. So, if you increase the number of collisions or the energy with which the particles collide, the reaction happens more quickly (i.e. the rate increases).

Increasing *Concentration* (or *Pressure*) *Increases Rate*

1) If a solution is made more concentrated it means there are more particles of reactant in the same volume. This makes collisions more likely, so the reaction rate increases.

2) In a gas, increasing the pressure means that the particles are more crowded. This means that the frequency of collisions between particles will increase — so the rate of reaction will also increase.

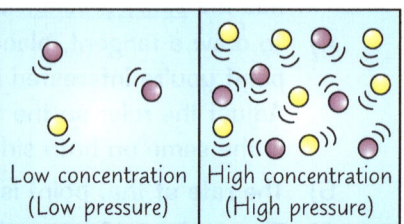
Low concentration (Low pressure) | High concentration (High pressure)

Smaller Solid Particles (or *More Surface Area*) *Means a Higher Rate*

1) If one reactant is a solid, breaking it into smaller pieces will increase its surface area to volume ratio (i.e. more of the solid will be exposed, compared to its overall volume).

2) The particles around it will have more area to work on, so the frequency of collisions will increase.

3) This means that the rate of reaction is faster for solids with a larger surface area to volume ratio.

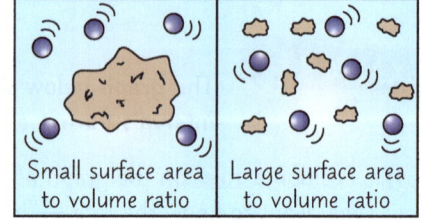
Small surface area to volume ratio | Large surface area to volume ratio

- You can see how decreasing particle size leads to a larger surface area to volume ratio by thinking about a cube with side lengths of 2 cm.

The volume of the cube is $2 \times 2 \times 2 = 8 \text{ cm}^3$.

The surface area of the cube is $6 \times (2 \times 2) = 24 \text{ cm}^2$.

So the surface area to volume ratio is 24 : 8, or <u>3 : 1</u>.

- The 2 cm cube can be broken down into 8 smaller cubes, each with side lengths of 1 cm.

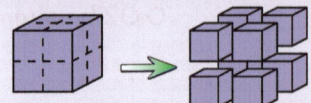

The total volume stays the same: $8 \times (1 \times 1 \times 1) = 8 \text{ cm}^3$.

But the surface area is now: $8 \times (6 \times (1 \times 1)) = 48 \text{ cm}^2$.

So the surface area to volume ratio is 48 : 8, or <u>6 : 1</u>.

Collision theory — it's always the other driver...

Remember — more collisions mean a faster reaction. But don't be fooled, as not every collision results in a reaction.

Q1   Describe the two factors, in terms of collisions, that affect the rate of reaction.   [2 marks]

Q2   Explain why breaking a solid reactant into smaller pieces increases the rate of a reaction.   [3 marks]

More Factors Affecting Rate of Reaction

As well as the effects of temperature, you also need to know about <u>catalysts</u>. Catalysts <u>increase reaction rate</u> and <u>reduce energy costs</u> in industrial reactions, so they're very important for <u>commercial reasons</u>.

Temperature *Also Affects the Number of Collisions*

1) When the <u>temperature is increased</u> the particles <u>move faster</u>. If they move faster, they're going to have <u>more collisions</u>.

2) Higher temperatures also increase the <u>energy</u> of the collisions, since the particles are moving <u>faster</u>. Reactions <u>only happen</u> if the particles collide with <u>enough energy</u>.

3) This means that at <u>higher</u> temperatures there will be more <u>successful collisions</u> (<u>more particles</u> will <u>collide</u> with <u>enough energy</u> to react). So <u>increasing</u> the temperature <u>increases</u> the rate of reaction.

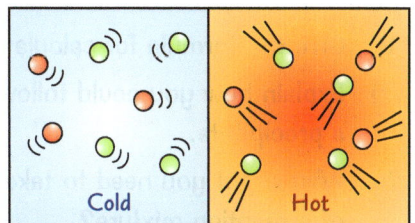

A *Catalyst Increases* the *Rate* of a Reaction

1) A <u>catalyst</u> is a substance which increases the <u>rate of a reaction</u>, <u>without</u> being chemically changed or used up in the reaction.

2) Using a catalyst <u>won't</u> change the products of the reaction — so the reaction <u>equation</u> will stay the <u>same</u>.

3) Because it <u>isn't</u> used up, you only need a <u>tiny bit</u> to catalyse large amounts of reactants.

4) Catalysts tend to be very <u>fussy</u> about which reactions they catalyse though — you can't just stick any old catalyst in a reaction and expect it to work.

A *Catalyst Lowers* the *Energy* Required for *Successful Collisions*

1) Catalysts work by <u>decreasing</u> the <u>energy</u> the particles need to have for a reaction to occur.

2) They do this by providing an <u>alternative reaction pathway</u>.

3) As a result, <u>more</u> of the particles have at least the <u>minimum amount of energy</u> needed for a reaction to occur when the particles collide.

4) This means there are more <u>successful</u> collisions, and so the <u>rate</u> of reaction <u>increases</u>.

Higher

Catalysts Need to be *Replaced Regularly*

1) Even though catalysts are <u>not</u> chemically changed or used up by the reactions they catalyse, they still need to be <u>replaced regularly</u> when they're used in industrial processes.

2) In <u>industrial processes</u>, there may be <u>impurities</u> present which do chemically change the catalyst.

3) These changes mean that over time the catalyst will <u>lose its activity</u> — it won't be able to increase the rate of reaction any more.

4) The reaction will <u>slow</u> back down to its <u>uncatalysed</u> rate until the catalyst is replaced.

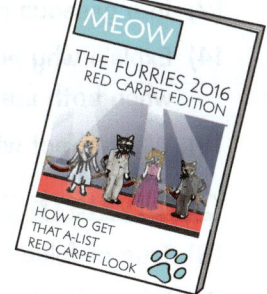

I wish there was a catalyst for making my takeaway arrive...

Catalysts are really handy. Some reactions take a very long time to happen by themselves, which isn't good for industrial reactions. Catalysts help to produce an acceptable amount of product in an acceptable length of time.

Q1   Give the definition of a catalyst.   [2 marks]

Q2   The decomposition of hydrogen peroxide can be catalysed by manganese dioxide. Explain why only a small amount of manganese dioxide is needed for the catalysis of this reaction, even when starting with a large quantity of hydrogen peroxide.   [1 mark]

Q3   Explain why catalysts used in industrial processes need to be replaced regularly.   [2 marks]

Revision Questions for Unit 2d

Nice short section that, so you should rattle through this page in no time.

- Try these questions and tick off each one when you get it right.
- When you've done all the questions for a topic and are completely happy with it, tick off the topic.

Measuring Rates of Reaction (p.88-91) ☑

1) Give the formula for calculating the rate of a reaction. ☐

2) Explain how you could follow the rate of a reaction where two colourless solutions react to form a precipitate. ☐

3) Why might you need to take safety precautions when measuring the change in mass of a reaction mixture? ☐

4) A student carries out a reaction which produces carbon dioxide gas.
He collects the carbon dioxide in a gas syringe. How will he know when the reaction has finished? ☐

5) Draw a diagram of the equipment you could use to measure the rate of reaction between hydrochloric acid and marble chips. ☑

6) How does the rate of the reaction between sodium thiosulfate and hydrochloric acid change with temperature? ☑

7) On a graph to find the rate of a reaction, which variable would you plot on:
a) the x-axis?
b) the y-axis? ☑

8) The results from two experiments carried out under different conditions are plotted on the same graph.
How could you tell from the graph which conditions produced the faster rate of reaction? ☐

9) Graphs to find the rate of a reaction are usually curved.
What does this tell you about the rate of a reaction over time? ☑

10) Explain how you would find the gradient of a curved graph at a certain point on the graph. ☑

Factors Affecting Rate of Reaction (p.92-93) ☐

11) Explain what a 'successful collision' between two particles is. ☑

12) How does concentration affect the rate of a reaction? ☑

13) In a gaseous reaction, why would a decrease in pressure result in a slower rate of reaction? ☑

14) Explain why powdered chalk reacts with hydrochloric acid more quickly than marble chips, when both are made of calcium carbonate ($CaCO_3$). ☐

15) What effect will raising the temperature have on the rate of a reaction? ☑

Catalysts (p.93) ☐

16) True or false? All catalysts work equally well for all reactions. ☑

17) What effect does a catalyst have on the energy needed for a reaction to take place? ☑

18) True or false? Catalysts are not used up, so never need replacing in industrial reactions. ☑

Circuits — The Basics

Here's a nice little introduction to circuits — make sure to read this page carefully and learn it off by heart.

A Voltage Pushes a Current Through a Resistance

1) Current is the rate of flow of electric charge (electrons) around a circuit. Current will only flow through an electrical component if there is a voltage across that component. The symbol for current is I and it's measured in amps, A.

2) Voltage (also called potential difference) is the driving force that pushes the current around. Its symbol is V and it's measured in volts, V.

3) Resistance is a measure of how easily charge can flow — the symbol for resistance is R and it's measured in ohms, Ω.

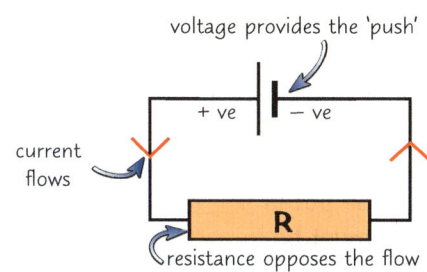

You can think about electrical circuits in terms of energy transfer — the battery (or power supply) transfers energy to the electrons and then the electrons transfer that energy to the electrical components.

There's a Formula Linking Voltage, Current and Resistance

$$\text{current (A)} = \frac{\text{voltage (V)}}{\text{resistance } (\Omega)}$$

As a formula triangle:

1) This equation shows that if the resistance is constant, then the current is proportional to the voltage ($I \propto V$) — the higher the voltage across a given component with a fixed resistance, the higher the current through it will be.

2) The equation also shows that if voltage is constant, then the current is inversely proportional to the resistance $\left(I \propto \frac{1}{R}\right)$ — the greater the resistance of a component, the smaller the current that flows through it.

You can Measure Current and Voltage

1) An AMMETER measures the current flowing through an electrical component. Ammeters should be connected inline with electrical components.

2) A VOLTMETER measures the voltage across an electrical component. It must be placed across the component in a circuit.

If you're doing Higher, you need to know that ammeters are connected in series and voltmeters are connected in parallel with components (see p.231).

Here are the Circuit Symbols You Should Know

There's more about a.c. and d.c. on p.101.

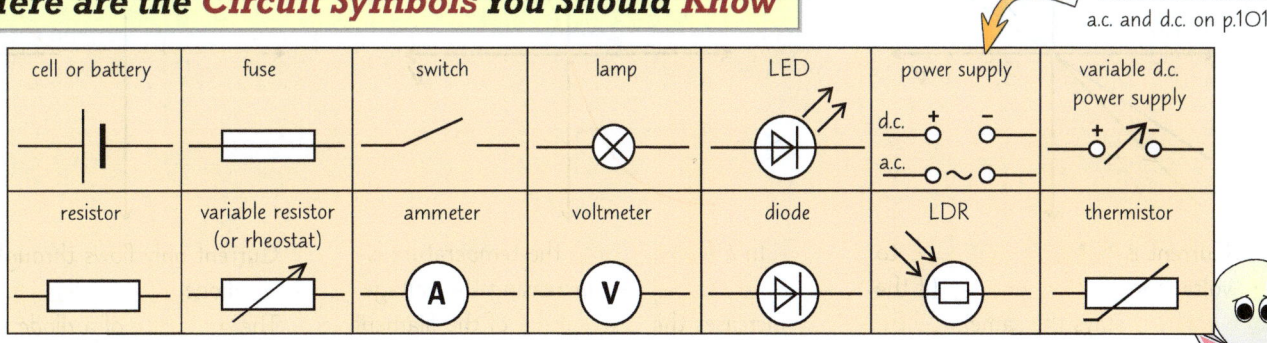

A lamp's favourite newspaper — full of current affairs...

Learn all those circuit symbols — you could be asked to draw a circuit using one or more of them in your exams.

Q1 Draw the circuit symbol for a variable resistor. [1 mark]

Q2 A voltage of 4.25 V is applied across a resistor, causing a current of 0.25 A to flow. Calculate the resistance, in ohms, of the resistor. [3 marks]

Investigating *I-V* Characteristics

Ooh experiments, you've gotta love 'em. Here's a simple experiment for investigating different components.

There's a *Simple Circuit* for *Investigating Components*

You can investigate how current changes with voltage for a range of components such as resistors, wires, filament lamps and diodes:

PRACTICAL

12 V d.c. power supply

component

1) Connect the circuit as shown on the right. The component you want to investigate, the ammeter and the variable resistor are all in series (p.98), which means they can be put in any order in the main circuit. (Remember the voltmeter must be in parallel (p.231) with the component under test.)

2) Varying the resistance of the variable resistor alters the current flowing through the circuit and the voltage across the component.

3) First set the resistance of the variable resistor to its highest value and measure the current and the voltage across the component.

4) Then decrease the resistance and repeat your measurements of the current and voltage. Repeat these measurements at a number of different resistances.

You could use a variable d.c. power supply instead of a regular power supply and a variable resistor.

5) Swap over the wires connected to the power supply to reverse the direction of the current. The voltmeter and ammeter should now show negative readings. Repeat steps 3 and 4 to get the results for the negative values.

6) Plot the current on the *y*-axis and the voltage on the *x*-axis to get *I-V* graphs like the ones below.

7) Make sure the circuit doesn't get too hot over the course of your experiment, as this will mess up your results. If the circuit starts to warm up, disconnect it for a while between readings so it can cool down. And, like any experiment, you should do repeats and calculate a mean.

You Need to Know Some *I-V* Characteristics

I-V graphs (known as *I-V* characteristics) show how the current through a component varies as you change the voltage across it. You can find the resistance for any point on an *I-V* graph by reading the voltage and current at that point and sticking them in the formula $R = V \div I$ (found from the equation on page 95). These are the results you should get from the experiment above:

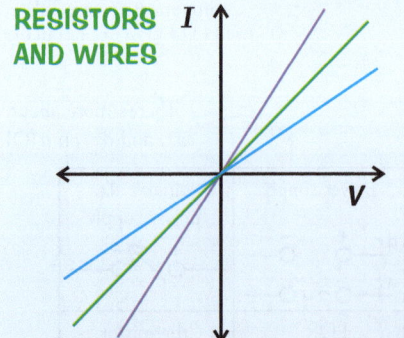

RESISTORS AND WIRES

Current is directly proportional to voltage in resistors or wires (if the temperature stays the same). Different resistors have different resistances, so their *I-V* graphs have different slopes.

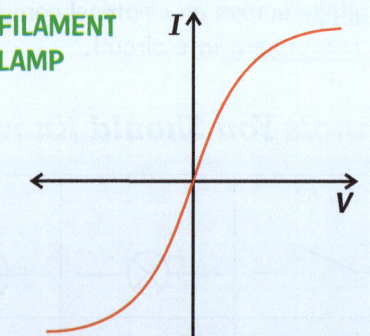

FILAMENT LAMP

In a filament lamp the temperature is not constant — increasing the voltage increases the temperature of the filament, which makes its resistance increase. This is what makes the *I-V* graph curved.

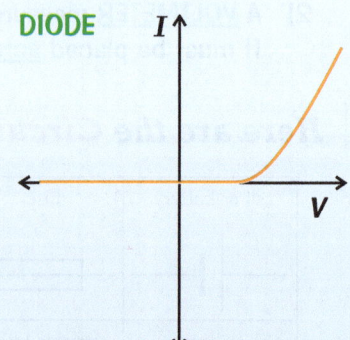

DIODE

Current only flows through a diode in one direction. The resistance of a diode isn't constant. There's more on diodes on the next page.

In the end you'll have to learn this — resistance is futile...

Make sure you can confidently draw those graphs, and that you understand why they look the way they do.

Q1   Draw a circuit that could be used to produce an *I-V* characteristic for a filament lamp.   [3 marks]

Circuit Devices

Lamps and resistors are all very well and good, but <u>diodes</u>, <u>LDRs</u> and <u>thermistors</u> are where the fun's really at.

Current Only Flows in *One Direction* through a *Diode*

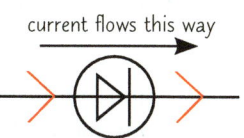

current flows this way

1) A diode is a special device that lets current flow freely through it in <u>one direction</u>, but <u>not</u> in the other (i.e. there's a very high resistance in the <u>reverse</u> direction). This is shown by the <u>*I-V* characteristic</u> on the previous page.

2) A diode will let current flow when a <u>positive voltage</u> is applied — this is called <u>forward bias</u>. The diode won't let current flow when a <u>negative voltage</u> is applied — this is called <u>reverse bias</u>.

3) The *I-V* characteristic also shows that a diode usually <u>won't conduct electricity</u> until it reaches a <u>certain voltage</u>. The *I-V* graph stays pretty <u>flat</u> until this certain voltage is reached.

You can Investigate the Resistance of *LDRs* and *Thermistors*

1) The <u>resistance</u> of some resistors is <u>dependent</u> on their <u>environment</u>.

2) If you set up the <u>circuit</u> shown on the right, you can <u>change the environment</u> the resistor is in to see the <u>effect</u> on its <u>resistance</u>.

3) To find the resistance of the component at any point, use the <u>voltmeter</u> and <u>ammeter</u> to measure the voltage and the current through the component, and then <u>calculate</u> the component's resistance by using $R = V \div I$ (found from rearranging the equation on p.95).

4) <u>Instead</u> of using an ammeter and voltmeter, you could use an <u>ohmmeter</u> (or <u>multimeter</u>), which measures <u>resistance directly</u>.

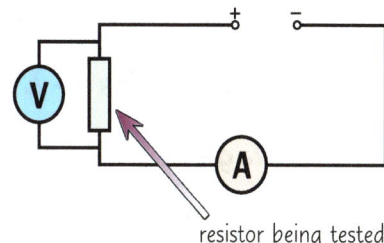

resistor being tested

A multimeter is an instrument that can measure lots of different properties. For example, it could be used as an ammeter, a voltmeter or an ohmmeter.

LDR Stands for *Light-Dependent Resistor*

1) An LDR is a resistor that's <u>dependent</u> on the <u>intensity</u> of <u>light</u>. At a <u>constant light level</u>, its <u>resistance</u> is <u>constant</u>.

2) In <u>darkness</u>, the resistance is <u>highest</u>. As light levels <u>increase</u> resistance <u>falls</u> so (for a given voltage) the <u>current</u> through the LDR <u>increases</u>.

3) You can <u>test</u> this by gradually <u>covering up</u> the surface of the LDR with a piece of thick paper.

4) They have lots of applications including <u>automatic night lights</u>, <u>outdoor lighting</u> and <u>burglar alarms</u>.

resistance / light intensity / dark / light

A *Thermistor* is a Type of *Temperature-Dependent Resistor*

1) In <u>hot</u> conditions, the resistance of an ntc thermistor <u>drops</u>. In <u>cool</u> conditions, the resistance goes <u>up</u>.

2) You can test this by placing a thermistor into a <u>beaker of hot water</u> and taking measurements of the resistance as the water cools down and the <u>temperature</u> of the thermistor <u>decreases</u>.

3) They're used as <u>temperature detectors</u> (e.g. <u>thermostats</u>, <u>irons</u> and <u>car engines</u>).

'ntc' stands for negative temperature coefficient — this just means that the resistance decreases as the temperature increases.

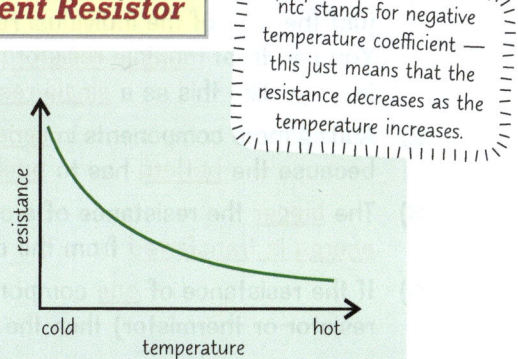

resistance / cold / temperature / hot

I'm a thermistor for ice cream — in heat my resistance drops...

Even more graphs to learn... Brilliant. Just keep drawing them out until they're completely stuck in your head.

Q1 How does the resistance of an LDR vary with light intensity? [1 mark]

Series and Parallel Circuits

Wiring a circuit in <u>series</u> or <u>parallel</u> can have a <u>big effect</u> on its behaviour.

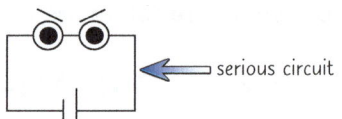

serious circuit

Series and Parallel Circuits are *Connected Differently*

1) In <u>series circuits</u>, the different components are connected <u>in a line</u>, <u>end to end</u>, between the +ve and −ve terminals of the power supply. Current has to flow through <u>all</u> of the components to get round the circuit, so if you <u>remove</u> one of them it can have a <u>big effect</u> on the others.

2) In <u>parallel circuits</u> each component is <u>separately</u> connected to the +ve and −ve terminals of the <u>supply</u>. This means if you remove or disconnect <u>one</u> of them, it will <u>hardly affect</u> the others at all.

3) Parallel circuits are usually the most sensible way to connect things, for example in <u>cars</u> and in <u>household electrics</u> (like the ring main, see page 102), where you have to be able to switch everything on and off <u>separately</u>. But you need to know all about both types of circuit I'm afraid.

4) If you add <u>more cells</u> to <u>any circuit</u>, connect them in <u>series</u>, not parallel. Connecting <u>several cells in series</u>, <u>all the same way</u> (+ to −) gives a <u>bigger total voltage</u> — because each charge in the circuit passes through each cell and gets a 'push' from each one. So <u>two 1.5 V</u> cells <u>in series</u> would supply <u>3 V in total</u>.

Series Circuits — *Everything in a Line*

Remember, always connect <u>ammeters</u> and <u>voltmeters</u> correctly (see p.95).

Voltage is Shared

1) In series circuits, the <u>total voltage</u> of the <u>supply</u> is <u>shared</u> between the various <u>components</u>. So the <u>voltages</u> round a series circuit always <u>add up</u> to equal the voltage across the <u>power supply</u>:

$$V = V_1 + V_2$$

2) This is because the total <u>energy transferred</u> to the charges in the circuit by the <u>power supply</u> equals the total <u>energy transferred</u> from the charges to the <u>components</u>.

Current is the Same Everywhere

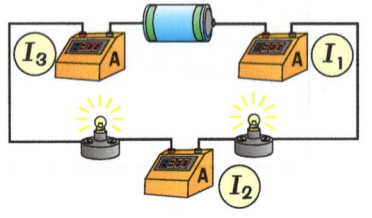

1) In series circuits the <u>same current</u> flows through <u>all parts</u> of the circuit:

$$I_1 = I_2 = I_3$$

2) The <u>size</u> of the current is determined by the <u>total voltage</u> of the power supply and the <u>total resistance</u> of the circuit: i.e. $I = V \div R$.

Resistance Adds Up

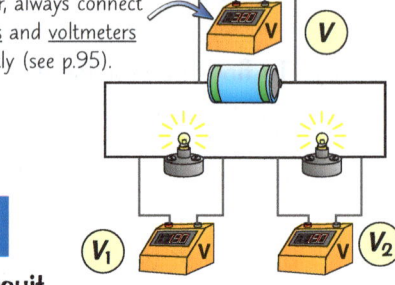

cell

$6\,\Omega$ $3\,\Omega$

total resistance, $R = 6 + 3 = 9\,\Omega$

1) In series circuits, the <u>total resistance</u> is just the <u>sum</u> of the individual resistances: You can treat <u>multiple resistors</u> connected in <u>series</u> like this as a <u>single resistor</u> with <u>equivalent resistance</u> *R*.

$$R = R_1 + R_2$$

2) Adding more components in <u>series increases</u> the circuit's total resistance because the <u>battery</u> has to <u>push each charge</u> through <u>more</u> components.

3) The <u>bigger</u> the resistance of a component, the bigger its <u>share</u> of the <u>total voltage</u> (because more <u>energy is transferred</u> from the charge when moving through a <u>large</u> resistance than a <u>small</u> one).

4) If the resistance of <u>one</u> component <u>changes</u> (e.g. if it's a variable resistor, light-dependent resistor or thermistor) then the <u>voltage</u> across <u>each</u> of the components will change too.

I like series circuits so much I bought the box set...

Series circuits are simple to make, but a real pain — if one of the bulbs in the diagrams above blew, it'd break the circuit, so they'd all go out. Sad times... That's one of the reasons they're not as popular as parallel circuits.

Q1   Three identical filament lamps are connected in series to a power supply of 3.6 V.
Calculate the voltage across each bulb.

[1 mark]

More on Series and Parallel Circuits

Parallel Circuits — *Independence* and *Isolation*

Voltage is the *Same* Across *All* Branches

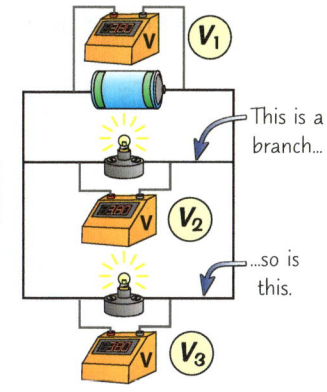

This is a branch...

...so is this.

1) In parallel circuits <u>all</u> branches get the <u>full supply voltage</u> so the voltage is the <u>same</u> across all branches: $V_1 = V_2 = V_3$

2) This is because <u>each charge</u> can only pass down <u>one branch</u> of the circuit, so it must <u>transfer all the energy</u> supplied to it by the <u>supply voltage</u> to whatever's on that branch.

Current is *Shared* Between Branches

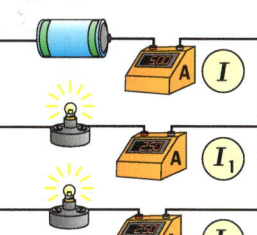

1) In parallel circuits the <u>total current</u> flowing through the power supply equals the <u>total</u> of all the currents through the <u>separate branches</u>: $I = I_1 + I_2$

2) You can find the current in a branch using <u>$I = V \div R$</u>, where *V* is the <u>voltage across the branch</u> (which is equal to the supply voltage) and *R* is the <u>resistance</u> of the <u>component on the branch</u> (or the <u>equivalent resistance</u> of the branch if there's more than one component on it).

3) In a parallel circuit, there are <u>junctions</u> where the current either <u>splits</u> or <u>rejoins</u>. The total current going <u>into</u> a junction has to equal the total current <u>leaving</u>.

Resistance is *Tricky*

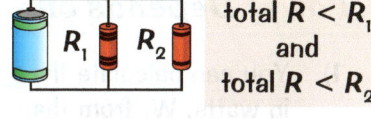

total $R < R_1$
and
total $R < R_2$

1) The <u>total resistance</u> of a parallel circuit is always <u>less</u> than that of the branch with the <u>smallest</u> resistance.

2) The resistance is lower because the charge has <u>more than one</u> branch to take — only <u>some</u> of the charge flows along each branch.

3) Adding components in parallel <u>decreases</u> the total resistance of a circuit as the charge has <u>more branches</u> through which it can flow.

4) The <u>total resistance</u>, *R*, can be calculated using:

$$\frac{1}{R} = \frac{1}{R_1} + \frac{1}{R_2}$$

You can *Combine Series* and *Parallel* Circuits

EXAMPLE:

For the circuit shown on the right, calculate:
a) the resistance of branch 1,
b) the total resistance of the circuit,
c) the current in the circuit.

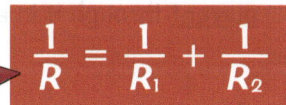

12 V
① 2 Ω 3 Ω
② 15 Ω

a) The resistors on branch 1 are in <u>series</u>, so use $R = R_1 + R_2$ (see the previous page) to find their <u>total resistance</u>.

b) The resistors on branch 1 can now be treated as a <u>single resistor</u> of 5 Ω. To calculate the <u>total resistance</u> of the circuit, use the <u>equation</u> $\frac{1}{R} = \frac{1}{R_1} + \frac{1}{R_2}$, where R_1 is the total resistance of <u>branch 1</u> and R_2 is the resistance of <u>branch 2</u>.

c) To find the <u>total current</u> in the circuit, use $I = V \div R$ (p.95) and <u>substitute</u> in the <u>supply voltage</u> and the <u>total resistance</u> of the circuit.

a) $R = R_1 + R_2$
$= 2 + 3 = 5 \ \Omega$

b) $\frac{1}{R} = \frac{1}{R_1} + \frac{1}{R_2}$
$= \frac{1}{5} + \frac{1}{15} = \frac{4}{15}$
$R = 1 \div \frac{4}{15} = 3.75 \ \Omega$

c) $I = 12 \div 3.75 = 3.2 \ A$

Higher

A current shared *(between identical components in parallel)* — is a current halved...

Remember, in parallel circuits, each branch has the same voltage, but the total current is shared between branches.

Q1 Three resistors of resistances 8 Ω, 4 Ω and 9 Ω are connected in parallel to a 6.0 V battery. Calculate the current through the 8 Ω resistor. [2 marks]

Energy and Power in Circuits

Power determines how quickly energy is transferred — like how motivation determines how quickly you revise...

Power is the Rate of Energy Transfer

1) The power of a component tells you how much energy it transfers per second.
Energy (E) and power (P) are related by the formula:

$$\underset{\text{in joules (J)}}{\text{energy transferred}} = \underset{\text{in watts (W)}}{\text{power}} \times \underset{\text{in seconds (s)}}{\text{time}}$$

2) Power is measured in watts (W). 1 W = 1 J/s (one joule of energy transferred per second).

> **EXAMPLE:** A 2 W electric toothbrush is used to clean for 2.5 minutes.
> Calculate how much energy is transferred by the toothbrush in this time.
>
> 1) First you need to convert the time from minutes to seconds.
>
> $2.5 \times 60 = 150$ seconds
>
> 2) Then substitute the values into the equation for energy transferred.
>
> Energy transferred = power × time
> $= 2 \times 150 = 300$ J

Power Depends on Current, Voltage and Resistance

1) You can calculate the power transferred by a component in watts, W, from the voltage across it in volts, V, and the current through it in amps, A, using the formula:

power = voltage × current

2) You know that current = voltage ÷ resistance (page 95). If you rearrange this for voltage, and then substitute into the formula above, you get another handy way to calculate power:

power = current² × resistance   or, in symbols: $P = I^2R$

> **EXAMPLE:** A toaster powered by a 230 V power supply has a current of 8.0 A through it.
> Calculate the power transferred by and the resistance of the toaster.
>
> 1) To find the power, substitute the values into $P = VI$.
>
> $P = VI = 230 \times 8.0$
> $= 1840 = 1800$ W (to 2 s.f.)
>
> 2) Rearrange $P = I^2R$ to find the resistance of the toaster.
>
> $R = P \div I^2 = 1840 \div (8)^2$
> $= 28.75 = 29\ \Omega$ (to 2 s.f.)
>
> You could also use $I = V \div R$ (p.95) to find the resistance of the toaster.

Watt's a good joke I could put here about power?

There's a lot of new equations here but don't panic, you'll be given them in the exam, so you won't need to remember them. You should get practising them though, so you feel totally comfortable rearranging and using them.

Q1   A 1.5×10^3 W hairdryer is turned on for 11 minutes. Calculate the energy transferred, in J.   [2 marks]

Q2   A 15 Ω resistor transfers energy at a rate of 375 W. Calculate the current through the resistor.   [3 marks]

Q3   A voltage of 2.5 V is applied across a resistor with a power of 8.5 W.
Calculate the current flowing through the resistor.   [3 marks]

Current and Mains Supply

Mains supply is the electricity that powers sockets and lights in homes, read on to find out more...

Mains Supply is a.c., Battery Supply is d.c.

1) There are two types of electric current — alternating current (a.c.) and direct current (d.c.).

2) In a.c. supplies the current is constantly changing direction. Alternating currents are produced by alternating voltages in which the positive and negative ends of the voltage keep alternating.

3) The UK domestic (mains) supply (the electricity in your home) is an a.c. supply at around 230 V.

4) The frequency of the a.c. mains supply is 50 cycles per second or 50 Hz.

5) By contrast, cells and batteries supply direct current.

6) Direct current is a current that is always flowing in the same direction. It's created by a direct voltage.

7) A CRO (cathode ray oscilloscope) can be connected to a circuit to show how the voltage in the circuit changes with time — the results are shown on the screen of the CRO:

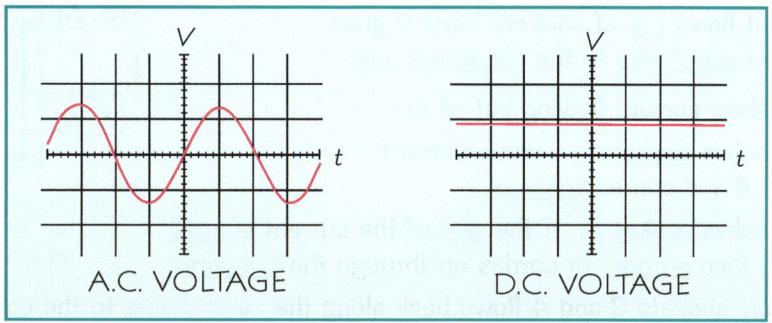

A.C. VOLTAGE   D.C. VOLTAGE

The Mains Supply uses Three Different Wires

1) **LIVE WIRE** (brown).
The live wire carries current at a high voltage to houses and their appliances.

2) **NEUTRAL WIRE** (blue). The neutral wire completes the circuit — normally, current flows through the live wire and the neutral wire. The neutral wire is always at a low voltage or 0 V.

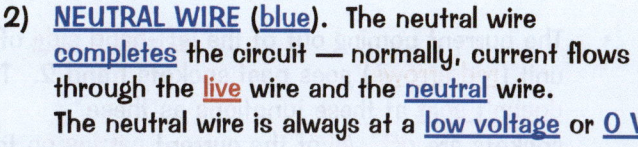

3) **EARTH WIRE** (green and yellow). The earth wire is for safety. It carries the current safely to the ground if there's a fault in an appliance with a metal casing (see page 103). It's also at 0 V.

You complete me.

Why are earth wires green and yellow — when mud is brown...?

I've always preferred d.c. voltage — a.c. voltage is so changeable. It's up and then it's down, it's happy then it's sad, it knows what it wants and then it changes its mind, it says it loves you but then never returns your calls. And no matter how much ice cream you eat, or how often friends say you're worth more than that, it still hurts.

Q1   Explain the difference between alternating current and direct current.   [2 marks]

Q2   Sketch the *V-t* graph that would be displayed on a CRO screen if the CRO was connected to an a.c. circuit.   [1 mark]

The Ring Main

The ring main supplies electricity to sockets around the house. The circuit is a tad tricky, but it's pretty neat.

Sockets on the Ring Main are in Parallel

1) The ring main is a looped parallel circuit that connects the plug sockets in a house to the consumer unit. The consumer unit is where the electricity supply for a house comes from.

2) The live, neutral and earth wires (see previous page) lead from the consumer unit to the sockets and then back to the consumer unit, as shown on the diagrams below.

3) Current can flow in both directions around the ring main.

4) First, let's look at how current might flow if a ring main contains four sockets that are all switched on:

The red arrows show current flowing out of the left-hand side of the consumer unit:

- The current splits at the junction for socket 1 — some current goes to socket 1 and some carries on.

- The current reaches socket 2. If the rest of the current is used by socket 2, then no current carries on through the live wire.

- The current that flows out of sockets 1 and 2 goes back along the neutral wire to the consumer unit.

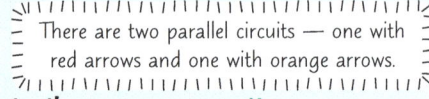

The orange arrows show current flowing out of the right-hand side:

- The current reaches socket 4 — some current goes to socket 4 and some carries on.

- The current reaches socket 3. If the rest of the current is used by this socket, then no current carries on through the live wire.

- The current from sockets 3 and 4 flows back along the neutral wire to the consumer unit.

There are two parallel circuits — one with red arrows and one with orange arrows.

How far each loop of current reaches depends on which sockets are switched on and what's plugged into them. For example, if an appliance that uses a lot of current was plugged into socket 4, the current might flow so that the red arrows reach sockets 1, 2, and 3 and the orange arrows only reach socket 4.

5) If sockets 1 and 2 are off, the current might flow like this:

- The current coming out of the left-hand side of the consumer unit (red arrows) goes past sockets 1 and 2. The current doesn't split at these junctions as these sockets are off. All of the current carries on to socket 3.

- All of the current passes through socket 3. It then travels back to the consumer unit along the neutral wire.

- The current coming out of the right-hand side of the consumer unit (orange arrows) travels along the live wire to socket 4 and then back to the consumer unit along the neutral wire.

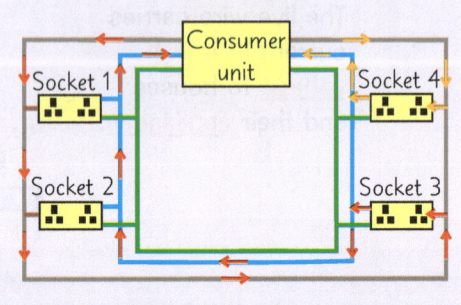

6) Lights in houses aren't connected to sockets, but they are connected in a similar circuit to the ring main.

The Ring Main has Lots of Advantages

1) Because the ring main is a parallel circuit, sockets can be placed anywhere in the circuit, and each socket can be operated independently.

2) Being in parallel also means that each socket on the ring receives the same voltage of 230 V (p.99).

3) Because current can take two paths around the ring main, there's less current flowing in each part of the cable, and so thinner wires can be used — so less metal is used for the wires, which saves money.

All this talk of ring mains is turning me loopy...

Those are some complicated diagrams. I reckon you should read this page again, try this question, then have a brew.

Q1   Why is it an advantage that current can flow two ways around the ring main?   [1 mark]

Fuses and Circuit Breakers

Fuses and circuit breakers are super handy — they help to stop electrical appliances from doing any damage.

Fuses *Prevent Electrical Overloads*

Surges (sudden increases) in current can be caused by a fault in an electrical appliance. Current surges can lead to circuits and wiring in appliances melting or causing a fire — faulty appliances can even cause deadly electric shocks. Fuses and earth wires are used in appliances to prevent this. This is how they work:

1) The earth wire is connected to the metal casing of an appliance. The earth wire has a low resistance.

2) If a fault develops and the live wire somehow touches the metal case, then there will be a surge in current as there is a low resistance path to ground, which is through the case and out down the earth wire.

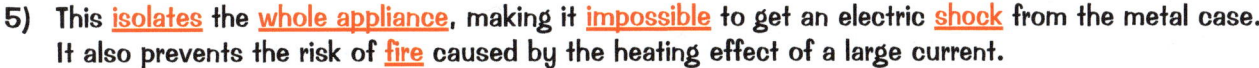

This is to certify that
THE MELTDOWN
is rated 5A

3) Fuses are connected to the live wire — this current surge blows the fuse (melts the strip of metal in the fuse) if the current is greater than the fuse rating (see below).

4) Breaking the fuse breaks the circuit and cuts off the live supply.

5) This isolates the whole appliance, making it impossible to get an electric shock from the metal case. It also prevents the risk of fire caused by the heating effect of a large current.

- Fuses should be rated as near as possible but just higher than the normal operating current.
- If the fuse rating is too low then the fuse will blow when the appliance is working normally.
- If the fuse rating is too high then the fuse won't blow when there's a surge in current.
- You may have to calculate the operating current of an appliance and then use this to find the most appropriate fuse rating for the appliance.

EXAMPLE: A 1000 W hairdryer is connected to a 230 V supply.
Suggest whether a 3 A, 5 A or 13 A fuse is needed.

1) Rearrange $P = VI$ (p.100) for I and substitute into the equation. $I = P \div V = 1000 \div 230 = 4.3... \text{ A}$

2) Choose the fuse rating just higher than the operating current calculated.   **So a 5 A fuse is needed.**

Circuit Breakers *Turn Off* a *Circuit* if *There's* a *Fault*

1) Circuit breakers can be used in the live wire instead of (or as well as) fuses.

2) Instead of melting a fuse, a large current may 'trip' (turn off) a circuit breaker.

3) Miniature circuit breakers (mcb) are one type of circuit breaker. They protect the circuit from damage if too much current flows.

4) An mcb contains an electromagnet — if the current is too big then the electromagnet will attract a switch. This opens the switch and breaks the circuit to isolate the appliance.

5) Another type of circuit breaker is a residual current circuit breaker (rccb):

- Normally exactly the same current flows through the live and neutral wires in an appliance. If someone touches the live wire a small but deadly current will flow through them to the earth. This means that the neutral wire carries less current than the live wire. The rccb detects this difference in the current and quickly opens a switch to cut off the power, protecting the person who touched the live wire.
- Rccbs even work for small current changes that might not be large enough to trip an mcb. This means that rccbs are more sensitive than mcbs.

6) One advantage of circuit breakers is that they can be reset by flicking a switch, which is much easier than having to replace a fuse.

This is all very con-fuse-ing...

Sorry, I had to... Learn the differences between an mcb and an rccb to make sure you don't mix them up.

Q1   A kettle is going to be connected to a 230 V supply. The kettle has a resistance of 25 Ω.
      Use $I = V \div R$ to suggest whether a 3 A, 5 A or 13 A fuse should be used in the kettle.   [3 marks]

Revision Questions for Unit 3a

Well, that wraps up Unit 3a — it's been a full-on topic, so now it's time to relax with some lovely questions...

- Try these questions and tick off each one when you get it right.
- When you've done all the questions for a topic and are completely happy with it, tick off the topic.

Circuits and Circuit Devices (p.95-97) ☐

1) What device is used in a circuit to measure current? ☐

2) Should a voltmeter be put in series or parallel with a component when measuring the voltage across a component? ☐

3) Draw the circuit symbol of a:
   a) lamp
   b) thermistor
   c) light dependent resistor (LDR)
   d) fuse ☐ ☐

4) Describe an experiment that could be done to find the I-V characteristic of a diode.

5) Sketch the I-V graph for a:
   a) wire at a constant temperature
   b) filament lamp
   c) diode ☐

6) What is the function of a diode? ☐

7) What does the resistance of an LDR depend on? ☐

8) Sketch a resistance-temperature graph for an ntc thermistor. ☐

Series and Parallel Circuits (p.98-99) ☐

9) True or false? Current is the same everywhere in a series circuit. ☐

10) Explain why adding components in series increases the total resistance of a circuit. ☐

11) What happens to the total resistance of a circuit as more resistors are added in parallel? ☐

Power in Circuits and Mains Electricity (p.100-103) ☑

12) What is meant by the power of a component? ☐

13) What is 1 W in J/s? ☐

14) Which type of electrical current is constantly changing direction — a.c. or d.c.? ☐

15) What is the voltage and frequency of the a.c. mains supply in the UK? ☑

16) Sketch what would be seen on a CRO screen if the CRO was connected to a d.c. circuit. ☑

17) Describe the function of the:
    a) live wire
    b) neutral wire
    c) earth wire ☑

18) Give one advantage of sockets in the ring main being in parallel. ☑

19) True or false? Fuses are placed in the earth wire. ☐

20) Describe how an mcb works. ☑

21) Describe how an rccb works. ☑

Efficiency and Sankey Diagrams

Efficiency is an important part of physics — we're always trying to make houses, industries, cars, etc. more efficient.

Most Energy Transfers Involve Some Energy Being Wasted

1) No device is 100% efficient — whenever work is done, some of the energy transferred is always wasted.

2) The less energy that is 'wasted', the more efficient the device is said to be.

3) The efficiency of any energy transfer can be worked out using this equation:

$$\% \text{ efficiency} = \frac{\text{energy (or power) usefully transferred}}{\text{total energy (or power) supplied}} \times 100$$

EXAMPLE: A food blender is 70% efficient. 6000 J of energy is transferred to it. Calculate the useful energy transferred by the blender.

1) Rearrange the equation for energy usefully transferred.

2) Stick in the numbers you're given.

energy usefully transferred
= (% efficiency ÷ 100) × total energy supplied
= (70 ÷ 100) × 6000 = 4200 J

4) The efficiency of any energy transfer can be increased by reducing unwanted energy transfers.

You can Use Sankey Diagrams to Show Efficiency

You can also sketch Sankey diagrams, where the width still represents the amount of energy transferred, but the diagram isn't to scale.

A Sankey diagram like the one below shows the energy transfers made by a device. From it you can work out the efficiency.

Diagram for an electric motor with 80% efficiency:

In this diagram, the width of one square on the grid represents 20 J. The thickness of the arrows represents how much energy is being transferred. The length has nothing to do with it.

The total energy transferred by the motor equals the sum of the energy usefully transferred and the energy wasted, because energy is always conserved (p.205).

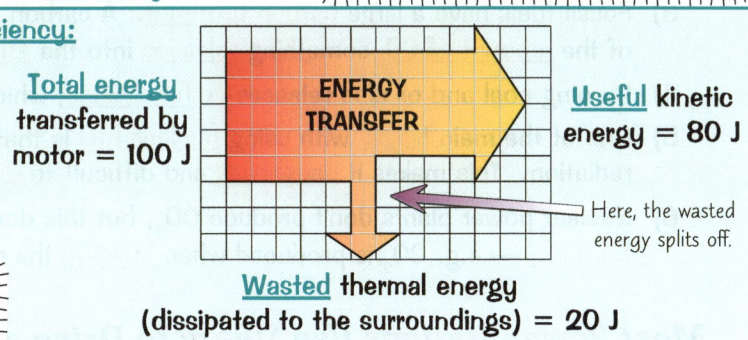

Total energy transferred by motor = 100 J

ENERGY TRANSFER

Useful kinetic energy = 80 J

Here, the wasted energy splits off.

Wasted thermal energy (dissipated to the surroundings) = 20 J

You Can Use the Kilowatt-hour (kWh) to Work Out Energy Costs

1) Electrical appliances transfer electrical energy into other forms.

2) Energy transferred (joules) = power (watts) × time (seconds) — see p.100.

3) When you're dealing with large amounts of electrical energy (e.g. the energy used by a home in one week), it's easier to think of power and time in kilowatts and hours — rather than in watts and seconds.

4) So the standard units of electrical energy are kilowatt-hours (kWh) — not joules.

A KILOWATT-HOUR is the amount of electrical energy converted by a 1 kW appliance in 1 HOUR.

units of energy used (kWh) = power (kW) × time (hours)

cost = units of energy used (kWh) × price per unit

A kilo-what? — For when you really don't understand...

Practise converting between kWh and J — first change kW to W (× 1000) then change hours to seconds (× 3600).

Q1 A washing machine has an average power of 750 W throughout its 2 hour cycle. A unit of energy costs 14p.
  a) Calculate the units of energy used per wash in kWh. [2 marks]
  b) What is the total cost of using the washing machine once a week for 10 weeks? [3 marks]

Energy Resources

We use A LOT of electricity. Just look around you — the energy to power it all has to come from somewhere.

Non-Renewable Energy Resources Will Eventually Run Out

1) We get some of our energy from non-renewable resources — resources that will run out one day.

2) The main non-renewable energy resources on Earth are the three fossil fuels (coal, oil and gas) and nuclear fuels (uranium and plutonium).

3) There are lots of advantages and disadvantages to all types of fuel. The main ones you need to think about are economic, environmental and sustainability issues.

4) You also need to think about the start-up time of a fuel source (how long before energy is produced) and their generating capacities (the maximum electric power they can create in normal conditions).

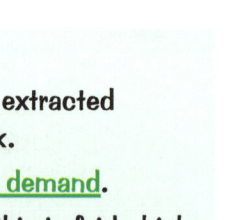

1) The main advantage of using these energy resources is that they're reliable.

2) There's enough fossil and nuclear fuels to meet current demand. Fossil fuels are extracted from the Earth at a fast enough rate that power stations always have fuel in stock.

3) This means that non-renewable power stations can respond quickly to changes in demand.

4) Coal, oil and gas are all about 50% efficient and nuclear power is about 40% — this is fairly high.

1) The main disadvantage of fossil fuels is that they damage the environment when they're used.

2) Coal, oil and gas release CO_2 into the atmosphere when they're burned. All of this CO_2 adds to the greenhouse effect, and contributes to global warming (p.85).

3) Fossil fuels have a large carbon footprint. A carbon footprint is a measure of the amount of CO_2 something releases into the atmosphere.

> Some environmental problems are unpredictable. E.g. oil spillages, that affect sea mammals and birds.

4) Burning coal and oil also releases sulfur dioxide, which causes acid rain.

5) One of the main issues with using nuclear fuel is that nuclear waste releases radiation. This makes it dangerous and difficult to dispose of — see p.221.

6) Nuclear power plants don't produce CO_2, but this doesn't mean they have no carbon footprint — e.g. CO_2 is produced when building the power stations and mining nuclear fuel.

Most Power Stations Use Steam to Drive a Turbine

The set-up costs for fossil fuel power stations are high, but the running costs are low. We currently generate some of our electricity using steam-driven turbines like this:

1) As the fossil fuel burns, the water is heated.

2) The water boils to form steam, which moves and turns a turbine.

3) The turbine is connected to an electrical generator, which generates a voltage across (and so a current through) a wire by spinning a magnet near to the wire (you don't need to know how this works).

4) The current produced by the generator flows through the national grid (p.110).

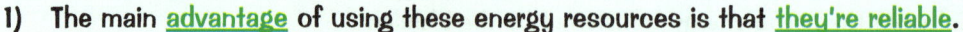

In power stations, energy changes between lots of different types:

- Chemical energy in the fuel is changed to heat energy when burned to create steam.

- The steam's heat energy is converted to the kinetic energy of the steam, which is converted to the kinetic energy of the turbine — heat energy is changed to kinetic energy.

- This drives a generator to produce electricity — kinetic energy is changed to electrical energy.

It all boils down to steam...

Fossil fuels damage the environment and will run out one day — that's why I use a solar powered calculator.

Q1   State two non-renewable energy resources.   [2 marks]

Renewable Energy Resources

Renewable energy resources never run out — and they are usually much better for the environment.

Wind Power — Lots of Wind Turbines

1) Each wind turbine has a generator inside it. The rotating blades turn the generator and produce electricity.

2) They have quite a high set-up cost but no fuel costs.

3) There's no pollution (except for a little bit when they're manufactured).

4) But some people think they spoil the view and they can be very noisy, which can be annoying for people living nearby. To avoid this, they can be placed offshore (which actually generates more energy, p.109).

5) Wind turbines only work when it's windy, so they can't always supply electricity, or respond to high demand. Also the output is variable because of changes in wind speed, so it's not as reliable as fossil fuels.

6) Wind power is fairly efficient, but not quite as efficient as non-renewable energy resources.

Solar Cells — Expensive but No Environmental Damage

1) Solar power is often used in remote places where there's not much choice (e.g. the Australian outback) and to power electric road signs and satellites.

2) Initial costs are high but after that the energy is free and running costs are almost zero.

Time to recharge.

3) There's no pollution when they're being used. (Although they do use quite a lot of energy to make.)

4) Solar cells are mainly used to generate electricity on a relatively small scale, e.g. in homes.

5) Solar power is most suitable for sunny countries, but it can be used in cloudy countries like Britain.

6) Solar power generation isn't constant throughout the year because the hours of sunlight vary a lot.

7) And, of course, you can't make solar power at night or increase production when there's extra demand.

8) Unfortunately, solar power isn't usually very efficient.

Biofuels are Made from Plants and Waste

1) Biofuels can be burnt to generate electricity or used to run cars in the same way as fossil fuels.

2) Burning them releases CO_2, but the plants you grow (either to burn or as animal feed) remove CO_2 from the atmosphere, so the carbon footprint appears to be zero. However there's debate about the net change of CO_2 — it would only be zero if you keep growing plants at at least the rate that you're burning things. It also doesn't take into account any CO_2 produced from growing, harvesting and processing the crops. Despite these issues, biofuels typically have a carbon footprint that is lower than that of fossil fuels.

3) Biofuels are fairly reliable as they can be produced fairly quickly and easily. But it's harder to respond to immediate energy demands, as crops take time to grow (you can stockpile biofuels to combat this).

4) The cost of making biofuels is very high and some worry that growing crops specifically for biofuels could lead to there not being enough space or water to grow enough crops for food for everyone.

5) In some places, large areas of land have been cleared to grow biofuels, resulting in species losing their habitats. The decay and burning of this vegetation also increases CO_2 and methane emissions.

6) Overall, biofuels aren't as efficient as fossil fuels. There are three main forms of biofuel:

Wood can be burned as a biofuel in many forms — firewood, charcoal, wood chips and sawdust. Wood is very readily available and can be easily grown. Unfortunately, burning wood produces a lot of carbon dioxide, soot and smoke.

Waste products from plants and animals will rot due to the action of bacteria. This produces biogas (e.g. methane) which can be burnt to generate electricity, burnt to heat water for heating systems or be used as fuel for vehicles.

Crops are often grown specifically to be used as biofuel. Some oil crops are grown for biodiesel (p.109).

Renewable energy — I'm a big fan...

Make sure you can describe all of the energy resources above and some of their advantages and disadvantages.

Q1   Give an advantage and a disadvantage of wind power.   [2 marks]

More Renewable Energy Resources

Good ol' water. Not only can we drink it, we can also use it to generate electricity. It's easy to get confused between wave and tidal power as they both involve the seaside — but don't. They are completely different.

Hydroelectric Power Uses Falling Water

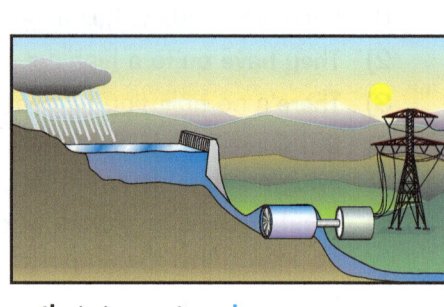

1) Hydroelectric power usually requires the flooding of a valley by building a big dam. Water is allowed out through turbines.

2) There is no pollution (as such), but there is a big impact on the environment due to flooding of the valley.

3) This can lead to rotting vegetation which releases methane and CO_2. It can also cause a loss of habitat for some animals and humans (sometimes the loss of whole villages).

4) Putting hydroelectric power stations in remote valleys tends to reduce their impact on humans.

5) A big advantage is that the dam can provide an immediate response to an increased demand for electricity.

6) Hydroelectric power is really efficient and there's no problem with reliability except in times of drought. Hydroelectric power stations have high generating capacities.

7) Initial costs are high, but there are no fuel costs and minimal running costs.

8) It can be a useful way to generate electricity on a small scale in remote areas.

Wave Power — Lots of Little Wave-Powered Turbines

1) Wave power needs lots of small wave-powered turbines located around the coast. Like with wind power (p.107), the moving turbines are connected to a generator.

2) There is no pollution. The main problems are disturbing the seabed and the habitats of marine animals, spoiling the view and being a hazard to boats.

3) They are fairly unreliable, since waves tend to die out when the wind drops. However, when waves are good they can be very efficient and have the potential for generating large amounts of electricity.

4) Initial costs are high, but there are no fuel costs and minimal running costs. Wave power is never likely to provide energy on a large scale, but it can be very useful on small islands.

Tidal Barrages — Using the Sun and Moon's Gravity

1) Tides are produced by the gravitational pull of the Sun and Moon.

2) Tides are used in lots of ways to generate electricity. The most common method is building a tidal barrage.

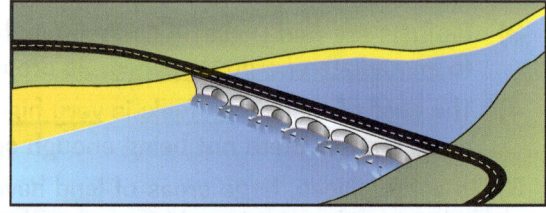

3) Tidal barrages are big dams built across river estuaries, with turbines in them. As the tide comes in and out, the water is allowed in and out through the turbines at a controlled speed.

4) There is no pollution. The main problems are preventing free access by boats, spoiling the view and altering the habitat of wildlife, e.g. wading birds, sea creatures and beasties who live in the sand.

5) Tides are pretty reliable in the sense that they happen twice a day without fail. The only drawback is that the height of the tide is variable so lower (neap) tides will provide significantly less energy than the bigger 'spring' tides. Barrages also don't work when the water level is the same either side of the barrage — this happens four times a day because of the tides.

6) Initial costs are moderately high, but there are no fuel costs and minimal running costs. Even though it can only be used in some of the most suitable estuaries, tidal power has the potential for generating a significant amount of energy at a very high efficiency.

I think I've hit a brick wall here — Dam...

Learn the differences between all of these water-based resources and everything will be hunky-dory.

Q1　　Give one negative environmental impact of wave power.　　　　　　　　　[1 mark]

Using Energy Resources

Saving money, saving the planet — there's a lot to think about when filling up your car or heating your home.

The Energy Output from Different Resources can Vary

1) You might need to analyse or interpret data on the energy output of an energy resource. (You might also need to evaluate how valid you think this data is — see p.5.)

2) For example, the table on the right shows some data for turbines in different locations.

3) The data shows that the length of the wind turbine blade and the location of the turbine make a huge difference to its energy output.

4) If you wanted a turbine with the highest possible energy output, you'd opt to build a large off-shore turbine, but you may be put off by the high start-up costs.

Location	Blade Length (m)	Power Output (MW)	Start-Up Costs (£ millions)
On-Shore	35	2.2	1.5
On-Shore	50	2.9	2.5
Off-Shore	35	2.8	37
Off-Shore	50	3.6	40

Remember power is the rate of transfer of energy (p.100).

Energy Resources are Needed for Transport and Heating

Transport

Most vehicles run on petrol and diesel, but some are starting to use electricity instead. Biodiesel can be mixed with regular diesel and used in regular diesel vehicles — biodiesel is typically made from plant products. The fuel vehicles use can have a big impact on how far you can go and how much it'll cost you.

1) Electric vehicles are usually more expensive to buy than petrol or diesel vehicles. However, electric vehicles are cheaper to run — they travel the furthest per unit cost of fuel. Biodiesel is the most expensive to buy, but some people produce it themselves at a low cost.

2) The maximum distance that a vehicle can travel on a full tank of fuel (or fully charged battery) is called its range. Petrol, diesel and biodiesel cars typically have a range of 300 to 400 miles, whereas electric cars have a lower range of around 100 miles.

Cost isn't the only thing that matters. You should also take into account the impact your vehicle will have on the environment.

3) A vehicle's efficiency (p.209) is how much of the energy stored in the fuel is converted to useful energy. Diesel and biodiesel vehicles have similar efficiencies, both are more efficient than petrol. Electric vehicles have a much higher efficiency, so they are cheaper to run in the long term.

Heating

How you choose to heat your home will affect your heating bills.

1) Most houses use a central heating system. Water is heated, usually in a large boiler, then pumped to radiators around the house.

2) The water may be heated by burning fuels such as fossil fuels (p.106) or biofuels (p.107). Electricity may be used to heat the water (but the electricity will have been generated using an energy resource, see previous three pages). Some homes use thermal solar panels that use radiation from the Sun to directly heat water.

3) How big your heating bill is depends on how cost-effective (p.114) your heating system is.

4) Gas central heating is usually a more cost-effective method of heating a house than electric central heating, and using a biomass boiler is typically less cost-effective than both of these methods.

5) The cost of buying and installing solar panels is quite high compared to a lot of other heating methods. But sunlight is free so there are no running costs, which means they can save you money (p.107). Not all days are sunny, so solar panels can be less reliable than other alternatives.

I'm a bit onshore about all of this energy stuff...

Make sure you're happy comparing energy sources for cars and fuel for homes — learn the pros and cons for each.

Q1   State one disadvantage of an electric vehicle compared to a petrol vehicle.   [1 mark]

The National Grid

The national grid is a giant web of wires that covers the whole of Britain, getting electricity from power stations to homes everywhere. Whoever you pay for your electricity, it's the national grid that gets it to you.

The National Grid Meets Electricity Demands

The national grid is a giant system of cables and transformers that covers the UK and connects power stations to consumers, transferring electrical power to homes and industries when it's needed.

1) Throughout the day electricity usage (demand) changes. Power stations have to produce enough electricity for everyone to have it when they need it. The minimum demand over a period of time (e.g. 1 week) is called the base load.

2) Some power stations need to have short start-up times (the time it takes to turn everything on and start producing electricity) so that they can quickly respond to changes in demand.

3) Power stations often run at well below their maximum power output. This is so that there's spare capacity to cope with a high demand, even if there's an unexpected shutdown of another station.

4) Smaller power stations that can start up quickly are kept in standby just in case. This makes the electricity supply reliable, as there are always more power stations that can be called upon.

5) If not enough electricity is available, or too much is produced, it's imported from or exported to foreign countries.

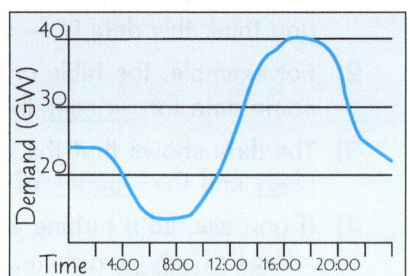

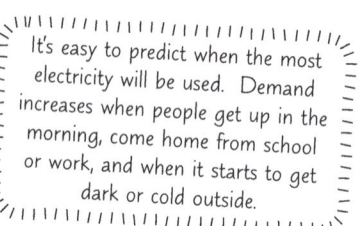

It's easy to predict when the most electricity will be used. Demand increases when people get up in the morning, come home from school or work, and when it starts to get dark or cold outside.

The National Grid Uses a High Voltage and a Low Current

1) To transmit the huge amount of power needed, you need either a high voltage or a high current (as $P = VI$, from p.100).

2) The problem with a high current is that you lose loads of energy as the wires heat up and energy is lost to the surroundings in the form of thermal energy.

3) It's cheaper to boost the voltage up really high (400 000 V) and keep the current as low as possible.

4) For a given power, increasing the voltage decreases the current, which decreases the energy lost by heating the wires and the surroundings. This makes the national grid an efficient way of transferring energy.

Voltage is Changed by a Transformer

1) Transformers have to step the voltage up at one end, for efficient transmission, and then bring it back down to safe, usable levels at the other end.

2) Step-up transformers increase the voltage and step-down transformers decrease the voltage.

3) Getting the voltage to 400 000 V for transmission requires transformers as well as big pylons with huge insulators — but it's still cheaper than using a lower voltage.

Transformers — NOT robots in disguise...

Transformers reduce energy losses in the national grid — they're essential for efficient power transmission.

Q1 Why is electricity in the national grid not transmitted at a high current? [2 marks]

Density and Matter

Density tells you how much <u>mass</u> is packed into a given <u>volume</u> — it depends on how particles are <u>arranged</u>.

Density is Mass per Unit Volume

1) <u>Density</u> is a measure of the '<u>compactness</u>' of a substance. It relates the <u>mass</u> of a substance to how much <u>space</u> it <u>takes up</u>.

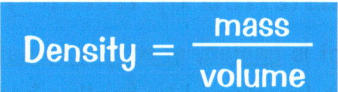

$$\text{Density} = \frac{\text{mass}}{\text{volume}}$$

The units of density are g/cm³ or kg/m³.

2) The density of an object depends on <u>what it's made of</u>. Density <u>doesn't vary</u> with <u>size</u> or <u>shape</u>.

Particle Theory is a Way of Explaining Density

1) In <u>particle theory</u>, you can think of the particles that make up matter as <u>tiny balls</u>. You can explain the ways that matter behaves in terms of how these tiny balls <u>move</u>, and the <u>forces</u> between them.

2) Three <u>states of matter</u> are <u>solid</u>, <u>liquid</u> and <u>gas</u>. The <u>particles</u> of a substance in each state are <u>the same</u> — only the <u>arrangement</u> and <u>energy</u> of the particles are <u>different</u>.

- Solids have a <u>high density</u> because their particles are packed very <u>tightly</u> together.
- Liquids also have <u>high densities</u>, but usually not quite as high as solids. This is because the particles in a liquid are also <u>close together</u> but are <u>randomly arranged</u> and can move around slightly.
- The particles in gases are <u>very far apart</u> — they have very <u>low densities</u>.

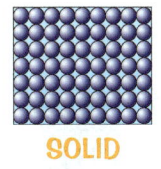
SOLID

LIQUID

GAS

You Can Measure the Density of Solids and Liquids

PRACTICAL

To find the density of a liquid

1) Record the mass of an <u>empty</u> measuring cylinder.

2) Fill it with a <u>known volume</u> of liquid (e.g. 20 cm³).

3) Record the <u>new mass</u> of the measuring cylinder — now if you <u>subtract</u> the empty mass from this it will give you the mass of your liquid.

4) You can then use the equation on this page to <u>find the density</u>.

5) This can be done with lots of different volumes of the same liquid and then you can take a <u>mean</u> of the densities. The mean is calculated by <u>adding up</u> all the values for density and then <u>dividing</u> by <u>how many values</u> you took (e.g. (1.1 + 1.0 + 1.2) ÷ 3 = 1.1).

To find the density of a solid object

1) Use a <u>balance</u> to measure the object's mass.

2) If it's a <u>regular shaped</u> solid then just calculate the <u>volume</u> (e.g. use width × height × length for a cuboid) and use the <u>formula</u> above for density.

3) For an <u>irregular shaped</u> solid, you can find its volume by <u>submerging</u> it in a measuring cylinder full of water.

4) Record the <u>volume of water</u> in the measuring cylinder and <u>then</u> put the object in.

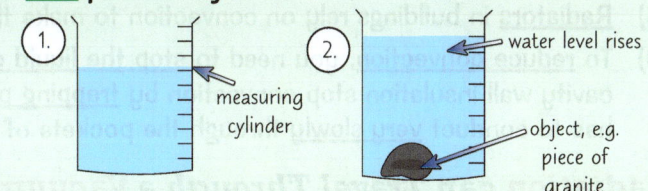
measuring cylinder
water level rises
object, e.g. piece of granite

5) Record the new volume of water and <u>subtract</u> the <u>original volume</u> — this is the volume of your object. Now you can use the <u>equation</u> above to calculate the object's <u>density</u>.

I'm feeling a bit dense after that lot...

There's a lot of maths on this page, so here's a practice question to sum it all up.

Q1   A class records the data for the volumes and masses of three cubes of copper in the table on the right. Calculate the mean density in g/cm³.   [3 marks]

Mass (g)	Volume (cm³)
178	20
119	14
93	10

Energy Transfer and Conduction

So you know energy can be transferred <u>by heating</u>, but what does that actually <u>mean</u>? I'm glad you asked...

Energy is Transferred by *Heating* in *Three* Different Ways

1) When an object is <u>heated</u>, <u>energy is transferred</u> and the object's <u>temperature increases</u>.

2) When energy is transferred by heating from a <u>hotter</u> object to a <u>cooler</u> object, the hotter object's <u>temperature</u> will <u>decrease</u> and the cooler object's <u>temperature</u> will <u>increase</u>.

3) The three ways that energy can be transferred <u>by heating</u> are: <u>conduction</u>, <u>convection</u> and <u>radiation</u>.

Conduction *Occurs Mainly in* Solids

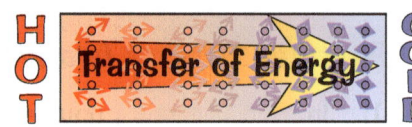

1) When an object is <u>heated</u> the energy transferred to the object is shared across the <u>kinetic</u> energies of the <u>particles</u> in the object.

2) The particles in the <u>hotter</u> part of the object <u>vibrate</u> more and <u>collide</u> with each other, transferring <u>kinetic energy</u> to <u>neighbouring particles</u>. These then also vibrate faster, <u>increasing</u> the <u>temperature</u> of that part of the object. This continues until the extra energy is <u>spread out evenly</u> across all the particles, and the <u>temperature</u> of the object is the <u>same</u> everywhere.

> <u>CONDUCTION</u> is the process where <u>vibrating particles</u> pass extra <u>energy</u> to neighbouring particles through <u>kinetic energy</u>.

3) Generally conduction occurs mainly in <u>solids</u>, as particles are held tightly together. Particles in <u>liquids</u> and <u>gases</u> are <u>further apart</u>, so conduction of energy is a lot <u>slower</u>.

4) <u>Metals</u> are good conductors because they have <u>free electrons</u> (electrons that are free to move around) which can carry this <u>kinetic energy</u> around the solid.

Higher

Convection *Occurs in* Fluids

1) Convection happens in <u>fluids</u> (liquids and gases) because the particles are <u>free</u> to <u>move around</u>.

2) When you <u>heat up</u> a liquid or gas, the particles gain energy and <u>move faster</u>. The fluid <u>expands</u> and becomes <u>less dense</u>.

Convection can't happen in solids because the particles can't move (just vibrate on the spot).

3) The <u>warmer</u>, <u>less dense</u> fluid <u>rises</u> above its <u>colder</u>, <u>denser</u> surroundings.

4) As the warm fluid rises, cooler fluid takes its place. The process continues until you end up with a <u>circulation</u> of fluid (<u>convection currents</u>).

> <u>CONVECTION</u> occurs when the particles with <u>more kinetic energy</u> move from the <u>hotter region</u> to the <u>cooler region</u> — and take their kinetic energy with them.

5) <u>Radiators</u> in buildings rely on convection to make the warm air <u>circulate</u> round the room.

6) To <u>reduce convection</u>, you need to <u>stop the liquid or gas moving</u>. Clothes, blankets and foam cavity wall insulation stop convection by <u>trapping pockets of air</u>. The air can't move so the energy has to conduct <u>very slowly</u> through the pockets of air, as well as the material in between.

Higher

Radiation *can Travel Through a* Vacuum

1) For energy to be transferred by conduction or convection, you need <u>particles</u>. But energy can also be transferred by <u>radiation</u>, which can travel through a <u>vacuum</u>. When energy is transferred by <u>heating</u> by radiation, the energy is carried by <u>infrared waves</u> (see page 122).

2) <u>All</u> objects continuously <u>emit and absorb</u> radiation — the <u>hotter</u> an object gets, the <u>more</u> radiation it <u>emits</u>.

3) <u>Cooler objects</u> will <u>absorb</u> the radiation emitted by hotter things, so their <u>temperature increases</u>.

4) <u>Matt black</u> surfaces are very <u>good absorbers and emitters</u> of radiation.

5) <u>Light-coloured</u>, <u>smooth</u> and <u>shiny</u> objects are <u>poor absorbers and emitters</u> of radiation.

Conduction — nothing to do with organising an orchestra...

Sometimes I'm just too funny for my own good. Pure gold this stuff.

Q1   Explain how conduction occurs in terms of particle collisions and the transfer of kinetic energy. [2 marks]

Investigating Energy Transfer by Heating

There are a bunch of <u>interesting experiments</u> that show the different methods of heat transfer — here are a few.

There are Lots of *Experiments* that Show *Heat Transfer*

Conduction

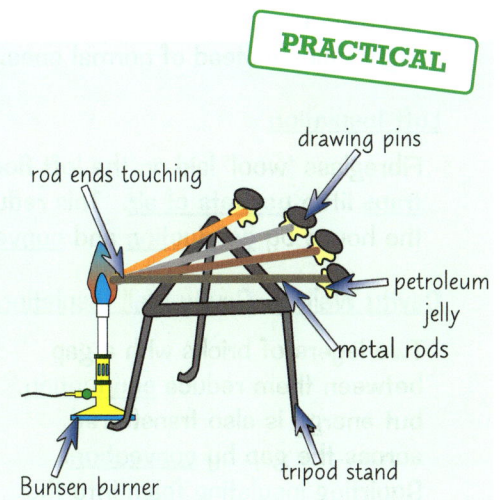

PRACTICAL

1) Set up this experiment using <u>4 different types of metal rod</u> (e.g. copper, iron, brass and aluminium) with a <u>drawing pin</u> stuck with petroleum jelly to the <u>end</u> of each rod — start with the Bunsen burner <u>turned off</u>.

2) Make sure the other ends of the rods are all <u>brought together</u> over the Bunsen burner so that they can be <u>heated equally</u>.

3) <u>Turn on</u> the Bunsen burner to the <u>blue flame</u> and let it heat the rods — <u>start a timer</u> when you turn on the burner.

4) When the heat reaches the end of the rod, it will <u>melt</u> the petroleum jelly and the drawing pin will <u>fall off</u>.

5) Record the <u>time</u> it takes for each of the drawing pins to fall off.

6) You can work out which metals are <u>more conductive</u> by seeing which drawing pins fell off <u>faster</u>.

rod ends touching
drawing pins
petroleum jelly
metal rods
Bunsen burner
tripod stand

Convection

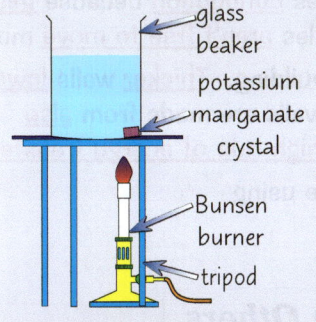

PRACTICAL

glass beaker
potassium manganate crystal
Bunsen burner
tripod

1) Fill a beaker with water and use forceps to put a crystal of <u>potassium manganate(VII)</u> into the <u>bottom</u> of <u>one side</u> of the beaker.

2) Light the Bunsen burner and set it to the <u>blue flame</u>.

3) Put the Bunsen flame <u>directly</u> underneath the crystal and <u>see what happens...</u>

4) The crystal will turn part of the water <u>purple</u>, and this purple water will follow the <u>convection currents</u> in the beaker.

Radiation

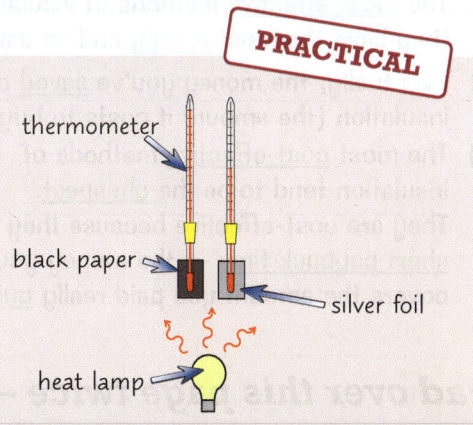

PRACTICAL

1) Use <u>tape</u> to attach <u>black paper</u> to the end of a thermometer, and <u>silver foil</u> to the end of another.

2) <u>Clamp</u> the thermometers the <u>same distance</u> away (e.g. 10 cm) from a heat lamp.

3) Record the <u>temperatures</u> on the two thermometers.

4) Switch on the <u>heat lamp</u> and record the temperature on the thermometers after <u>10 minutes</u>.

5) You can tell which colour is the better <u>absorber of heat</u> by which thermometer has gone up <u>more</u>.

thermometer
black paper
silver foil
heat lamp

Who doesn't love a good experiment...

Make sure to think about the different safety precautions you need to take during these practicals.

Q1   A student has two materials, A and B. Briefly describe an experiment that the student could do to determine which material is the better absorber of heat.

[4 marks]

Reducing Unwanted Energy Transfers

A house can lose energy by convection, conduction and radiation, but there are a few ways you can stop this.

Insulating Your House Reduces Energy Loss

1) Energy in the home can be transferred usefully (e.g. by radiators) and wasted (e.g. by windows).

2) To save energy, you can use appliances that have been made more efficient, e.g. use energy-saving light bulbs instead of normal ones. You can also design your house to reduce energy losses:

Loft Insulation

Fibreglass 'wool' laid on the loft floor and ceiling traps little pockets of air. This reduces energy loss from the house by conduction and convection.

Cavity Walls & Cavity Wall Insulation

Two layers of bricks with a gap between them reduce conduction, but energy is also transferred across the gap by convection. Squirting insulating foam into the gap traps pockets of air to minimise this convection.

> Energy is still lost from the walls by radiation. Also, if there are any spaces where air is not trapped, there'll still be some convection too.

Hot Water Tank Jacket

Reduces conduction, keeping the water hot.

Double Glazing

Reduces conduction using two layers of glass with an air gap between them.

Thick Curtains

Reduce heat loss by convection and conduction through the windows.

Draught-proofing

Strips of foam and plastic around doors and windows stop hot air going out and cold air coming in — reducing convection.

3) Lots of these insulation methods use 'trapped air' — this massively reduces conduction because gases don't conduct heat well, and it reduces convection because the gas particles aren't free to move much.

4) The thickness of walls affects how quickly energy is transferred out of a building. Thicker walls lower the rate of energy transfer. The thermal conductivity of the material the walls are made from also affects the rate of energy transfer. A high thermal conductivity means a high rate of energy transfer.

5) It's important for the environment to insulate your house properly because using less energy for heating reduces your carbon footprint (see page 106).

Some Insulating Methods are More Cost-Effective Than Others

1) The most effective methods of insulation are ones that give you the biggest annual saving — they save the most energy and so save you the most money each year on your heating bills.

2) Eventually, the money you've saved on heating bills will equal the initial cost of putting in the insulation (the amount it costs to buy and install). The time this takes is called the payback time.

3) The most cost-effective methods of insulation tend to be the cheapest. They are cost-effective because they have a short payback time — the money you save covers the amount you paid really quickly.

$$\text{payback time} = \frac{\text{installation cost}}{\text{annual saving}}$$

Read over this page twice — double gazing...

Learn all of these insulating methods off by heart — make sure you understand which method of energy transfer each insulation type reduces, and don't forget that some methods reduce more than one type of heat loss.

Q1 The cost of installing cavity wall insulation is £700. The insulation saves £200 per year.
Another insulating method is draught-proofing, which costs a household £150 and saves £25 per year.
a) Calculate the payback times for the two insulation methods. [2 marks]
b) Which method is the more cost-effective? [1 mark]

Evaluating Energy Costs

There are lots of ways to <u>investigate</u> energy costs, including looking on the internet, or just looking on a label.

Domestic *Wind* and *Solar Power* can *Save You Money*

There are several pros and cons to using <u>wind turbines</u> or <u>solar panels</u> — see p.107.
A big advantage of using them <u>at home</u> is that they can <u>save you money</u> and even <u>make you money</u>:

1) Homeowners who <u>generate electricity</u> from <u>renewable energy</u> get <u>paid</u> for energy <u>they produce</u> under a scheme called '<u>Feed-in Tariff</u>' (FIT). They are paid for the energy they <u>produce</u> and <u>use</u> themselves.

2) An <u>export tariff</u> is paid for any electricity they <u>don't use</u> but instead put into the <u>national grid</u>.

3) They will also see their energy bills <u>fall</u> because they are <u>using less energy</u> from the national grid.

There are <u>advantages</u> and <u>disadvantages</u> to using domestic <u>wind and solar power</u>:

- Wind and solar power have <u>expensive start-up costs</u> and <u>long payback times</u> — but eventually you could make a <u>profit</u>.
- The UK doesn't have the best weather for these — it's not very <u>sunny</u> and not always very <u>windy</u>...
- <u>Maintenance costs</u> are <u>low</u>.
- Some people <u>don't like</u> how wind turbines or solar panels <u>look</u>.

Type of domestic power	Solar	Wind
Initial cost (£)	6000	15 000
Annual saving (£)	200	320
Feed-in tariff (£)	240	430
Payback time (years)	13.5	20

Energy Bands and Power Ratings *Give You Information About Efficiency*

Energy Bands

1) <u>Energy banding</u> shows how <u>energy efficient</u> an appliance is. Lots of <u>household appliances</u> such as washing machines and light bulbs will have an energy band <u>label</u> on them.

2) An energy band label has 7 '<u>bands</u>' from A to G, <u>A</u> is the <u>best</u> and <u>G</u> is the <u>worst</u>.

3) If the appliance is in the A band then it is <u>very energy efficient</u> and will have <u>low running costs</u>.

4) Lower down in the G band, the appliance is <u>not energy efficient</u>, so the <u>running costs</u> might be <u>higher</u>.

Energy Efficiency

1) Electrical appliances have <u>power ratings</u> that show what <u>power</u> the appliance works at for a <u>certain voltage</u>.

2) The <u>efficiency</u> of an appliance tells you <u>how much</u> of this power is <u>useful</u>.

> A <u>kettle</u> has a power rating of 2.4 kW. If a kettle has an energy efficiency of <u>80%</u> then 80% of the power is being used to <u>boil water</u>. If <u>two kettles</u> have the <u>same power rating</u> but <u>different efficiencies</u>, the kettle with the <u>higher efficiency</u> boils water <u>quicker</u>. The higher efficiency kettle uses <u>less energy</u> overall because it's switched on for less time.

3) Light bulbs in your house also have <u>different powers</u> and <u>efficiencies</u>. A more efficient light bulb needs <u>less power</u> to give off the <u>same brightness</u>.

4) <u>Cheaper</u> light bulbs tend to have a <u>high wattage</u>, <u>cost more</u> to run and <u>need replacing</u>

Type of bulb	Price of bulb (£)	Wattage needed	Monthly cost (10 hours a day) (£)	Life span (hours)
Filament	1	60	2.16	1000
Halogen	1.5	45	1.62	3000
LED	5	10	0.36	24000

more often — it's often worth <u>paying more</u> for a bulb because it'll <u>save you money</u> in the long run.

Make sure your revising efficiency is high...

Learn how to use terms such as efficiency and power output when investigating electrical appliances.

Q1   State what is meant by the 'Feed-in Tariff' scheme.   [1 mark]

Revision Questions for Unit 3b

Well, that wraps up <u>Unit 3b</u> — take a little breather (you've earned it) and come back and try these.

- Try these questions and <u>tick off each one</u> when you <u>get it right</u>.
- When you've done <u>all the questions</u> for a topic and are <u>completely happy</u> with it, tick off the topic.

Efficiency and Energy Resources (p.105-109) ☑

1) What is the equation for % efficiency?
2) Give the equation for calculating the units of energy used in kWh.
3) Name the three main fossil fuels.
4) What is meant by the term carbon footprint?
5) Give a disadvantage of burning fossil fuels.
6) Which gas from burning coal causes acid rain?
7) What is used to drive turbines at most power stations?
8) True or false? Renewable energy has no carbon footprint.
9) Give three examples of renewable energy resources.

The National Grid (p.110) ☐

10) When in the day does the demand for electricity increase?
11) What is meant by the 'base load'?
12) What happens to any extra electricity Britain produces?
13) How is energy lost when transmitting electricity at a high current?
14) What is increased by a step-up transformer?

Density and Matter (p.111) ☐

15) What is the equation for density?
16) What typically has the highest density — solids, liquids or gases?
17) How would you measure the density of an irregularly shaped object?

Energy Transfer (p.112-115) ☐

18) What state of matter is the best at conducting heat?
19) What type of energy is transferred in heat transfer?
20) Why are metals such good conductors of heat?
21) Why can't convection happen in solids?
22) Why does the warm fluid rise above the cold fluid in convection?
23) What type of waves carry heat radiation?
24) Which is a better absorber and emitter of heat radiation — a matt black object or a shiny object?
25) Describe an experiment to demonstrate conduction.
26) Give three examples of ways to insulate a house.
27) Do cost-effective methods have a short or long payback time?
28) Give an advantage and disadvantage of installing solar panels on your home.
29) How many levels are there to the energy banding system?

Wave Basics

Waves transfer <u>energy</u> from one place to another without transferring any <u>matter</u> (stuff). Clever so and sos.

Waves *Transfer Energy* in the *Direction* they are *Travelling*

When waves travel through a medium, the <u>particles</u> of the medium <u>vibrate</u> and <u>transfer energy</u> between each other. BUT overall, the particles stay in the <u>same place</u> — <u>only energy</u> is transferred.

> For example, if you drop a twig into a calm pool of water, <u>ripples</u> form on the water's surface. The ripples <u>don't</u> carry the <u>water</u> (or the twig) away with them though. Similarly, if you strum a <u>guitar string</u> and create <u>sound waves</u>, the sound waves don't carry the <u>air</u> away from the guitar and create a <u>vacuum</u>.

1) The <u>amplitude</u> of a wave is the <u>displacement</u> from the <u>rest position</u> to a <u>crest</u> or <u>trough</u>.

2) The <u>wavelength</u> is the length of a <u>full cycle</u> of the wave, e.g. from <u>crest to crest</u> (or from <u>compression</u> to <u>compression</u> — see below).

3) <u>Frequency</u> is the <u>number of complete waves or cycles</u> passing a certain point <u>per second</u>. Frequency is measured in <u>hertz</u> (<u>Hz</u>). 1 Hz is <u>1 wave per second</u>.

4) Sources can emit waves with a <u>varying</u> wavelength. You might be asked to find the <u>mean wavelength</u>.

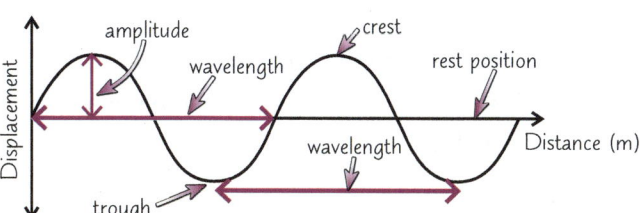

EXAMPLE: Calculate the mean wavelength of the waves shown.

To calculate the mean wavelength, divide the total length of all the waves by the number of full wave cycles.

There are 4 full wave cycles. So mean wavelength = 2.0 ÷ 4 = 0.5 m

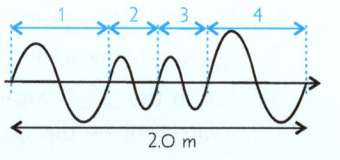

Transverse Waves *Have Sideways* Vibrations

1) In <u>transverse waves</u>, the vibrations are <u>perpendicular</u> (at 90°) to the <u>direction</u> the wave travels.

2) <u>Most waves</u> are transverse, including <u>all electromagnetic waves</u> (p.120), e.g. light, and <u>ripples</u> and waves in <u>water</u>.

3) There are <u>two</u> types of transverse wave graph:

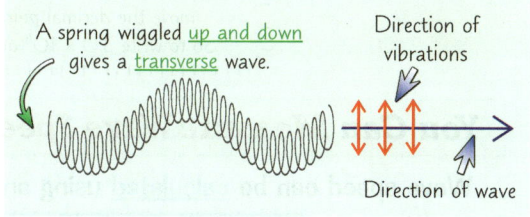

A spring wiggled <u>up and down</u> gives a <u>transverse</u> wave.

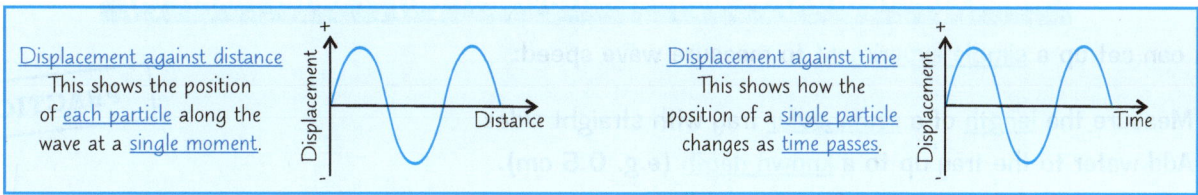

<u>Displacement against distance</u>
This shows the position of <u>each particle</u> along the wave at a <u>single moment</u>.

<u>Displacement against time</u>
This shows how the position of a <u>single particle</u> changes as <u>time passes</u>.

Longitudinal Waves *Have Parallel* Vibrations

1) In <u>longitudinal waves</u>, the vibrations are <u>parallel</u> to the <u>direction</u> the wave travels.

2) <u>Sound waves</u> are longitudinal waves.

3) Longitudinal waves <u>squash up</u> and <u>stretch out</u> the arrangement of particles in the medium they pass through, making <u>compressions</u> (<u>high pressure</u>, lots of particles) and <u>rarefactions</u> (<u>low pressure</u>, fewer particles).

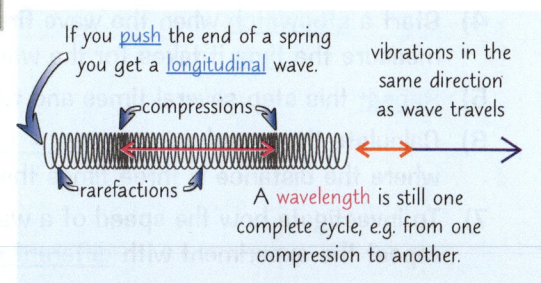

If you <u>push</u> the end of a spring you get a <u>longitudinal</u> wave.

A wavelength is still one complete cycle, e.g. from one compression to another.

What about Mexican waves...

You won't get far unless you understand these wave basics. Try a question to test your knowledge.

Q1   Give an example of   a) a transverse wave   b) a longitudinal wave   [2 marks]

Wave Speed

Now it's time to bring a little bit of maths into all of this — there's not too much though, don't worry...

Wavelength and Frequency are linked — so are Energy and Amplitude

1) For a wave at a given speed, the wavelength of the wave is inversely proportional to its frequency — as the wavelength increases the frequency decreases.

2) The energy of a wave is linked to its amplitude — a higher energy wave has a bigger amplitude.

Wave Speed = Wavelength × Frequency

1) Wave speed is how fast a wave is moving.

2) It is the speed at which energy is being transferred through the medium.

3) The wave speed equation can be used for all types of wave, including water, sound and electromagnetic waves.

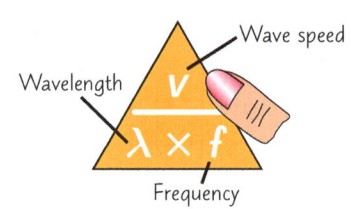

wave speed (m/s) = wavelength (m) × frequency (Hz)

EXAMPLE:
A radio wave has a frequency of 12 MHz.
Find its wavelength. (The speed of radio waves in air is 3.0 × 10⁸ m/s.)

This number is given with a prefix. The M in front of Hz means mega — mega means 1 000 000.

1) Change the frequency into hertz.
2) Rearrange the wave speed equation for wavelength.
3) Put in the values you've been given.
   Watch out — the speed is in standard form (see below).

$12 \times 1\,000\,000 = 12\,000\,000$ Hz
wavelength = wave speed ÷ frequency
$= (3.0 \times 10^8) \div (12\,000\,000)$
$= 25$ m

Standard form is used for writing very big or very small numbers in a more manageable way. To write a number in standard form out in full, you move the decimal point. How to move it depends on the power of 10 — if it's positive, move the decimal point that number of places right, and if it's negative, move it that number of places left. So to write 3.0×10^8 out in full, move the decimal point 8 places to the right, which gives 300 000 000.

You Can Measure Wave Speed

Wave speed can be calculated using an equation like the speed equation on page 197.

wave speed (m/s) = distance travelled (m) ÷ time taken (s)

You can set up a simple experiment to measure wave speed:

PRACTICAL

1) Measure the length of a rectangular tray with straight sides.

2) Add water to the tray up to a known depth (e.g. 0.5 cm).

3) Lift one end of the tray up a few cm and then put it back down — a wave should start moving along the surface of the water.

4) Start a stopwatch when the wave first hits the end of the tray and measure the time it takes for the wave to travel three lengths of the tray.

5) Repeat this step several times and take the mean of your results.

6) Calculate the speed using speed = distance ÷ time, where the distance is three times the length of the tray.

7) To investigate how the speed of a water wave changes with depth, repeat the experiment with different depths of water.

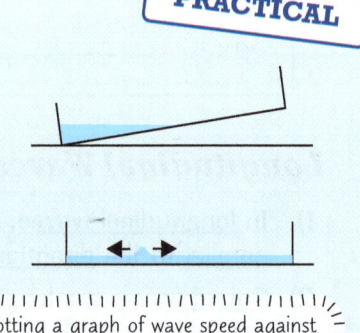

Plotting a graph of wave speed against water depth should give you points that can be joined by a smooth curve.

Increasing wave speed increases risk of wrist injury...

Make sure you understand each step of the practical above — you could be tested on it in the exams.

Q1   Calculate the frequency of a sound wave with a wave speed of 340 m/s and a wavelength of 20 cm. [2 marks]

Reflection and Refraction

All waves <u>reflect</u> and <u>refract</u>. 'What does that mean?' you ask. Read on...

Waves are *Transmitted* and *Reflected* at *Boundaries*

When a <u>wave</u> meets a <u>boundary</u> between two materials, various things can happen. Here are two of them:

1) The wave may be <u>TRANSMITTED</u> through the second material — the wave <u>carries on travelling</u> through the new material. This often leads to <u>refraction</u> (see below).

2) The wave may be <u>REFLECTED</u> — this is where the incoming ray isn't <u>transmitted</u>, but instead is '<u>sent back</u>' away from the second material.

What actually happens depends on the wavelength of the wave and the properties of the materials involved.

Refraction — *Waves Changing Direction* at a *Boundary*

1) Waves travel at <u>different speeds</u> in different materials. When a wave crosses a <u>boundary</u> between materials it <u>changes speed</u>.

2) The <u>frequency</u> of a wave <u>stays the same</u> (it can't change) as it crosses a boundary from one medium (material) to another. As $v = \lambda f$, this means if the <u>speed</u> of the wave changes, the <u>wavelength</u> must also change. The change in wavelength is <u>proportional</u> to the change in wave speed — the wavelength <u>decreases</u> if the wave <u>slows down</u>, and <u>increases</u> if it <u>speeds up</u>.

3) If the wave hits the boundary at an <u>angle</u> to the normal, this change of <u>speed</u> causes a <u>change in direction</u> — this is <u>refraction</u>. If the wave is travelling <u>along the normal</u> it will <u>change speed</u>, but it's <u>NOT refracted</u>.

The normal is an imaginary line at right angles to the surface at the point the wave hits it.

4) The <u>wavefront diagrams</u> below show a wave slowing down as it crosses a boundary.

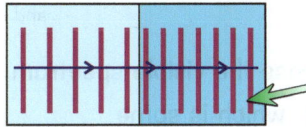

The wavefronts are closer together, showing a decrease in wavelength (and so a decrease in speed).

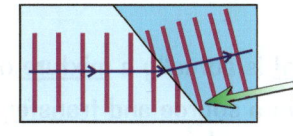

The wave hits a different medium at an angle, so the wave changes direction.

A wavefront is a line used to represent a crest (or trough) of a wave.

5) The <u>greater</u> the <u>change</u> in speed, the <u>more</u> a wave <u>bends</u> (changes direction).

6) The angle between the incident wave and the normal is the <u>angle of incidence</u>.

7) The angle between the refracted wave and the normal is the <u>angle of refraction</u>.

8) The wave bends <u>towards the normal</u> if it <u>slows down</u>, and <u>away</u> from the normal if it <u>speeds up</u>.

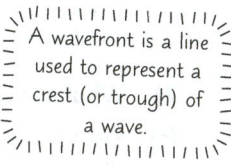

Water Waves *Reflect and Refract*

The best thing about water waves is that you can actually <u>see</u> the <u>wavefronts</u>. A <u>ripple tank</u> can be used to demonstrate their reflection and refraction.

A sudden change in water depth acts as a boundary.

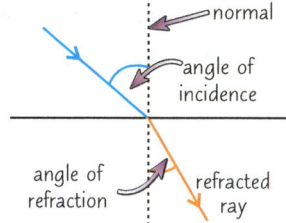

REFRACTION:

When water waves pass into <u>shallower</u> water, they <u>slow down</u> and their <u>wavelength decreases</u> (their frequency doesn't change). If they're at an angle to the normal, they <u>refract</u>. If they pass into <u>deeper</u> water, they <u>speed up</u> and their <u>wavelength increases</u>.

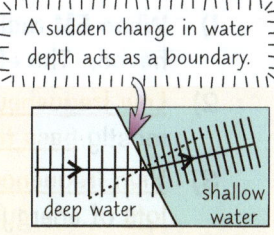

REFLECTION:

When water waves hit an object, they are <u>reflected</u>. The <u>angles</u> the incident and reflected waves make with the normal are always <u>equal</u>. (The angle between the normal and the reflected wave is called the <u>angle of reflection</u>.)

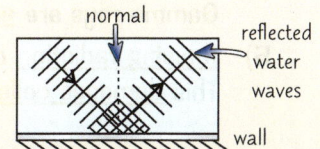

I'll give you some time to reflect on this page...

So the angle at which a wave hits a boundary determines whether it refracts or not. How fantabulous.

Q1 A wave slows down as it passes a boundary into a different medium. With reference to the wave speed equation, explain the change of the wavelength of the wave.

[2 marks]

Electromagnetic Waves

You know that light is a wave, but did you know that light's just one small part of the EM spectrum...

There's a Continuous Spectrum of EM Waves

Electromagnetic waves are vibrations of electric and magnetic fields (rather than vibrations of particles). This means they can travel through a vacuum.

1) Electromagnetic (EM) waves are transverse waves (p.117).

2) They all travel at the same speed of 3×10^8 m/s through space (a vacuum). This speed is very fast, but finite (so it always takes EM waves some time to travel from one point to another). However, they travel at different speeds in different materials.

3) EM waves vary in wavelength from around 10^{-15} m to more than 10^4 m, and those with shorter wavelengths have higher frequencies (from $v = \lambda f$ on page 118).

4) We group them based on their wavelength and frequency — there are seven basic types, but the different groups merge to form a continuous spectrum.

5) Our eyes can only detect a small part of this spectrum — visible light. Different colours of light have different wavelengths. From longest to shortest — red, orange, yellow, green, blue, indigo, violet.

6) Electromagnetic waves are also known as electromagnetic radiation.

wavelength	RADIO WAVES	MICRO WAVES	INFRA RED	VISIBLE LIGHT	ULTRA VIOLET	X-RAYS	GAMMA RAYS
	1 m $- 10^4$ m	10^{-2} m	10^{-5} m	10^{-7} m	10^{-8} m	10^{-10} m	10^{-15} m

Long wavelength, low frequency and low energy. → Short wavelength, high frequency and high energy.

7) What we see as white light is actually a mixture of all of the colours across the visible spectrum.

8) EM waves spread out from a source and transfer energy to an absorber, which is some distance away. For example, when you warm yourself by an electric heater, infrared waves transfer thermal energy from the heater (the source) to you (the absorber).

9) The higher the frequency of the EM wave, the more energy it transfers.

Some EM Radiation Can be Harmful to People

1) When EM radiation enters living tissue — like you — it's often harmless, but sometimes it creates havoc. The effects of each type of radiation are based on how much energy the wave transfers.

2) Low frequency waves, like radio waves, don't transfer much energy and mostly pass through soft tissue without being absorbed.

'Radiation' can refer to electromagnetic waves, or energy given out by a radioactive source.

3) High frequency waves like UV, X-rays and gamma rays all transfer lots of energy and so can cause lots of damage.

4) X-rays, high energy UV rays and gamma rays are types of ionising radiation. Gamma rays are emitted by some radioactive substances (p.217).

5) Ionising radiation can interact with atoms, knocking electrons off them. This damages cells — it can cause gene mutation or cell destruction, and cancer.

Learn about the EM spectrum and wave goodbye to exam stress...

Here's a handy mnemonic for the order of EM waves: 'Rock Music Is Very Useful for eXperiments with Goats'.

Q1   State one possible effect of the human body being exposed to ionising radiation.   [1 mark]

Q2   Put the following in order of increasing wavelength: microwaves, X-rays, visible light.   [1 mark]

Uses of Electromagnetic Waves

EM waves are always being used around us for day-to-day activities — here are some examples.

Radio Waves are Used Mainly for Communication

1) Radio and TV signals can be sent by radio waves.
2) Very short wavelength radio waves are used for FM radio and TV.
3) Longer wavelength radio waves can be used to send radio signals around the world.

Microwaves are Used for Satellites and Cooking

1) Communication with satellites uses microwaves, e.g. for satellite TV and mobile phones.
2) A signal is sent into space to a satellite dish high above the Earth.
3) The satellite sends the signal back to Earth in a different direction.
4) A satellite dish on the ground receives the signal.
5) It's best to use a frequency of microwave that can pass through Earth's watery atmosphere

1) Microwave ovens use microwaves to cook food.
2) The oven produces microwaves, which are absorbed by water in the food.
3) Energy carried by the microwaves is transferred to the water molecules, causing them to heat up.
4) This causes the rest of the food to heat up and quickly cook.

Geosynchronous Satellites Orbit the Earth Once in 24 Hours

Higher

1) Satellites in geosynchronous orbits take 24 hours for one full orbit of Earth. This is the same as the time taken for the Earth itself to rotate once.

2) So a geosynchronous satellite will only be in the exact same position above the Earth once every 24 hours.

3) A geostationary satellite is a special type of geosynchronous satellite. It orbits above the Earth's equator.

4) Because the satellite's orbit is in the same plane as the Earth's rotation, it stays in the same position above Earth always.

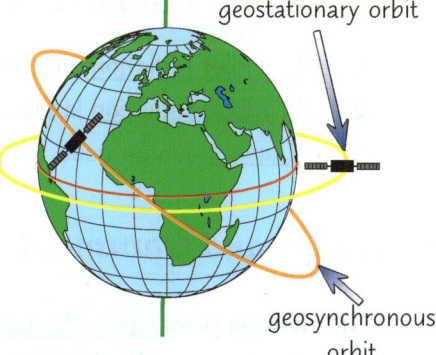

geostationary orbit

geosynchronous orbit

5) The advantage of this is that the satellite can remain in constant communication with a base station on Earth. You don't even have to move any satellite dishes, because the satellite is in the same position above the Earth at all times.

6) A satellite can only communicate with part of the Earth at one time. So multiple satellites are used to send signals between distant points on Earth. E.g. in the diagram below, neither satellite can 'see' both points A and C due to the curvature of the Earth. So signals between these points must be 'bounced' between the two satellites and an additional receiving/transmitting station located at point B.

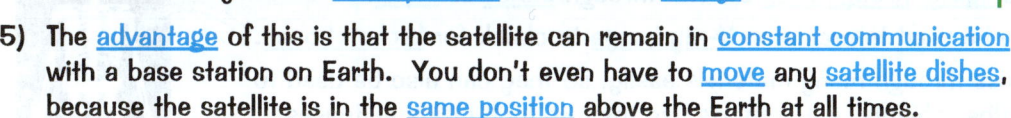

7) When a signal travels from the Earth to a satellite directly above it and back down to the same point again, it travels twice the height of the satellite's orbit. So if a satellite is at 36 000 km above Earth, a signal sent between two points close together on Earth will actually travel 36 000 × 2 = 72 000 km.

What washes up on tiny beaches? Microwaves...

Who knew we used microwaves for more than cooking chips in less than 3 minutes? Turns out, they're dead handy.

Q1 Give an advantage of geostationary satellites compared to non-geostationary satellites.　　　[1 mark]

More Uses of Electromagnetic Waves

This page gives you even more uses of <u>EM waves</u>... Oh when will it end? (hint: on the next page)

Infrared Radiation Can be Used to Heat Things

TV remote controls use infrared radiation to send signals to the TV.

1) <u>Infrared</u> (IR) radiation is <u>given out</u> by <u>all objects</u>.

2) The <u>hotter</u> the object, the <u>more</u> infrared radiation it gives out.

3) When an object <u>absorbs</u> infrared radiation, <u>thermal energy</u> is transferred to the object and it <u>warms up</u>.

4) Infrared radiation can be <u>used</u> in many ways:

> 1) <u>Infrared cameras</u> detect IR radiation and create a <u>picture</u>.
> 2) This is useful for seeing where a house is <u>losing energy</u>.
> 3) It can also allow you to see <u>hot objects</u> in the <u>dark</u>.

> 1) Infrared radiation can be used to <u>warm things</u>.
> 2) <u>Electric heaters</u> and some <u>cookers</u> use IR radiation.

The different colours mean different amounts of IR radiation are being detected from those areas. Here, the redder the colour, the more infrared radiation is being detected.

Optical Fibres Use Visible Light to Send Data

IR radiation can be used in optical fibres too.

1) <u>Light</u> is used to <u>see things</u>, but it's also used for <u>communication</u>.

2) <u>Optical fibres</u> are thin <u>glass or plastic tubes</u> that can <u>carry data</u> over long distances.

3) They're often used to send information to <u>telephones</u> or <u>computers</u>.

4) Optical fibres are also used to <u>see inside</u> a person's body during surgery.

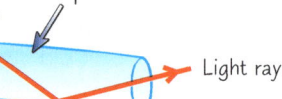

Optical fibre

Light ray

Ultraviolet Radiation Gives You a Suntan

1) <u>Ultraviolet radiation</u> can be used in hospitals to kill microbes and <u>sterilise</u> surgical equipment.

2) <u>Ultraviolet radiation</u> is also produced by <u>the Sun</u>. It's what gives you a <u>suntan</u>.

3) <u>UV lamps</u> can be used to give people a <u>suntan</u> without the Sun (but this can be <u>dangerous</u>).

X-rays and Gamma Rays are Used in Medicine

1) X-rays pass <u>easily through flesh</u> but not through <u>bones</u> or <u>metal</u>.

2) So they can be used to create an <u>X-ray image</u> to check for <u>broken bones</u>.

3) They can pass through many materials easily, so they can also be used to <u>see inside</u> other objects, e.g. airports use them to look inside suitcases.

4) <u>X-rays</u> can also treat people with <u>cancer</u> because they can <u>kill cells</u>.

> 1) <u>Gamma rays</u> (p.120) can also <u>kill cells</u> so they can be used to <u>treat cancer</u> in the same way as X-rays.
> 2) They can also be used to <u>sterilise</u> (kill germs on) food and medical equipment.
>   The food or equipment is <u>blasted</u> with <u>gamma rays</u>, which <u>kills</u> any <u>living</u> things on it.
> 3) Gamma rays are also used in <u>medical imaging</u> to <u>see inside</u> your body (see p.222).

Don't lie to an X-ray — they can see right through you...

I hate to say it, but go back over the last pages and read all of the uses of EM waves again to really learn 'em.

Q1 State two uses of X-rays.   [2 marks]

Q2 State one use of ultraviolet light.   [1 mark]

Revision Questions for Unit 3c

Wave goodbye to Unit 3c — there's a lot of complicated stuff in this unit, so best make sure it's sunk in...

• Try these questions and tick off each one when you get it right.
• When you've done all the questions for a topic and are completely happy with it, tick off the topic.

Wave Basics (p.117-118) ☐

1) Define the terms amplitude, wavelength and frequency of a wave. ☐
2) What is a transverse wave? ☐
3) Sketch a distance-displacement graph for a transverse wave. ☐
4) What is a longitudinal wave? ☐
5) What type of wave is a sound wave? ☐
6) Describe the relationship between the frequency of a wave and its wavelength. ☐
7) Describe the relationship between the amplitude of a wave and its energy. ☐
8) What are the two equations used to calculate wave speed? ☐
9) Describe an experiment that can be used to measure the wave speed of a water wave. ☐

Reflection and Refraction (p.119) ☐

10) Name two things that can happen to a wave when it meets a boundary. ☐
11) Sketch a diagram showing the wavefronts of a water wave as it reflects. ☐
12) True or false? The frequency of a wave doesn't change at a boundary. ☐
13) During refraction, what happens to the wavelength of a wave if it speeds up? ☐
14) What is the angle of incidence of a wave? ☐

Electromagnetic Waves (p.120-122) ☐

15) Are electromagnetic waves transverse or longitudinal? ☐
16) What are the seven types of EM radiation in order from longest to shortest wavelength? ☐
17) Which types of EM radiation can be harmful to people? ☐
18) Describe the orbit of a geostationary satellite. ☐
19) A signal sent from Earth to a satellite and back again will travel a distance equal to
   a) the satellite's orbit height   or   b) twice the satellite's orbit height? ☐
20) Name one use of each of the following:
   a) Infrared radiation
   b) Visible light
   c) Ultraviolet light
   d) X-rays
   e) Gamma rays
   f) Microwaves ☐

Classification

It seems to be a basic human urge to want to classify things — that's the case in biology anyway...

Classification is Organising Living Organisms into Groups

1) There are millions of different organisms living on Earth and they come in a huge range of shapes and sizes — from small and simple (like bacteria) to large and complex (like blue whales). They also have a wide variety of physical features — e.g. wings, beaks, claws, teeth, leaves, branches, etc.

2) All of these organisms can be organised into groups. For example:
   - Plants can be divided into two major groups — flowering plants (e.g. daisies) and non-flowering plants (such as ferns and mosses).
   - Animals can also be divided into two major groups — invertebrates (which lack a backbone, e.g. insects) and vertebrates (which have a backbone, e.g. mammals).

3) There are different ways of classifying organisms, and all organisms are part of more than one group.

Organisms with Similar Features can be Classified into the Same Group

1) Organisms can be classified based on similarities in their morphological characteristics — these are features of their internal and external structure, e.g. whether something has lungs or gills, how many legs it has, what colour it is, etc.

2) Organisms can also be classified using DNA analysis — this involves looking for similarities in their DNA.

3) Morphological characteristics are used to classify organisms in the five kingdom classification system. In this system, living organisms are first divided into five groups called kingdoms. These are:

   > 1) Animals — fish, mammals, reptiles, etc.
   > 2) Plants — grasses, trees, etc.
   > 3) Fungi — mushrooms and toadstools, yeasts, all that mouldy stuff on your loaf of bread (yuck).
   > 4) Bacteria — single-celled organisms without a nucleus.
   > 5) Single-celled organisms with a nucleus, e.g. algae.

   Kingdom
   Phylum
   Class
   Order
   Family
   Genus
   Species

4) The kingdoms are then subdivided into smaller and smaller groups that have common features — these are phylum, class, order, family, genus and species. This is called a taxonomic hierarchy. Here's how humans are classified:

Kingdom	Phylum	Class	Order	Family	Genus	Species
Animalia	Chordata	Mammalia	Primates	Hominidae	*Homo*	*sapiens*

The groups in a classification system (from kingdom to species) are called taxa.

5) Having a systematic approach to classification helps scientists to better understand the huge variety of living organisms on Earth, as well as the relationships between them.

Each Organism Has its Own Two-Part Scientific Name in Latin

1) The first part of a scientific (Latin) name refers to the genus that the organism belongs to. This gives you information on the organism's ancestry. The second part refers to the species. E.g. humans are known as *Homo sapiens*. '*Homo*' is the genus and '*sapiens*' is the species.

2) This naming system is used worldwide and means that scientists in different countries or who speak different languages all refer to a particular species by the same name. This helps to avoid the confusion of using common or local names. E.g. over 100 different plant species are commonly called raspberries.

Why did the beaver invite the mushroom to his party?

... because he's a fun-gi. Biologists have the best jokes. Sometimes the genus in a two-part scientific name is abbreviated to a capital letter with a full stop after it. E.g. *Escherichia coli* is often written as *E. coli*.

Q1   What genus does the Eurasian beaver, *Castor fiber*, belong to?   [1 mark]

Adaptations

Life exists in so many different environments because the organisms that live in them have adaptations.

Adaptations *Allow* Organisms *to Survive*

Organisms, including microorganisms, are adapted to live in different environmental conditions. The features or characteristics that allow them to do this are called adaptations. Adaptations can be:

1) Morphological

These are features of an organism's body structure — such as shape or colour. For example:

Arctic animals like the Arctic fox have white fur so they're camouflaged against the snow. This helps them sneak up on prey. Like other animals living in cold places, Arctic foxes also have adaptations to help them retain heat. These include:

- a thick layer of body fat and thick fur,
- a relatively large body mass,
- a rounded shape and compact features (e.g. small ears), which gives them a small surface area compared to their volume.

Surface area can be compared to volume in a ratio, so you can also talk about large or small surface area to volume ratios.

Animals that live in hot places, like the fennec fox, have adaptations to help them lose heat. For example, fennec foxes have:

- a thin layer of body fat,
- large ears, which give them a large surface area compared to their volume.

2) Behavioural

These are ways that organisms behave. For example:

Some animals, such as antelope, live in groups. This means that there are more eyes to look out for predators, which increases an individual antelope's chance of survival.

Some species (e.g. birds) migrate to warmer climates during the winter to avoid the problems of living in cold conditions.

In a nutshell, it's horses for courses...

In the exam, you might have to say how an organism is adapted to its environment. Look at its characteristics (e.g. colour/shape) as well as the conditions it has to cope with (e.g. predation/temperature) and you'll be sorted.

Q1   The figure on the right shows a penguin. Penguins live in the cold, icy environment of the Antarctic. They swim in the sea to hunt for fish to eat. Some penguins also huddle together in large groups to keep warm.

a) What type of adaptation is being described when penguins 'huddle together'?   [1 mark]

b) Explain one morphological adaptation a penguin has to its environment.   [2 marks]

Factors Affecting Population Size

It's tough in the wild — there's always <u>competition</u> for <u>food</u> and other resources.
In fact, competition is one of the <u>key factors</u> affecting <u>population size</u>.

Organisms *Compete* for Resources *to Survive*

1) Organisms need things from their <u>environment</u> and from <u>other organisms</u> in order to <u>survive</u> and <u>reproduce</u>:

   - <u>Plants</u> need <u>light</u>, <u>space</u>, <u>water</u> and <u>minerals</u> from the soil.
   - <u>Animals</u> need <u>space (territory)</u>, <u>shelter</u>, <u>food</u>, <u>water</u> and <u>mates</u>.

2) The <u>size</u> of a <u>population</u> is <u>limited</u> by <u>competition</u> for these <u>resources</u>, as well as by factors such as <u>predation</u> and <u>disease</u> (see below).

3) Organisms often compete with <u>other species</u> (known as <u>interspecific</u> competition) and with members of their <u>own species</u> (called <u>intraspecific</u> competition) for the <u>same resources</u>. For example:

> A population is all the organisms of one species in a habitat (see page 43).

> Red and grey <u>squirrels</u> live in the <u>same habitat</u> and eat the <u>same food</u>. <u>Competition</u> with the grey squirrels for these resources in some areas means there's <u>not enough food</u> for the reds — so the <u>population</u> of red squirrels is <u>decreasing</u>, partly as a result of this <u>interspecific</u> competition.

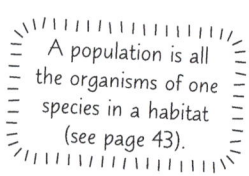

> <u>Plants</u> growing near to each other <u>compete</u> for <u>light</u>. The <u>fastest growing</u> plants reach the light first and start to grow <u>larger</u>, <u>shading</u> the ground below. This <u>reduces</u> the amount of <u>light</u> available for other, <u>smaller plants</u> of the <u>same species</u> (<u>intraspecific competition</u>) and <u>restricts</u> the <u>population size</u> of that species in the area.

Population Size *is also* Affected *by the Following* Factors:

1) *Pollutants*

1) <u>Pesticides</u> can <u>build up</u> in food chains through <u>bioaccumulation</u> (see page 48), reducing the population size of organisms at the top of the food chain.

2) <u>Excess fertilisers</u> released into <u>lakes</u> and <u>ponds</u> cause <u>increased growth</u> of <u>algae</u> (see page 48). The algae <u>block sunlight</u> from plants, which die. Microorganisms feeding on the dead plants use up O_2 in the water, leading to the <u>death</u> of other organisms (e.g. fish).

3) <u>Air pollution</u> (in the form of, e.g. sulfur dioxide released from car exhausts and power stations) can <u>kill</u> sensitive <u>plant species</u> and <u>lichens</u> (see page 49).

2) *Number of Predators*

For example, if the <u>number of lions</u> (predators) <u>decreases</u> then the number of <u>gazelles</u> (prey) might <u>increase</u> because <u>fewer</u> of them will be <u>eaten</u> by the lions.

3) *Disease*

For example, if a <u>new pathogen</u> was introduced into the community then populations may <u>decrease</u> due to <u>illness</u>.

Revision — a factor causing stress in my environment...

Organisms like everything to be just right — temperature, light, food... I'd never get away with being that fussy.

Q1   Give two factors that could affect population size.   [2 marks]

Unit 4a — Classifying Organisms and Biodiversity

Biodiversity

This page is all about the variety of life, and what we can do to maintain it.

Earth's Biodiversity is Important

1) Biodiversity is the variety of different species in an area. It also takes into account the number of individuals within each species — so an area with high biodiversity has many different species living there and each species is present in large numbers.

2) A high level of biodiversity (whether globally or just in a small area) is a good thing — it means that if the environment changes in some way, there's a good chance that at least some species will be able to survive. It also means that we humans can get the most out of the world's resources.

Maintaining Biodiversity Benefits Humans

1) It could provide future medicines — many of the medicines we use today come from plants. Undiscovered plant species may contain new medicinal chemicals. If these plants are allowed to become extinct, perhaps through rainforest destruction, we could miss out on valuable medicines.

2) It helps to provide industrial materials and fuels — plant and animal species are involved in the production of industrial materials (e.g. wood, paper, adhesives and oils) and some fuels. If these species become extinct, these important resources may become more difficult to produce.

3) It provides us with food. For example, maintaining insect biodiversity helps to ensure crop plants are pollinated. Undiscovered plant species could also provide us with potential new food sources.

4) It helps to improve human well-being. For example, people enjoy visiting unspoilt landscapes with a variety of animal and plant species. As well as providing enjoyment and relaxation, these landscapes bring money to an area through tourism and provide job opportunities for local people.

Biodiversity and Endangered Species can be Protected

There are many ways in which we help to protect biodiversity and endangered species. These include:

1) Seed banks — these help to conserve biodiversity by storing the seeds (and therefore genetic material) from lots of different species of plant. Similarly, sperm banks store sperm from endangered animal species to preserve the genetic material of animals that may no longer exist in the future.

2) Captive breeding programmes — breeding animals in captivity (e.g. zoos) can increase the number of a species before releasing them back into the wild.

3) National parks and Sites of Special Scientific Interest (SSSIs) — keeping species in protected areas such as National parks and SSSIs helps to keep them safe from harmful activities like hunting or habitat destruction.

4) The Convention on International Trade in Endangered Species (CITES) — this is an agreement between governments which aims to protect endangered plants and animals by restricting or preventing their international trade.

5) Local Biodiversity Action Plans — these are conservation plans put in place to protect species and restore habitats in a particular area.

The Use of Legislation to Protect Biodiversity can Create Problems...

Protecting biodiversity by law is great for wildlife, but can have negative impacts on people. For example:

> Creating protected areas such as SSSIs (Sites of Special Scientific Interest) preserves local wildlife, but restricts further development, including agricultural development in the area. This could cause problems for farmers who need to expand in order to keep their farm in profit.

If my bank accepted seeds, I wouldn't have to write these gags...

Well who knew protecting biodiversity had so many advantages. That's the last time I vacuum up a spider...

Q1 Explain three ways in which biodiversity and endangered species can be protected. [3 marks]

Investigating Ecosystems

This is where the <u>fun</u> starts. Studying ecology gives you the chance to <u>rummage around</u> in bushes. Hurrah.

Organisms Live in Different Places

1) The <u>abundance</u> of an organism is <u>how many</u> individuals you find in an area (i.e. <u>population size</u>).

2) The <u>distribution</u> of an organism is <u>where</u> an organism is <u>found</u> in a habitat, e.g. in a part of a field.

3) You need to know how to <u>investigate</u> the distribution and abundance of organisms in a <u>habitat</u>.

4) Most of the time it would be <u>too time consuming</u> to measure the <u>number of individuals</u> and <u>distribution</u> of every species in the area you're investigating. So instead you take <u>samples</u>.

5) <u>Abundance</u> can be estimated by <u>counting</u> the number of individuals in the samples taken. These results then need <u>scaling up</u> for the total area (see below).

6) There are a couple of ways to study the <u>distribution</u> of an organism. You can:

   - Measure <u>how common</u> an organism is in <u>two sample areas</u> (e.g. using <u>quadrats</u>) and <u>compare</u> them.

   - Study how the <u>distribution changes</u> across an area, e.g. by placing quadrats <u>along a transect</u> (p.129).

7) You need to know about the <u>sampling methods</u> coming up below and on the next page.

Use a Quadrat to Study The Abundance of Small Organisms

A <u>quadrat</u> is a <u>square</u> frame enclosing a <u>known area</u>, e.g. 1 m².
To estimate the population size of an organism in an area, just follow these simple steps:

1) Place a <u>quadrat</u> on the ground at a <u>random point</u> within your chosen sample area. E.g. divide the area into a <u>grid</u> and use a <u>random number generator</u> to pick <u>coordinates</u>. Otherwise, if all your samples are in <u>one spot</u> and everywhere else is <u>different</u>, the results you get won't be <u>valid</u>.

2) <u>Count</u> all the organisms you're interested in <u>within</u> the quadrat.

3) <u>Repeat</u> steps 1 and 2 lots of times. The <u>larger</u> the <u>sample size</u> the <u>better</u>, because bigger samples are more likely to be <u>representative</u> of the <u>whole population</u> — see page 5. This also helps to make sure your results are <u>valid</u>.

4) <u>Work out</u> the <u>mean</u> number of organisms per m².

5) Then <u>scale up</u> to estimate the total population of the habitat.

A quadrat

Whether you're working in the lab or outdoors, it's important to do a risk assessment before carrying out any practical work. Risks in field work include things like poisonous plants and tripping on uneven ground.

 **EXAMPLE:** Students used quadrats with an area of 0.25 m² to randomly sample daisies on an open field. The students found a mean of 5.5 daisies per quadrat. The field had an area of 800 m². Estimate the population of daisies on the field.

1) Work out the <u>mean number of organisms per m²</u>.

   1 m² ÷ 0.25 m² = 4
   4 × 5.5 = 22 daisies per m²

2) Then <u>multiply</u> the mean by the <u>total area</u> (in m²) of the habitat.

   800 × 22 = 17 600
   daisies on the open field

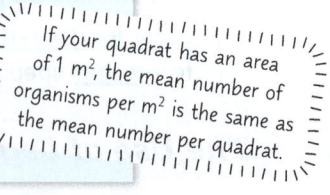

If your quadrat has an area of 1 m², the mean number of organisms per m² is the same as the mean number per quadrat.

6) You use this method to estimate the population size of a species in <u>two different areas</u> and then <u>compare</u> the figures. This could give you an idea of how <u>environmental factors</u> affect the <u>distribution</u> of that species, e.g. you might find <u>more daisies</u> growing in a <u>sunny</u> area than in a <u>shaded</u> one.

Drat, drat and double drat — my favourite use of quadrats...

Estimating population size isn't always accurate as it relies on human judgement when recording the data.

Q1 A field was randomly sampled for buttercups using quadrats with an area of 0.25 m². The field had an area of 1200 m². A mean of 0.75 buttercups were found per quadrat. Estimate the total population of buttercups in the field. [2 marks]

More on Investigating Ecosystems

Here's a bit more on studying the distribution and abundance of organisms. I'm sure you're thrilled to bits...

Use Transects to Study The Distribution of Organisms Along a Line

You can use lines called transects to help find out how organisms (like plants) are distributed across an area — e.g. if an organism becomes more or less common as you move from a hedge towards the middle of a field. Here's what to do:

PRACTICAL

1) Mark out a line in the area you want to study using a tape measure.

2) Then collect data along the line.

3) You can do this by just counting all the organisms you're interested in that touch the line.

4) Or, you can collect data by using quadrats (see previous page). These can be placed next to each other along the line or at intervals, for example, every 2 m.

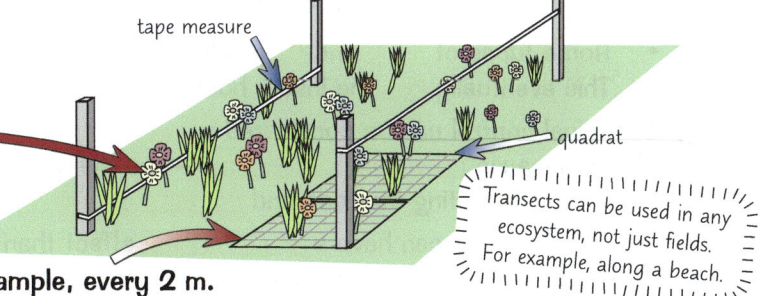

tape measure

quadrat

Transects can be used in any ecosystem, not just fields. For example, along a beach.

5) You can also take measurements of environmental factors, such as light intensity (using a light meter) or soil pH (using a pH probe), at regular intervals along the transect. This will allow you to investigate how these factors affect the distribution of organisms in the habitat.

You can Estimate Animal Population Sizes Using Capture-Recapture

1) Capture a sample of the population and mark the animals in a harmless way. For example, to capture insects you could use a pitfall trap like this one.

2) Release them back into the environment.

3) Recapture another sample of the population. Count how many of this sample are marked.

4) Then estimate population size with this equation:

You don't need to remember the equation for the exam.

cover propped up with stones

jar

food

A pitfall trap in the ground

$$\text{Population Size} = \frac{\text{number in first sample} \times \text{number in second sample}}{\text{number in second sample previously marked}}$$

Higher

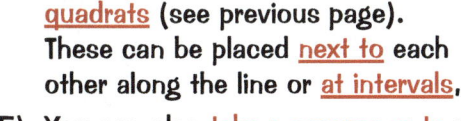
EXAMPLE:

A pitfall trap was set up in an area of woodland. 30 woodlice were caught in an hour and marked on their shell, before being released back into the environment. The next day, 35 woodlice were caught in an hour, only 5 of which were marked. Estimate the population size.

All you need to do is put the numbers into the population size equation (shown above).

Population size = (30 × 35) ÷ 5 = 210 woodlice

number in the first sample | number in the second sample | number in the second sample previously marked

When using the capture-recapture method you have to make a number of assumptions. These include:

1) There has been no change in population size between the samples — e.g. no births or deaths and no immigration or emigration (animals moving into or out of the same area).

2) The marking hasn't affected individuals' chance of survival (e.g. making them more visible to predators). For this reason, marking is non-toxic and not usually permanent.

Capture-recapture — it's just like taking selfies...

Transects often involve using quadrats in a very organised way. It's exciting, I know, so here's a question to tackle...

Q1   Some students want to measure how the distribution of dandelions changes from a hedgerow to the middle of a field. Describe a method they could use to do this.   [3 marks]

Biological Control and Invasive Species

Biological control is growing more popular, as people get fed up with the problems caused by pesticides.

Biological Control Involves Living Organisms

1) Biological control is an alternative to using pesticides. It involves using other organisms (called biological control agents) to reduce the numbers of pests. This is done by encouraging wild organisms or adding new ones. For example:

   - Aphids are a pest because they eat roses and vegetables. Ladybirds are aphid predators, so people release them into their fields and gardens to keep aphid numbers down.
   - Some types of wasp and fly produce larvae which develop on (or in, yuck) a host insect. This eventually kills the insect host. Lots of insect pests have parasites like this.

2) Biological control can be considered a safer alternative to pesticides. This is because no chemicals are used — so there's less pollution, a lower risk to people eating the food and no passing of chemicals along food chains.

3) Biological control can have a longer-lasting effect than spraying pesticides, so there's often no need to keep repeating the treatment.

4) However, biological control can cause problems...

Biological Control Agents can Become Invasive

1) An invasive species is any species that is introduced into an area where it doesn't naturally occur and starts to cause problems for local wildlife.

   E.g. cane toads were introduced to Australia as biological control agents to eat beetles, but they're now a major pest because they poison the native species that eat them.

   > Non-native species that are introduced to an area are also known as alien species. If an alien species starts to cause problems, it's invasive.

2) There are several ways in which an invasive species can cause problems. For example:

   - Invasive species may grow faster than native species and upset the natural ecosystem. E.g. Japanese knotweed was introduced to the UK as an ornamental plant, but due to its fast growth rate, it quickly takes over an area, preventing other plants from growing and reducing biodiversity.
   - Native species may not be able to compete with invasive species for resources such as food and shelter. E.g. signal crayfish were introduced to the UK for food, but they prey on and out-compete many native river species. They also carry a disease that kills native crayfish. This has led to a decline in the population size of some native species.

3) Biological control agents that become invasive are introduced to an area deliberately, but other invasive species may be introduced accidentally (e.g. as a stowaway in international cargo).

Research is Carried Out into the Use of Biological Control Agents

1) Before a biological control agent is introduced to a new area, scientists spend lots of time researching the agent so that they understand it and know how best to control it.

2) This research involves trials which assess the effect of the biological control agent on non-targeted native species (i.e. species which the agent is not supposed to be controlling).

We come in peace — but we might cause some major issues...

It might surprise you to learn that alien species aren't from outer space like in the movies. Instead, species such as Japanese knotweed are quite possibly transported from place to place on the bottom of your shoes.

Q1   Explain two ways in which invasive species can become a problem.   [4 marks]

Revision Questions for Unit 4a

You've reached the end of Unit 4a — now you should know all about classification and biodiversity.

- Try these questions and tick off each one when you get it right.
- When you've done all the questions for a topic and are completely happy with it, tick off the topic.

Classification (p.124) ☐

1) Give two major groups that plants can be divided into. ☐
2) On what basis are organisms sorted into groups in the five kingdom classification system? ☐
3) The biggest group in the five kingdom classification system is a kingdom.
   Name the other six groups in order of size. ☑
4) What does the second part of an organism's scientific name refer to? ☐
5) Why are organisms given a scientific name? ☑

Adaptations and Factors Affecting Population Size (p.125-126) ☐

6) Give two examples of morphological adaptations. ☑
7) Give two examples of behavioural adaptations. ☑
8) What do animals compete for? ☐
9) What is intraspecific competition? What is interspecific competition? ☑
10) Describe one way in which pollution could limit the size of a population. ☐

Biodiversity (p. 127) ☐

11) What is meant by the term biodiversity? ☑
12) Why is a high level of biodiversity important for an area? ☑
13) Give two ways in which maintaining biodiversity benefits humans. ☑
14) Give one way in which protecting biodiversity by law can have a negative impact on humans. ☑

Investigating Ecosystems (p.128-129) ☐

15) What is meant by the abundance of an organism? ☑
16) What is meant by the distribution of an organism? ☑
17) Describe how a quadrat can be used to investigate the abundance of a species in a sample area. ☑
18) What is a transect? ☑
19) Give two assumptions that are made when using the capture-recapture method
    to estimate the population size of an animal species. ☑

Biological Control and Invasive Species (p. 130) ☐

20) What is biological control an alternative to? ☑
21) Give two ways in which a biological control agent might work. ☑
22) What is an invasive species? ☑
23) Why is it important to carry out trials on biological control agents
    before they are fully introduced to a new area? ☑

Chromosomes and Mitosis

In order to survive and grow, our cells have got to be able to divide. And that means our DNA as well...

Chromosomes *Contain Genetic Information*

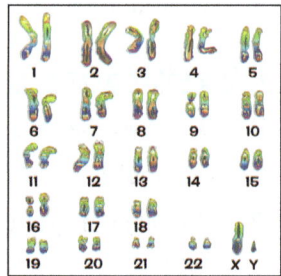

1) Most cells in your body have a nucleus. The nucleus contains your genetic material in the form of chromosomes.

2) Chromosomes are coiled up lengths of DNA molecules.

3) Each chromosome carries a large number of genes. The genes are arranged one after the other on the chromosome, in a long line (the posh way of saying this is that the genes have a 'linear arrangement'). Different genes control the development of different characteristics, e.g. hair colour.

4) Body cells normally have two copies of each chromosome — one from the organism's 'mother', and one from its 'father'. So, humans have two copies of chromosome 1, two copies of chromosome 2, etc.

5) The diagram shows the 23 pairs of chromosomes from a human cell.

Mitosis *Makes New Cells for Growth, Development and Repair*

1) Body cells in multicellular organisms divide to produce new cells during mitosis.

2) Multicellular organisms use mitosis to grow, replace cells that have worn out, and repair damaged tissue.

Mitosis is when a cell reproduces itself by dividing to form two identical offspring.

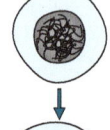
The cell has two copies of its DNA all spread out in long strings.

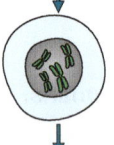
Before the cell divides, the DNA forms X-shaped chromosomes. Each 'arm' of a chromosome is an exact copy of the other.

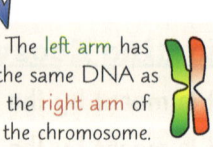
The left arm has the same DNA as the right arm of the chromosome.

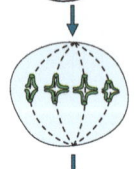
The chromosomes then line up at the centre of the cell and cell fibres pull them apart. The two arms of each chromosome go to opposite ends of the cell.

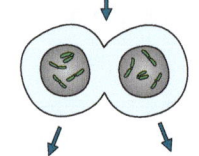
Membranes form around each of the sets of chromosomes. These become the nuclei of the two new cells.

Lastly, the cytoplasm divides.

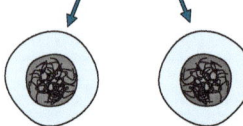
You now have two new cells containing exactly the same DNA — they're genetically identical to each other and to the parent cell.

Cancer *is a Case of Uncontrolled Mitosis*

1) The rate at which cells divide by mitosis is controlled by the cells' genes.

2) If there's a change in one of the genes that controls cell division, a cell may start dividing uncontrollably. This can result in a mass of abnormal cells called a tumour.

3) If the tumour invades and destroys surrounding tissue it is called cancer.

A cell's favourite computer game — divide and conquer...

Mitosis can seem tricky at first. But don't worry — just go through it slowly, one step at a time.

Q1   What is mitosis?   [1 mark]

Meiosis

If you've ever wondered why you look <u>a bit like</u> your mum and <u>a bit like</u> your dad but not exactly like your <u>brothers</u> and <u>sisters</u> (unless you're an identical twin), then today's your lucky day...

Gametes *Are Produced* by *Meiosis*

1) <u>Gametes</u> are sex cells (e.g. male <u>sperm cells</u> and female <u>egg cells</u> in humans).
2) They only have <u>one copy</u> of each <u>chromosome</u>, so when a male and a female gamete <u>fuse together</u> at <u>fertilisation</u> (see page 142), you get the <u>right number</u> of <u>chromosomes</u> again (two copies of each).
3) To make <u>gametes</u>, cells divide by <u>meiosis</u>. This process involves <u>two cell divisions</u>.

Meiosis *Produces Cells Which Have* Half *the Normal Number* of *Chromosomes*

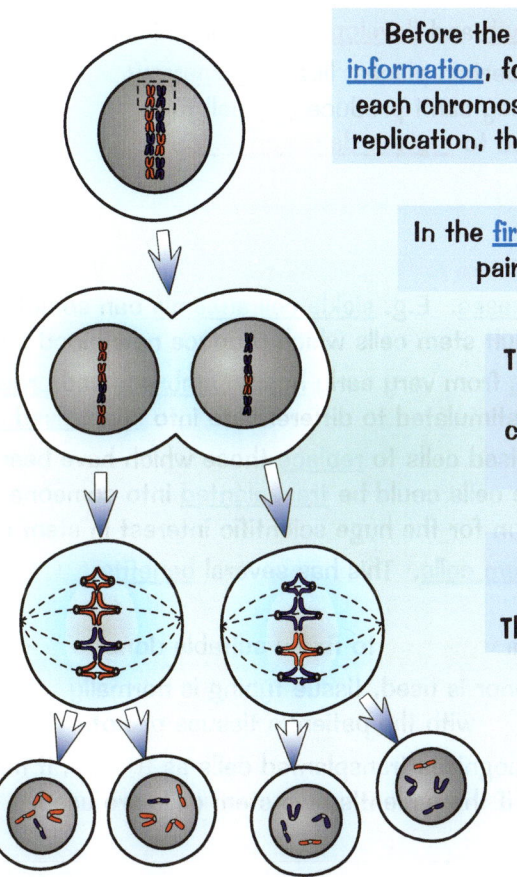

Before the cell starts to divide, it <u>duplicates</u> its <u>genetic information</u>, forming two armed chromosomes — one arm of each chromosome is an <u>exact copy</u> of the other arm. After replication, the chromosomes arrange themselves into <u>pairs</u>.

In the <u>first division</u> in meiosis, the chromosome pairs <u>line up</u> in the centre of the cell.

The pairs are then <u>pulled apart</u> so each new cell only has one copy of each chromosome. <u>Some</u> of the father's chromosomes (shown in blue) and <u>some</u> of the mother's chromosomes (shown in red) go into each new cell.

In the <u>second division</u>, the chromosomes <u>line up</u> again in the centre of the cell. The arms of the chromosomes are <u>pulled apart</u>.

You get <u>four</u> daughter cells, which are <u>gametes</u>. Each has <u>half</u> the number of chromosomes of the parent cell. Each of the gametes is <u>genetically different</u> from the others because the chromosomes all get <u>shuffled up</u> during meiosis and each gamete only gets <u>half</u> of them, at random.

You Need to be Able to *Compare Mitosis* and *Meiosis*

	Mitosis	Meiosis
Number of divisions	1	2
Number of daughter cells	2	4
No. of chromosomes in daughter cells	Full set (46 in humans)	Half set (23 in humans)
Daughter cells are...	Genetically identical	Genetically different

Now that I have your undivided attention...

Don't get mitosis and meiosis mixed up — go over the differences until you're mumbling them in your sleep.

Q1   How many cell divisions take place in meiosis?   [1 mark]

Stem Cells

Your body is made up of all sorts of weird and wonderful cells. This page tells you where they all came from...

Stem Cells can Differentiate into Different Types of Cells

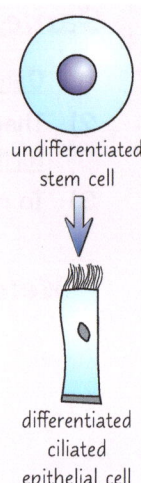

undifferentiated stem cell

differentiated ciliated epithelial cell

1) Differentiation is the process by which a cell becomes specialised for its job.

2) In the cells of most mature tissues, the ability to differentiate is lost. But some animal and plant cells don't lose the ability to differentiate.

3) Undifferentiated cells are called stem cells — they can divide by mitosis to become new cells, which then differentiate into different cell types.

4) Stem cells are found in early human embryos. These embryonic stem cells have the potential to divide and produce any kind of cell. This makes sense — all the different types of cell found in a human have to come from those few cells in the early embryo.

5) This means stem cells are really important for the growth and development of organisms.

6) Adults also have stem cells, but they're only found in certain places, like bone marrow. These aren't as versatile as embryonic stem cells — they can't produce any cell type, only certain ones. In animals, adult stem cells are used to replace damaged cells.

Stem Cells Can be Used in Medicine

1) Doctors already use adult stem cells to cure some diseases. E.g. sickle cell anaemia can sometimes be cured with a bone marrow transplant (containing adult stem cells which produce new blood cells).

2) Scientists have experimented with extracting stem cells from very early human embryos and growing them. Under certain conditions the stem cells can be stimulated to differentiate into specialised cells.

3) It might be possible to use stem cells to create specialised cells to replace those which have been damaged by disease or injury, e.g. new cardiac muscle cells could be transplanted into someone with heart disease. This potential for new cures is the reason for the huge scientific interest in stem cells.

4) Some diseases can be treated using a person's own stem cells. This has several benefits:

- There's no need to find a donor — it can take a long time to find a suitable donor.
- There's no need for tissue typing — when a donor is used, tissue typing is normally needed to see if the donor tissues are compatible with the patient's tissues or not.
- There's no rejection — if the patient's body recognises transplanted cells as foreign, it may try to get rid of them, but this doesn't happen if the patient's own stem cells are used.

Some People Are Against Stem Cell Research

1) Some people are against stem cell research because they feel that human embryos shouldn't be used for experiments since each one is a potential human life.

2) Others think that curing existing patients who are suffering is more important than the rights of embryos.

3) One argument in favour of this point of view is that the embryos used in the research are usually unwanted ones from fertility clinics which, if they weren't used for research, would probably just be destroyed. However, campaigners for the rights of embryos usually want this practice banned too.

4) These campaigners feel that scientists should concentrate more on finding and developing other sources of stem cells, so people could be helped without having to use embryos.

5) In some countries, stem cell research is banned. It's allowed in the UK as long as it follows strict guidelines.

But florists cell stems, and nobody's against that...

Whatever your opinion is, make sure you know the benefits of stem cells and the ethical issues of using them.

Q1   What is differentiation?   [1 mark]

DNA

Right, time to find out exactly what this genetic material is all about and why it's so blummin' important...

Chromosomes are Really Long Molecules of DNA

1) As you know from page 132, your nucleus contains chromosomes and each chromosome is one very long, coiled up molecule of DNA.

2) DNA contains coded information — basically all the instructions to put an organism together and make it work.

3) So it's what's in your DNA that determines what characteristics you have.

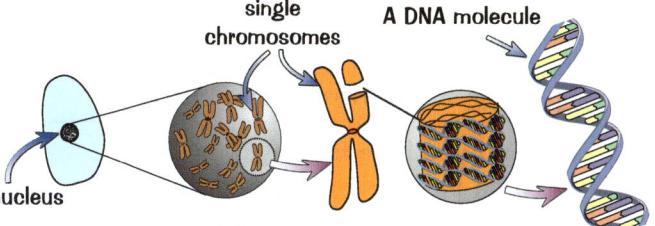

single chromosomes   A DNA molecule

cell nucleus

DNA is Made Up of Sugar and Phosphate Molecules

1) DNA strands are made up of long chains of sugar and phosphate molecules.

2) The sugar and phosphate molecules alternate and form the 'backbone' to the DNA strands.

3) One of four different bases joins to each sugar. The bases are: A, T, C and G.

4) A stands for Adenine, T stands for Thymine, C stands for Cytosine and G stands for Guanine.

5) A DNA molecule has two strands coiled together in the shape of a double helix (a double stranded spiral).

6) Each base links to a base on the opposite strand in the helix. This gives DNA a structure like a ladder, with the bases as rungs.

7) A always pairs up with T, and C always pairs up with G. This is called complementary base pairing.

8) The complementary base pairs are joined together by weak hydrogen bonds.

9) In 1953, Watson and Crick were the first scientists to build a model of DNA, showing DNA as a double helix of two strands wound together, with bases occurring in pairs.

H

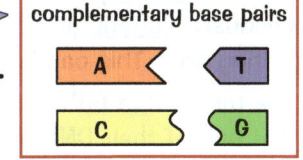

complementary base pairs

A — T

C — G

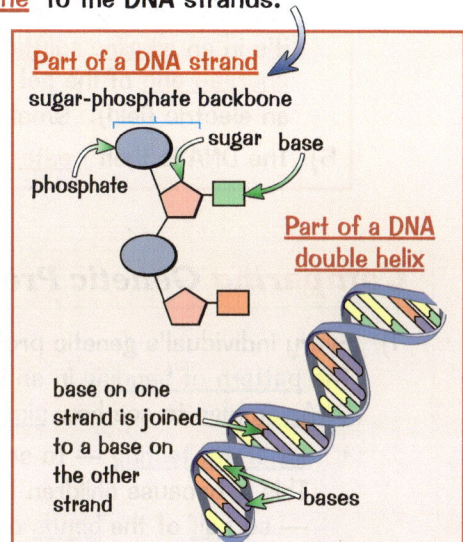

Part of a DNA strand

sugar-phosphate backbone

phosphate   sugar   base

Part of a DNA double helix

base on one strand is joined to a base on the other strand   bases

The Order of Bases in a Gene Codes for a Protein

1) A gene is a small section of DNA found on a chromosome.

2) It's the order of bases in a gene that decides the order of amino acids in a protein.

3) Each amino acid is coded for by a sequence of three bases in the gene called a triplet. For example, the triplet AGG codes for the amino acid arginine. The sequence AGGCTT codes for arginine, then leucine.

4) The amino acids are joined together to make various proteins, depending on the order of triplets in the gene. The properties and function of each protein are determined by the particular amino acids it contains and the order they're present in.

5) DNA is really big so can't move out of the cell nucleus — instead a molecule is used to relay the triplet code from the DNA to the cell cytoplasm where proteins are synthesised.

Higher

A triplet of bases — three-tiered cheesecake anyone...

This all sounds rather complicated... but you'll be okay if you get a handle on the basics. Chromosomes are made up of long strands of DNA. DNA contains a sequence of bases and the order of bases determines the protein.

Q1   Which bases pair up according to complementary base pairing?   [2 marks]

Genetic Profiling

You can tell people apart using their genetic profile — particularly useful if you want to find out whodunnit...

DNA is Unique

1) Almost everyone's DNA is unique. The only exceptions are identical twins and clones.

2) Genetic profiling (or DNA profiling) is a way of cutting up a person's DNA into small sections and then separating them. Here's how it works:

---

1) First you have to extract the DNA from the cells in the blood, semen etc.

2) The DNA is then cut up into fragments.

3) This produces lots of different sized bits of DNA. The number of each size will be different for everyone because of the way it's cut.

4) The DNA bits are separated by size, using gel electrophoresis. They're suspended in an alkaline gel, and an electric current is passed through the gel. DNA is negatively charged when it's in an alkaline solution, so it moves towards the positively charged end of the gel (because charged particles move in an electric field). Small bits travel faster than big bits, so they get further through the gel.

5) The DNA is then treated to make it visible — this is the DNA profile.

DNA moves towards the positive end, with smallest fragments moving furthest

−ve end

DNA fragment

alkaline gel

+ve end

Comparing Genetic Profiles has Many Uses

1) Every individual's genetic profile has a unique pattern (unless they're identical twins or clones of course). The pattern of banding in an individual's genetic profile is compared to that of genetic profiles from other DNA samples to see how similar they are. This can be useful for a variety of reasons, for example:

- Paternity testing — to see if a man is the father of a particular child. This is because children inherit half of their DNA from their mum and half from their dad — so half of the bands on their DNA profile will be the same as their father's.

- Species classification — the more closely-related two individuals are, the more similar their DNA profiles will be (e.g. more bands will match), which means that species can be sorted into groups (see page 124).

- Forensic science — DNA (from hair, skin flakes, blood, semen etc.) taken from a crime scene is compared with a DNA sample taken from a suspect. In the diagram, suspect 2's DNA has the same pattern as the DNA from the crime scene — so suspect 2 was probably at the crime scene.

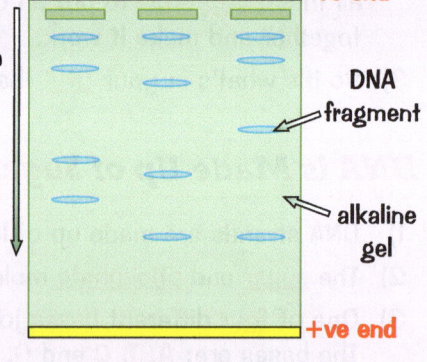

Unknown DNA from crime scene   DNA from suspect 1   DNA from suspect 2

2) Genetic profiles can also be used to help doctors diagnose diseases and to find out if a person is at a higher risk of a getting a particular disease. If doctors know about certain genes that are associated with a disease or disorder, they can identify these genes in a person's genetic profile. Earlier diagnosis can lead to better treatment for patients.

Some people would like there to be a national genetic database of everyone's genetic profile in the country. But others think that storing genetic profiles is a big invasion of privacy. They worry the data could be stolen and that if insurances companies gained access to the information they may refuse to insure people based on their genetic profile (e.g if a person has genes that are associated with a disease).

So the trick is — frame your twin and they'll never get you...

Genetic profiling gives us more information about people than ever, but we need to be careful with how it's stored.

Q1   Why do DNA fragments separate into bands during genetic profiling?   [2 marks]

Sex Determination

Now for a couple of <u>very</u> important little chromosomes...

Your Chromosomes Control Whether You're Male or Female

There are <u>23 pairs</u> of chromosomes in every human body cell. Of these, <u>22</u> are <u>matched pairs</u> of chromosomes that just control <u>characteristics</u>. The <u>23rd pair</u> are labelled <u>XY</u> or <u>XX</u>. They're the two chromosomes that <u>decide</u> your <u>sex</u> — whether you turn out <u>male</u> or <u>female</u>.

<u>Males</u> have an <u>X</u> and a <u>Y</u> chromosome: XY
The <u>Y chromosome</u> causes <u>male characteristics</u>.

<u>Females</u> have <u>two X chromosomes</u>:   XX
The <u>XX combination</u> allows <u>female characteristics</u> to develop.

1) When making sperm, the **X** and **Y** chromosomes are drawn apart in the first division in <u>meiosis</u> (see page 133).

2) There's a <u>50% chance</u> each sperm cell gets an <u>X-chromosome</u> and a <u>50% chance</u> it gets a <u>Y-chromosome</u>.

3) A similar thing happens when making eggs. But the original cell has <u>two X-chromosomes</u>, so all the eggs have <u>one X-chromosome</u>.

4) One sperm cell and one egg cell combine <u>randomly</u> at fertilisation.

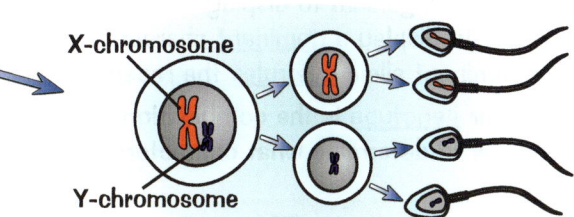

X-chromosome

Y-chromosome

Punnett Squares Show the Possible Gamete Combinations

1) To find the <u>probability</u> of getting a boy or a girl, you can draw a <u>Punnett square</u>.

2) Punnett squares are just <u>models</u> that are used to show all the possible genetic <u>outcomes</u> when you <u>cross together</u> different genes or chromosomes.

3) Put the <u>possible gametes</u> (eggs or sperm) from <u>one</u> parent down the side, and those from the <u>other</u> parent along the top.

4) Then in each middle square you <u>fill in</u> the letters from the top and side that line up with that square. The <u>pairs of letters</u> in the middle show the possible combinations of the gametes.

5) There are <u>two XX results</u> and <u>two XY results</u>, so there's the same probability of getting a boy or a girl.

6) Don't forget that this <u>50:50 ratio</u> is only a <u>probability</u> at each pregnancy.

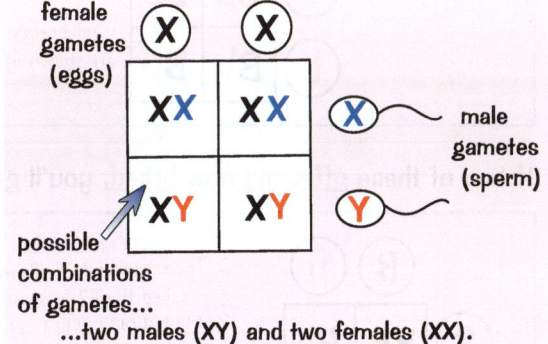

female gametes (eggs)

male gametes (sperm)

possible combinations of gametes...

...two males (XY) and two females (XX).

Have you got the Y-factor...

Most Punnett squares you'll see in exams concentrate on a gene instead of a chromosome.
But the principle's the same. Don't worry — there are other examples of Punnett squares on the next page.

Q1   What combination of sex chromosomes do human females have?   [1 mark]

Q2   What sex is a person with an X and a Y chromosome?   [1 mark]

Inheritance

You can use Punnett squares to predict what characteristics offspring will inherit...

Some Characteristics are Controlled by Single Genes

1) What genes you inherit control what characteristics you develop.

2) Some characteristics are controlled by a single gene — this is called single gene inheritance.

3) However, it's not always quite this simple — most characteristics are actually controlled by multiple genes.

4) All genes exist in different versions called alleles (which are represented by letters in genetic diagrams).

5) You have two versions (alleles) of every gene in your body — one on each chromosome in a pair.

6) If an organism has two alleles for a particular gene that are the same, then it's homozygous for that trait. If its two alleles for a particular gene are different, then it's heterozygous.

7) If the two alleles are different, only one can determine what characteristic is present. The allele for the characteristic that's shown is called the dominant allele (use a capital letter for dominant alleles — e.g. 'C'). The other one is called recessive (and you show these with small letters — e.g. 'c').

8) For an organism to display a recessive characteristic, both its alleles must be recessive (e.g. cc). But to display a dominant characteristic the organism can be either CC or Cc, because the dominant allele overrules the recessive one if the plant/animal/other organism is heterozygous.

9) Your genotype is the combination of alleles you have. Your alleles work at a molecular level to determine what characteristics you have — your phenotype.

Punnett Squares Show the Possible Alleles of Offspring

Suppose you start breeding hamsters with superpowers. The allele which causes hamsters to have superpowers is recessive ("b"), whilst normal (boring) behaviour is due to a dominant allele ("B").

1) A superpowered hamster must have the genotype bb. But a normal hamster could be BB or Bb.

2) Here's what happens if you breed from two homozygous hamsters:

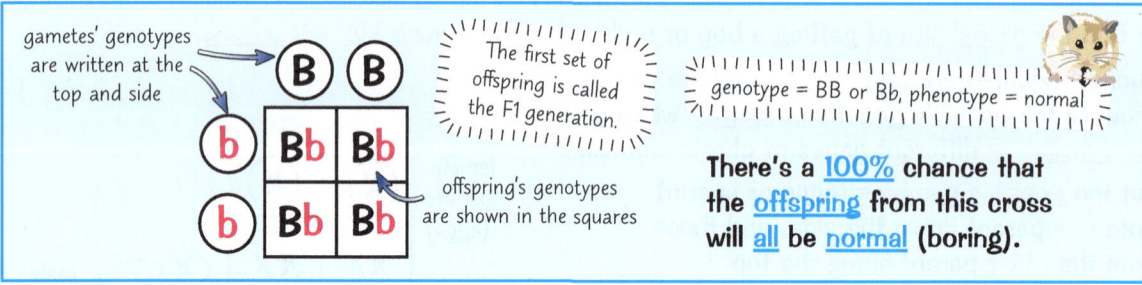

gametes' genotypes are written at the top and side

The first set of offspring is called the F1 generation.

offspring's genotypes are shown in the squares

genotype = BB or Bb, phenotype = normal

There's a 100% chance that the offspring from this cross will all be normal (boring).

3) If two of these offspring now breed, you'll get the next generation:

The second set of offspring is called the F2 generation.

Superpowered!

- There's a 3 in 4 (75%) chance that the offspring will be normal.

- There's a 1 in 4 (25%) chance that the offspring will have superpowers.

But remember — Punnett squares only tell you probabilities. They don't say definitely what'll happen.

That's a 3:1 ratio of normal to superpowered offspring in this generation (a 1 in 4 or 25% probability of superpowers).

Your meanotype determines how nice you are to your sibling...

You need to be able to produce and interpret Punnett squares — so persevere practising those puzzling Punnetts.

Q1   Define genotype and phenotype.   [2 marks]

Genetic Modification

Genetic modification is an interesting area of science with <u>exciting possibilities</u>, but there might be <u>dangers</u> too...

Genetic Modification *Transfers Genes Between Organisms*

The basic idea of genetic modification is to artificially <u>transfer</u> a <u>gene</u> responsible for a <u>desirable characteristic</u> from one organism into <u>another</u> organism, so that it also has the <u>desired characteristic</u>.

1) A useful gene is <u>isolated</u> (cut) from one organism's genome using <u>enzymes</u> and is inserted into a <u>vector</u>.

2) The vector is usually a <u>virus</u> or a <u>bacterial plasmid</u> (a fancy piece of circular DNA found in bacterial cells), depending on the type of organism that the gene is being transferred to.

3) When the vector is <u>introduced</u> to the target organism, the <u>useful gene</u> is <u>inserted</u> into its cell(s).

Genetic Modification *Has Many Benefits...*

1) In <u>agriculture</u>, <u>crops</u> can be genetically modified to be <u>resistant to herbicides</u> (chemicals that kill plants). Making crops <u>herbicide-resistant</u> means farmers can <u>spray</u> their crops to <u>kill weeds</u>, <u>without</u> affecting the crop itself, and as such, can <u>increase crop yield</u>.

2) Crops can also be <u>genetically modified</u> to be <u>resistant</u> to <u>insect pests</u>. This can <u>improve crop yields</u> and reduce the need for chemical pesticides.

3) Some crops can be modified to combat certain <u>deficiency diseases</u>, e.g. <u>Golden Rice</u> has been genetically engineered to produce a chemical that's converted in the body to <u>vitamin A</u>.

4) In <u>medicine</u>, researchers have genetically modified <u>bacteria</u> to produce human <u>insulin</u>.

5) They've also managed to transfer <u>human genes</u> that produce <u>useful proteins</u> into <u>sheep</u> and <u>cows</u>. E.g. human <u>antibodies</u> used in therapy for illnesses like <u>arthritis</u>. These proteins can then be <u>extracted</u> from the animal, e.g. from their <u>milk</u>.

...But It Also Comes With Risks

There are <u>concerns</u> about growing genetically modified crops...

1) <u>Transplanted genes</u> may get out into the <u>environment</u>. E.g. a herbicide resistance gene may be picked up by weeds, creating new 'superweeds'.

2) Another concern is that genetically modified crops could adversely affect <u>food chains</u> — or even <u>human health</u>.

3) Some people are against <u>genetic modification</u> altogether. They <u>worry</u> that changing an organism's genes might create unforeseen <u>problems</u> — which would then get passed on to <u>future generations</u>.

4) Some people say that growing genetically modified crops will affect the number of <u>weeds</u> and <u>flowers</u> (and therefore wildlife) that usually live in and around the crops — <u>reducing</u> farmland <u>biodiversity</u> (number and variety of species in an ecosystem).

> People in developed countries, e.g. those in Europe, tend to be more concerned about the potential risks because food shortages are not as big an issue as in developing countries.

I say it's great.

Genetic Modification Raises *Ethical Issues*

You need to know about the <u>ethical issues</u> surrounding genetic modification too:

1) Some people think it's <u>wrong</u> to genetically modify other organisms purely for <u>human benefit</u>. This is a particular problem in the genetic modification of <u>animals</u>, especially if the animal <u>suffers</u> as a result.

2) People worry that we won't <u>stop</u> at modifying <u>plants</u> and <u>animals</u>. In the future, those who can afford genetic modification might be able to decide the characteristics they want their <u>children</u> to have — and those who can't afford it may become a '<u>genetic underclass</u>'.

3) Some people think genetic modification is <u>irresponsible</u> when there's <u>uncertainty</u> about the consequences.

If only there was a gene to make revision easier...

Genetic modification is a serious issue — its not just designer food. Make sure you know the pros and cons.

Q1   Give two potential risks of growing genetically modified crops.   [2 marks]

Variation

You'll probably have noticed that <u>not all</u> people are <u>identical</u>. There are reasons for this.

Organisms of the *Same Species* Have *Differences*

1) Different species look... well... different — my dog definitely doesn't look like a daisy.

2) But even organisms of the <u>same species</u> will usually look at least <u>slightly</u> different — e.g. in a room full of people you'll see different <u>colour hair</u>, individually <u>shaped noses</u>, etc.

3) These differences are called the <u>variation</u> within a species, and there are <u>two</u> types of variation — <u>genetic variation</u> and <u>environmental variation</u>.

Different Genes Cause Genetic *Variation*

1) All plants and animals have <u>characteristics</u> that are in some ways similar to their <u>parents'</u>.

2) This is because an organism's <u>characteristics</u> are determined by the <u>genes inherited</u> from their <u>parents</u>. (There's more about genes on page 135.)

3) In sexually reproducing species genes are passed on in <u>gametes</u>, from which the offspring develop (see page 142).

4) Most animals (and quite a lot of plants) get <u>some</u> genes from the <u>mother</u> and <u>some</u> from the <u>father</u>.

5) This combining of genes from two parents causes <u>genetic variation</u> — no two members of the species are <u>genetically identical</u> (other than identical twins).

6) <u>Some</u> characteristics are determined <u>only</u> by genes (e.g. violet flower colour). In <u>animals</u> these include: <u>eye colour</u>, <u>blood group</u> and <u>inherited disorders</u> (e.g. haemophilia or cystic fibrosis).

Characteristics are also Influenced by the *Environment*

1) The <u>environment</u>, including the <u>conditions</u> that organisms <u>live and grow</u> in, also causes <u>differences</u> between members of the same species — this is called <u>environmental variation</u>.

2) Environmental variation covers a <u>wide range</u> of differences — from <u>losing your toes</u> in a piranha attack, to getting a <u>suntan</u>, to having <u>yellow leaves</u> (never happened to me yet though), and so on.

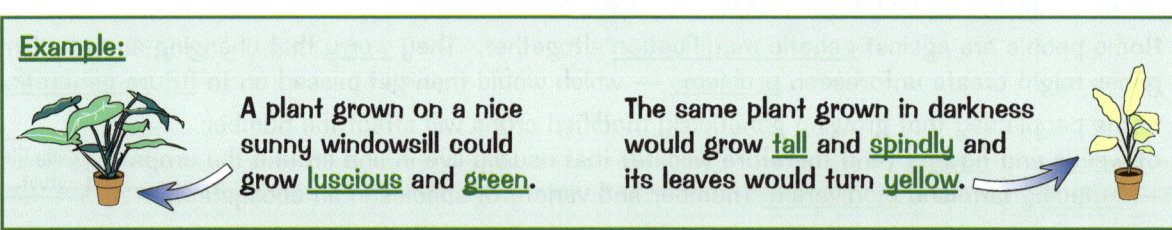

Example:

A plant grown on a nice sunny windowsill could grow <u>luscious</u> and <u>green</u>.

The same plant grown in darkness would grow <u>tall</u> and <u>spindly</u> and its leaves would turn <u>yellow</u>.

Most Characteristics are Due to *Genes AND* the *Environment*

1) <u>Most characteristics</u> (e.g. body weight, height, skin colour, condition of teeth, academic or athletic prowess, etc.) are determined by a <u>mixture</u> of <u>genetic</u> and <u>environmental</u> factors.

2) For example, the <u>maximum height</u> that an animal or plant could grow to is determined by its <u>genes</u>. But whether it actually grows that tall depends on its <u>environment</u> (e.g. how much food it gets).

My mum's got no trousers — cos I've got her jeans...

So you can't blame all of your faults on your parents — the environment usually plays a role too.

Q1   Explain what is meant by environmental variation. [2 marks]

More on Variation

Yep, there's <u>more</u> you need to learn about <u>variation</u> I'm afraid — including a practical...

Variation can be Continuous

1) <u>Continuous variation</u> is when the individuals in a population <u>vary within a range</u> — there are <u>no distinct categories</u>, e.g. humans can be any <u>height</u> within a range, not just tall or short.

2) Other examples include an organism's <u>mass</u>, and the <u>number of leaves</u> on a tree.

3) Characteristics that are influenced by <u>more than one gene</u> or that are influenced by <u>both genetic</u> and <u>environmental factors</u> usually show continuous variation.

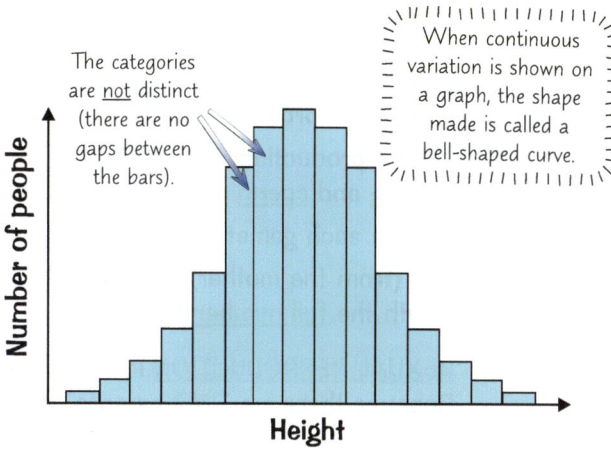

The categories are <u>not</u> distinct (there are no gaps between the bars).

When continuous variation is shown on a graph, the shape made is called a bell-shaped curve.

Variation can be Discontinuous

1) <u>Discontinuous variation</u> is when there are <u>two or more distinct categories</u> — each individual falls into <u>only one</u> of these categories, there are <u>no intermediates</u>.

2) For example, humans can <u>only</u> be <u>blood group</u> A, B, AB or O.

3) Characteristics that are only influenced by <u>one gene</u> and that <u>aren't</u> influenced by the <u>environment</u> are likely to show discontinuous variation.

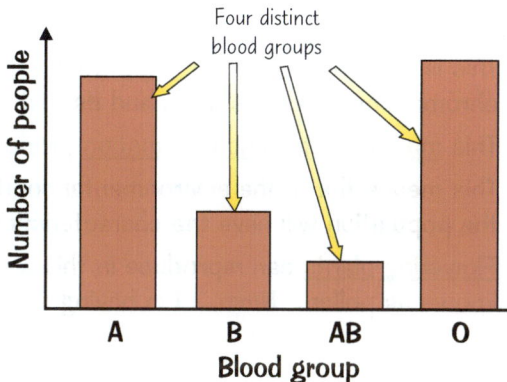

Four distinct blood groups

You can Investigate Variation in Organisms

PRACTICAL

You can investigate <u>variation</u> by collecting data on the <u>height</u> of <u>everyone</u> in a group, e.g. your class. To do this, follow this method:

1) Ask each person to <u>remove</u> their shoes.

2) Use a <u>measuring tape</u> to measure from the <u>top</u> of a person's head to the <u>ground</u>. (Ask a partner to help you hold one end of the measuring tape if needed.)

3) <u>Record</u> the <u>height</u> of the person.

4) <u>Plot your data</u> of height against number of people, and <u>compare</u> its shape to the graph at the top of this page.

You could also follow the above method and record whether the person is <u>male or female</u> at step 3. This would allow you to plot the height of a group of females and a group of males on <u>separate graphs</u>, which could then be <u>compared</u>.

Environmental variation — pretty much sums up British weather...

Remember, variation can be continuous or discontinuous and they are both shown on different types of graph.

Q1   Explain the difference between continuous and discontinuous variation.   [2 marks]

Asexual and Sexual Reproduction

Ooo err, reproduction... Surely you knew it'd come up at some point. Read on my friend..

Sexual Reproduction Produces Genetically Different Cells

1) Sexual reproduction is where genetic information from two organisms (a father and a mother) is combined to produce offspring which are genetically different to either parent.

2) In sexual reproduction, the mother and father produce gametes by meiosis — e.g. egg and sperm cells in animals (see p.133).

3) In humans, each gamete contains 23 chromosomes — half the number of chromosomes in a normal cell.

4) The egg (from the mother) and the sperm cell (from the father) then fuse together (fertilisation) to form a cell with the full number of chromosomes (half from the father, half from the mother).

> SEXUAL REPRODUCTION involves the fusion of male and female gametes. Because there are TWO parents, the offspring contain a mixture of their parents' genes.

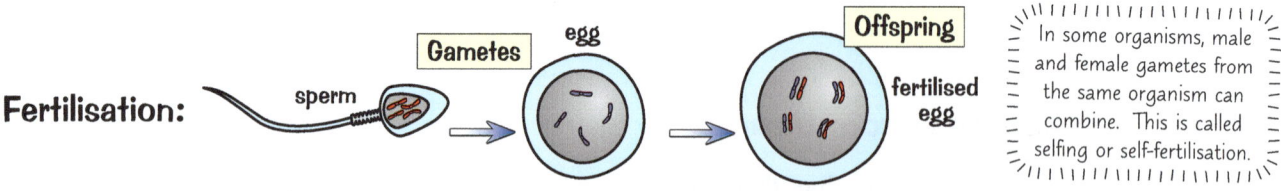

Fertilisation:

In some organisms, male and female gametes from the same organism can combine. This is called selfing or self-fertilisation.

5) This is why the offspring inherits features from both parents — it's received a mixture of chromosomes from its mum and its dad (and it's the chromosomes that decide how you turn out).

6) This mixture of genetic information produces variation in the offspring. Pretty cool, eh.

7) This means that if the environmental conditions change, it's more likely that at least some individuals in the population will have the characteristics needed to survive the change.

8) Flowering plants can reproduce in this way too. They also have egg cells, but their version of sperm is known as pollen. Hmm... I'm having second thoughts about frolicking in that meadow now.

Asexual Reproduction Produces Genetically Identical Cells

1) In asexual reproduction there's only one parent so the offspring are genetically identical to that parent.

2) Asexual reproduction happens by mitosis — an ordinary cell makes a new cell by dividing in two (see page 132).

3) The new cell has exactly the same genetic information (i.e. genes) as the parent cell — it's called a clone.

> In ASEXUAL REPRODUCTION there's only ONE parent. There's no fusion of gametes, no mixing of chromosomes and no genetic variation between parent and offspring. The offspring are genetically identical to the parent — they're clones.

4) No genetic variation between offspring in the population means that is the environment changes and conditions become unfavourable, the whole population may be affected.

A handsome bunch — even if I do say so myself...

5) Bacteria, some plants and some animals reproduce asexually.

You need to reproduce these facts in the exam...

The main messages on this page are that: 1) sexual reproduction needs two parents and forms cells that are genetically different to the parents, so there's lots of genetic variation. And 2) asexual reproduction needs just one parent to make genetically identical cells, so there's no genetic variation in the offspring.

Q1   Explain why there is variation in the offspring of sexual reproduction.   [2 marks]

Mutations

Sometimes the <u>sequence</u> of <u>DNA bases</u> can be changed. These changes are called <u>mutations</u>. Read on...

Mutations are Changes to the Sequence of DNA Bases

1) <u>Occasionally</u> a gene may <u>mutate</u>. A mutation is a random <u>change</u> in an organism's <u>DNA</u>.

2) <u>New alleles</u> (versions of genes) can arise from <u>mutations</u> in <u>existing alleles</u>.
These <u>new alleles</u> can sometimes be <u>inherited</u>.

3) Mutations occur <u>continuously</u> and they can occur <u>spontaneously</u>.

4) The <u>number</u> of mutations that occur in a gene or organism over time is known as the <u>mutation rate</u>.

5) The <u>mutation rate</u> is <u>increased</u> by exposure to <u>ionising radiation</u> —
the <u>greater</u> the <u>dose</u> of ionising radiation, the <u>greater</u> the chance of <u>mutation</u>.

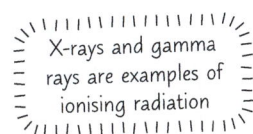
X-rays and gamma rays are examples of ionising radiation

Mutations May Have No Effect on an Organism

1) As the <u>sequence</u> of DNA bases <u>codes</u> for the sequence of <u>amino acids</u> that make up a <u>protein</u> (see page 135), mutations to a gene <u>sometimes</u> lead to <u>changes</u> in the protein that it codes for.

2) Most mutations have <u>very little</u> or <u>no effect</u> on the protein.

3) Some mutations will change it to such a <u>small extent</u> that its function or appearance is <u>unaffected</u>.

Some Mutations May be Beneficial...

1) Some mutations can <u>seriously affect</u> a protein — e.g. they can make an enzyme <u>more</u> or <u>less active</u>.

2) These can <u>benefit</u> an organism, for example:

> Some bacterial enzymes <u>break down</u> certain antibiotics.
> Mutations in the genes that code for these enzymes could make
> them work on a <u>wider range</u> of antibiotics. This is <u>beneficial</u> to the
> <u>bacteria</u> because <u>antibiotic resistance</u> can help them to <u>survive</u>.

... or Harmful

Mutations that seriously affect a protein can also have a <u>negative</u> effect, for example:

> People with the genetic disorder <u>cystic fibrosis</u> have a mutation that causes a
> <u>protein</u> to <u>stop</u> working properly. This protein controls the movement of <u>salt</u> and
> <u>water</u> into and out of cells. So this disorder leads to the production of thick,
> sticky <u>mucus</u> in the lungs and digestive system, which can make it <u>difficult to
> breathe and digest food</u>. (There's more on cystic fibrosis on the next page.)

Mutations that cause genetic disorders can be <u>passed on</u> in families (see the next page for more).

Mutations — like mutants in movies, but in stealth mode...

It might seem a bit surprising, but it's important to remember that most mutations don't actually end up having much of an effect on a protein — and if a mutation doesn't change a protein, it won't affect the organism either.

Q1 What is a mutation? [1 mark]

Q2 Give one factor that can increase mutation rate. [1 mark]

Cystic Fibrosis

Cystic fibrosis can be inherited from your parents — read on to find out more...

Cystic Fibrosis is Caused by a Recessive Allele

Cystic fibrosis is a genetic disorder of the cell membranes. It is caused by the mutation of a single gene and results in the body producing a lot of thick sticky mucus in the bronchioles and in the pancreas.

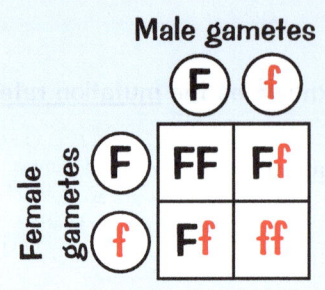

1) The allele which causes cystic fibrosis is a recessive allele, 'f', carried by about 1 person in 25.

2) Because it's recessive, people with only one copy of the allele (Ff) won't have the disorder — they're known as carriers.

3) For a child to have the disorder, both parents must be either carriers or have the disorder themselves.

4) As the diagram shows, there's a 1 in 4 chance of a child having the disorder (ff) if both parents are carriers.

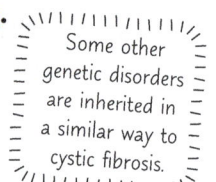

Some other genetic disorders are inherited in a similar way to cystic fibrosis.

A Family Tree can Show How Cystic Fibrosis is Inherited in a Family

Below is a family tree for a family that includes carriers of cystic fibrosis. The lines on the tree link the parents to each other (horizontal) and to their children (vertical).

1) You can see from the family tree that the allele for cystic fibrosis isn't dominant because plenty of the family carry the allele but don't have the disorder.

2) There is a 1 in 4 (25%) chance that the new baby will have cystic fibrosis and a 1 in 2 (50%) chance that it will be a carrier because both of its parents are carriers but don't have the disorder.

3) The case of the new baby is just the same as in the genetic diagram above — so the baby could be unaffected (FF), a carrier (Ff) or have the disorder (ff).

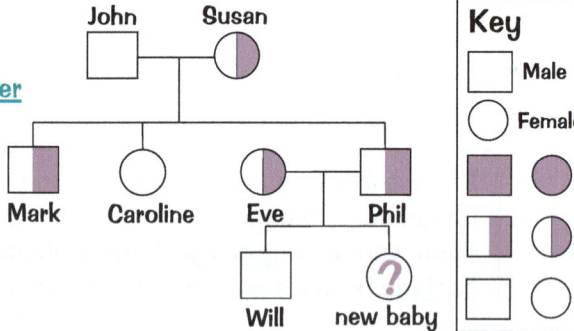

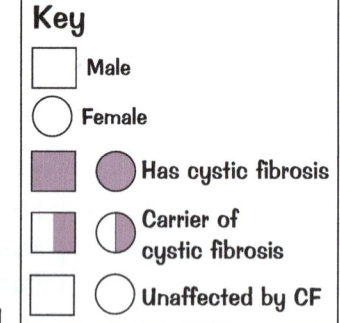

Key

- ☐ Male
- ○ Female
- Has cystic fibrosis
- Carrier of cystic fibrosis
- Unaffected by CF

Gene Therapy Could Be Used to Treat Cystic Fibrosis

1) Gene therapy involves altering a person's genes in an attempt to cure genetic disorders.

2) Scientists are working on using gene therapy as a treatment for cystic fibrosis.

3) The treatment involves inserting copies of the non-mutated allele into the cells lining the lungs.

4) An inhaler is used to deliver the treatment to the patient's lung tissue.

5) However, it is difficult to get these 'new' alleles into the correct cells and working normally in the body to produce a protein.

6) It is also not a cure for cystic fibrosis because the treated cells are replaced by the body over time.

7) Any offspring would still be able to inherit cystic fibrosis, because the alleles in the gametes wouldn't be affected.

Family trees are enough to make you go cross-eyed...

You need to know how cystic fibrosis could be inherited and how gene therapy could be used as a treatment.

Q1 Use the family tree above for the following question. Mark and his wife (who is not shown in the diagram) have a baby with cystic fibrosis. What are the possible genotypes of Mark's wife? [1 mark]

Natural Selection

Evolution is the <u>slow and continuous change</u> of organisms from one generation to the next.

Natural Selection *Increases Advantageous* Characteristics

<u>Evolution</u> occurs by a process called <u>natural selection</u>. This process accounts for the vast <u>diversity</u> of <u>living organisms</u> on Earth, and is the reason why <u>all organisms</u> are <u>related</u>, to varying degrees.

1) Organisms in a species show <u>wide variation</u> in their characteristics due to differences in their <u>alleles</u> — the <u>versions</u> of <u>genes</u> they <u>inherit</u> (see page 138 for more on alleles).

2) Organisms also have to <u>compete</u> for <u>limited resources</u> in an ecosystem.

3) Therefore organisms with the most <u>suitable characteristics</u> for the <u>environment</u> will be <u>more successful competitors</u> and will be <u>more likely to survive</u>.

4) The successful organisms that <u>survive</u> are more likely to <u>reproduce</u> and <u>pass on</u> the allele for the characteristics that made them successful to their <u>offspring</u>.

5) The organisms that are <u>less well adapted</u> will be <u>less likely to survive</u> and <u>reproduce</u>, so they are less likely to pass on their alleles to the next generation.

6) Over time, <u>beneficial characteristics</u> become <u>more common</u> in the population and the species <u>changes</u> — it <u>evolves</u>.

> Once upon a time maybe all rabbits had <u>short ears</u> and managed OK. Then one day a <u>mutated allele</u> meant that one rabbit popped out with <u>big ears</u>. This rabbit could hear better and was always the first to dive for cover at the sound of a predator. Pretty soon he's fathered a whole family of rabbits with <u>big ears</u>, all diving for cover before the other rabbits, and before you know it, there are only <u>big-eared</u> rabbits left — because the rest just didn't hear trouble coming quick enough.
>
> FOX!

You *Can Use a* Model *to Mimic Natural Selection*

1) Biologists can use <u>models</u> to mimic the <u>effect of characteristics</u> that help individuals to <u>survive</u> in their environment and therefore <u>breed</u> more <u>successfully</u>.

2) Here's an example of a model that mimics the effect of <u>camouflage</u> on a prey species.

> • 30 <u>blue</u> objects and 30 <u>red</u> objects (the 'prey') are randomly placed on a <u>blue</u> background (the 'environment').
> • A person (the 'predator') <u>picks up</u> as many objects as they can in <u>ten seconds</u>.
> • The number of red and blue objects <u>left</u> are counted and the <u>number recorded</u>.
> • For each object that has not been picked up, <u>another object</u> of the <u>same colour</u> is <u>added</u> to the background (the prey have 'reproduced').
> • The process is <u>repeated twice</u> more.

3) The results should show that, over time, more of the <u>blue objects accumulate</u> on the <u>blue background</u> because they're better camouflaged than the red objects. '<u>Natural selection</u>' has taken place.

4) However, this model has its limitations, for example:
   • <u>Other factors</u> would <u>affect survival</u> in real life, e.g. how fast the prey can move.
   • The <u>colour difference</u> between the prey and the environment would be <u>less extreme</u> in real life.
   • Many organisms <u>produce more than one offspring</u> in real life.

Also, the person choosing may be biased, because they know what the results should be.

"Natural selection" — sounds like vegan chocolates...

Natural selection's all about the organisms with the best characteristics surviving to pass on their alleles.

Q1 Musk oxen have thick fur, which is advantageous in the cold climate in which they live. Explain how the musk oxen may have developed this characteristic over many years. [4 marks]

More On Natural Selection

It was two clever chaps — <u>Darwin</u> and <u>Wallace</u> — who first developed the <u>theory of evolution by natural selection</u>. Little did they know we'd still be harping on about them <u>150 years later</u>...

Darwin Came up With The Theory of Evolution by Natural Selection...

<u>Charles Darwin</u> is well known as the guy who came up with the <u>theory of evolution by natural selection</u>. The <u>development</u> of the theory is a good example of how scientific <u>theories</u> arise. Darwin made <u>observations</u>, collected <u>evidence</u>, looked at the work of <u>other scientists</u> to <u>check</u> and <u>improve</u> his explanations, then <u>shared</u> his theory with the <u>scientific community</u>. This is how he did it:

1) He spent 5 years on a <u>voyage</u> around the world <u>studying plants</u> and <u>animals</u> on a ship called <u>HMS Beagle</u>.

2) He noticed that there was <u>variation</u> in members of the <u>same species</u> and that those with characteristics <u>most suited</u> to the <u>environment</u> were more likely to <u>survive</u>.

3) He also noticed that characteristics could be <u>passed on</u> to offspring.

4) Back in England, he carried out <u>experiments</u> to show how selection of particular <u>characteristics</u> could lead to the development of <u>new varieties</u> of an organism.

5) He wrote his <u>theory of evolution by natural selection</u> to explain his observations.

Charles Darwin

DNA and genes hadn't been discovered when Darwin was doing his work, so he didn't know exactly how characteristics were passed on — these details were added to the theory much later on.

...and Wallace Contributed Too

1) <u>Alfred Russel Wallace</u> was a scientist working at the <u>same time</u> as Darwin.

2) He also came up with the idea of natural selection, <u>independently</u> of Darwin.

3) He and Darwin <u>published</u> their papers on evolution <u>together</u> and <u>acknowledged</u> each other's work — although they didn't always <u>agree</u> on the <u>mechanisms</u> involved in <u>natural selection</u>.

4) Wallace's <u>observations</u> provided lots of <u>evidence</u> to help support the theory of evolution by natural selection. E.g. he realised that <u>warning colours</u> are used by some species (e.g. butterflies) to <u>deter predators</u> from eating them — an example of a <u>beneficial characteristic</u> that had <u>evolved</u> by natural selection.

5) But it was <u>Darwin's famous book</u> 'On the Origin of Species' (published in 1859) that made other scientists pay attention to the theory. In this book Darwin gave lots of <u>evidence</u> to support the theory and <u>expanded on it</u>. This book is partly why <u>Darwin</u> is usually <u>better remembered</u> than Wallace.

If Natural Selection is Too Slow, Species Could Become Extinct

1) Many species <u>don't exist any more</u> — these species are said to be <u>extinct</u>.

2) This can happen when the <u>environment changes</u> too quickly, e.g. due to the destruction of a habitat.

3) The process of natural selection is often <u>too slow</u> for organisms to <u>adapt</u> to <u>rapid</u> environmental changes.

Darwin was a darlin', and Wallace was well ace...

Biology wouldn't be what it is today without Darwin and Wallace, but at the time their ideas were revolutionary.

Q1   Describe Wallace's role in developing the theory of evolution by natural selection.   [2 marks]

Evidence For Evolution

There's a lot of modern evidence for the theory of evolution by natural selection.

Evolution is Ongoing and There is Evidence From...

As you know from page 146, evolution is a process in which organisms naturally change and adapt over time. There is lots of evidence to support that evolution is still happening, such as:

1) Antibiotic Resistance

1) Like all organisms, bacteria sometimes develop random mutations in their DNA. These can create new alleles, which can change the bacteria's characteristics — e.g. a bacterium could become less affected by a particular antibiotic (a drug designed to kill bacteria or prevent them from reproducing).

2) For the bacterium, the ability to resist this antibiotic is a big advantage. In a host who's being treated to get rid of the infection, a resistant bacterium is better able to survive than a non-resistant bacterium — and so it lives for longer and reproduces many more times.

3) This leads to the allele for antibiotic resistance being passed on to lots of offspring — it's just natural selection.

> MRSA is a type of antibiotic-resistant bacteria.

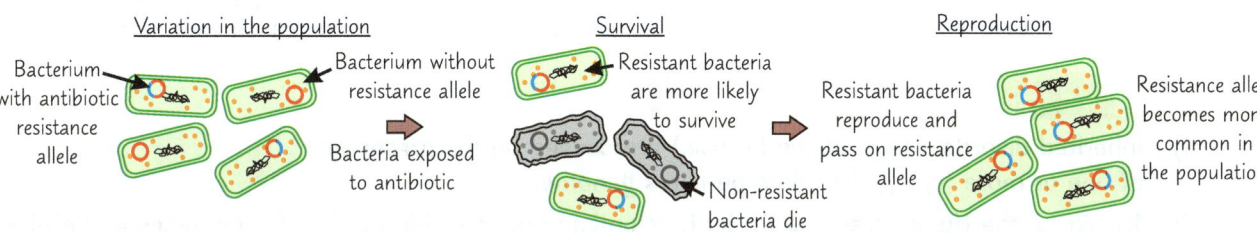

Variation in the population — Bacterium with antibiotic resistance allele — Bacterium without resistance allele — Bacteria exposed to antibiotic

Survival — Resistant bacteria are more likely to survive — Non-resistant bacteria die

Reproduction — Resistant bacteria reproduce and pass on resistance allele — Resistance allele becomes more common in the population

2) Warfarin Resistance

1) Warfarin used to be the main ingredient in rat poison.

2) Some rats are resistant to warfarin due to random mutations in their DNA creating new alleles.

3) This means rats which are resistant to warfarin have an advantage over non-resistant rats. So in an environment where there is warfarin, rats with warfarin resistance will be more able to survive and reproduce, whereas rats without warfarin resistance will be less able to survive.

4) This means the alleles that provide warfarin resistance are passed on to the next generation.

3) Pesticide Resistance

1) Some insects have evolved resistance to chemical pesticides due to random mutations in their DNA, which created new alleles.

2) This means insects which are resistant to pesticides have an advantage over non-resistant insects. So in an environment where pesticides are present, insects with pesticide resistance will be more likely to survive and reproduce, compared to non-resistant insects.

3) This means the alleles that provide pesticide resistance are passed on to the next generation.

All of these examples provide evidence for evolution because they make the organism better adapted to an environment. And as a result, antibiotic resistance, warfarin resistance and pesticide resistance become more common in the population over time.

Human evolution — from cave-man to desk-man...

So the evidence for evolution is all around us... But you've got to know what you're looking for.

Q1 Describe how antibiotic-resistant bacteria provide evidence for evolution. [2 marks]

The Human Genome

The <u>Human Genome Project</u> is one of the most exciting things to have happened in science in recent years.

Researchers Managed to Map Over 20 000 Human Genes

1) <u>Genome</u> is just the fancy term for the <u>entire set of genetic material</u> in an organism.

2) The <u>Human Genome Project</u> aimed to map all of the genetic material in <u>humans</u> — thousands of scientists from all over the world <u>collaborated</u> (worked together) to find <u>every single</u> human gene.

3) The project officially started in 1990 and a complete map of the human genome, including the locations of around <u>20 500 genes</u>, was completed in 2003.

4) Now that the genes have all been found, scientists are trying to figure out <u>what they all do</u>.

5) So far, the project has helped to identify about <u>1800 genes</u> related to disease, which has huge potential <u>benefits</u> for <u>medicine</u> (see below).

There are Lots of Medical Applications for the Project's Research

Prediction and prevention of diseases

Many <u>common diseases</u> like cancers and heart disease are caused by the <u>interaction</u> of <u>different genes</u>, as well as <u>lifestyle factors</u>. If doctors knew <u>what genes</u> predisposed people to <u>what diseases</u>, we could all get <u>individually tailored</u> advice on the best diet and lifestyle to avoid our likely problems. Doctors could also <u>check us</u> regularly to ensure <u>early treatment</u> if we do develop the diseases we're susceptible to.

Testing and treatment for inherited disorders

1) Inherited disorders (e.g. cystic fibrosis) are caused by the presence of one or more <u>faulty alleles</u> in a person's genome.

2) Thanks to the Human Genome Project, scientists are now able to <u>identify</u> the genes and alleles that are suspected of causing an inherited disorder <u>much more quickly</u> than they could do in the past.

3) Once an allele that causes an inherited disorder has been identified, people can be <u>tested</u> for it and it may be possible to <u>develop better treatments</u> or even (eventually) a <u>cure</u> for the disease.

New and better medicines

1) Genome research has highlighted some <u>common genetic variations</u> between people. Some variations affect how our individual bodies will <u>react</u> to certain <u>diseases</u> and to the possible <u>treatments</u> for them.

2) Scientists can use this knowledge to <u>design new drugs</u> that are specifically <u>tailored</u> to people with a <u>particular genetic variation</u>. They can also determine <u>how well an existing drug will work</u> for an individual. Tests can already identify whether or not someone with breast cancer will <u>respond</u> to a particular drug, and what <u>dosage</u> is most <u>appropriate</u> for certain drugs in different patients.

3) More generally, knowing how a disease affects us on a <u>molecular level</u> should make it possible to design <u>more effective</u> treatments with <u>fewer side-effects</u>.

But There Could Also be Drawbacks

1) <u>Increased stress</u> — if someone knew from an early age that they're susceptible to a nasty brain disease, they could <u>panic</u> every time they get a <u>headache</u> (even if they never get the disease).

2) <u>Gene-ism</u> — people with genetic problems could come under <u>pressure</u> not to have children.

3) <u>Discrimination</u> by <u>employers</u> and <u>insurers</u> — <u>life insurance</u> could become impossible to get (or blummin' <u>expensive</u> at least) if you have any <u>genetic likelihood</u> of serious disease. And employers may <u>discriminate</u> against people who are genetically likely to get a disease.

DNA lipstick is part of my genetic make-up...

The Human Genome Project has resulted in some pretty useful discoveries, but there's still loads of work to do.

Q1   How could information from human genome mapping be used
to help prevent individuals from developing certain diseases?   [2 marks]

Revision Questions for Unit 4b

Hurrah. It's the end of Unit 4b — hopefully you're feeling really confident with genetics and evolution now.

- Try these questions and tick off each one when you get it right.
- When you've done all the questions for a topic and are completely happy with it, tick off the topic.

Cell Division and Stem Cells (p.132-134) ☐

1) Give three reasons why multicellular organisms carry out mitosis. ☐
2) Explain how mitosis can result in cancer. ☐
3) What type of cell division produces gametes? ☐
4) How many daughter cells are produced by meiosis. ☑
5) What is a 'stem cell'? ☐

DNA and Genetic Profiling (p.135-136) ☐

6) Name the four bases that make up DNA. ☐
7) What shape does DNA form? ☐
8) What does a triplet of bases code for? ☑
9) Give two uses of genetic profiling. ☐

Sex Determination, Inheritance and Genetic Modification (p.137-139) ☐

10) What is the probability that offspring will have the **XX** combination of sex chromosomes? ☑
11) What combination of sex chromosomes do human males have? ☐
12) What is an 'allele'? ☑
13) What does it mean if an organism is:
  a) homozygous for a gene?
  b) heterozygous for a gene? ☑
14) Are most characteristics controlled by multiple genes or single gene inheritance? ☐
15) Briefly explain how genetic modification is carried out. ☑

Variation and Reproduction (p.140-142) ☐

16) What is variation? ☑
17) What shape of graph is shown by continuous variation? ☑
18) Which type of reproduction produces genetically identical cells? ☑

Mutations and Cystic Fibrosis (p.143-144) ☐

19) What effect do most mutations have on an organism? ☑
20) What problem does cystic fibrosis cause in the lungs? ☑
21) How is gene therapy for cystic fibrosis delivered to a patient's lung? ☑

Natural Selection and Evolution (p.145-147) ☐

22) Explain how beneficial characteristics can become more common in a population over time. ☑
23) Name the scientist who came up with the idea of natural selection at the same time as Charles Darwin. ☑
24) Give three examples that show evidence of evolution. ☑

The Human Genome (p.148) ☑

25) What is the human genome? ☑
26) Give two examples of medical applications of the human genome project. ☑

The Nervous System

The nervous system is what lets you react to what goes on around you, so you'd find life tough without it.

The Brain and Spinal Cord Make Up the Central Nervous System (CNS)

1) The spinal cord is a long column of neurones (nerve cells) that run from the base of the brain down the spine. At several places down the cord, neurones branch off and connect with other parts of the body. The spinal cord relays information between the brain and the rest of the body.

2) The brain is made up of billions of interconnected neurones.

The CNS Coordinates a Response

1) The nervous system is made up of neurones (nerve cells) which go to all parts of the body.

2) The sense organs are organs that contain receptors — groups of cells that can detect a change in your environment (a stimulus). Different receptors detect different stimuli. For example, receptors in your eyes detect light, receptors in your ear detect sound, receptors on your tongue detect chemicals and receptors in your skin detect touch (pressure) and temperature change.

3) When a stimulus is detected by receptors, the information is converted to an electrical (nervous) impulse and sent along neurones to the CNS.

4) The CNS coordinates the response (in other words, it decides what to do about the stimulus and tells something to do it).

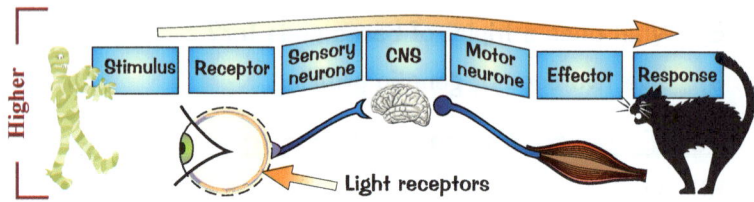

5) Impulses then travel along neurones to an effector (muscle or gland). The effector responds accordingly — e.g. a muscle may contract or a gland may secrete a hormone.

6) The time it takes you to respond to a stimulus is called your reaction time.

You Can Measure Reaction Time   PRACTICAL

Caffeine is a drug that can speed up a person's reaction time. The effect of caffeine on reaction time can be measured like this...

1) The person being tested should sit with their arm resting on the edge of a table.

2) Hold a ruler vertically between their thumb and forefinger. Make sure that the zero end of the ruler is level with their thumb and finger. Then let go without giving any warning.

3) The person being tested should try to catch the ruler as quickly as they can.

4) Reaction time is measured by the number on the ruler where it's caught — the further down the ruler it's caught, the slower their reaction time.

5) Repeat the test several times then calculate the mean distance that the ruler fell.

6) Repeat steps 1 to 5 ten minutes after the person being tested has had a caffeinated drink.

7) You need to control any variables to make sure that this is a fair test. E.g. you should use the same person to catch the ruler each time, and that person should always use the same hand to catch the ruler. Also, the ruler should always be dropped from the same height, and you should make sure that the person being tested has not had any caffeine (or anything else that may affect their reaction time) before the start of the experiment.

You can use a conversion table or a bit of maths to work out the reaction time in seconds from the mean distance.

Ready... Steady...   ... Ah, too slow.

Q1   A student was measuring her reaction time using a computer test. She had to click the mouse when the screen changed from red to green. She repeated the test five times. Her results were as follows:
242 ms, 256 ms, 253 ms, 249 ms, 235 ms.
Calculate the mean reaction time of the student.   [2 marks]

Reflexes

Information is passed between neurones <u>really quickly</u>, especially when there's a <u>reflex</u> involved...

Synapses *Connect Neurones*

1) The <u>junction</u> between <u>two neurones</u> is called a <u>synapse</u>.
2) The nerve impulse is transferred by <u>chemicals</u> which <u>diffuse</u> (move) across the gap.
3) The chemicals then set off a <u>new electrical signal</u> in the <u>next</u> neurone.
4) The <u>transmission</u> of a nervous <u>impulse</u> is <u>very fast</u>, but it is <u>slowed down</u> a bit at the synapse because the <u>diffusion</u> of chemicals across the gap takes <u>time</u>.

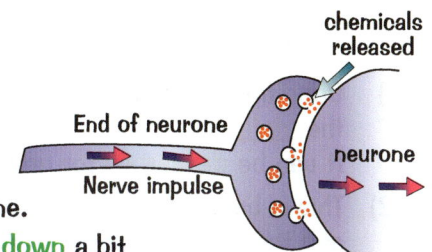

chemicals released

End of neurone

neurone

Nerve impulse

Higher

Reflexes *Help* Prevent Injury

1) <u>Reflexes</u> are <u>automatic</u>, <u>rapid</u> responses to stimuli. Reflexes can be <u>protective</u> — they can reduce the chances of being injured. An example of this is the <u>withdrawal reflex</u> in response to a painful stimulus — like when you move your hand away from a bee that stings you.
2) The passage of information in a reflex (from receptor, to coordinator, to effector) is called a <u>reflex arc</u>.
3) The neurones in reflex arcs go through the <u>spinal cord</u> or through an <u>unconscious part of the brain</u>.
4) When a <u>stimulus</u> (e.g. a bee sting) is detected by <u>receptors</u> (in this example, they're in the skin), <u>impulses</u> are sent along a <u>sensory neurone</u> to a <u>relay neurone</u> in the CNS.
5) When the impulses reach a <u>synapse</u> between the sensory neurone and the relay neurone, they trigger <u>chemicals</u> to be released (see above). These cause impulses to be sent along the <u>relay neurone</u>.
6) When the impulses reach a <u>synapse</u> between the relay neurone and a motor neurone, the same thing happens. Chemicals are released and cause impulses to be sent along the <u>motor neurone</u>.
7) The impulses then travel along the motor neurone to the <u>effector</u> (in this example it's a muscle, but it could be a gland).
8) The <u>muscle</u> then <u>contracts</u> and moves your hand away from the bee.

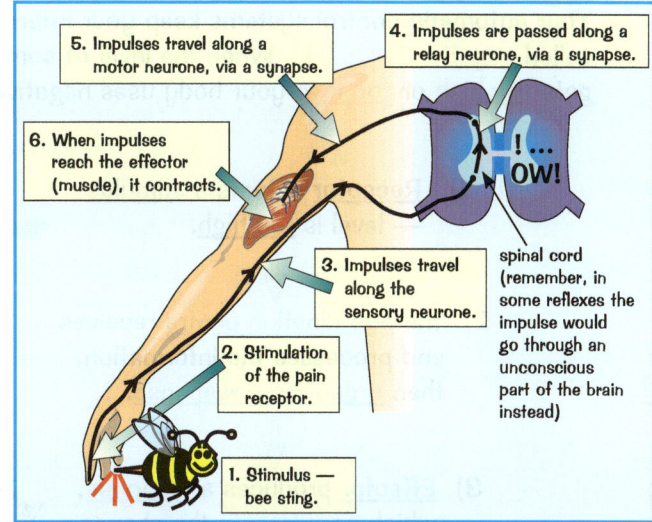

5. Impulses travel along a motor neurone, via a synapse.

4. Impulses are passed along a relay neurone, via a synapse.

6. When impulses reach the effector (muscle), it contracts.

!... OW!

3. Impulses travel along the sensory neurone.

spinal cord (remember, in some reflexes the impulse would go through an unconscious part of the brain instead)

2. Stimulation of the pain receptor.

1. Stimulus — bee sting.

9) Because you don't have to spend time thinking about the response, it's <u>quicker</u> than normal responses.

Higher

Reflexes *Help to* Protect the Eye

1) <u>Very bright light</u> can <u>damage</u> the eye — so you have a reflex to protect it.
2) <u>Light receptors</u> in the eye detect very bright light and send a message along a <u>sensory neurone</u> to the brain.
3) The message then travels along a <u>relay neurone</u> to a <u>motor neurone</u>, which tells <u>circular muscles</u> in the <u>iris</u> (the coloured part of the eye) to <u>contract</u>, making the pupil smaller.
4) <u>Blinking</u> is also a protective <u>reflex</u>. It closes the eye to stop it being <u>damaged</u> by anything <u>touching</u> it.

Bright light

iris

circular muscle contracted

pupil

Don't get all twitchy — just learn it...

Reflexes bypass conscious parts of your brain completely when a super quick response is essential — your body just gets on with things. If you had to stop and think first, you'd end up a lot more sore (or worse).

Q1   A chef touches a hot tray. A reflex reaction causes him to immediately move his hand away. Describe the pathway of the reflex arc from receptors to effector.   [4 marks]

Homeostasis

Homeostasis involves balancing body functions to maintain a 'constant internal environment'. Smashing.

Homeostasis *is* Maintaining *a* Constant Internal Environment

1) Conditions in your body need to be kept steady — this is really important so that all the metabolic reactions vital for keeping you alive can continue at an appropriate rate. It can be dangerous for your health if conditions vary too much from normal levels.

2) This is because metabolism only works if temperature and pH are within a certain range, and the body has enough of the right nutrients and water.

3) To maintain a constant internal environment, your body needs to respond to both internal and external changes whilst balancing inputs (stuff going into your body) with outputs (stuff leaving).

4) Things that you need to keep steady include:

> • Blood glucose (sugar) concentration — you need to make sure the amount of glucose in your blood doesn't get too high or too low (see page 154).
>
> • Body temperature — you need to make sure it doesn't get too high or too low (see next page).

Negative Feedback *Counteracts Changes*

Your automatic control systems keep your internal environment stable using a mechanism called negative feedback. When the level of something (e.g. blood glucose or temperature) gets too high or too low, your body uses negative feedback to bring it back to normal.

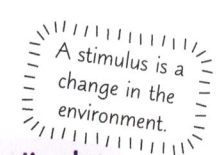
A stimulus is a change in the environment.

1) Receptor detects a stimulus — level is too high.

2) The coordination centre receives and processes the information, then organises a response.

3) Effector produces a response, which counteracts the change and restores the optimum level — the level decreases.

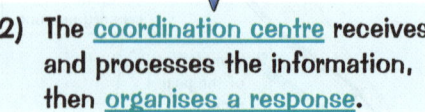
level decreases   level increases

1) Receptor detects a stimulus — level is too low.

2) The coordination centre receives and processes the information, then organises a response.

3) Effector produces a response, which counteracts the change and restores the optimum level — the level increases.

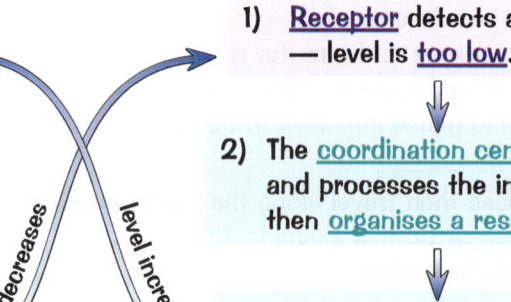
The effectors will just carry on producing the responses for as long as they're stimulated by the coordination centre. This might cause the opposite problem — making the level change too much (away from the ideal). Luckily the receptor detects if the level becomes too different and negative feedback starts again.

This process happens without you thinking about it — it's all automatic.

Higher

If you do enough revision, you can avoid negative feedback...

Negative feedback is a fancy-sounding name for a not-very-complicated idea. It's common sense really. For example, if you looked sad, I'd try and cheer you up. And if you looked really happy, I'd probably start to annoy you by flicking the backs of your ears. It stops things getting out of balance, I think.

Q1   Why do the internal conditions of your body need to be regulated?   [1 mark]

Q2   Name the component of a negative feedback mechanism that detects stimuli.   [1 mark]

Temperature Regulation

The body has to keep its insides at around 37 °C — the optimum temperature for enzymes in the body.

Body Temperature *Must be Kept* Constant

1) The body has to balance the amount of energy gained (e.g. through respiration) and lost to keep the core body temperature constant.

2) There is a thermoregulatory centre in the brain, which contains receptors that are sensitive to the temperature of the blood flowing through the brain.

3) The thermoregulatory centre also receives nervous impulses from temperature receptors in the skin, giving information about skin temperature.

> Core body temperature is the temperature inside your body, where your internal organs are.

Higher

1) Temperature receptors detect that core body temperature is too high.

2) The thermoregulatory centre acts as a coordination centre — it receives information from the temperature receptors and sends nervous impulses to trigger the effectors automatically.

3) Effectors, e.g. sweat glands, produce a response (see below) and counteract the change.

body cools down *body warms up*

1) Temperature receptors detect that core body temperature is too low.

2) The thermoregulatory centre acts as a coordination centre — it receives information from the temperature receptors and sends nervous impulses to trigger the effectors automatically.

3) Effectors, e.g. muscles, produce a response (see below) and counteract the change.

The *Body* has Some Nifty Tricks for *Altering* its Temperature

When You're *Too Hot...*

1) Erector muscles relax, so hairs lie flat.

2) Lots of sweat is produced — when the sweat evaporates, it transfers energy from your skin to the environment, cooling you down.

3) Blood vessels close to the surface of the skin dilate (widen). This is called vasodilation. It allows more blood to flow near the surface, so it can transfer more energy into the surroundings, which cools you down.

When You're *Too Cold...*

1) Erector muscles contract. Hairs stand on end to trap an insulating layer of air.

2) Very little sweat is produced.

3) Blood vessels near the surface of the skin constrict (narrow). This is called vasoconstriction. It means less blood flows near the surface, so less energy is transferred to the surroundings.

4) When you're cold you shiver too (your muscles contract automatically). This needs respiration, which transfers some energy to warm the body.

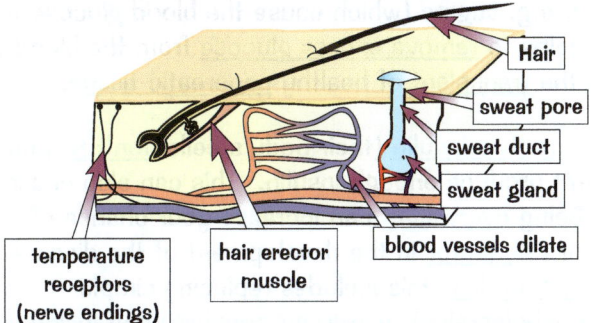

Hair
sweat pore
sweat duct
sweat gland
temperature receptors (nerve endings)
hair erector muscle
blood vessels dilate

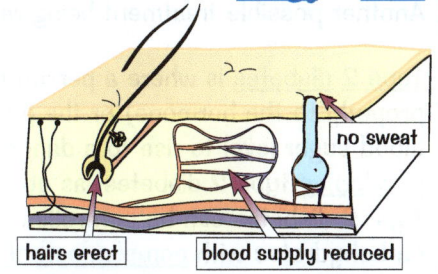

no sweat
hairs erect
blood supply reduced

Learn about temperature regulation — and keep your cool...

Controlling temperature is really important for keeping processes in your body ticking over nicely. Make sure you learn why temperature needs to be controlled, and can explain how your body responds to changes in temperature.

Q1   Explain how blood flow through the skin is affected when a person is too cold.   [2 marks]

Controlling Blood Sugar Level and Diabetes

Blood sugar level is controlled as part of homeostasis. Insulin and glucagon are the two hormones involved.

Hormones Are Chemical Messengers That Control Many Body Functions

Hormones are chemicals released directly into the blood. They are carried in the blood to other parts of the body, but only affect particular cells in particular organs. Hormones control things that need constant adjustment. For example, insulin (a protein) and glucagon control blood glucose (sugar) level:

1) Eating foods containing carbohydrate puts glucose into the blood from the small intestine.

2) Exercise and the normal metabolism of cells removes glucose from the blood.

3) Excess glucose is converted to insoluble glycogen in the liver. It's then stored in the liver and muscles.

4) When these stores are full, the excess glucose is stored as lipid (fat) in the tissues.

5) The level of glucose in the blood must be kept steady to prevent damage to the body. Changes in blood glucose are monitored and controlled by the pancreas using the hormones insulin and glucagon. It's a negative feedback mechanism (see p.152).

You only need to know about negative feedback and glucagon if you're sitting the Higher tier papers.

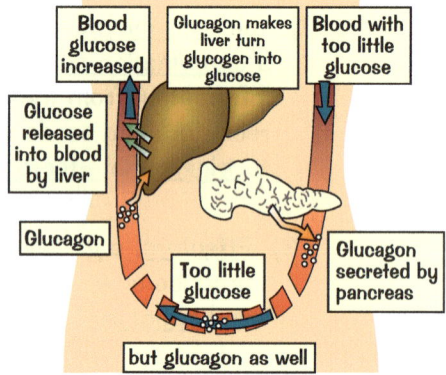

Having Diabetes Means You Can't Control Your Blood Sugar Level

Diabetes is a condition that affects your ability to control your blood sugar level, so that it becomes too high. Finding glucose in urine is a symptom of diabetes. Urine samples can be tested for glucose using Benedict's reagent (see page 28). There are two types of diabetes:

TYPE 1 Type 1 diabetes is where the pancreas stops producing insulin. The result is that a person's blood glucose level can rise to a level that can kill them. People with type 1 diabetes need insulin therapy. This usually involves having insulin injections several times a day (often at mealtimes). This makes sure that glucose is removed from the blood quickly once food has been digested. This stops the level of glucose in the blood from getting too high and is a very effective treatment. The amount of insulin needed depends on the person's diet and how active they are. As well as insulin therapy, people with type 1 diabetes need to think about limiting their intake of food rich in simple carbohydrates, e.g. sugars (which cause the blood glucose to rise rapidly) and taking regular exercise (which helps to remove excess glucose from the blood). Another possible treatment being researched is the transplant of healthy pancreatic tissue.

TYPE 2 Type 2 diabetes is where a person becomes resistant to insulin (their body's cells don't respond properly to the hormone) or the pancreas doesn't produce enough insulin. This can also cause blood sugar level to rise to a dangerous level. Being overweight can increase your chance of developing type 2 diabetes, as obesity is a major risk factor in the development of the disease. Type 2 diabetes can be controlled by eating a healthy diet (this includes replacing simple carbohydrates with complex carbohydrates, e.g. wholegrains), exercising regularly and losing weight if necessary. Some people with type 2 diabetes also have medication or insulin injections.

And people used to think the pancreas was just a cushion...

This stuff can seem a bit confusing at first, but if you understand those two diagrams, it'll all become a lot easier.

Q1   Describe how the level of insulin production differs in type 1 and type 2 diabetes.   [2 marks]

Lifestyle Choices

Some <u>lifestyle choices</u> that people make can have an impact on <u>health</u>.

Alcohol and Drug Abuse Can Affect Chemical Processes in the Body

Alcohol is a Depressant Drug

1) Alcohol has an effect on many <u>chemical processes</u> in the body. For example, it <u>reduces</u> the activity of the <u>nervous system</u> and <u>slows down reaction times</u> — it's a <u>depressant</u>.

2) Drinking too much alcohol leads to <u>impaired judgement</u>, <u>poor balance</u>, <u>poor coordination</u>, <u>slurred speech</u>, <u>blurred vision</u> and <u>sleepiness</u>.

3) <u>Alcohol</u> is <u>poisonous</u>. It's <u>broken down</u> by <u>enzymes</u> in the liver and some of the <u>products</u> are <u>toxic</u>. If you drink <u>too much</u> alcohol over a <u>long period</u> of time, these toxic products can cause the <u>death</u> of liver cells, forming <u>scar tissue</u> that stops <u>blood</u> reaching the liver — this is called <u>cirrhosis</u>.

4) If the liver can't do its normal job of <u>cleaning the blood</u>, dangerous substances start to <u>build up</u> and <u>damage</u> the rest of the body.

5) Drinking too much alcohol also <u>increases blood pressure</u> which can lead to <u>circulatory</u> and <u>heart diseases</u>.

6) Many <u>cancers</u>, including those of the <u>mouth</u>, <u>throat</u>, <u>bowels</u> and <u>liver</u>, have all been linked to alcohol consumption because the toxic products <u>damage DNA</u> and cause cells to <u>divide faster</u> than normal.

7) Alcohol is <u>addictive</u> — some people become <u>dependent</u> on alcohol in their <u>daily lives</u>. It can be difficult for these people to give up alcohol, as they often experience severe <u>withdrawal symptoms</u> (e.g. depression, anxiety, nausea, hand tremors).

Some Drugs are Misused

Not all drugs are used by people with <u>illnesses</u> — some are used to <u>boost sporting performance</u>, whilst others are used for <u>enjoyment</u>. This is <u>drug misuse</u> and it can have a wide range of <u>negative</u> effects.

1) <u>Illegal</u> drugs can be divided into <u>two main classes</u> — <u>soft</u> (e.g. cannabis) and <u>hard</u> (e.g. heroin and ecstasy). <u>Hard</u> drugs are really <u>addictive</u> and are typically more <u>harmful</u> than <u>soft</u> drugs.

2) Both hard and soft drugs can cause <u>serious health problems</u> or even <u>death</u>. For example, heroin, ecstasy and cannabis can all cause <u>heart</u> and <u>circulatory</u> problems. Cannabis can also increase the risk of developing <u>mental health problems</u>.

3) <u>Anabolic steroids</u> can be used as <u>performance-enhancing</u> drugs that are sometimes taken by athletes. These drugs can have negative impacts on the body, including <u>high blood pressure</u>.

Diet Can Negatively Impact the Body

The <u>food</u> we eat can have an impact on how our <u>body functions</u>. For example, eating too much can lead to <u>obesity</u>. It's thought that obesity can directly cause <u>type 2 diabetes</u> by making the body <u>less sensitive</u> or <u>resistant</u> to insulin, meaning that it struggles to <u>control</u> the <u>concentration</u> of <u>glucose</u> in the blood (see previous page).

"I was doing research, man" — tell that to the judge...

In the exam, you might be asked to interpret data about how lifestyle choices affect health. These sorts of questions quite often come with a graph. See page 10 for a few tips on what you can and can't say in your answer.

Q1   Explain how lifestyle choices can affect the incidence of type 2 diabetes.   [2 marks]

Revision Questions for Unit 4c

Ah... the final page of Unit 4c — I hope this section hasn't left you feeling too nervous...

* Try these questions and tick off each one when you get it right.
* When you've done all the questions for a topic and are completely happy with it, tick off the topic.

The Nervous System (p.150) ☐

1) What makes up the central nervous system and what does it do? ☐
2) What is a stimulus? ☐
3) How is information transmitted around the nervous system? ☐
4) What is reaction time? ☐
5) How can the effect of caffeine on reaction time be measured? ☐

Reflexes (p.151) ☐

6) What is a synapse? ☐
7) What is the purpose of a reflex action? ☐
8) Describe the series of events that take place during a reflex action. ☐
9) State two reflex actions that protect the eye. ☐

Homeostasis (p.152-154) ☐

10) What is homeostasis? ☐
11) Name two conditions in the body that need to be kept steady. ☐
12) How does negative feedback help to maintain a stable environment? ☐
13) Give three things the body can do to reduce heat loss if it gets too cold. ☐
14) What is a hormone? ☐
15) Where is glycogen stored in the body? ☐
16) True or false? Insulin is a protein. ☐
17) What effect does the hormone glucagon have on blood glucose level? ☐
18) What type of mechanism controls blood glucose levels? ☐
19) How is urine tested for glucose? ☐
20) How are type 1 diabetes usually controlled? How is type 2 diabetes usually controlled? ☐

Lifestyle Choices (p.155) ☐

21) How does alcohol affect reaction time? ☐
22) Give one disease caused by excessive alcohol consumption. ☐
23) Name a disease that can be caused by obesity. ☐

Pathogens

Well, here are loads of ways you can catch diseases. As if I wasn't feeling paranoid enough already...

Pathogens Cause Diseases

Micro-organisms are everywhere. Most won't do you any harm — in fact, many carry out really important functions, like helping you digest food. But some micro-organisms cause communicable diseases (diseases that can spread between organisms). These micro-organisms are called pathogens — there are four types:

1) **BACTERIA** — very small cells (about 1/100th the size of your body cells), which can reproduce rapidly. They make you feel ill by producing toxins (poisons) that damage your cells and tissues.

2) **VIRUSES** — these are not cells. They're really tiny, about 1/100th the size of a bacterium. They replicate themselves inside the infected organism's cells. These cells then burst, releasing the viruses.

3) **PROTISTS** — these are usually single-celled and vary in size.

4) **FUNGI** — some fungi are single-celled while others have a body, which is made up of thread-like structures called hyphae. These hyphae can grow and penetrate human skin and the surface of plants, causing diseases. They can also produce spores, which can be spread to other plants and animals.

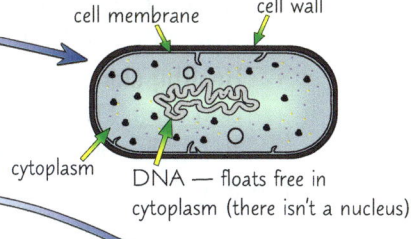

cell membrane   cell wall

cytoplasm   DNA — floats free in cytoplasm (there isn't a nucleus)

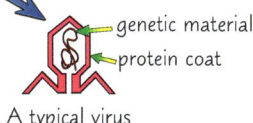

genetic material
protein coat

A typical virus

Communicable Diseases are Spread in Different Ways

Pathogens infect both animals and plants and can spread in different ways. For example:

Water	Some pathogens can be picked up by drinking or bathing in water that contains them.
Aerosol (in the air)	Some pathogens are carried in the air (e.g. fungal spores blown between plants by the wind). Airborne pathogens can also be carried in droplets produced when you cough or sneeze — so other people can breathe them in.
Contact	Some pathogens can be picked up by touching contaminated surfaces. E.g. athlete's foot is a fungus which makes skin itch and flake off. It's most commonly spread by touching the same things as an infected person, e.g. shower floors and towels.
Body fluids	Some pathogens are spread by body fluids such as blood (e.g. by sharing needles to inject drugs), breast milk (through breast feeding) and semen (through sexual contact).
Insects	Insects can spread disease. E.g. malaria is caused by a protist. Mosquitoes pick up the malarial protist when they feed on an infected animal. Every time the mosquito feeds on another animal, it infects it by inserting the protist into the animal's blood vessels.
Food	Some pathogens are picked up by eating contaminated food. E.g. *Salmonella* bacteria are found in some foods, e.g. raw meat. You could get food poisoning from eating these foods.

Some Things Help to Prevent You Getting a Disease

1) Good hygiene practices (e.g. hand-washing) and using clean water can help protect you from disease.

2) Having a healthy diet (see p.31) can also help your immune system to function effectively, which keeps diseases at bay and reduces the risk of developing diseases linked to an unhealthy diet (see p.37).

3) Other diseases can be prevented with vaccines (see page 159) or with drugs (e.g. anti-malarial medication can reduce the chance of you getting malaria).

4) Drugs are also used to treat diseases (e.g. antibiotics treat bacterial infections), which can help to prevent a disease spreading to other people.

Ahh...Ahh... Ahhhhh Choooooooo — urghh, this page is catching...

Pathogens are usually really small — you often need a microscope to see them — but they don't half get about...

Q1   Give three ways in which communicable diseases can be spread.   [3 marks]

Fighting Disease

Your body has some pretty neat features when it comes to fighting disease.

Your Body Defends *Itself* Against Disease

1) Your body's first line of defence includes barriers that try to prevent pathogens getting in. For example:
   - The skin is an intact, physical barrier to pathogens, and, if it gets damaged, blood clots quickly seal cuts and keep micro-organisms out.
   - Healthy skin is also naturally covered in millions of micro-organisms, which are collectively known as skin flora. The skin flora helps to protect the body from disease by making it difficult for pathogens to survive on the skin, e.g. by out-competing the pathogens for the resources they need to survive.

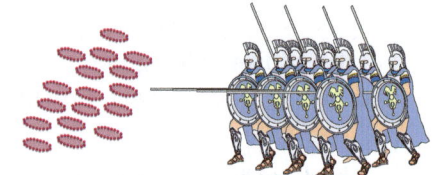

2) But if pathogens do manage to make it past the barriers and into your body, then it's left to the immune system to defend you against disease.

Your Immune System *Can* Attack Pathogens *that* Enter *the Body*

The most important part of your immune system is the white blood cells. They travel around in your blood, constantly patrolling for pathogens. When they find an invading pathogen they have three lines of attack:

1. Ingesting *Them*

Some white blood cells (phagocytes) have a flexible membrane and contain lots of enzymes. This enables them to engulf foreign cells and digest them.

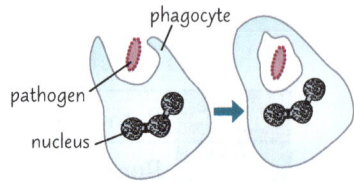
phagocyte
pathogen
nucleus

2. Producing Antibodies

1) Every cell has unique molecules on its surface called antigens. In a healthy person, white blood cells recognise antigens on pathogens as foreign (non-self) and antigens on normal body cells as self.

2) When lymphocytes (a type of white blood cell) come across a foreign antigen, they will start to produce proteins called antibodies to lock onto the invading cells. The antibodies produced are specific to that type of antigen — they won't lock on to any others.

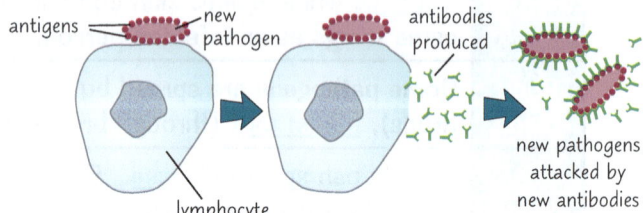
antigens
new pathogen
antibodies produced
lymphocyte
new pathogens attacked by new antibodies

3) The lymphocytes divide many times so you end up with lots of clones (exact copies) of the lymphocytes, all producing the same antibodies. This results in lots of the antibodies being carried around the body to lock on to all similar pathogens.

4) The antibodies can inactivate the pathogens and help phagocytes find the pathogens. The phagocytes then engulf the pathogens.

5) Some white blood cells, called memory cells, stay around in the blood after the pathogen has been fought off. If the person is infected with the same pathogen again, the white blood cells will rapidly produce lots of the antibody to help destroy it. The pathogen will be fought off much faster than the first time it was encountered — the person is naturally immune to that specific pathogen and won't get ill.

Memory cells are also produced following a vaccination — see next page.

3. Producing Antitoxins

These are produced by lymphocytes and counteract toxins produced by invading bacteria.

Fight disease — give your nose a blow with boxing gloves...

The body makes antibodies against the antigens on pathogens. There, don't say I never help you. Right, tea...

Q1   Explain the role of blood clots in defending the body against disease.   [2 marks]

Unit 4d — Disease

Vaccinations

An ounce of <u>prevention</u> is worth a pound of <u>cure</u>. That's what my mum says, anyhow.

Vaccinations Can Stop You Getting Infections

1) When you're infected with a <u>new</u> pathogen it can take your white blood cells a while to produce the <u>antibodies</u> to deal with it. In that time you can get <u>very ill</u>, or maybe even die.

2) To avoid this you can be <u>vaccinated</u> (immunised) against some <u>bacterial</u> or <u>viral</u> diseases, e.g. tuberculosis or measles.

3) To <u>make</u> a vaccine, the <u>pathogen</u> (e.g. bacteria or virus) that causes the disease is <u>identified</u> and <u>grown</u> in a lab. The pathogens are then either <u>killed</u>, <u>inactivated</u> or <u>weakened</u>, or the <u>antigens</u> they carry are <u>isolated</u>. The pathogens or isolated antigens are then made into a <u>vaccine</u> that can be administered to a person, usually as an <u>injection</u>.

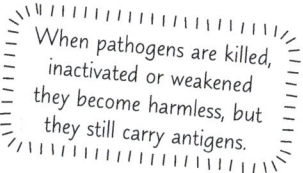

When pathogens are killed, inactivated or weakened they become harmless, but they still carry antigens.

4) The presence of the pathogen's <u>antigens</u> in a person's bloodstream triggers an <u>immune response</u> — white blood cells (lymphocytes) produce <u>antibodies</u> to attack them.

5) Some of these white blood cells will remain in the blood as <u>memory cells</u>, so if <u>live</u> pathogens of the <u>same type</u> ever appear, the antibodies that <u>help destroy them</u> will be produced immediately.

Higher

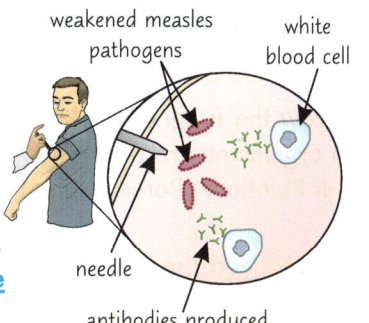

weakened measles pathogens
white blood cell
needle
antibodies produced

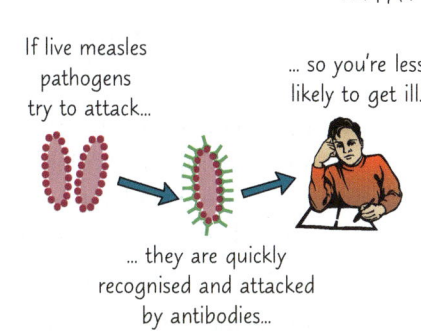

If live measles pathogens try to attack...
... so you're less likely to get ill.
... they are quickly recognised and attacked by antibodies...

Parents Decide Whether or Not to Have Children Vaccinated

People are <u>normally</u> vaccinated as <u>children</u>. This means it's usually up to <u>parents</u> to <u>decide</u> whether or not to have their <u>child</u> vaccinated. There are arguments <u>for</u> and <u>against</u> vaccination they should consider:

Arguments FOR

1) Vaccines <u>protect</u> a child from getting some very nasty <u>diseases</u>.

2) Big outbreaks of disease (<u>epidemics</u>) can be prevented if a <u>large percentage</u> of the population is vaccinated. That way, even the people who aren't vaccinated are <u>unlikely</u> to catch the disease as there are <u>fewer</u> people able to <u>pass it on</u>. But if a significant number of people <u>aren't</u> vaccinated, the disease can <u>spread</u> quickly through them and lots of people will be <u>ill</u> at the same time.

3) Parents may be influenced by <u>media campaigns</u> which <u>encourage</u> vaccinations — these are usually run by health organisations such as the <u>NHS</u>.

Arguments AGAINST

1) Vaccines don't always work — sometimes they <u>don't</u> give a child <u>immunity</u>.

2) Children can sometimes have a <u>bad reaction</u> to a vaccine (e.g. swelling, or maybe something more serious like a fever or seizures). Bad reactions are very <u>rare</u> but parents may read articles about them in the <u>media</u> which make them <u>worry</u>.

3) Some parents worry about <u>links</u> to <u>other conditions</u>. For example, in 1998, there was a big <u>media story</u> surrounding a scientist who claimed to have found a link between the <u>MMR vaccine</u> (for measles, mumps and rubella) and <u>autism</u>. This meant many parents <u>stopped</u> their children from being vaccinated, leading to a <u>rise</u> in the number of children catching <u>measles</u>. However, the results have <u>never</u> been reproduced and health authorities have now <u>concluded</u> that the vaccine is <u>safe</u>.

Take that, you evil antigen...

The way that vaccines are portrayed in the media is important — a biased article can influence a lot of people.

Q1   Explain how lymphocytes respond to vaccinations.   [2 marks]

Antibiotics

Your immune system is pretty impressive, but sometimes it just needs a helping hand to fight off disease.

Antibiotics *Can Cure Diseases Caused by Bacteria*

1) Sometimes the body might not be able to fight off a disease on its own. In this case, it might be necessary to use medicines to help things along.

2) Antibiotics (e.g. penicillin) actually kill or prevent the growth of the bacteria causing the problem without killing your own body cells. Different antibiotics attack different types of bacteria, so it's important to be treated with the right one.

3) Many antibiotics are produced naturally by fungi and other living organisms. For example:

- Alexander Fleming was clearing out some Petri dishes containing bacteria. He noticed that one of the dishes of bacteria also had mould on it and the area around the mould was free of the bacteria.

- He found that the mould (*Penicillium notatum*) on the Petri dish was producing a substance that diffused through the agar jelly it was growing on and killed the bacteria — this substance was penicillin.

4) Pharmaceutical companies can grow the fungi or other organisms on a large scale in the lab and extract the antibiotics. Antibiotics from organisms are often modified in the lab to make them more effective — these are called semi-synthetic antibiotics. Some antibiotics are created by chemists in a lab — these are called synthetic antibiotics.

5) The use of antibiotics has greatly reduced the number of deaths from bacterial communicable diseases.

6) But antibiotics don't destroy viruses (e.g. flu or cold viruses). Viruses reproduce using your body cells, which makes it very difficult to develop drugs that destroy just the virus without killing the body's cells.

Overuse *of Antibiotics May Make Some Diseases Difficult to Treat*

1) Some bacteria are naturally resistant to certain antibiotics.

2) The overuse of antibiotics can increase the rate of development of these resistant strains. For example:

Doctors may prescribe antibiotics when they're not really needed, e.g. for minor infections or viral infections. This will kill some bacteria in the patient's body, but resistant bacteria may survive the antibiotic. Once the non-resistant bacteria have been killed, the resistant strains will have less competition and will be able to grow and reproduce and become more common.

Using antibiotics in animal feed helps keep livestock healthy but it could lead to the development of antibiotic-resistant bacteria in farm animals. The resistant bacteria could then enter the human food chain when we eat meat or when we eat crops that have been fertilised with animal manure.

3) Because of the misuse of antibiotics, very resistant strains of bacteria have developed, e.g. MRSA (the hospital 'superbug') is a well-known example of an antibiotic-resistant strain. The development of these very resistant strains means that the antibiotics we currently use are becoming less effective.

4) Since superbugs like MRSA can be very dangerous, doctors have to balance their patient's well-being with the well-being of other people in society when they decide whether or not to prescribe antibiotics — e.g. they may not prescribe antibiotics if they're not really needed.

5) Hospitals also have many control measures to help to reduce the spread of MRSA. These include thoroughly cleaning hospital wards, staff washing their hands between contact with different patients and increasing the use of alcohol gels (which can kill MRSA) in hospitals. Some hospitals also carry out MRSA screening — a simple test to check if patients entering the hospital carry the MRSA bacteria.

Aaargh, a giant earwig! Run from the attack of the superbug...

The reality of 'superbugs' is even scarier than giant earwigs. Micro-organisms that are resistant to all of our drugs are a worrying thought. It'll be like going back in time to before antibiotics were invented.

Q1 Explain why many antibiotics are becoming less effective as treatments for infections. [3 marks]

Developing New Drugs

As you saw on the previous page, living organisms can produce chemicals that we can use as drugs. When scientists develop a new drug, the process often starts with them extracting and purifying the active chemicals they've found. The drugs then have to be extensively tested before they can be given to the general public.

There are Three Main Stages in Drug Testing

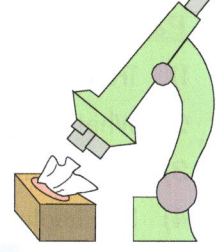

①

1) In preclinical testing, drugs are tested on human cells and tissues in the lab.

2) However, you can't use human cells and tissues to test drugs that affect whole or multiple body systems, e.g. testing a drug for blood pressure must be done on a whole animal because it has an intact circulatory system.

②

1) The next step in preclinical testing is to test the drug on live animals. This is to test efficacy (whether the drug works and produces the effect you're looking for), to find out about its toxicity (how harmful it is) and to find the best dosage (the concentration that should be given, and how often it should be given).

2) The law in Britain states that any new drug must be tested on two different live mammals. However, this raises some ethical issues. For example:

> • Some people think it's cruel to test on animals because experiments can cause them pain and distress.
>
> • Some people also think that animals are so different from humans that testing on animals is pointless.
>
> • Others believe that testing on animals is the safest way to make sure a drug isn't dangerous before it's given to humans.
>
> • Some people believe animal testing is okay because scientists have to follow strict rules stating that animals must be properly looked after and measures must be taken to minimise their discomfort.

3) There are alternatives to using animals in research, e.g. using computer models to predict the effects of drugs. As technology advances, it is possible that new technologies could supersede (replace) animal testing in the future.

③

1) If the drug passes all the preclinical tests then it's tested on human volunteers in a clinical trial.

2) First, the drug is tested on healthy volunteers. This is to make sure that it doesn't have any harmful side effects when the body is working normally. The side effects of the drug may not happen to everyone, so it needs to be tested on a large number of people.

Although drug trials involve lots of people, sometimes side effects don't show up until the drug is on the market and being taken by lots more people.

3) If the results of the tests on healthy volunteers are good, the drugs can be tested on people suffering from the illness. The optimum dose is found — this is the dose of drug that is the most effective and has few side effects.

4) The results of drug testing aren't published until they've been through peer review (see p.2). This helps to prevent false claims.

Being involved in a drug trial can be risky — although the drug has already been tested before it reaches humans, there's still the risk that the drug could have unexpected harmful effects. However, drug trials are strictly regulated to help make sure that everyone taking part is as safe as possible. The benefits of being able to collect data which leads to the development of new and improved drugs usually outweighs the risks associated with the trials.

Crikey — and I used to think that school kids were tested a lot...

Researchers work really hard carrying out rigorous, large-scale drug trials so that you can benefit from new and improved medicines — so the least you can do to pay them back is learn how they do it by reading this page.

Q1   Give one argument for and one argument against using animal testing during drug development. [2 marks]

Revision Questions for Unit 4d

You'll be pleased to know that's <u>Unit 4d</u> done — now you can celebrate by seeing how much you've learnt...

- Try these questions and <u>tick off each one</u> when you <u>get it right</u>.
- When you've done <u>all the questions</u> for a topic and are <u>completely happy</u> with it, tick off the topic.

<u>Pathogens (p.157)</u> ☐

1) True or False? All micro-organisms cause disease. ☐
2) What is a pathogen? ☐
3) Name four types of pathogen. ☐
4) In a bacterial cell, where is the DNA found? ☐
5) Give one reason why having a healthy diet helps to protect you from getting a disease. ☐
6) Other than having a healthy diet, give two things that can be done to help protect you from getting a disease. ☐

<u>Fighting Disease (p.158)</u> ☐

7) Describe two ways in which the skin helps to defend the body against disease. ☐
8) Describe the role of phagocytes in the immune system. ☐
9) What is an antigen? ☐
10) Which type of white blood cell produces antibodies? ☐
11) True or False? One type of antibody can lock on to many different types of pathogen. ☐
12) Explain why you may not get ill the second time a specific pathogen enters your body. ☐
13) Describe the role of antitoxins in defending the body against pathogens. ☐

<u>Vaccinations (p.159)</u> ☐

14) Give two types of pathogen which the body can be vaccinated against. ☐
15) Describe how a pathogen is made into a vaccine. ☐
16) Explain how having a vaccination protects a person against disease. ☐
17) Give one argument for and one argument against a parent having their child vaccinated. ☐

<u>Antibiotics (p.160)</u> ☐

18) How can antibiotics cure a disease? ☐
19) True or False? Some antibiotics originally come from fungi. ☐
20) State two ways in which antibiotics are being over used. ☐
21) Give three examples of control measures that can reduce the spread of MRSA. ☐

<u>Developing New Drugs (p.161)</u> ☑

22) True or False? New drugs have to be tested on animals before they can be approved for use in humans. ☑
23) Give an example of a new technology that could be used instead of animal testing. ☑
24) In terms of side effects, why is it important that drug trials involve a large number of people? ☑
25) Why is it important that the results of drug trials are peer reviewed before being published? ☑

Metallic Bonding

Right, time to take a look at the bonding in different substances. First up — metals.

Metallic Bonding Involves Delocalised Electrons

1) Metals consist of a giant structure.

2) The electrons in the outer shell of the metal atoms are delocalised (free to move around). There are strong forces of electrostatic attraction between the lattice of positive metal ions and the shared sea of negative electrons.

3) These forces of attraction hold the atoms together in a regular structure and are known as metallic bonding. Metallic bonding is very strong.

I don't think he's from round here.

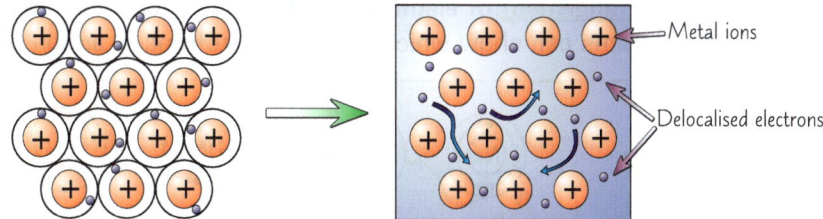

Metal ions

Delocalised electrons

4) Substances that are held together by metallic bonding include metallic elements and alloys (see p.180).

5) It's the delocalised electrons in the metallic bonds which produce many of the properties of metals.

Most Metals are Solid at Room Temperature

1) The electrostatic forces between the metal atoms and the delocalised sea of electrons are very strong, so need lots of energy to be broken.

2) This means that most compounds with metallic bonds have very high melting and boiling points, so they're generally solid at room temperature.

Metals aren't soluble — they don't dissolve in water.

3) Ions with higher charges have more delocalised electrons. This means they have stronger electrostatic forces of attraction. So metals that contain ions with higher charges generally have higher melting and boiling points than those that contain ions with lower charges.

4) E.g. aluminium contains Al^{3+} ions, so has a higher melting point than magnesium, which contains Mg^{2+} ions. Both aluminium and magnesium have higher melting points than sodium, which contains Na^+ ions.

Higher

Metals are Good Conductors of Electricity and Heat

The delocalised electrons carry electrical charge and thermal (heat) energy through the whole structure, so metals are good conductors of electricity and heat.

Most Metals are Malleable and Ductile

1) The layers of atoms in a metal can slide over each other, making metals malleable — this means that they can be bent or hammered or rolled into flat sheets.

2) The layers of atoms within metals also make them ductile. This means that metals can be drawn out into thin wires without breaking.

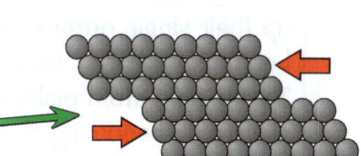

I saw a metal on the train once — he was the conductor...

If your knowledge of metals is still feeling a bit delocalised, the questions below will help...

Q1   Copper is a metallic element. Describe and explain what property of copper makes it suitable for use in electrical circuits.   [2 marks]

Q2   Explain why magnesium has a higher melting point than sodium.   [3 marks]

Ionic Bonding

Now you've cracked metallic bonding, you must be dying to know what happens when a metal and non-metal react.

Ionic Bonding — Transfer of Electrons

When a metal and a non-metal react together, the metal atom loses electrons to form a positively charged ion and the non-metal gains these electrons to form a negatively charged ion. These oppositely charged ions are strongly attracted to one another by electrostatic forces. This attraction is called an ionic bond.

Dot and Cross Diagrams Show How Ionic Compounds are Formed

Dot and cross diagrams show the arrangement of electrons in an atom or ion. Each electron is represented by a dot or a cross. So these diagrams can show which atom the electrons in an ion originally came from.

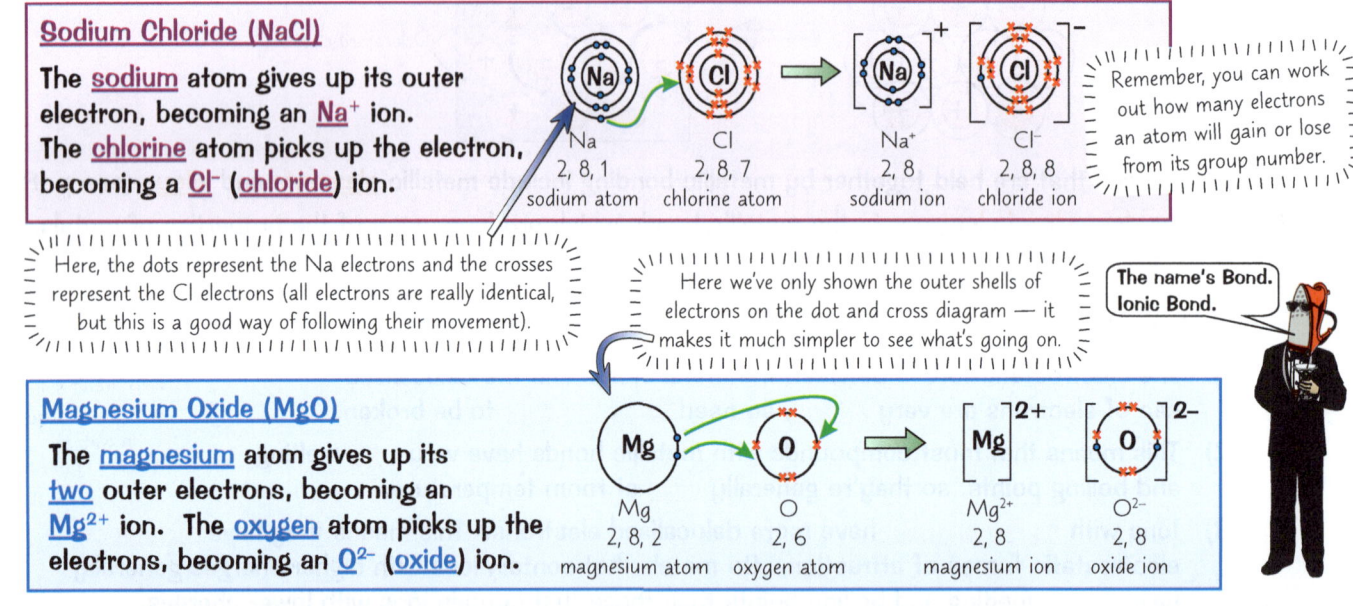

Sodium Chloride (NaCl)
The sodium atom gives up its outer electron, becoming an Na^+ ion.
The chlorine atom picks up the electron, becoming a Cl^- (chloride) ion.

Remember, you can work out how many electrons an atom will gain or lose from its group number.

Here, the dots represent the Na electrons and the crosses represent the Cl electrons (all electrons are really identical, but this is a good way of following their movement).

Here we've only shown the outer shells of electrons on the dot and cross diagram — it makes it much simpler to see what's going on.

The name's Bond. Ionic Bond.

Magnesium Oxide (MgO)
The magnesium atom gives up its two outer electrons, becoming an Mg^{2+} ion. The oxygen atom picks up the electrons, becoming an O^{2-} (oxide) ion.

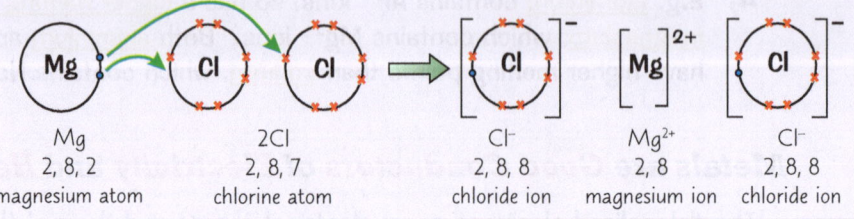

Magnesium Chloride (MgCl₂)
The magnesium atom gives up its two outer electrons, becoming an Mg^{2+} ion. The two chlorine atoms pick up one electron each, becoming two Cl^- (chloride) ions.

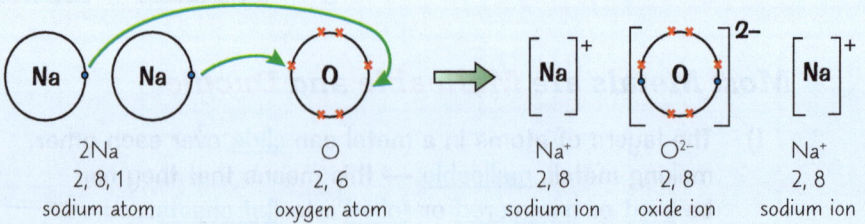

Sodium Oxide (Na₂O)
Two sodium atoms each give up their single outer electron, becoming two Na^+ ions. The oxygen atom picks up the two electrons, becoming an O^{2-} ion.

Stop slacking — I've got my ion you...

You need to be able to describe how ionic compounds are formed using both words and dot and cross diagrams. It gets easier with practice, so here are some questions to get you started.

Q1 Describe, in terms of electron transfer, how calcium and fluorine react to form calcium fluoride (CaF_2). [2 marks]

Q2 Draw a dot and cross diagram to show how potassium (a Group 1 metal) and bromine (a Group 7 non-metal) form potassium bromide (KBr). [3 marks]

Ionic Compounds

I'd take everything on this page with a pinch of salt if I were you... Ho ho ho — I jest, it's important really.

Ionic Compounds *Have a Regular Lattice* Structure

1) Ionic compounds have a structure called a giant ionic lattice.

2) The ions form a closely packed regular lattice arrangement and there are very strong electrostatic forces of attraction between oppositely charged ions, in all directions in the lattice.

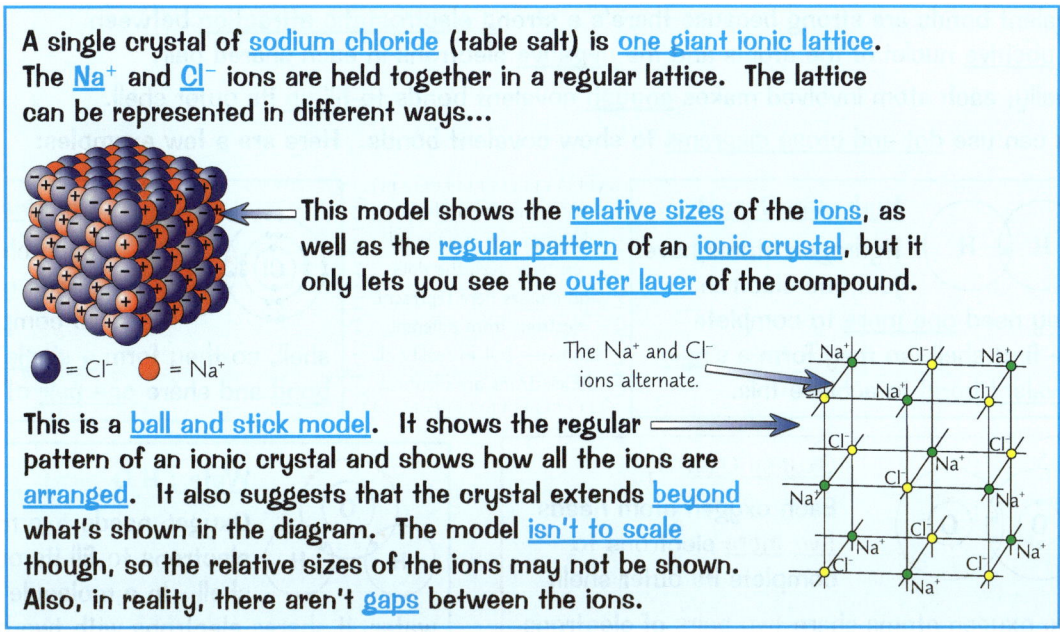

A single crystal of sodium chloride (table salt) is one giant ionic lattice. The Na^+ and Cl^- ions are held together in a regular lattice. The lattice can be represented in different ways...

This model shows the relative sizes of the ions, as well as the regular pattern of an ionic crystal, but it only lets you see the outer layer of the compound.

= Cl^- = Na^+

The Na^+ and Cl^- ions alternate.

This is a ball and stick model. It shows the regular pattern of an ionic crystal and shows how all the ions are arranged. It also suggests that the crystal extends beyond what's shown in the diagram. The model isn't to scale though, so the relative sizes of the ions may not be shown. Also, in reality, there aren't gaps between the ions.

Ionic Compounds *All Have* Similar Properties...

1) They all have high melting points and high boiling points due to the many strong bonds between the ions. It takes lots of energy to overcome this attraction.

2) When they're solid, the ions are held in place, so the compounds can't conduct electricity. When ionic compounds melt, the ions are free to move and they'll carry electric charge.

3) Some ionic compounds also dissolve in water. The ions separate and are all free to move in the solution, so they'll carry electric charge.

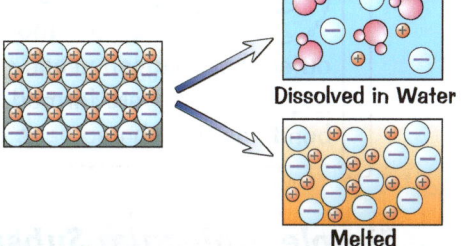

Dissolved in Water

Melted

... *But Some Have* Higher Melting Points *and* Boiling Points *Than Others*

Higher

1) Magnesium oxide and sodium chloride are both ionic compounds. However magnesium oxide has a higher melting point (and also a higher boiling point) than sodium chloride.

2) This is because the charges on the ions in magnesium oxide (Mg^{2+} and O^{2-}) are greater than the charges on the ions in sodium chloride (Na^+ and Cl^-). This makes the electrostatic forces of attraction stronger.

3) This means the ionic bonding in magnesium oxide is stronger than the bonding in sodium chloride. The ions are therefore harder to break apart and the melting and boiling points are higher.

Giant ionic lattices — all over your chips...

Okay, that's the final salt joke — I promise. Here's some more practice questions for you to have a crack at.

Q1   Caesium chloride is an ionic compound. Explain why it has a high melting point.   [1 mark]

Simple Molecules

These molecules might be <u>simple</u>, but you've still gotta know about them. I know, the world is a cruel place.

Covalent Bonds — Sharing Electrons

1) When <u>non-metal atoms</u> combine together, they form <u>covalent bonds</u> by <u>sharing</u> pairs of electrons.

2) This way, <u>both atoms</u> feel that they have <u>a full outer shell</u>, and that makes them happy.

3) <u>Each</u> covalent bond provides <u>one extra</u> shared electron for each atom.

4) Covalent bonds are strong because there's a strong <u>electrostatic attraction</u> between the <u>positive</u> nuclei of the atoms and the <u>negative</u> electrons in each shared pair.

5) Usually, each atom involved makes <u>enough</u> covalent bonds to <u>fill up</u> its outer shell.

6) You can use <u>dot and cross diagrams</u> to show covalent bonds. Here are a few examples:

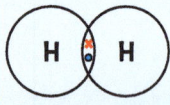

Hydrogen Gas: H$_2$
Hydrogen atoms have just one electron. They need <u>one more</u> to complete the first shell, so they form a <u>single covalent bond</u> to achieve this.

As in the dot and cross diagrams for ionic bonds on page 164, the dots and crosses here represent electrons from different atoms — but in reality all the electrons are identical.

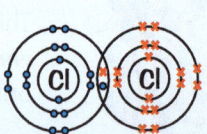

Chlorine Gas: Cl$_2$
Each chlorine atom needs <u>one electron</u> to complete its outer shell, so they form <u>a single covalent bond</u> and share <u>one pair</u> of electrons.

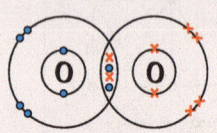

Oxygen Gas: O$_2$
Each oxygen atom needs <u>two more</u> electrons to complete its outer shell.
<u>Two</u> oxygen atoms share <u>two pairs</u> of electrons with each other making a <u>double covalent bond</u>.

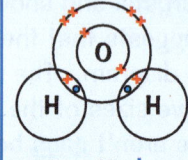

Water: H$_2$O
Oxygen needs <u>two</u> more electrons to fill its outer shell. In a molecule of water, it <u>shares</u> electrons with two hydrogen atoms, forming two single covalent bonds.

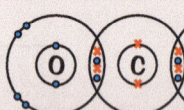

Carbon Dioxide: CO$_2$
Carbon needs <u>four</u> more electrons to fill its outer shell, oxygen needs <u>two</u>. So <u>two double covalent bonds</u> are formed. A double covalent bond has <u>two shared pairs</u> of electrons.

Higher

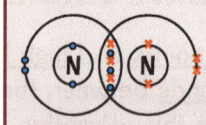

Nitrogen: N$_2$
Nitrogen atoms need <u>three more</u> electrons to fill their outer shells, so <u>two</u> nitrogen atoms share <u>three pairs</u> of electrons. This creates a <u>triple bond</u>.

Higher

Simple Molecular Substances Have Low Melting and Boiling Points

1) Substances formed with <u>covalent bonds</u> usually have <u>simple molecular structures</u>, like CO$_2$ and H$_2$O.

2) The atoms within the molecules are held together by <u>very strong covalent bonds</u>.

3) By contrast, the forces of attraction <u>between</u> these molecules are <u>very weak</u>. It's these <u>feeble intermolecular forces</u> that you have to overcome to melt or boil a simple covalent compound.

4) So the melting and boiling points are <u>very low</u>, because the molecules are <u>easily parted</u> from each other.

5) Most simple molecular substances are <u>gases or liquids</u> at room temperature.

6) Simple molecular substances <u>don't conduct electricity</u>, because they <u>don't</u> have free electrons or ions.

7) Simple molecular substances are usually quite <u>insoluble</u> in water.

weak intermolecular forces

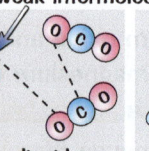

Carbon dioxide

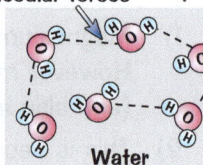

Water

May the intermolecular force be with you...

Remember — a covalent bond is just a shared pair of electrons. Easy-peasy.

Q1   In a molecule of ammonia, NH$_3$, a nitrogen atom is covalently bonded to three hydrogen atoms.
Draw a dot and cross diagram to show the bonding in an ammonia molecule.   [1 mark]

Giant Covalent Structures and Fullerenes

I hope you didn't think simple molecules would be the end of covalent bonding. Time to think giant.

Most Giant Covalent Structures Have Certain Properties

1) In giant covalent structures, all the atoms are bonded to each other by strong covalent bonds.

2) They have very high melting and boiling points as lots of energy is needed to break the covalent bonds.

3) They generally don't contain charged particles, so they don't conduct electricity. ← Apart from graphite and graphene.

4) They aren't soluble in water.

5) The following examples are all carbon-based giant covalent structures.

DIAMOND
- Diamond is made up of a network of carbon atoms that each form four covalent bonds.
- The strong covalent bonds take lots of energy to break, so diamond has a high melting point.
- The strong covalent bonds also hold the atoms in a rigid lattice structure, making diamond really hard — it's used to strengthen cutting tools (e.g. saw teeth and drill bits).
- It doesn't conduct electricity because it has no free electrons or ions.

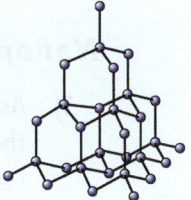

GRAPHITE
- In graphite, each carbon atom has three covalent bonds, creating sheets of carbon atoms arranged in hexagons.
- There aren't any covalent bonds between the layers — they're only held together weakly, so they're free to move over each other.
- This makes graphite soft and slippery, so it's ideal as a lubricating material.
- Graphite's got a high melting point — the covalent bonds in the layers need loads of energy to break.
- Only three out of each carbon's four outer electrons are used in bonds, so each carbon atom has one electron that's delocalised (free) and can move. So graphite conducts electricity.

GRAPHENE
- Graphene is one layer of graphite.
- It's a sheet of carbon atoms joined together in hexagons.
- The sheet is just one atom thick, making it a two-dimensional compound.
- Graphene is one of the strongest materials ever tested. Like graphite, it has delocalised electrons which make it an excellent electrical conductor. However, it's not yet available in any products.

Fullerenes Form Spheres and Tubes

1) Fullerenes are molecules of carbon that form cage structures, like closed tubes or hollow balls.

2) They're made up of carbon atoms arranged in rings.

3) Fullerenes can be used to 'cage' other molecules. The fullerene structure forms around another atom or molecule, which is then trapped inside. This could be used to deliver a drug directly to cells in the body.

4) Fullerenes have a huge surface area, so they could help make great industrial catalysts — individual catalyst molecules could be attached to the fullerenes.

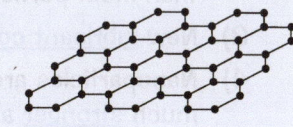
Buckminsterfullerene has the molecular formula C_{60} and forms a hollow sphere made up of 20 hexagons and 12 pentagons. It's a stable molecule that forms soft brownish-black crystals.

← Catalysts speed up the rates of reactions without being used up (see page 93).

5) As well as drug delivery and catalyst uses, scientists are investigating fullerenes for use in lubricants.

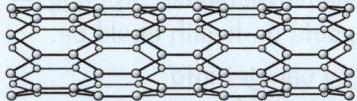
Nanotubes are also fullerenes. They are tiny tubes of graphene — so they have delocalised electrons meaning they conduct electricity. Their strong covalent bonds mean they have a high tensile strength (they don't break when stretched). They also have a very low density, so they can be used to strengthen materials without adding much weight.

Fullerenes are forever — doesn't quite have the same ring to it...

Did you know that buckminsterfullerene is the state molecule of Texas? True story...

Q1 Explain why graphite conducts electricity but diamond does not. [2 marks]

Nanoparticles

There are loads of really <u>useful properties</u> of <u>nanoparticles</u> for you to learn.

Nanoparticles are Really Really Really Really Tiny

1) Really tiny particles, <u>1–100 nanometres</u> across, are called '<u>nanoparticles</u>' (1 nm = 0.000 000 001 m). Nanoparticles contain roughly <u>a few hundred atoms</u> — so they're <u>bigger</u> than <u>atoms</u> (atoms are around 0.1–0.5 nm) and <u>simple molecules</u>, but smaller than pretty much anything else.

2) A nanoparticle has very <u>different properties</u> from the 'bulk' chemical that it's made from — e.g. <u>fullerenes</u>, <u>carbon nanotubes</u>, <u>diamond</u>, <u>graphite</u> and <u>graphene</u>. all have <u>different properties</u> even though they all just contain <u>carbon atoms</u>.

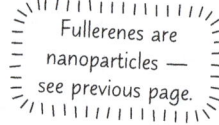
Fullerenes are nanoparticles — see previous page.

Nanoparticles Have a High Surface Area to Volume Ratio

1) As particles <u>decrease</u> in size, the size of their surface area <u>increases</u> in relation to their volume — so their surface area to volume ratio <u>increases</u>.

> surface area to volume ratio = surface area ÷ volume

2) Nanoparticles have a really <u>high</u> surface area to volume ratio compared to larger particles.

3) This is what causes the <u>properties</u> of a material to be different depending on whether it's a <u>nanoparticle</u> or whether it's <u>in bulk</u>.

Nanoparticles Can Modify the Properties of Materials

Using nanoparticles is known as <u>nanoscience</u>. Many <u>new uses</u> of nanoparticles are being developed:

1) They have a <u>huge surface area to volume ratio</u>, so they can make good <u>catalysts</u> (see p.93).

2) <u>Nanomedicine</u> is a hot topic. The idea is that tiny fullerenes are <u>absorbed</u> more easily by the body than most particles. This means they could <u>deliver drugs</u> right into the cells where they're needed.

3) New <u>lubricant coatings</u> using fullerenes could be used in, e.g. <u>artificial joints</u> and <u>gears</u>.

4) Nanoparticles are added to <u>plastics</u> in <u>sports equipment</u>. They make the plastic much <u>stronger</u> and <u>more durable</u>, without adding much <u>mass</u>.

As with carbon nanoparticles, silver nanoparticles have different properties to those in 'bulk' silver.

- <u>Silver nanoparticles</u> have <u>antibacterial</u>, <u>antiviral</u> and <u>antifungal</u> properties. They can be added to the polymer fibres used to make <u>surgical masks</u> and <u>wound dressings</u>.

- They can also be used in <u>antiseptic sprays</u>, <u>refrigerator linings</u>, <u>socks</u> and <u>deodorants</u>.

- <u>Titanium dioxide</u> nanoparticles are being used in <u>sun creams</u>. They are better than the materials in traditional sun creams at <u>protecting skin</u> from harmful <u>UV rays</u>. They also give better <u>skin coverage</u> than traditional sun creams, and are <u>transparent</u> (which lots of people prefer).

- <u>Titanium dioxide</u> nanoparticles are also used as a <u>coating</u> for <u>self-cleaning glass</u>.

The Effects of Nanoparticles on Health Aren't Fully Understood

1) Although nanoparticles are useful, the way they affect <u>the body</u> isn't fully understood, so it's important that any new products are <u>tested</u> thoroughly to minimise the risks.

2) Some people are worried that <u>products</u> containing nanoparticles have been made available <u>before</u> any possible <u>harmful</u> effects on <u>human health</u> have been investigated <u>properly</u> — in other words, we don't know what the <u>side effects</u> or <u>long-term</u> impacts on health could be.

3) For example, it's not yet clear whether the nanoparticles in <u>sun creams</u> can get into your <u>body</u>, and, if they do, whether they might <u>damage cells</u>. It's also possible that when they are <u>washed away</u> they might <u>damage the environment</u>.

The large surface area to volume ratio could be making them more toxic.

Higher

Nanofarticles — when ants get into that old tin of baked beans...

It seems like small particles are big business — but as with any new tech there are pros and cons.

Q1   State one use of titanium dioxide nanoparticles.   [1 mark]

Smart Materials

Scientists are constantly developing <u>new materials</u>, such as smart materials, to fit <u>new uses</u>.

Smart Materials *Change When Their* Environment *Changes*

1) <u>Smart materials</u> react to <u>changes</u> in their <u>environment</u>.
2) This means that <u>one or more</u> of their properties can be changed by an <u>external condition</u> such as <u>temperature</u>, <u>light</u>, <u>pH</u>, etc.
3) The change that a smart material makes is <u>reversible</u> — the material will <u>go back</u> to how it was.
4) These <u>properties</u> make smart materials very <u>useful</u>.

Thermochromic *Pigments*

1) Thermochromic pigments <u>change colour</u> or <u>become transparent</u> when <u>heated or cooled</u>.
2) Baby products, like <u>bath toys</u> and <u>baby spoons</u>, often have them added as a <u>safety feature</u> — you can tell at a glance if the baby's bath water or food is <u>too hot</u>.

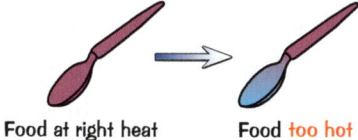

Food at right heat   Food too hot

Photochromic *Pigments*

1) Photochromic pigments <u>change colour</u> when <u>light intensity</u> changes.
2) Photochromic materials can be used in <u>sunglasses</u> — exposure to sunlight makes the lenses of the glasses <u>darken</u> to protect the eyes.

Polymer Gels

1) Polymer gels (also known as <u>hydrogels</u>) can <u>expand</u> or <u>shrink</u> by up to <u>1000 times</u> in <u>volume</u> by absorbing or giving out <u>water</u>.
2) This volume change happens as a result of a change in <u>pH</u> or <u>temperature</u>.
3) Polymer gels have uses in <u>medicine</u>.

Shape Memory *Alloys*

1) An alloy is a <u>mixture</u> of two elements, one of which is a <u>metal</u> (p.180).
2) Some smart alloys have a <u>shape memory</u> property — they "<u>remember</u>" their original shape.
3) If you <u>bend</u> a wire made of a smart alloy, it'll go back to its <u>original shape</u> when it's <u>heated</u>.
4) Shape memory alloys are handy for things like <u>glasses frames</u> — if they get bent (or sat on) they can <u>easily</u> be <u>reshaped</u>.

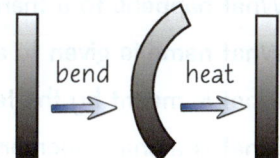

bend   heat

Shape Memory *Polymers*

1) These work the <u>same</u> as shape memory alloys, but are made out of <u>polymers</u> instead.
2) A polymer is a <u>very large molecule</u> made of a chain of <u>smaller repeated molecules</u> (p.193).
3) Shape memory polymers return to their <u>original shape</u> when <u>heated</u>.

Not smart enough to do the exam for you though...

Hmm, so scientists can faff about with materials until they can make them do exactly what they want. Well, I'd like a gold ring that can cook meals, do the washing up and tidy rooms.

Q1   A student was given samples of two different metals. Both had been bent. Describe what the student could do to find out which metal is a shape memory alloy and state what would be observed.   [2 marks]

Revision Questions for Unit 5a

Well, that's the end of Unit 5a — well, nearly the end. You know what's coming next...
*   Try these questions and tick off each one when you get it right.
*   When you've done all the questions for a topic and are completely happy with it, tick off the topic.

Metallic Bonding (p.163) ☐

1)   What is metallic bonding?
2)   Explain why most metals are solid at room temperature.
3)   Why are metals good conductors of heat?
4)   Why are metals malleable?

Ionic Bonding and Ionic Compounds (p.164-165) ☐

5)   Describe how an ionic bond forms.
6)   Sketch dot and cross diagrams to show the formation of:
     a) sodium chloride   b) magnesium oxide   c) magnesium chloride   d) sodium oxide
7)   Describe the structure of a crystal of sodium chloride.
8)   List the main properties of ionic compounds.
9)   Explain why magnesium oxide has a higher melting point than sodium chloride.

Covalent Bonding and Nanoparticles (p.166-168) ☐

10) Describe how a covalent bond forms.
11) Why do simple molecular substances have low melting and boiling points?
12) List three typical properties of giant covalent structures.
13) Name three substances that have a giant covalent structure.
14) What are nanoparticles?
15) How do you calculate surface area to volume ratio?
16) Give a use of silver nanoparticles.

Smart Materials (p.169) ☐

17) True or false? When a change occurs in a smart material, the change is reversible.
18) What happens to a thermochromic material when it is heated or cooled?
19) What name is given to a pigment that changes colour depending on light intensity?
20) What is meant by the term 'alloy'?
21) What is a shape memory alloy?

Acids and Bases

Testing the pH of a solution means using an indicator — and that means pretty <u>colours</u>...

The *pH Scale* Goes From *0 to 14*

1) The <u>pH scale</u> is a measure of how <u>acidic</u> or <u>alkaline</u> a solution is.
2) The <u>lower</u> the pH of a solution, the <u>more acidic</u> it is.
3) The <u>higher</u> the pH of a solution, the more <u>alkaline</u> it is.
4) A <u>neutral</u> substance (e.g. pure water) has <u>pH 7</u>.

Strong acids have pHs of 0-2, whilst strong alkalis have pHs of 12-14. There's more on acid and alkali strength on the next page.

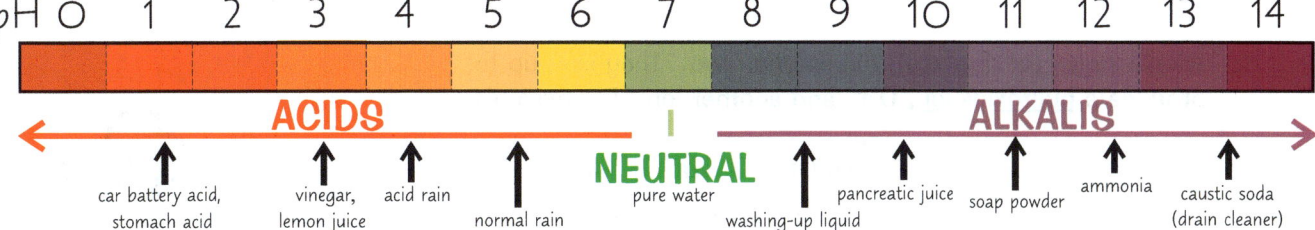

You Can *Measure* the pH of a Solution

1) An <u>indicator</u> is a <u>dye</u> that <u>changes colour</u> depending on whether it's <u>above or below a certain pH</u>. Some indicators contain a <u>mixture of dyes</u> that means they <u>gradually change colour</u> over a broad range of pH. These are useful for <u>estimating</u> the pH of a solution. For example, <u>universal indicator</u> gives the colours shown above.

2) A <u>pH probe</u> attached to a <u>pH meter</u> can also be used to measure pH <u>electronically</u>. The probe is placed in the solution you are measuring and the pH is given on a digital display as a <u>numerical value</u>, meaning it's more accurate than an indicator.

Acids and *Bases* Neutralise Each Other

1) An <u>acid</u> is a substance that forms <u>aqueous solutions</u> with a pH of <u>less than 7</u>. Acids form H^+ <u>ions</u> in <u>water</u>.

2) A <u>base</u> is a substance with a pH <u>greater than 7</u>.

3) An <u>alkali</u> is a base that <u>dissolves in water</u> to form a solution with a pH <u>greater than 7</u>. Alkalis form OH^- <u>ions</u> in <u>water</u>.

I have literally no idea what I'm doing.

The reaction between acids and bases is called <u>neutralisation</u>:

$$\text{acid} + \text{base} \rightarrow \text{salt} + \text{water}$$

Neutralisation between acids and alkalis can be seen in terms of <u>H$^+$</u> and <u>OH$^-$ ions</u> like this:

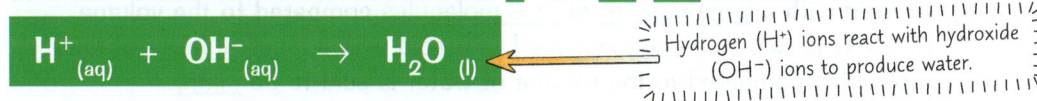

$$H^+_{(aq)} + OH^-_{(aq)} \rightarrow H_2O_{(l)}$$

Hydrogen (H$^+$) ions react with hydroxide (OH$^-$) ions to produce water.

When an acid neutralises a base (or vice versa), the <u>products</u> are <u>neutral</u>, i.e. they have a <u>pH of 7</u>. An indicator can be used to show that a neutralisation reaction is over.

<u>Neutralisation</u> reactions of <u>strong</u> acids and alkalis can be used to calculate the <u>concentration</u> of an acid or alkali by <u>titration</u> — there is more about this technique on page 174.

This page should have all bases covered...

pHew, you finished the page... This stuff isn't too bad really, and pH is worth knowing about — it's important to the chemistry in our bodies. For example, here's an interesting(ish) fact — your skin is slightly acidic (pH 5.5).

Q1   A student uses universal indicator to test the pH of some lemon juice.
      What colour would you expect the indicator to turn?   [1 mark]

Q2   The pH of an unknown solution is found to be 8. Is the solution acidic or alkaline?   [1 mark]

Acid and Alkali Strength

Right then. More on <u>acids</u> and <u>alkalis</u>. Brace yourself...

Acids *Produce Hydrogen Ions* in *Water*

1) All acids can <u>ionise</u> (or <u>dissociate</u>) in solution — that means splitting up
to produce a <u>hydrogen ion</u>, H$^+$, and another ion. For example:

$$HCl \rightarrow H^+ + Cl^-$$
$$HNO_3 \rightarrow H^+ + NO_3^-$$

HCl and HNO$_3$ don't produce hydrogen ions until they meet water.

2) Alkalis <u>ionise</u> (or <u>dissociate</u>) in solution too. They split up to
produce a <u>hydroxide ion</u>, OH$^-$, and another ion. For example:

$$NaOH \rightarrow Na^+ + OH^-$$
$$KOH \rightarrow K^+ + OH^-$$

Acids and Alkalis Can be *Strong* or *Weak*

1) The strength of <u>acids</u> can be measured by the proportion of <u>hydrogen ions</u> they <u>release</u>.

2) <u>Strong acids</u> (e.g. sulfuric, hydrochloric and nitric acids) <u>ionise almost completely</u> in water, i.e. a <u>large</u>
proportion of the acid molecules dissociate to release H$^+$ ions. They tend to have low <u>pHs</u> (pH 0-2).

3) <u>Weak acids</u> (e.g. ethanoic, citric and carbonic acids) <u>do not fully ionise</u> in solution, i.e. only a <u>small</u>
proportion of the acid molecules dissociate to release H$^+$ ions. Their <u>pHs</u> tend to be around 2-6.

4) The strength of <u>alkalis</u> can be measured by the proportion of <u>hydroxide ions</u> they <u>release</u>.

5) <u>Strong alkalis</u> ionise almost completely in water. A <u>large proportion</u> of the alkali
molecules dissociate to release OH$^-$ ions. Strong alkalis have a <u>pH</u> of about 12-14.

6) <u>Weak alkalis</u> don't fully ionise in water. Only a <u>small proportion</u> of the alkali
molecules dissociate to release OH$^-$ ions. Weak alkalis have a <u>pH</u> of about 8-12.

Don't Confuse *Strong* Acids with *Concentrated* Acids

1) Acid <u>strength</u> (i.e. strong or weak) tells you <u>what proportion</u> of the acid molecules <u>ionise</u> in water.

2) The <u>concentration</u> of an acid is different. Concentration measures <u>how much acid</u>
there is in a litre (1 dm^3) of water. Concentration is basically how <u>watered down</u> your acid is.

3) An acid with a <u>large number</u> of <u>acid molecules</u> compared to the volume
of water is said to be <u>concentrated</u>. An acid with a <u>small number</u> of acid
molecules compared to the volume of water is said to be <u>dilute</u>.

Concentration is measured in g/dm^3 or mol/dm^3.

4) Note that concentration describes the <u>total number</u> of dissolved acid
molecules — <u>not</u> the number of acid molecules that produce hydrogen ions.

5) The more grams (or moles) of acid per dm^3, the <u>more concentrated</u> the acid is.

6) So you can have a <u>dilute strong</u> acid, or a <u>concentrated weak</u> acid.

Weak acid or strong acid? I know which goes better with chips...

Acids are acidic because of H$^+$ ions. And strong acids are strong because they let go of all their H$^+$ ions at the drop
of a hat... Well, at the drop of a drop of water. The same goes for alkalis too — but they let go of OH$^-$ ions.

Q1   What ion is released when an alkali dissociates in water?   [1 mark]

Q2   Explain the difference between a strong acid and a weak acid.   [2 marks]

Reactions of Acids

Now you've learnt the basics of what acids are, lets see what they can do...

Salts Form When Acids React with Bases

1) A salt is formed during a neutralisation reaction (a reaction between an acid and a base).
2) A neutralisation reaction is always exothermic (p.183)
3) In general, hydrochloric acid produces chloride salts, sulfuric acid produces sulfate salts and nitric acid produces nitrate salts.
4) You need to be able to remember what happens when you add acids to various bases...

Acid + Metal Oxide → Salt + Water

Examples:
$2HCl + CuO \rightarrow CuCl_2 + H_2O$ (Copper chloride)
$H_2SO_4 + ZnO \rightarrow ZnSO_4 + H_2O$ (Zinc sulfate)
$2HNO_3 + MgO \rightarrow Mg(NO_3)_2 + H_2O$ (Magnesium nitrate)

Metal oxides and metal hydroxides are bases.

Acid + Metal Hydroxide → Salt + Water

Examples:
$HCl + NaOH \rightarrow NaCl + H_2O$ (Sodium chloride)
$H_2SO_4 + Zn(OH)_2 \rightarrow ZnSO_4 + 2H_2O$ (Zinc sulfate)
$HNO_3 + KOH \rightarrow KNO_3 + H_2O$ (Potassium nitrate)

Salts Also Form When Acids React With Metals or Metal Carbonates

You also need to know what happens when you react an acid with a metal or a metal carbonate:

Acid + Metal → Salt + Hydrogen

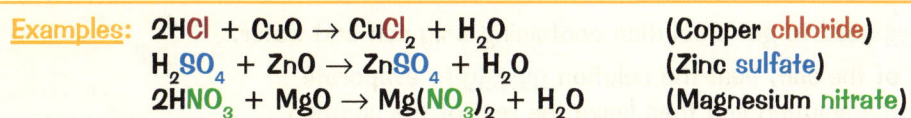

Examples:
$2HCl + Mg \rightarrow MgCl_2 + H_2$ (Magnesium chloride)
$H_2SO_4 + Mg \rightarrow MgSO_4 + H_2$ (Magnesium sulfate)

The reaction of nitric acid with metals can be more complicated — you get a nitrate salt, but instead of hydrogen gas, the other products are usually a mixture of water, NO and NO_2.

Whether or not a metal will react with an acid depends on its position in the reactivity series compared to hydrogen — metals above hydrogen in the reactivity series will react with acids, metals below hydrogen will not. There's more on the reactivity series of metals on page 176.

Acid + Metal Carbonate → Salt + Water + Carbon Dioxide

Examples:
$2HCl + Na_2CO_3 \rightarrow 2NaCl + H_2O + CO_2$ (Sodium chloride)
$H_2SO_4 + K_2CO_3 \rightarrow K_2SO_4 + H_2O + CO_2$ (Potassium sulfate)
$2HNO_3 + ZnCO_3 \rightarrow Zn(NO_3)_2 + H_2O + CO_2$ (Zinc nitrate)

You can use this reaction as a test to see if an acid or carbonate is present — the solution will effervesce (fizz) as CO_2 gas is produced.

Test for Sulfate Ions Using Barium Chloride Solution

1) To test for sulfate ions in solution, first add some dilute hydrochloric acid to the test sample — this stops any precipitation reactions not involving sulfate ions from taking place.
2) Then add some barium chloride solution. If there are sulfate ions in the solution, a white precipitate of barium sulfate will form:

barium ions + sulfate ions → barium sulfate
$Ba^{2+}_{(aq)} + SO_4^{2-}_{(aq)} \rightarrow BaSO_{4(s)}$

Nitrates — much cheaper than day-rates...

What a lot of reactions. Better take a peek back at page 55 for help with writing and balancing chemical equations.

Q1 Write a balanced chemical equation for the reaction of hydrochloric acid with calcium carbonate. [2 marks]

Making Salts

You met the reactions for making salts on the previous page. Now it's time for the experiments.

Making *Soluble Salts* Using an *Acid* and an *Insoluble Reactant*

1) You can make soluble salts (salts that dissolve in water) by reacting an acid with a metal, an insoluble base (normally a metal hydroxide or a metal oxide) or a metal carbonate. To get a particular salt, you need to pick the right reactants.

2) Add an excess of the insoluble substance to the acid — they will react to produce a soluble salt (plus either water, hydrogen, or water and carbon dioxide).

3) You will know when all the acid has reacted because the excess solid will just sink to the bottom of the flask.

> You sometimes need to heat the reaction mixture during this step to get everything to react faster.

4) Then filter off the excess solid to get a solution containing only salt and water.

5) To make small crystals of the salt, heat the solution quickly to evaporate off about two thirds of the solution and then leave the rest of the solution to cool to form crystals. Filter off the crystals and leave them to dry.

6) To make big crystals, leave the solution to evaporate slowly over a few days.

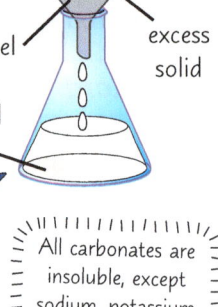

filter paper
filter funnel
salt and water
excess solid

> All carbonates are insoluble, except sodium, potassium and ammonium carbonates.

> **Example:** You can add copper carbonate to sulfuric acid to make copper sulfate:
> $$CuCO_{3(s)} + H_2SO_{4(aq)} \rightarrow CuSO_{4(aq)} + H_2O_{(l)} + CO_{2(g)}$$

You Can Make *Soluble Salts* Using *Acid/Alkali Reactions*

1) Soluble salts can also be made by reacting an acid with an alkali.

2) But, in this case, you can't tell whether the reaction has finished — there's no signal that all the acid has been neutralised. You also can't just add an excess of alkali to the acid, because the salt is soluble and would be contaminated with the excess alkali.

3) Instead, you need to work out exactly the right volume of alkali to neutralise the acid. For this, you need to do a titration using an indicator. Here's what you do...

- Measure out a set volume of acid into a conical flask using a pipette. Add a few drops of indicator.

- Slowly add alkali to the acid, using a burette, until you reach the end point — this is when the acid's been exactly neutralised and the indicator changes colour.

- Then, carry out the reaction using exactly the same volumes of alkali and acid but with no indicator, so the salt won't be contaminated with indicator.

- The solution that remains when the reaction is complete contains only the salt and water.

- Slowly evaporate off some of the water and then leave the solution to crystallise. Filter off the solid and dry it — you'll be left with a pure, dry salt.

> For a titration, you should use an indicator with a single, clear colour change (like phenolphthalein or methyl orange). Universal indicator is no good as its colour change is too gradual.

4) You can tell if the acid is more concentrated than the base (or the other way round) by the relative volume that was needed to neutralise it.

I was attacked by a nasty copper sulfate — it was a salt...

Yet more salts for you to make. If I were you though, I'd just get my salts from a sachet at the local chippy...

Q1   Copper sulfate is a soluble salt that can be made from copper carbonate and sulfuric acid.
     Suggest a method you could use to make a pure sample of copper sulfate from these reactants.   [3 marks]

Revision Questions for Unit 5b

Well, that wraps up Unit 5b — a nice short section. Don't be fooled though — there are still questions to do.
*   Try these questions and tick off each one when you get it right.
*   When you've done all the questions for a topic and are completely happy with it, tick off the topic.

Acids and Bases (p.171) ☐

1)   What pH value would a neutral substance have? ☐
2)   State whether the following pH values are acidic, alkaline or neutral.
     a) 9   b) 2   c) 6 ☐
3)   What colour of universal indicator would you expect to see for a weak acid? ☐
4)   What is an alkali? ☐
5)   Give the general word equation for the reaction between an acid and a base. ☐
6)   What type of reagent could be used to show that an acid or base has been completely neutralised? ☐

Acid and Alkali Strength and the Reactions of Acids (p.172-173) ☑

7)   What ion is released when an acid ionises in water? ☐
8)   What ions would sodium hydroxide, NaOH, produce when in solution? ☐
9)   Is a neutralisation reaction exothermic or endothermic? ☐
10) Write an equation to show how hydrochloric acid reacts with copper oxide. ☐
11) What are the products of a reaction between a metal carbonate and an acid? ☐
12) How can you test for sulfate ions? ☐

Making Salts (p.174) ☑

13) How can you change the size of the salt crystals produced from a solution of
     a soluble salt and water? ☐
14) Describe a method you could use to make a soluble salt from an acid and an alkali. ☐

Metal Ores and The Reactivity Series

A few unreactive metals, like gold, are found in the Earth as the metals themselves, rather than as a compound. The rest of the metals we get by extracting them from rocks — and I bet you're just itching to find out how...

Ores Contain Enough Metal to Make Extraction Worthwhile

1) A metal ore is a rock which contains enough metal to make it economically worthwhile extracting the metal from it. The metal ore is a metal compound — in many cases the ore is an oxide of the metal.

> **Example:** the main aluminium ore is called bauxite — it's aluminium oxide (Al_2O_3).

You can tell what metals are in an ore by looking at its chemical formula.

2) Most of the metals that we use are found in their ores in the Earth's crust. The ores are mined and the metals can then be extracted from the ores.

3) Some unreactive metals, such as gold and silver, are present in the Earth's crust in their native forms (as uncombined elements). These metals can be mined straight out of the ground, but they usually need to be refined before they can be used.

4) The more reactive a metal, the harder they are to extract from their ores.

Row faster men!

We can't — it's these cursed metal oars.

Some Metals can be Extracted by Reduction with Carbon

Oxidation can mean the reaction with, or addition of oxygen. Reduction can be the removal of oxygen.

Reduction and oxidation can also be to do with electrons (see page 178).

> **E.g.** $2Fe_2O_3 + 3C \rightarrow 4Fe + 3CO_2$
> - Iron oxide is reduced to iron (as oxygen is removed).
> - Carbon is oxidised to carbon dioxide (as oxygen is added).

A metal can be extracted from its ore by reduction with carbon. The position of the metal in the reactivity series determines whether it can be extracted in this way.

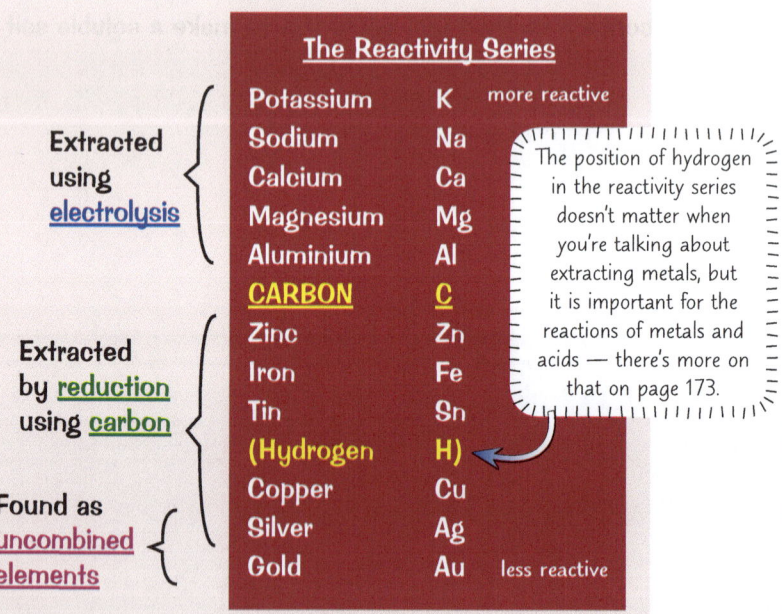

- Metals higher than carbon in the reactivity series have to be extracted using electrolysis (see p.179) which is expensive.
- Metals below carbon in the reactivity series can be extracted by reduction using carbon. For example, iron oxide is reduced in a blast furnace to make iron.
- This is because carbon can only take the oxygen away from metals which are less reactive than carbon itself is.

The Reactivity Series

Potassium	K	more reactive
Sodium	Na	
Calcium	Ca	
Magnesium	Mg	
Aluminium	Al	
CARBON	**C**	
Zinc	Zn	
Iron	Fe	
Tin	Sn	
(Hydrogen	H)	
Copper	Cu	
Silver	Ag	
Gold	Au	less reactive

Extracted using electrolysis

Extracted by reduction using carbon

Found as uncombined elements

The position of hydrogen in the reactivity series doesn't matter when you're talking about extracting metals, but it is important for the reactions of metals and acids — there's more on that on page 173.

[Please insert ore-ful pun here]...

Make sure you've got that reactivity series sorted in your head. If a metal's below carbon in the reactivity series, then it's less reactive than carbon and can be extracted from its ore by reduction using carbon. Phew... got it?

Q1   How would you extract tin from its metal ore? Explain your answer.   [2 marks]

Q2   Write a balanced chemical equation to describe the reaction that occurs when carbon is used to extract zinc from its ore, zinc oxide (ZnO).   [2 marks]

Extracting Iron

Iron is a <u>very common element</u> in the Earth's crust, but good iron ores are only found in <u>a few select places</u> around the world, such as Australia, Canada and Millom. Iron is extracted by reduction in a <u>blast furnace</u>.

The Raw Materials are *Iron Ore*, *Coke* and *Limestone*

1) The <u>iron ore</u> contains the <u>iron</u> — which is pretty important.

2) The <u>coke</u> is a fuel — it's almost <u>pure carbon</u>. It's used to produce carbon monoxide for the reduction of the <u>iron oxide</u> to <u>iron metal</u>.

3) The <u>limestone</u> takes away <u>impurities</u> in the form of <u>slag</u>.

Reducing the *Iron Ore to Iron:*

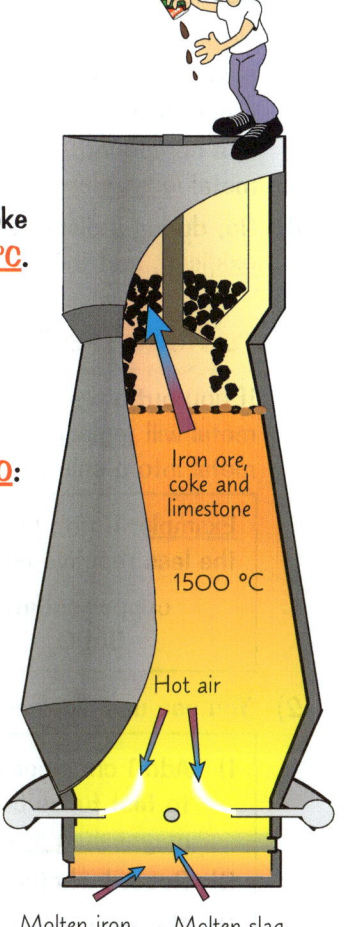

Iron ore, coke and limestone

1500 °C

Hot air

Molten iron   Molten slag

1) <u>Hot air</u> is blasted into the furnace. This provides oxygen and makes the coke <u>burn much faster</u> than normal. This raises the <u>temperature</u> to about <u>1500 °C</u>.

2) The <u>coke burns</u> in a <u>combustion</u> reaction and produces <u>carbon dioxide</u>:

$$C \; + \; O_2 \; \rightarrow \; CO_2$$
carbon + oxygen → carbon dioxide

3) The <u>CO_2</u> then reacts with <u>unburnt coke</u> in a combustion reaction to form <u>CO</u>:

$$CO_2 \; + \; C \; \rightarrow \; 2CO$$
carbon dioxide + carbon → carbon monoxide

4) The <u>carbon monoxide</u> then <u>reduces</u> the <u>iron ore</u> to <u>iron</u>:

$$3CO \; + \; Fe_2O_3 \; \rightarrow \; 3CO_2 + 2Fe$$
carbon monoxide + iron(III) oxide → carbon dioxide + iron

5) The <u>iron</u> is <u>molten</u> at this temperature and it's also very <u>dense</u>, so it runs straight to the <u>bottom</u> of the furnace where it's <u>tapped off</u>.

Removing the *Impurities:*

1) The <u>main impurity</u> is <u>sand</u> (silicon dioxide). This is still <u>solid</u>, even at 1500 °C, and would tend to stay <u>mixed in</u> with the iron. <u>The limestone removes it</u>.

2) The <u>limestone</u> is <u>decomposed</u> by the <u>heat</u> into <u>calcium oxide</u> and <u>CO_2</u>.

$$CaCO_3 \; \rightarrow \; CaO + CO_2$$
calcium carbonate → calcium oxide + carbon dioxide

3) The <u>calcium oxide</u> then reacts with the <u>sand</u> in a <u>neutralisation reaction</u> to form <u>calcium silicate</u>, or <u>slag</u>, which is molten and can be tapped off:

$$CaO + SiO_2 \; \rightarrow \; CaSiO_3$$
calcium oxide + silicon dioxide → calcium silicate (slag)

> This is a continuous process — the iron ore, coke and limestone are continuously added to the furnace as the molten iron and molten slag are removed. This means that you don't need to get the furnace up to temperature each time as the reaction doesn't stop. This saves time and money.

Learn the facts about iron extraction — it's a blast...

This is all important and could be tested in the exam, including the equations. Cover it up and try repeating the facts back to yourself. If you're in a public place people might think you're mad. But that's OK.

Q1   Write the balanced equation for carbon monoxide reducing iron ore, Fe_2O_3, to iron.   [1 mark]

Metal Displacement Reactions

You can directly compare the reactivity of metals using <u>displacement reactions</u>. Exciting stuff I tell ya.

Displacement Reactions are Redox Reactions

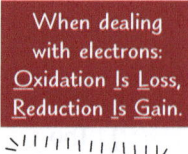

When dealing with electrons:
Oxidation Is Loss,
Reduction Is Gain.

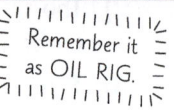

Remember it as OIL RIG.

1) As well as talking about <u>reduction</u> and <u>oxidation</u> in terms of the loss and gain of <u>oxygen</u> (as on page 176), you can also talk about them in terms of <u>electrons</u>.

2) <u>Oxidation</u> can be the <u>loss of electrons</u>, and <u>reduction</u> can be the <u>gain of electrons</u>.

3) Reduction and oxidation happen <u>simultaneously</u> — hence the name <u>redox</u> reactions.

4) <u>Displacement reactions</u> are examples of redox reactions.

5) In displacement reactions, a <u>more reactive element</u> reacts to take the place of a <u>less reactive element</u> in a compound. In metal displacement reactions, the more reactive metal <u>loses electrons</u> and the less reactive metal <u>gains electrons</u>.

6) So, during a displacement reaction, the <u>more reactive metal</u> is <u>oxidised</u>, and the <u>less reactive metal</u> is <u>reduced</u>. For example:

copper is reduced

$$Zn + CuSO_4 \rightarrow ZnSO_4 + Cu$$

zinc is oxidised

More Reactive Metals Displace Less Reactive Ones

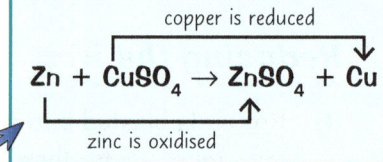

PRACTICAL

1) If you put a <u>reactive metal</u> into a solution of a <u>less reactive metal salt</u>, the reactive metal will <u>replace</u> the <u>less reactive metal</u> in the salt. If you put a less reactive metal into a solution of a more reactive metal salt, <u>nothing will happen</u>.

> <u>Example:</u> if you put an <u>iron nail</u> in a solution of <u>copper sulfate</u>, the more reactive iron will "<u>kick out</u>" the less reactive copper from the salt. You end up with <u>iron sulfate solution</u> and <u>copper metal</u>.
>
> copper sulfate + iron → iron sulfate + copper
> $$CuSO_4 + Fe \rightarrow FeSO_4 + Cu$$
>
> Copper is reduced and iron is oxidised.

2) You can use displacement reactions to <u>work out</u> where in the reactivity series a metal should go. E.g.

> 1) Add 1 cm pieces of <u>copper</u>, <u>magnesium</u> and <u>zinc</u> to test tubes containing 5 cm³ <u>copper(II) sulfate</u>, <u>magnesium sulfate</u> and <u>zinc sulfate</u> solutions.
>
> 2) Record whether any <u>reactions</u> happen.
>
> 3) The table shows the results you'd get.
>
> | | copper(II) sulfate | magnesium sulfate | zinc sulfate |
> | --- | --- | --- | --- |
> | copper | no reaction | no reaction | no reaction |
> | magnesium | magnesium sulfate and copper formed | no reaction | magnesium sulfate and zinc formed |
> | zinc | zinc sulfate and copper formed | no reaction | no reaction |
>
> 4) You can use the table to work out an <u>order of reactivity</u> for the metals:
>
> • Magnesium <u>displaces</u> both <u>copper</u> and <u>zinc</u>, so it must be <u>more reactive</u> than both.
> • Copper <u>is displaced by</u> both <u>magnesium</u> and <u>zinc</u>, so it must be <u>less reactive</u> than both.
> • Zinc <u>can displace copper</u>, but <u>not magnesium</u>, so it must go between them.
>
> The <u>order of reactivity</u>, from <u>most to least</u>, is: <u>magnesium, zinc, copper</u>.

3) If you heat a <u>reactive metal</u> with a less reactive <u>metal oxide</u>, the more reactive metal will <u>remove oxygen</u> from it. This is called a <u>competition reaction</u>.

> <u>Example:</u> if you heat <u>iron(III) oxide</u> with <u>aluminium</u>, the more reactive aluminium will <u>remove</u> the <u>oxygen</u> from the iron(III) oxide. You end up with <u>aluminium oxide</u> and <u>iron metal</u>.
>
> iron(III) oxide + aluminium → aluminium oxide + iron
> $$Fe_2O_3 + 2Al \rightarrow Al_2O_3 + 2Fe$$
>
> This is called the thermit reaction.

And that's why Iron Man never goes swimming in copper sulfate...

See, experiments aren't just for fun — they can give you a thrilling insight into the relative reactivities of elements.

Q1 State whether silver would displace iron from iron(II) chloride solution and explain your answer. [1 mark]

Electrolysis

Electrolysis uses an <u>electrical current</u> to cause a reaction. It's actually pretty cool. No, really...

Electrolysis Means 'Splitting Up with Electricity'

1) During electrolysis, an electric current is passed through an electrolyte (a <u>molten</u> or <u>dissolved</u> ionic compound). The ions move towards the electrodes, where they react, and the compound <u>decomposes</u>.

2) The <u>positive ions</u> in the electrolyte will move towards the <u>cathode</u> (–ve electrode) and <u>gain</u> electrons (they are <u>reduced</u>).

3) The <u>negative ions</u> in the electrolyte will move towards the <u>anode</u> (+ve electrode) and <u>lose</u> electrons (they are <u>oxidised</u>).

> An electrolyte is just a liquid or solution that can conduct electricity. An electrode is a solid that conducts electricity and is submerged in the electrolyte

4) This creates a <u>flow of charge</u> through the <u>electrolyte</u> as ions travel to the electrodes.

5) As ions gain or lose electrons, they form the uncharged element and are <u>discharged</u> from the electrolyte.

Electrolysis of Molten Ionic Solids Forms Elements

1) An <u>ionic solid can't</u> be electrolysed because the ions are in fixed positions and <u>can't move</u>.

> The electrodes should be inert so they don't react with the electrolyte.

2) <u>Molten ionic compounds can</u> be electrolysed because the ions can <u>move freely</u> and conduct electricity.

3) Molten ionic compounds, e.g. <u>lead bromide</u>, are always broken up into their <u>elements</u>.

4) Positive <u>metal</u> ions are <u>reduced</u> to the element at the <u>cathode</u>, e.g.

$$Pb^{2+} + 2e^- \rightarrow Pb$$

5) Negative <u>non-metal</u> ions are <u>oxidised</u> to the element at the <u>anode</u>, e.g.

$$2Br^- \rightarrow Br_2 + 2e^-$$

Metals can be Extracted From Their Ores Using Electrolysis

If a metal is <u>too reactive</u> to be <u>reduced</u> with <u>carbon</u> (page 176) or reacts with carbon, then electrolysis can be used to extract it. Extracting metals via this method is very <u>expensive</u> as lots of energy is required to melt the ore and produce the required current.

1) Aluminium is extracted from its ore by <u>electrolysis</u>. The ore contains <u>alumina</u> (aluminium oxide), Al_2O_3.

2) Aluminium oxide has a <u>very high</u> melting temperature so it's dissolved in <u>molten cryolite</u> to lower the melting point. This saves energy.

> Cryolite is an aluminium-based compound with a lower melting point than aluminium oxide.

3) The <u>molten mixture</u> contains <u>free ions</u> — so it'll <u>conduct electricity</u>.

4) The <u>positive Al^{3+} ions</u> are attracted to the <u>negative electrode</u> where they <u>each pick up three electrons</u> and turn into neutral <u>aluminium atoms</u>. These then <u>sink</u> to the bottom of the electrolysis tank.

5) The <u>negative O^{2-} ions</u> are attracted to the <u>positive electrode</u> where they <u>each lose two electrons</u>. The neutral oxygen atoms will then <u>combine</u> to form O_2 molecules.

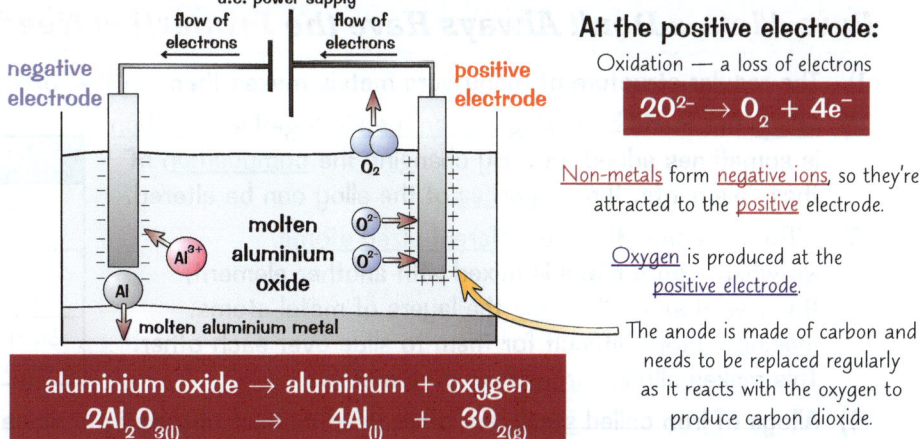

At the negative electrode:

Reduction — a gain of electrons:

$$Al^{3+} + 3e^- \rightarrow Al$$

<u>Metals</u> form <u>positive ions</u>, so they're attracted to the <u>negative</u> electrode.

<u>Aluminium</u> is produced at the <u>negative electrode</u>.

At the positive electrode:

Oxidation — a loss of electrons

$$2O^{2-} \rightarrow O_2 + 4e^-$$

<u>Non-metals</u> form <u>negative ions</u>, so they're attracted to the <u>positive</u> electrode.

<u>Oxygen</u> is produced at the <u>positive electrode</u>.

The anode is made of carbon and needs to be replaced regularly as it reacts with the oxygen to produce carbon dioxide.

Overall Equation:

aluminium oxide → aluminium + oxygen
$$2Al_2O_{3(l)} \rightarrow 4Al_{(l)} + 3O_{2(g)}$$

Faster shopping at the supermarket — use Electrolleys...

It might be useful for your exams to learn how to work out the products of the electrolysis of ionic compounds...

Q1   A student carries out electrolysis on molten sodium chloride. What is produced at:
      a) the anode? b) the cathode?   [2 marks]

Uses of Metals

Iron, aluminium, titanium and copper are some of the most used metals in the whole world. Time to learn why.

Iron, Aluminium, Titanium and Copper have Properties in Common

Iron, aluminium, titanium and copper have the same basic properties — they are all metals after all.

1) They are dense and lustrous (i.e. shiny) and have high melting points — iron melts at 1538 °C, aluminium melts at 660 °C, titanium melts at 1668 °C and copper melts at 1085 °C.

2) They have high tensile strength — they're strong and hard to break.

3) But they can also be hammered into a different shape (they're malleable).

4) They are good conductors of electricity and of heat energy too.

There's more on the properties of metals on page 163.

The Uses of Metals Depend on their Properties

- Iron has all the properties you'd expect a metal to have.
  Adding other materials to the iron can change its properties though (see below).

- Wrought iron is almost completely pure iron. It's malleable, so it's used to make gates and railings.

- The main problem with iron is that it corrodes easily (i.e. it rusts).

- Aluminium is also a typical metal. However, unlike iron, it doesn't corrode easily.

- The aluminium reacts very quickly with oxygen in the air to form aluminium oxide. A nice protective layer of aluminium oxide sticks firmly to the aluminium below and stops any further reaction taking place.

- Because aluminium doesn't corrode it's useful for products that come in contact with water, e.g. window frames. This also means it is non-toxic — it's good for food cans.

- Aluminium is also much less dense than iron, which makes it lighter.

- This makes it useful when the weight of the metal is important, e.g. in bicycle frames and aeroplanes.

- Copper is malleable and ductile, and it is an especially good conductor of heat and electricity.

- It is used in electrical components and wiring as it has low resistance and so is efficient at transferring electricity. It is also used in heating systems, such as underfloor heating, as it allows speedy transfer of heat to the surroundings.

- Copper also has an attractive colour and lustre (a bright, shiny glow) so it gets used as decoration.

- Titanium has a very low density and it doesn't corrode easily. It's also very hard.

- It is very lightweight, so it's used for bicycle frames and aeroplanes — like aluminium.

Pure Metals Don't Always Have the Properties Needed

1) The regular structure of many pure metals makes them soft — often too soft for everyday uses.

2) Alloys are made by mixing molten metals together. Carbon is sometimes added too. By changing the composition of these elements, the properties of the alloy can be altered.

3) Different elements have different sized atoms.
   So when a pure metal is mixed with another element, the new atoms will distort the layers of metal atoms, making it more difficult for them to slide over each other. This makes alloys harder than pure metals.

TYPE OF STEEL	PROPERTIES	USE
Low carbon steel (0.1–0.3% carbon)	easily shaped	car bodies
High carbon steel (0.22–2.5% carbon)	very strong, inflexible, brittle	bridges
Stainless steel (chromium added, and sometimes nickel)	corrosion-resistant, hard	cutlery

4) Alloys of iron called steels are often used instead of pure iron, since they are harder and stronger. Steels are made by adding small amounts of carbon and sometimes other metals to iron.

If Iron Man and the Silver Surfer teamed up, they'd be great alloys...

Different metals have different properties, which make them suited to different uses. The same goes for alloys too.

Q1   Give one use of steel.   [1 mark]

Transition Metals

Transition metals have plenty of different properties that you need to know — grab a cup of tea and read on...

The Transition Metals Sit in the Middle of the Periodic Table

A lot of everyday metals are transition metals (e.g. copper, iron, zinc, gold, silver, platinum) — but there are loads of others as well.

If you get asked about a transition metal you've never heard of — don't panic. These 'new' transition metals will follow all the properties you've already learnt for the others.

These are the transition metals

Sc	Ti	V	Cr	Mn	Fe	Co	Ni	Cu	Zn
Y	Zr	Nb	Mo	Tc	Ru	Rh	Pd	Ag	Cd
La	Hf	Ta	W	Re	Os	Ir	Pt	Au	Hg
Ac	Rf	Db	Sg	Bh	Hs	Mt	Ds	Rg	Cn

Transition metals can be called transition elements.

Transition Metals Have Typical Metallic Properties

1) The transition metals have all the typical properties of metals (see page 163) — they're relatively hard, strong, shiny and malleable materials that conduct heat and electricity well.

2) They have high melting and boiling points (except mercury, which is liquid at room temperature).

3) They also have high densities. For example, at room temperature, potassium (a Group 1 metal) has a density of 0.9 g/cm³, while copper has a density of 9.0 g/cm³, and iron has a density of 7.9 g/cm³.

4) The properties of some transition metals make them really useful. For example, gold is used in jewellery because it's shiny and malleable, but it's also a great electrical conductor and really corrosion resistant, so it's used in some electronic components. Copper is used for water pipes because it's malleable and corrosion resistant. It's another good electrical conductor, so it's used in a lot of electrical wiring.

5) Transition metals have more than one ion. For example, iron forms Fe^{2+} and Fe^{3+} ions.

Transition Metals and Their Compounds Make Good Catalysts

1) A catalyst speeds up the rate of a reaction without being changed or used up itself — see page 93 for more about catalysts.

2) Iron is the catalyst used in the Haber process for making ammonia.

3) Platinum is the catalyst used in catalytic converters.

Did you send for me?

No, I said iron catalyst.

Transition Metal Compounds are Very Colourful

The compounds of transition metals are colourful. What colour they are depends on what transition metal ion they contain — e.g. compounds containing Fe^{2+} ions are usually pale green, ones with Fe^{3+} ions are brown (e.g. rust) and those with Cu^{2+} ions are often blue.

Higher

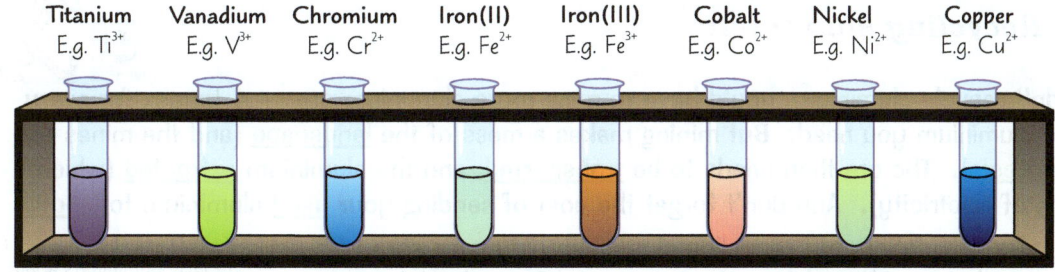

| Titanium E.g. Ti^{3+} | Vanadium E.g. V^{3+} | Chromium E.g. Cr^{2+} | Iron(II) E.g. Fe^{2+} | Iron(III) E.g. Fe^{3+} | Cobalt E.g. Co^{2+} | Nickel E.g. Ni^{2+} | Copper E.g. Cu^{2+} |

You need to make sure you know the colours of compounds containing Fe^{2+}, Fe^{3+}, and Cu^{2+} ions for the exam.

You can't get much more colourful than transition metal ions...

Transition metals are everywhere. They make good catalysts, iron's used to make steel for construction, copper's used in electrical wiring, and you can even use their pretty compounds to colour stained glass.

Q1 Name one industrial process that uses a transition metal catalyst. Name the catalyst used. [1 mark]

Q2 Explain how a scientist could tell apart samples of iron(II) chloride and iron(III) chloride. [2 marks]

Sustainability of Metal Extraction

There's loads of things to take into account before building a metal extraction plant — where to build the plant, how to save fuel and energy costs, how to... oh the list is too long, just read the page.

It's Important to Choose the Right Site for a Metal Extraction Plant

There are lots of factors that affect where a metal extraction plant is set up. You have to take into account the economic benefits and sustainability of the extraction process when deciding on a site:

1) Plants are usually built near to the coast so raw materials can be easily imported into the plant.

2) Plants can't be built too close to urban areas — it's likely that local residents would oppose this. Metal extraction plants can create noise and air pollution, as well as a loss of natural landscape.

3) They need to be close enough to towns and cities that workers can travel easily from their homes.

4) Aluminium plants need a lot of electricity to run, so it's important that there is a direct power supply from a nearby power station.

> Anglesey Aluminium was an aluminium plant in Wales — when running it would use 10-15% of all the electricity used in Wales. When their closest power supply, Wylfa Power Station, was decommissioned, Anglesey Aluminium no longer had a guaranteed direct supply of electricity. This meant that the aluminium plant became uneconomical and had to close down.

5) The finished product from metal extraction plants needs to be transported all over the country (and possibly the world) to buyers. It's essential that the location has good transport links — nearby railway lines and motorways will influence the siting of a plant.

Metal Extraction Plants Need to be Sustainable

1) Metal extraction plants need be sustainable, both in economic and environmental terms.

2) Sometimes the cost of importing materials from other countries is lower than mining the raw materials near to the extraction plant.

> Wales has produced iron and steel for a very long time because all of the raw materials can be found there. However the plant at Port Talbot imports their raw materials instead. It isn't sustainable to use the raw materials available in Wales due to the cost and environmental impact of quarrying.

3) Extracting raw materials uses large amounts of energy, lots of which comes from burning fossil fuels.

4) Recycling materials saves energy as the process often only uses a small fraction of the energy needed to extract and refine the material from scratch. This reduces greenhouse gas emissions (p.85).

5) As there's a finite amount of most raw materials, recycling also conserves resources.

6) It's beneficial to the economy to recycle metals that are expensive to extract or buy.

Example: Recycling Aluminium

1) If you didn't recycle aluminium, you'd have to mine more aluminium ore — 4 tonnes for every 1 tonne of aluminium you need. But mining makes a mess of the landscape (and the mines can be in rainforests). The ore then needs to be transported, and the aluminium extracted (which uses loads of electricity). And don't forget the cost of sending your used aluminium to landfill.

2) It's a complex calculation, but recycling aluminium only uses about 5% of the energy that you'd need to extract the metal from aluminium ore.

In fact, aluminium's about the most cost-effective metal to recycle.

Let's see if I can find a good joke to recycle here...

Sustainability's a hot topic. We don't have an infinite amount of materials to keep on making things from, so recycling is really important to make sure we don't run out of lots of important raw materials.

Q1   Give an advantage and a disadvantage of building a metal extraction plant near to a town.   [2 marks]

Endothermic and Exothermic Reactions

So, endothermic and exothermic reactions are all about taking in and giving out energy to the surroundings. I think endothermic reactions are a bit self-centred really — they just take, take, take...

Reactions are *Exothermic or Endothermic*

Combustion reactions (p.189) and neutralisation reactions (p.171) are always exothermic.

An **EXOTHERMIC** reaction is one which gives out energy to the surroundings, usually in the form of heat and usually shown by a rise in temperature of the surroundings.

An **ENDOTHERMIC** reaction is one which takes in energy from the surroundings, usually in the form of heat and usually shown by a fall in temperature of the surroundings.

Reaction Profiles *Show if a Reaction's* Exo- *or Endothermic*

Reaction profiles show the energy levels of the reactants and the products in a reaction. You can use them to work out if energy is released (exothermic) or taken in (endothermic).

1) This shows an exothermic reaction — the products are at a lower energy than the reactants.
2) The difference in height represents the energy given out in the reaction.

EXOTHERMIC

Energy is released

1) This shows an endothermic reaction because the products are at a higher energy than the reactants.
2) The difference in height represents the energy taken in during the reaction.

ENDOTHERMIC

Energy is absorbed

Activation Energy *is the Energy Needed to* Start *a Reaction*

1) The activation energy is the minimum amount of energy needed for bonds to break (see page 184) and for a reaction to start.
2) On a reaction profile, it's the energy difference between the reactants and the highest point on the curve.
3) It's a bit like having to climb up one side of a hill before you can ski/snowboard/sledge/fall down the other side.
4) If the energy input is less than the activation energy there won't be enough energy to start the reaction — so nothing will happen.

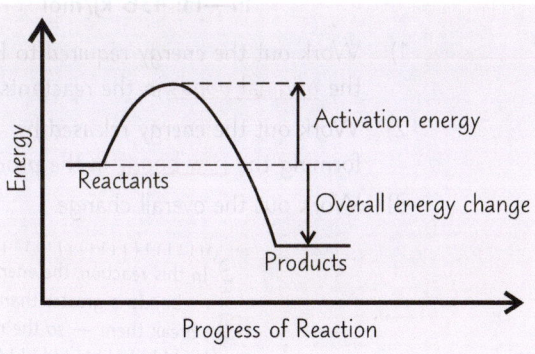

Endothermic reactions — they just get cooler and cooler...

Remember, "exo-" = exit, "-thermic" = heat, so an exothermic reaction is one that gives out heat — and endothermic means just the opposite. To make sure you really understand these terms, try this question.

Q1   A student carries out an experiment which results in a change in temperature of the reaction mixture. Use the energy profile for the reaction, shown on the right, to help explain whether the temperature of the reaction mixture increased or decreased.

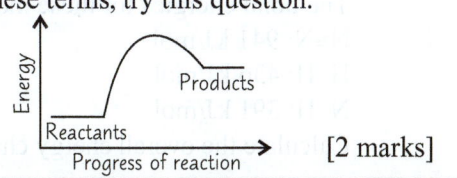

[2 marks]

Unit 5c — Metals, Extraction and Energy

Bond Energies

Energy transfer in chemical reactions is all to do with <u>making and breaking bonds</u>.

There's more on energy transfer on page 92.

Energy Must Always be *Supplied* to Break Bonds

1) During a chemical reaction, <u>old bonds are broken</u> and <u>new bonds are formed</u>.
2) Energy must be <u>supplied</u> to break <u>existing bonds</u> — so bond breaking is an <u>endothermic</u> process.
3) Energy is <u>released</u> when new bonds are <u>formed</u> — so bond formation is an <u>exothermic</u> process.

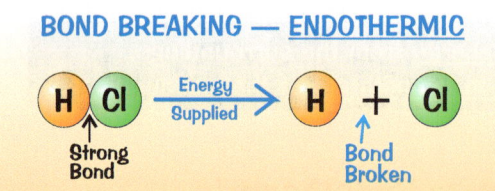

BOND BREAKING — ENDOTHERMIC

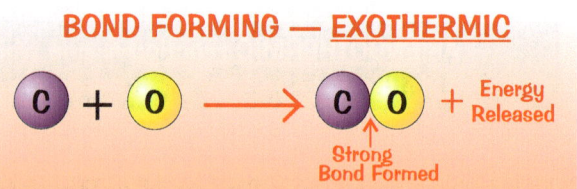

BOND FORMING — EXOTHERMIC

4) In <u>endothermic</u> reactions, the energy <u>used</u> to break bonds is <u>greater</u> than the energy <u>released</u> by forming them.
5) In <u>exothermic</u> reactions, the energy <u>released</u> by forming bonds is <u>greater</u> than the energy <u>breaking</u> 'em.

Bond Energy Calculations — *Need to be Practised*

1) <u>Every</u> chemical bond has a particular <u>bond energy</u> associated with it. This <u>bond energy</u> varies slightly depending on the <u>compound</u> the bond occurs in.
2) You can use these <u>known bond energies</u> to calculate the <u>overall energy change</u> for a reaction.

overall energy change	=	energy required to break bonds	−	energy released by forming bonds

3) A <u>positive</u> energy change means an <u>endothermic</u> reaction and a <u>negative</u> energy change means an <u>exothermic</u> reaction.

4) You need to <u>practise</u> a few of these, but the basic idea is really very simple...

 **EXAMPLE:**

Using the bond energy values below, calculate the energy change for the following reaction, where hydrogen and chlorine react to produce hydrogen chloride:

$$H—H + Cl—Cl \rightarrow 2H—Cl$$

H—H: 436 kJ/mol   Cl—Cl: 242 kJ/mol   H—Cl: 431 kJ/mol

1) Work out the energy required to break the <u>original bonds</u> in the reactants.

(1 × H—H) + (1 × Cl—Cl) = 436 + 242
= 678 kJ/mol

2) Work out the energy released by forming the <u>new bonds</u> in the products.

(2 × H—Cl) = 2 × 431
= 862 kJ/mol

3) Work out the overall change.

overall energy change = energy required to break bonds −
energy released by forming bonds
= 678 − 862 = −184 kJ/mol

In this reaction, the energy released by forming bonds is greater than the energy used to break them — so the reaction is exothermic.

A student and their mobile — a bond that can never be broken...

This stuff might look hard at the moment, but with a bit of practice it's dead easy and it'll win you easy marks if you understand all the theory behind it. See how you get on with this question:

Q1 During the Haber Process, N_2 reacts with H_2 in the following reaction: $N_2 + 3H_2 \rightarrow 2NH_3$
The bond energies for these molecules are:
N≡N: 941 kJ/mol
H–H: 436 kJ/mol
N–H: 391 kJ/mol

N≡N + H—H ⟶
H—H

H—H   H   H
N   +   N
H   H   H   H

Calculate the overall energy change for the reaction.

[3 marks]

Revision Questions for Unit 5c

Well, that's Unit 5c finished — now it's time for the greatest quiz on earth. Try not to get too excited...

- Try these questions and tick off each one when you get it right.
- When you've done all the questions for a topic and are completely happy with it, tick off the topic.

Extracting Metals From Their Ores (p.176-179) ☐

1) What is a metal ore and where are they usually found? ☐
2) How are metals more reactive than carbon usually extracted from their ores? ☐
3) Describe how metals less reactive than carbon are usually extracted from their ores. ☐
4) What are the three raw materials used to extract iron from its ore in the blast furnace? ☐
5) Write out word equations for the three reactions that are used to extract iron from iron ore. ☐
6) Describe oxidation and reduction in terms of electrons. ☐
7) Describe what happens during a displacement reaction. ☐
8) During electrolysis, which electrode are the positive ions attracted to? ☐
9) Why can ionic solids not undergo electrolysis? ☐
10) Do ions get reduced or oxidised at the anode? ☐
11) During the manufacture of aluminium from alumina, which electrode is aluminium formed at? ☐

Metals and Their Uses (p.180-181) ☐

12) Give three properties that aluminium, copper, iron and titanium have in common. ☐
13) Give a different property of aluminium and link this to a particular use. ☐
14) What is an alloy? ☐
15) Name an element that is added to iron to make steel. ☐
16) Explain why alloys are usually harder than pure metals. ☐
17) a) Give two properties that transition metals have in common with most other metals.
    b) Give two typical properties of transition metals that they don't share with most other metals. ☐
18) What colour are Fe^{3+} compounds? ☐

Metal Extraction Plants (p.182) ☑

19) Why are metal extraction plants usually sited close to the coast? ☑
20) Why do metal extraction plants need a direct power supply from a nearby power station? ☑
21) Why is it more sustainable to recycle metals than extract more of the raw materials? ☐

Reactions and Bond Energy (p.183-184) ☐

22) What change in the temperature of the surroundings
    would you expect to observe in an exothermic reaction? ☑
23) Draw a reaction profile for an endothermic reaction. ☐
24) What is activation energy? ☑
25) Is energy required for the breaking of bonds or the forming of bonds? ☑
26) What is the equation for calculating the overall energy change for a reaction? ☑

Fractional Distillation of Crude Oil

Fossil fuels like coal, oil and gas are called non-renewable fuels — they take so long to make that they're being used up much faster than they're being formed. They're finite resources — one day they'll run out.

Crude Oil is Separated into Different Hydrocarbon Fractions

1) Crude oil is our main source of hydrocarbons and is used as a raw material (sometimes called a feedstock) to create lots of useful substances used in the petrochemical industry.

2) It's formed underground, over millions of years (at high temperatures and pressures) from the buried remains of marine organisms. It's a non-renewable (finite) resource, so one day it will run out.

3) Crude oil is a complex mixture of lots of different hydrocarbons — compounds which contain just carbon and hydrogen. The hydrocarbons found in crude oil have their carbon atoms arranged in either chains or rings and are mostly alkanes (hydrocarbons with the general formula C_nH_{2n+2}).

4) Crude oil can be separated out into fractions — simpler, more useful mixtures containing groups of hydrocarbons of similar lengths (i.e. they have similar numbers of carbon and hydrogen atoms). The fractions from crude oil, e.g. petrol, kerosene and diesel, are examples of non-renewable fossil fuels.

5) The different fractions in crude oil are separated by fractional distillation. The oil is heated until most of it has turned into gas. The gases enter a fractionating column (and the liquid bit, bitumen, is drained off at the bottom).

6) In the column there's a temperature gradient (i.e. it's hot at the bottom and gets cooler as you go up).

7) The longer hydrocarbons have higher boiling points. They turn back into liquids and drain out of the column early on, when they're near the bottom. The shorter hydrocarbons have lower boiling points. They turn to liquid and drain out much later on, near to the top of the column where it's cooler.

8) You end up with the crude oil mixture separated out into different fractions. Each fraction contains a mixture of hydrocarbons, mostly alkanes with similar boiling points.

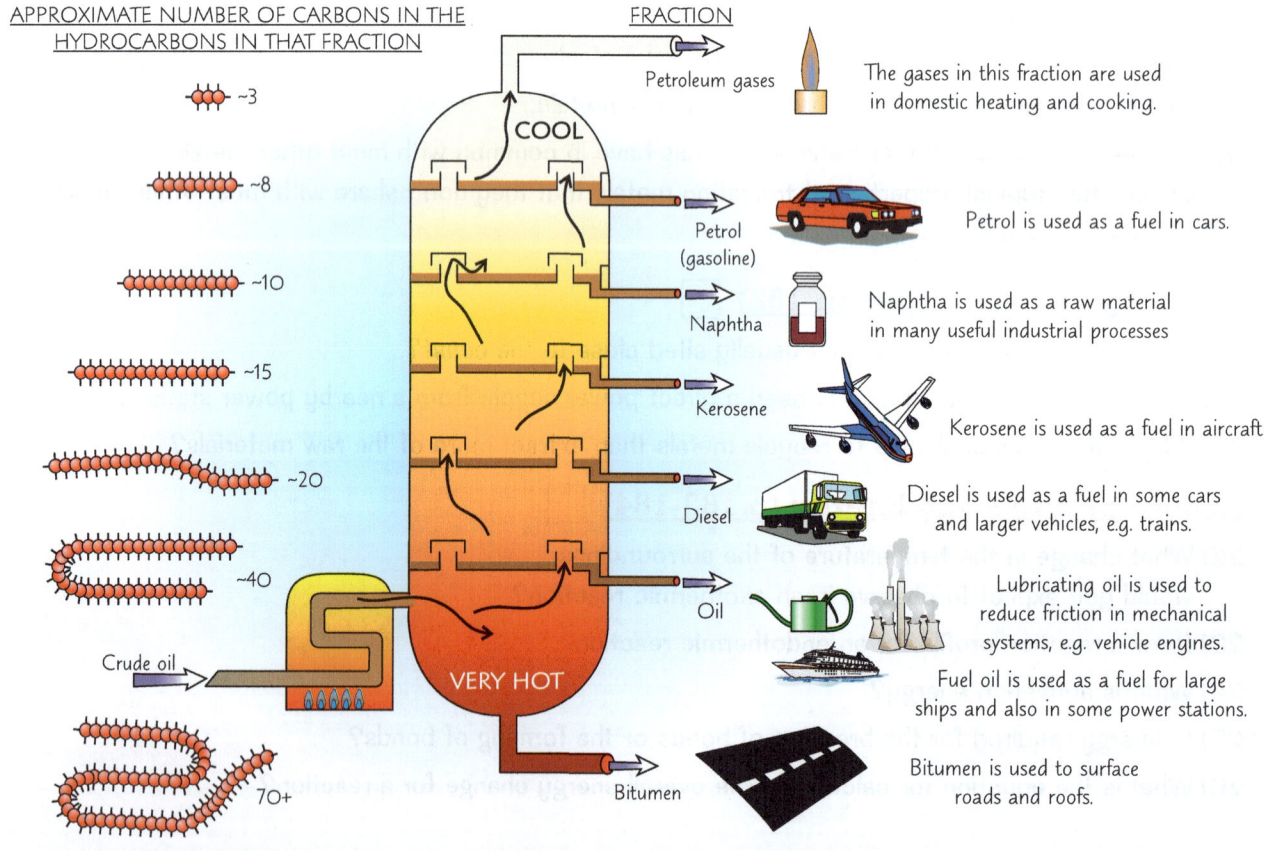

APPROXIMATE NUMBER OF CARBONS IN THE HYDROCARBONS IN THAT FRACTION

FRACTION

~3

~8

~10

~15

~20

~40

Crude oil

70+

COOL

VERY HOT

Petroleum gases — The gases in this fraction are used in domestic heating and cooking.

Petrol (gasoline) — Petrol is used as a fuel in cars.

Naphtha — Naphtha is used as a raw material in many useful industrial processes

Kerosene — Kerosene is used as a fuel in aircraft.

Diesel — Diesel is used as a fuel in some cars and larger vehicles, e.g. trains.

Oil — Lubricating oil is used to reduce friction in mechanical systems, e.g. vehicle engines. Fuel oil is used as a fuel for large ships and also in some power stations.

Bitumen — Bitumen is used to surface roads and roofs.

How much petrol is there in crude oil? Just a fraction...

You'll need to know the names and uses of all the fractions for your exam, so best have a good read of this page.

Q1   Petrol drains further up a fractionating column than diesel. What does this suggest about the boiling points of the hydrocarbons which make up petrol compared to those in diesel?   [1 mark]

Crude Oil and Cracking

Crude oil really improves our lives in lots of ways but we're using up our supplies way too quickly...

Crude Oil Provides Important Fuels for Modern Life

1) Crude oil provides the energy needed to do lots of vital things — generating electricity, heating homes...

2) Oil provides the fuel for most modern transport — cars, trains, planes, the lot. It also provides the raw materials needed to make various chemicals, including plastics.

3) However, crude oil supplies are limited and non-renewable.

4) New reserves are sometimes found, and new technology means we can get to oil that was once too difficult to extract. But one day we'll just run out.

5) Some people think we should stop using oil for fuel (where we have alternatives) and keep it for making plastics and other chemicals (e.g. medicines). This could lead to conflict for resources between the fuel and chemical industries.

But There Are Economic and Environmental Issues With Using It

1) As Earth's population increases, and as countries like India and China become more developed, more fossil fuels are burned to provide electricity — both for increased home use and to run manufacturing industries. This increasing use of crude oil isn't sustainable in the long run.

2) As the demand for fossil fuels increases, prices go up. It's not just heating and transport that get more expensive though — the prices of food and other goods are affected by energy costs too.

3) Burning fossil fuels also leads to environmental problems like global warming (p.85) and acid rain (p.86). The effects of these issues aren't just felt in the countries using the energy.

Cracking Means Splitting Up Long–Chain Hydrocarbons

1) Fractional distillation produces many large alkane molecules which are not in great demand — we don't need them nearly as much as some of the smaller hydrocarbon fractions like petrol and diesel.

2) A lot of the longer alkane molecules produced from fractional distillation are turned into smaller, more useful ones by a process called cracking.

3) During cracking, the hydrocarbons are heated until they become a vapour and passed over a powdered catalyst, which causes them to split apart.

4) Cracking is a form of thermal decomposition — the hydrocarbon breaks down when it is heated. You need lots of energy for this because you're breaking the strong covalent bonds within the molecule.

5) As well as alkanes, cracking also produces another type of hydrocarbon called alkenes (see page 192). Alkenes (e.g. ethene) are used as a starting material when making the polymers for plastics (see p.193).

> The number of C and H atoms in the large alkane should equal the total number of C and H atoms in the products. So when writing a cracking equation, make sure both sides balance.

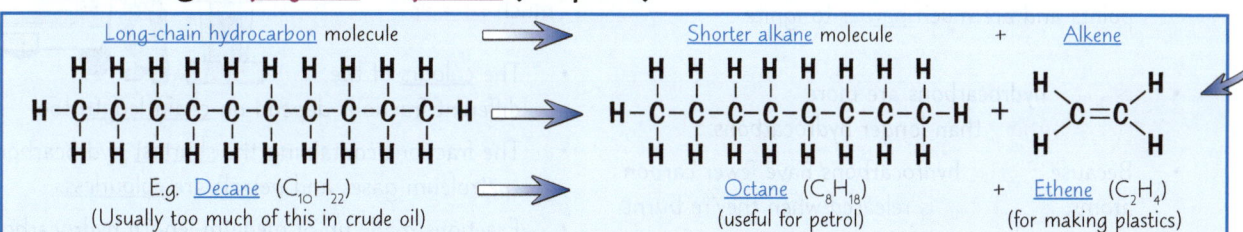

6) If we didn't use cracking — lots more crude oil would need to be extracted to meet the demands for certain hydrocarbons (e.g. petrol) and a lot of the longer chain hydrocarbons would go to waste.

I'm not one to brag, but this really is a cracking page...

Demand for fossil fuels is rising, but supplies are running ever lower and prices are going up. That's why cracking is so important — we can eke out our resources until we've developed our technology to run on alternatives.

Q1   A molecule of dodecane, $C_{12}H_{26}$, was cracked, producing two products. One of the products had the molecular formula C_9H_{20}. Give the molecular formula for the other product.   [1 mark]

Hydrocarbons

The physical properties of crude oil fractions all depend on how big the hydrocarbons in that fraction are.

There are Trends in the Properties of Fractions

1) Crude oil fractions contain alkanes — see p.191.
2) For each additional carbon atom in the alkane molecule, there is an extra CH_2 unit in the molecular formula.
3) Different alkanes have similar chemical properties.
4) The physical properties of the alkanes vary between the different molecules. For example, the bigger a molecule is, the higher the boiling point will be (see below).

Alkane	Molecular formula	Boiling point (°C)	Fraction in crude oil
Methane	CH_4	−162	Gases
Ethane	C_2H_6	−89	Gases
Dodecane	$C_{12}H_{26}$	216	Kerosene
Icosane	$C_{20}H_{42}$	343	Diesel
Tetracontane	$C_{40}H_{82}$	524	Fuel Oil

5) The properties of alkenes (p.192), which are also found in fractions, are related in a similar way.

The Size of a Hydrocarbon Determines its Properties

1) The size of a hydrocarbon determines which fraction of crude oil it will separate into (see page 186).
2) Each fraction contains hydrocarbons (mostly alkanes) with similar numbers of carbon atoms, so all of the molecules in a fraction will have similar properties and behave in similar ways.
3) The physical properties are determined by the intermolecular forces that hold the chains together.

- The intermolecular forces of attraction break a lot more easily in small molecules than they do in bigger molecules. That's because the forces are much stronger between big molecules than they are between small molecules.

- It makes sense if you think about it — even if a big molecule can overcome the forces attracting it to another molecule at a few points along its length, it's still got lots of other places where the force is still strong enough to hold it in place.

- That's why big molecules have higher boiling points than small molecules.

not many intermolecular forces to break

lots of intermolecular forces to break

- Shorter hydrocarbons are easy to ignite because they have lower boiling points, so tend to be gases at room temperature.
- These gas molecules mix with oxygen in the air to produce a gas mixture which bursts into flames if it comes into contact with a spark.
- Longer hydrocarbons are usually liquids at room temperature. They have higher boiling points and are much harder to ignite.

- Viscosity measures how easily a substance flows.
- The stronger the force is between hydrocarbon molecules, the harder it is for the liquid to flow.
- Fractions containing longer hydrocarbons have a higher viscosity — they're thick like treacle.
- Fractions made up of shorter hydrocarbons have a low viscosity and are much runnier.

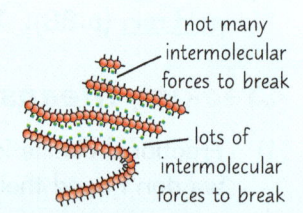

- Shorter hydrocarbons are more clean-burning than longer hydrocarbons.
- Because shorter hydrocarbons have fewer carbon atoms, less carbon is released when they're burnt.
- Shorter hydrocarbons burn with a blue flame, but when longer hydrocarbons are burned, the flame is yellow and smoky.

- The colours of the different fractions depend on chain length too.
- The fractions containing the shortest hydrocarbons (petroleum gases and petrol) are colourless.
- Fractions made up of medium-length hydrocarbons, such as naphtha, kerosene and diesel, are yellow.
- Fuel oil and bitumen, which have the longest hydrocarbons, are brown.

My sister has a high viscosity — she's pretty thick...

So there are trends in the properties of crude oil fractions — as the length of the hydrocarbons increases, boiling point and viscosity increase, ease of ignition and cleanliness of burn decrease, and the colour generally gets darker.

Q1   Explain why dodecane ($C_{12}H_{26}$) has a higher boiling point than methane (CH_4).   [2 marks]

Burning Fuels

Combustion reactions can be really useful, but you've got to be able to stop them if things get out of hand...

Fuels Release Energy in Combustion Reactions

1) Hydrocarbons make great fuels because the combustion reactions that happen when you burn them in oxygen give out lots of energy — the reactions are very exothermic (see page 183).

2) When you burn hydrocarbons in plenty of oxygen, the only products are carbon dioxide and water — this is called complete combustion.

Hydrocarbon + oxygen → carbon dioxide + water
E.g. C_3H_8 + $5O_2$ → $3CO_2$ + $4H_2O$

Hydrogen Can be Used as a Clean, Renewable Fuel

Hydrogen gas has been used as rocket fuel for years, and is now being used in fuel cells to power cars.

Pros: Hydrogen is a very clean fuel. In a hydrogen fuel cell, hydrogen combines with oxygen to produce energy, and the only waste product is water — no nasty pollutants that cause global warming or acid rain (which are produced when fossil fuels are burnt). Hydrogen's obtained from water which is a renewable resource, so it's not going to run out (unlike fossil fuels). Hydrogen can even be obtained from the water produced by the cell when it's used in fuel cells.

hydrogen + oxygen → water
$2H_2$ + O_2 → $2H_2O$

Cons: You need a special, expensive engine. Hydrogen gas is produced from the electrolysis of water, which is expensive and uses large amounts of electricity — this electricity is often generated by burning fossil fuels, which produces pollutants. Also, hydrogen's hard to store (it requires large, pressurised containers) and it can be dangerous as it forms an explosive mixture with air.

The Fire Triangle Shows the Three Things Needed for a Fire to Burn

1) A fire needs fuel, oxygen and heat to burn.

2) Fire is just the combustion reaction between the fuel and the oxygen.

3) However, this reaction has a high activation energy, so can only start at high temperatures — you need heat too.

Check out page 183 if you're feeling uncertain about activation energy.

The fire triangle is used to prevent and to fight fires. A fire can only start and keep burning if all three elements from the fire triangle are present. If you take away one or more elements, the fire will go out (or won't start in the first place).

FUEL:
- In industry, safer alternatives to highly flammable materials are used wherever possible.
- Forest fires are often tackled by chopping down and removing trees in the path of the fire. Without these as a source of fuel, the fire (eventually) goes out.

OXYGEN:
- Covering a fire with a fire blanket or damp cloth stops the oxygen in the air from getting to it.
- Some fire extinguishers use foam or powder to block the oxygen in a similar way.
- Carbon dioxide fire extinguishers work by replacing the air (and so oxygen) around the fire.

HEAT:
- Storing flammable materials away from sources of heat is an important method of fire prevention.
- Pouring water over a fire, or spraying it from a hose or extinguisher, cools the fire down.

Water should never be used on fires involving electricity or flammable liquids — it just makes things worse.

I'm burning to know more...

The fire triangle could literally save your life. If that's not a good reason to learn this page, I don't know what is.

Q1   Explain how putting a fire blanket over a fire helps to put the fire out.   [2 marks]

Measuring Energy Changes  PRACTICAL

You can see for yourself just how <u>exothermic</u> combustion reactions are by doing this nice simple <u>experiment</u> (and a little bit of <u>maths</u>...). Probably not in your bedroom though — health and safety and all that...

You Can Measure the Energy Released in Combustion Reactions

To measure the amount of energy released when a fuel is burnt, you can simply burn the fuel and use the flame to <u>heat up some water</u>.

1) Put 100 cm³ of water into a conical flask and <u>record its temperature</u>.

2) Clamp the flask in place.

3) <u>Weigh the spirit burner</u> (filled with fuel) and the lid.

4) Put the spirit burner underneath the flask, and light the wick. Heat the water, <u>stirring constantly</u>, until the temperature has increased by about <u>40 °C</u>.

5) <u>Put out the flame</u> using the burner lid, and measure the <u>final temperature</u> of the water.

6) <u>Weigh</u> the spirit burner and lid <u>again</u>.

7) You can then use the measurements you've taken to <u>calculate the energy change</u> (see below).

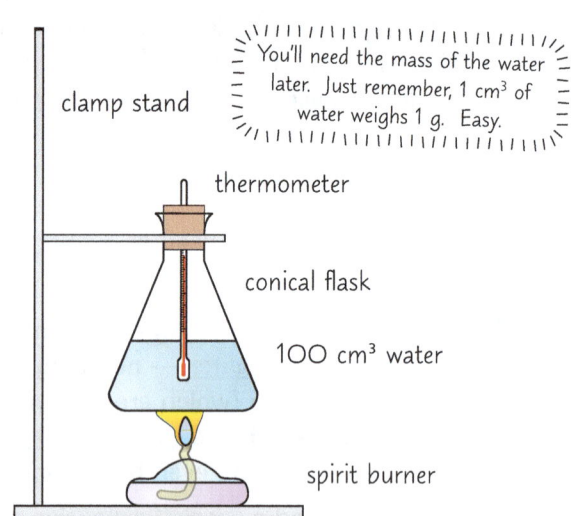

You'll need the mass of the water later. Just remember, 1 cm³ of water weighs 1 g. Easy.

clamp stand

thermometer

conical flask

100 cm³ water

spirit burner

You Calculate the Energy Released Per Gram of Fuel

1) The <u>combustion</u> experiment above involves <u>heating water</u> by burning a <u>liquid fuel</u>.

2) If you measure (i) <u>how much fuel</u> you've burned and (ii) the <u>temperature change</u> of the water, you can work out how much energy is supplied by <u>each gram of fuel</u>. You need this equation:

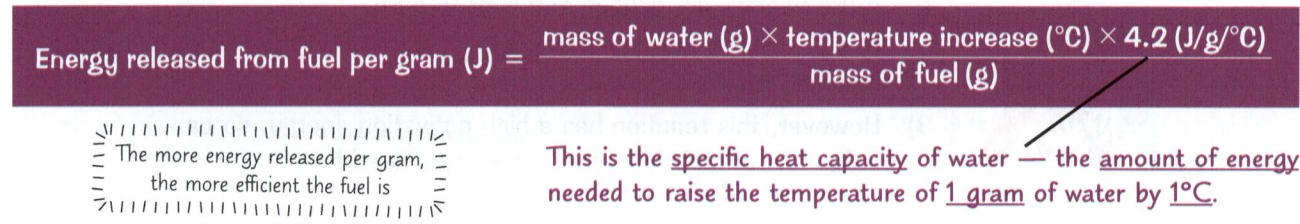

$$\text{Energy released from fuel per gram (J)} = \frac{\text{mass of water (g)} \times \text{temperature increase (°C)} \times 4.2 \text{ (J/g/°C)}}{\text{mass of fuel (g)}}$$

The more energy released per gram, the more efficient the fuel is

This is the <u>specific heat capacity</u> of water — the <u>amount of energy</u> needed to raise the temperature of <u>1 gram</u> of water by <u>1°C</u>.

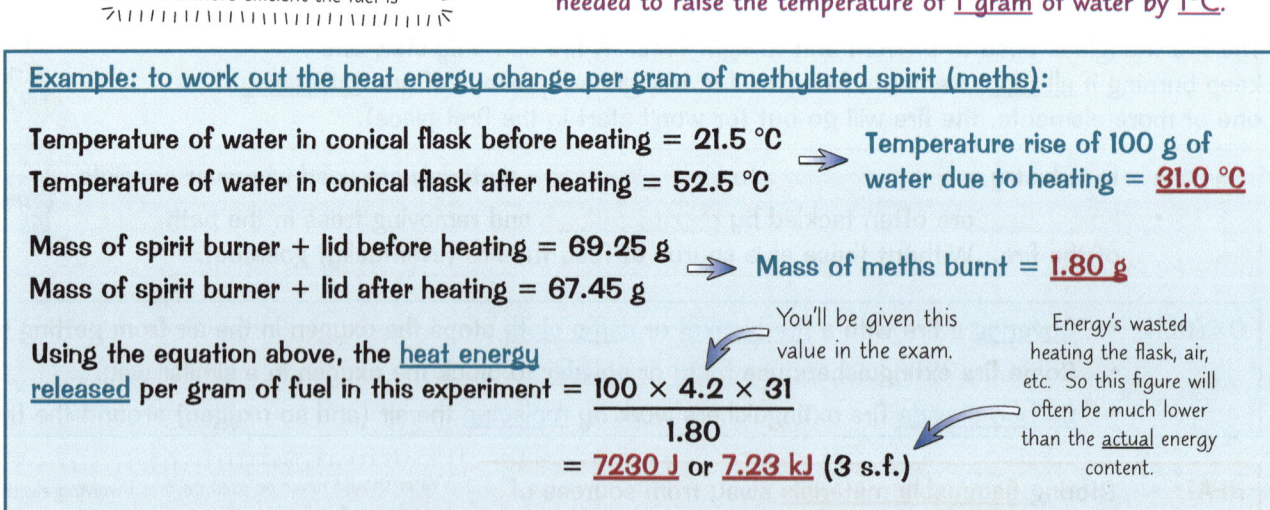

<u>Example: to work out the heat energy change per gram of methylated spirit (meths):</u>

Temperature of water in conical flask before heating = 21.5 °C
Temperature of water in conical flask after heating = 52.5 °C
➡ Temperature rise of 100 g of water due to heating = <u>31.0 °C</u>

Mass of spirit burner + lid before heating = 69.25 g
Mass of spirit burner + lid after heating = 67.45 g
➡ Mass of meths burnt = <u>1.80 g</u>

Using the equation above, the <u>heat energy released</u> per gram of fuel in this experiment = $\dfrac{100 \times 4.2 \times 31}{1.80}$

You'll be given this value in the exam.

Energy's wasted heating the flask, air, etc. So this figure will often be much lower than the <u>actual</u> energy content.

= <u>7230 J</u> or <u>7.23 kJ</u> (3 s.f.)

Specific revision capacity — biscuits per student per mark...

If you're using this method to compare different fuels, you need to make sure it's a fair test. So you want to use the same conical flask each time, keep it the same distance from the flame, use the same type of burner, etc., etc...

Q1   In an experiment, 0.2 g of butane is burnt and raises the temperature of 100 g of water by 18.7 °C.
      Use the formula above to calculate the energy in kJ given out per gram of butane burnt.   [3 marks]

Alkanes

We're now going to look at the different types of hydrocarbons you can get. First up is the alkanes...

Alkanes are *Saturated Hydrocarbons*

1) Alkanes are hydrocarbons — they're chains of carbon atoms surrounded by hydrogen atoms.
2) Different alkanes have chains of different lengths.
3) Alkanes have the general formula C_nH_{2n+2}.
4) You need to know the names and the structural formulae of the first five alkanes.

> Alkanes = C_nH_{2n+2}

n is just the number of carbon atoms there are in the molecule

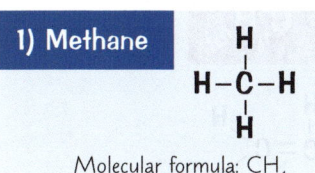

1) Methane

Molecular formula: CH_4

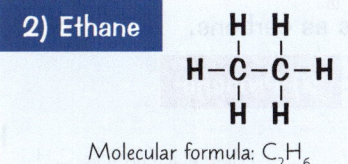

2) Ethane

Molecular formula: C_2H_6

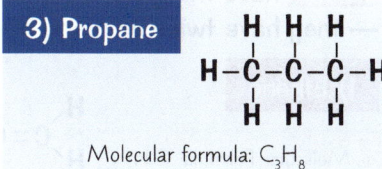

3) Propane

Molecular formula: C_3H_8

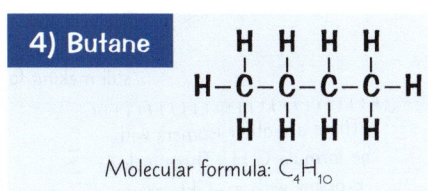

4) Butane

Molecular formula: C_4H_{10}

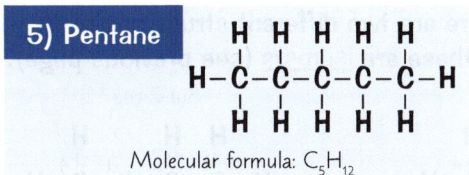

5) Pentane

Molecular formula: C_5H_{12}

To help remember the names of the first four alkanes just remember: Mice Eat Peanut Butter. Pentane is five, just like a pentagon, so you'll have to remember that one on its own.

5) Carbon atoms must always form four bonds. This means they can bond to up to four other atoms.
6) The diagrams above show that all the atoms have formed bonds with as many other atoms as they can. There are only single bonds between the carbon atoms — this means the molecules are saturated.

In *Isomers* the Atoms Are *Arranged Differently*

1) Two molecules are isomers of one another if they have the same molecular formula but the atoms are arranged differently.
2) This means their structural formulae are different.
3) Isomers of alkanes have differently shaped carbon chains.
4) The carbons could be arranged as a straight chain or a branched chain (one of the carbons being bonded to more than two other carbons).

Alkane, Al saw, Al conquered.

Give it a rest, Alan!

There Are *Two Isomers* of C_4H_{10} and *Three Isomers* of C_5H_{12}

And you need to be able to draw all of them.

C_4H_{10} has one straight chain isomer and one branched chain isomer.

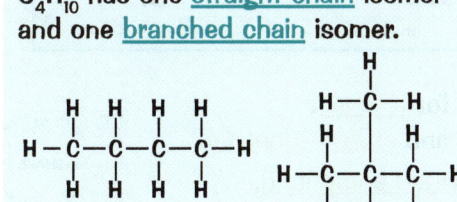

C_5H_{12} has one straight chain and two different branched chain isomers

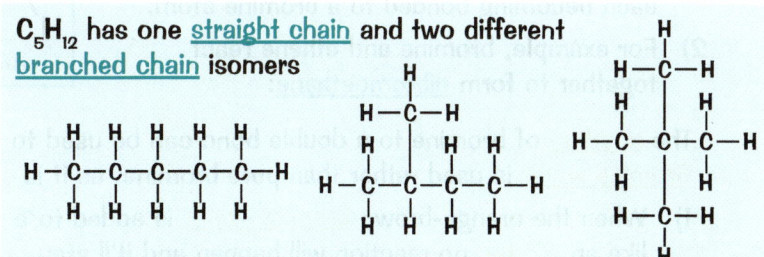

Higher

My brain during exam revision is a bit like alkanes — saturated...

I guess you're after a useful tip? OK here goes: Make sure you learn the general formula of alkanes and how to draw the first five alkanes. It could be super helpful in your exam, hint hint...

Q1   A molecule of the alkane octane contains eight carbon atoms. Give octane's molecular formula.   [1 mark]

Alkenes

Alkenes are another type of hydrocarbon. They are different to alkanes because they contain a double bond.

Alkenes Have a C=C Double Bond

1) Alkenes are hydrocarbons which have a double bond between two of the carbon atoms in their chain.

2) They are unsaturated molecules because they can make more bonds — the double bond can open up, allowing the two carbon atoms to bond with other atoms (see below). This is an addition reaction.

3) The first three alkenes are ethene (with two carbon atoms), propene (three Cs) and butene (four Cs).

4) Alkenes have the general formula: C_nH_{2n} — they have twice as many hydrogens as carbons.

Alkenes = C_nH_{2n}

1) Ethene

$$H{\diagdown}C=C{\diagup}^H_H \quad H{\diagup}\ \ {\diagdown}H$$

Molecular Formula: C_2H_4

2) Propene

Molecular Formula: C_3H_6

This is a double bond — so each carbon atom is still making four bonds.

3) Butene

There are two different structures for butene — these are isomers (see previous page).

But-1-ene

Molecular Formula: C_4H_8

But-2-ene

Molecular Formula: C_4H_8

There are other isomers with the formula C_4H_8. These include propene with a $-CH_3$ group attached to the second carbon.

• But-1-ene and but-2-ene are the systematic names for these isomers.

• You find the systematic name by numbering the carbon chain so that one of the carbons in the C=C group has the lowest possible number.

• In but-1-ene the C=C group starts at carbon 1 and in but-2-ene it starts at carbon 2.

R is just the rest of the molecule. It isn't involved in the reaction so it doesn't matter what it's like.

Alkenes Can React with Hydrogen...

Hydrogen can react with the double-bonded carbons to open up the double bond and form the equivalent, saturated, alkane.

The alkene is reacted with hydrogen in the presence of a catalyst:

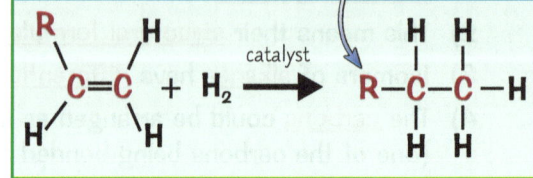

...And Also with Bromine

1) Alkenes will also react in addition reactions with bromine. The molecules formed are saturated bromoalkanes, with the C=C carbons each becoming bonded to a bromine atom.

2) For example, bromine and ethene react together to form dibromoethane:

ethene + bromine → dibromoethane

There are two bromine atoms so it's called dibromoethane.

The addition of bromine to a double bond can be used to test for alkenes.
Bromine water is used rather than pure bromine, as it is safer and easier to handle.

1) When the orange-brown bromine water is added to a saturated compound, like an alkane, no reaction will happen and it'll stay orange-brown.

2) If it's added to an alkene the bromine will add across the double bond, making a colourless dibromo-compound — so the bromine water is decolourised.

SHAKE

bromine water + an alkene   solution goes colourless

Double the carbon bonds, double the fun...

Don't go mixing up your alkanes and alkenes — remember, the double bond in alkenes makes them 'kene' to react.

Q1   Give the structural formula of the product of the reaction between propene and hydrogen.   [1 mark]

Addition Polymers

Polymers are made by joining lots of <u>little molecules</u> together in <u>long chains</u>. Magic.

Addition Polymers are Made From *Unsaturated Monomers*

1) <u>Polymers</u> are long molecules made by joining up lots of small repeating units called <u>monomers</u>. The monomers that make up <u>addition polymers</u> have a <u>double covalent bond</u> — this makes them very reactive.

2) Lots of <u>unsaturated monomer molecules</u> (<u>alkenes</u> — see last page) can open up their <u>double bonds</u> and join together to form <u>polymer chains</u>. This is called <u>addition polymerisation</u>.

3) The <u>name</u> of the polymer comes from the <u>type of monomer</u> it's made from — you just put <u>brackets</u> around it and stick the word "<u>poly</u>" in front of it. So <u>propene</u> becomes <u>poly(propene)</u>, etc.

4) To get the <u>formula</u> of the polymer, you just put the formula of the <u>monomer</u> in brackets and put a little 'n' after it. So C_3H_6 becomes $(C_3H_6)_n$. Simple.

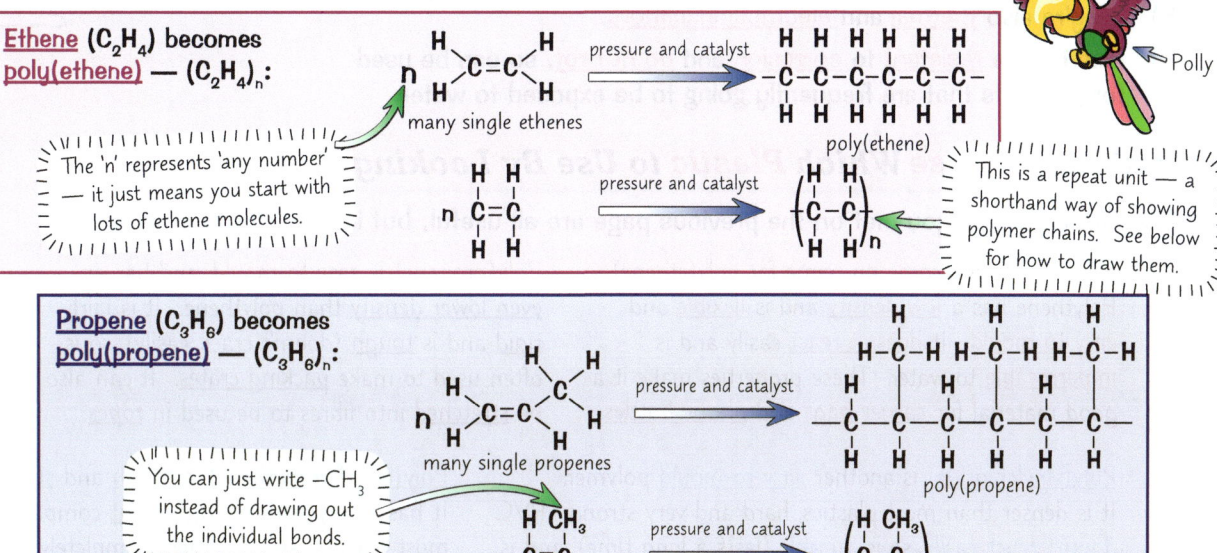

5) Drawing the <u>structural formula</u> of an <u>addition polymer</u> from the structural formula of its <u>monomer</u> is easy. Join the carbons together in a <u>row</u> with <u>no</u> double bonds between them, stick a pair of <u>brackets</u> around the repeating bit, and put an '<u>n</u>' after it (to show that there are lots of monomers). You should also draw a bond going through the brackets at each end — this shows the chain continues.

6) To get from the <u>structural formula</u> of the <u>polymer</u> to the structural formula of the <u>monomer</u>, just do the reverse. Draw out the <u>repeating bit</u>, get rid of the two bonds going through the brackets and put a <u>double bond</u> between the <u>carbons</u>.

Which polymer is good for making a cuppa? Poly(putthekettleon)...

You'll need to be able to draw the structural formulae of all of the monomers and polymers shown on this page.

Q1   Explain why propene can undergo addition polymerisation but propane cannot.   [2 marks]

Uses of Plastics

Materials made up of lots of individual <u>polymer molecules</u> are known as <u>plastics</u>.
You need to know all about their <u>properties</u> and <u>uses</u>.

Plastics *Are Really* Adaptable

Plastics have lots of different properties that make them useful in a wide range of applications.

1) They're often <u>cheaper</u> than most other materials.
2) They're generally <u>strong</u>.
3) They tend to be <u>less dense</u> than most metals or ceramics, so they're often used when designing products that need to have a low mass.
4) Some plastics are <u>flexible</u>, so they can be bent without breaking, and can be <u>easily moulded</u> into almost any shape.
5) They're also <u>thermal</u> and <u>electrical insulators</u>.
6) Plastics are <u>resistant</u> to <u>corrosion</u> and <u>do not rot</u>, so can be used for products that are frequently going to be exposed to water.

You Can Choose *Which* Plastic *to Use By Looking at Its* Properties

The four polymers you met on the previous page are all useful, but in very different ways...

<u>Polythene</u> is the common name for poly(ethene). Polythene has a <u>low density</u> and is <u>flexible</u> and <u>easy to mould</u>. It <u>doesn't react</u> easily and is <u>impermeable</u> to water. These properties make it a good material for <u>carrier bags</u> and <u>plastic bottles</u>.

<u>Poly(propene)</u> is <u>easy to mould</u>, and has an <u>even lower density</u> than polythene. It is fairly <u>rigid</u> and is <u>tough</u> (doesn't crack easily), so is often used to make <u>packing crates</u>. It can also be <u>stretched</u> into fibres to be used in <u>ropes</u>.

<u>Poly(vinylchloride)</u> is another <u>easy-to-mould</u> polymer. It is denser than most plastics, hard and very strong. PVC <u>doesn't react easily</u>, so is <u>durable</u> (lasts a long time), and is highly <u>fire resistant</u>. For these reasons, it is often used in construction, particularly for <u>drainpipes</u> and <u>window frames</u>.

<u>Poly(tetrafluoroethene)</u> is <u>tough</u> and <u>strong</u>. It has a <u>very high melting point</u> compared to most plastics, and is almost completely <u>unreactive</u>. It also has a <u>very slippery</u> surface. These properties make it great at <u>making pans non-stick</u>.

You Need to Be Able to Compare *Plastics with* Other Materials

Chemists <u>use information</u> about the properties of materials to <u>assess</u> their <u>suitability</u> for different uses. You might need to do this in the exam too...

EXAMPLE: A company is investigating the best material to make a camping cup. The cup needs to be lightweight, able to withstand the temperature of hot drinks and shouldn't be brittle. Using the data in the table, suggest which material from the table the company should use.

Material	Melting point (°C)	Density (g/cm³)	Brittleness
Aluminium	660	2.7	Low
Glass	700 (softens)	2.6	High
Poly(propene)	171	0.94	Medium
LDPE	110 (but softens from 80)	0.92	Medium

- Aluminium can be ruled out — it has a high melting point and isn't brittle but it's the densest material.
- Glass has a high softening point and is less dense than aluminium, but it's brittle, so breaks easily.
- The density and brittleness of LDPE and poly(propene) are similar, but LDPE starts softening at 80 °C. A hot drink could be up to 100 °C, so LDPE wouldn't be any good.
- Poly(propene) melts above 100 °C, is lightweight and not too brittle. So **poly(propene)** is the best material for the job.

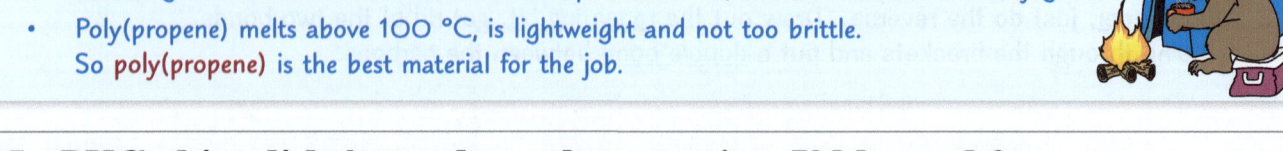

My PVC skirt didn't produce the reaction I'd hoped for...

Plastics can be used for all kinds of things, but you need to make sure you get the right one for the job.

Q1   State two properties of poly(tetrafluoroethene) which make it suitable for coating non-stick pans. [2 marks]

Disposing of Polymers

It's easy to throw away old plastic bottles and plastic packaging without giving much thought — but we need to start thinking about the <u>impact</u> it's having on the <u>environment</u> today and the <u>availability</u> of plastics in the future.

Polymers are Made From Crude Oil

1) <u>Plastics</u> are a type of <u>polymer</u> which are made from <u>crude oil</u>.
   Crude oil is a <u>finite</u> resource — eventually, it will all get used up and run out.

2) The more we use up our crude oil resources, the more <u>expensive</u> crude oil will become — this will then <u>increase the price</u> of crude oil products.

3) Crude oil isn't just used to make <u>plastics</u> — we need it for lots of different things, such as petrol for cars and heating our homes. As resources dry up, we will face the dilemma of how to use the remaining oil. One way we can help delay this problem is by <u>recycling</u> our polymers.

The Disposal of Polymers Comes with Many Problems

In the UK, over <u>2 million</u> tonnes of plastic waste are generated each year.
It's important to find ways to get rid of this waste while <u>minimising environmental damage</u>.

Disposal of Polymers in Landfill Sites:

1) A lot of plastics get dumped in <u>landfill sites</u>. This is usually when different polymers are too <u>difficult</u> or <u>expensive</u> to <u>separate</u> and recycle.

2) Lots of <u>valuable land</u> is quickly getting used up for use as landfill sites.

3) Most polymers are <u>non-biodegradable</u> — they're not broken down by microorganisms. This means that they will sit in landfill for years and years and years and years...

Disposal of Polymers by Combustion:

1) <u>Burning plastics</u> produces a lot of <u>energy</u> and this can be used to <u>generate electricity</u>. But it's not all rainbows and smiles...

2) If not carefully controlled, <u>toxic gases</u> can be released from the combustion of plastics. For example, when polymers that contain chlorine (such as PVC) are burned, they produce HCl — this has to be removed.

3) <u>Carbon dioxide</u> is also produced and this contributes to <u>global warming</u>.

Recycling Polymers Has Both Pros and Cons

1) <u>Recycling</u> polymers is a great way to limit the amount of crude oil we're using and avoid the <u>environmental impact</u> of burning and landfills.

2) Unfortunately, recycling is not as <u>simple</u> as throwing all the plastic rubbish together and then melting and remoulding it all...

Stop trying to recycle your brother, Mark.

ADVANTAGES	DISADVANTAGES
• <u>Reduces</u> the amount of <u>non-biodegradable</u> waste filling up landfill sites.	• Polymers must be <u>separated</u> by type before they can be <u>melted</u> and <u>reformed</u> into a new product — this can be <u>difficult</u> and <u>expensive</u>.
• <u>Reduces emissions</u> of greenhouse and toxic gases which can be released from burning polymers.	• If polymers are <u>mixed</u> together, the <u>quality</u> of the final recycled polymer product could be <u>reduced</u>.
• Recycling generally uses up <u>less water</u> and <u>energy resources</u> than when making new plastics.	• Polymers can only be recycled a <u>finite</u> number of times. Over time, the <u>strength</u> of the polymer can decrease.
• <u>Reduces</u> the amount of <u>crude oil</u> needed to produce more plastics.	• Melting polymers can release dangerous gases into the atmosphere. These are <u>harmful</u> to plants and animals.
• Recycling generally <u>saves money</u> and <u>creates jobs</u>.	

I hear plastic cars are the way forward — they don't break down...

So, if you didn't realise how important recycling polymers was, you should definitely know now. I, for one, can't imagine a life without plastics or petrol, but if we carry on the way we are going, it could soon become reality...

Q1   Give two disadvantages of burning waste plastics.   [2 marks]

Q2   Explain why the price of polymer products could increase if we don't recycle polymers.   [3 marks]

Revision Questions for Unit 5d

Phew! That unit was a wild ride. Time to see how much you can remember...

- Try these questions and tick off each one when you get it right.
- When you've done all the questions for a topic and are completely happy with it, tick off the topic.

Crude Oil and its Fractions (p.186-188) ☐

1) How is crude oil formed?
2) What does non-renewable mean?
3) What is a fraction in terms of crude oil?
4) Put these fractions in order of increasing chain length: kerosene, petroleum gases, bitumen, petrol.
5) What is naphtha used for?
6) What is the purpose of cracking?
7) How do the boiling points of the alkanes change as the size of the molecule increases?
8) How does the size of a hydrocarbon affect how easy it is to ignite?
9) Are longer or shorter hydrocarbons associated with a low viscosity?
10) A hydrocarbon burns with a yellow, smoky flame and leaves behind a sooty residue.
Is the hydrocarbon likely to have a long or short chain?

Burning Fuels (p.189-190) ☐

11) Give the products of the complete combustion of a hydrocarbon.
12) Give two advantages and two disadvantages of using hydrogen as a fuel.
13) Name the three sides of the fire triangle.
14) Draw a diagram of the set-up you would use to measure the energy transferred when a fuel is burnt.

Alkanes and Alkenes (p.191-192) ☐

15) Give the general formula of alkanes.
16) List the first five alkanes.
17) What are isomers?
18) Draw all the isomers of C_5H_{12}.
19) Explain why alkenes are known as unsaturated molecules.
20) Name the alkene that contains three carbon atoms.
21) Draw and name the two isomers of butene.
22) What is used to test for alkenes?

Polymers (p.193-195) ☑

23) What is a monomer?
24) Draw the repeat unit of poly(vinyl chloride).
25) List three properties of poly(ethene).
26) Give a disadvantage associated with the disposal of polymers in landfills.

Speed, Velocity and Acceleration

This page will set you up for the rest of the topic. <u>Learn it</u>, don't forget it, and <u>do the questions</u> at the end.

Scalars are Just Numbers, but Vectors Have Direction Too

1) <u>Distance</u> and <u>displacement</u> are different things. They both measure how <u>far</u> something has travelled, but <u>displacement</u> also says which <u>direction</u> something has travelled in. For example, you could say a car has travelled a <u>distance</u> of <u>10 m</u>, but it has a <u>displacement</u> of <u>10 m north</u>.

2) To measure the <u>speed</u> of an object, you only need to measure <u>how fast</u> it's going — the <u>direction</u> is <u>not important</u>. E.g. <u>speed = 30 mph</u>.

3) <u>Velocity</u> is a <u>more useful</u> measure of <u>motion</u>, because it describes both the <u>speed and direction</u>. E.g. <u>velocity = 30 mph due north</u>.

4) Quantities like <u>speed</u> and <u>distance</u>, that are only <u>numbers</u>, are called <u>scalar</u> quantities. ⟶ <u>Scalar quantities</u>: speed, distance, mass, time, etc.

5) Quantities like <u>velocity</u> and <u>displacement</u>, that have a <u>direction as well</u>, are <u>vector</u> quantities. ⟶ <u>Vector quantities</u>: velocity, displacement, force, acceleration, etc.

> When we use <u>vectors</u>, we often talk about there being a <u>positive</u> and a <u>negative direction</u>. E.g. a <u>car</u> moving in one direction could have a <u>velocity</u> of <u>3 m/s</u>, but moving in the <u>opposite direction</u> it will have a velocity of <u>− 3 m/s</u>. In this example, the car has a <u>speed</u> of <u>3 m/s</u> in <u>both directions</u>. You can often <u>pick</u> a positive direction that makes the <u>calculations easier</u>.

Speed, Distance and Time — the Formula

You really ought to get <u>pretty slick</u> with this <u>equation</u>, it pops up a lot...

$$\text{speed (m/s)} = \text{distance (m)} \div \text{time (s)}$$

The equation for calculating displacement is: velocity (m/s) = displacement (m) ÷ time (s).

EXAMPLE: A cat skulks 20 m in 50 s. Find: a) its speed, b) how long it takes to skulk 32 m.

1) <u>Substitute</u> the numbers given into the equation above.

2) Now that the speed has been calculated, you can find the time, *t*, taken to travel a different distance at the <u>same speed</u>.

$s = \dfrac{d}{t} = 20 \div 50 = 0.4 \text{ m/s}$

$t = \dfrac{d}{s} = 32 \div 0.4 = 80 \text{ s}$

Acceleration is How Quickly You're Speeding Up

1) Acceleration is definitely <u>not</u> the same as <u>velocity</u> or <u>speed</u>.

2) Acceleration is the <u>change in velocity</u> in a certain amount of <u>time</u>.

3) You can find the <u>average acceleration</u> of an object using:

Acceleration (m/s²) ⟶ $a = \dfrac{\Delta v}{t}$ ⟵ Change in velocity (m/s)

⟵ Time (s)

EXAMPLE:

A cat accelerates at 2.5 m/s² from 2.0 m/s to 6.0 m/s. Find the time it takes to do this.

$t = \Delta v \div a$
$\quad = (6.0 - 2.0) \div 2.5 = 1.6 \text{ s}$

4) <u>Deceleration</u> is just <u>negative</u> acceleration (if something <u>slows down</u>, the change in velocity is <u>negative</u>).

Try not to speed through these pages...

Know the difference between vectors and scalars — scalars have a size, vectors have a size AND a direction.

Q1 A cyclist has a constant speed. Calculate their speed if they cycle 660 m in 2.0 minutes. [2 marks]

Q2 Calculate the acceleration of a car that reaches 10.0 m/s from rest after 3.5 seconds. [2 marks]

Distance-Time Graphs

A graph speaks a thousand words, so drawing one can be better than writing 'An object starts at rest, then moves at a steady speed of 10 m/s for 2 s until it reaches a distance of 20 m, then remains stationary for 5 s before increasing its velocity with a constant acceleration for 2.5 s.'

Distance-Time (d-t) Graphs Tell You How Far Something has Travelled

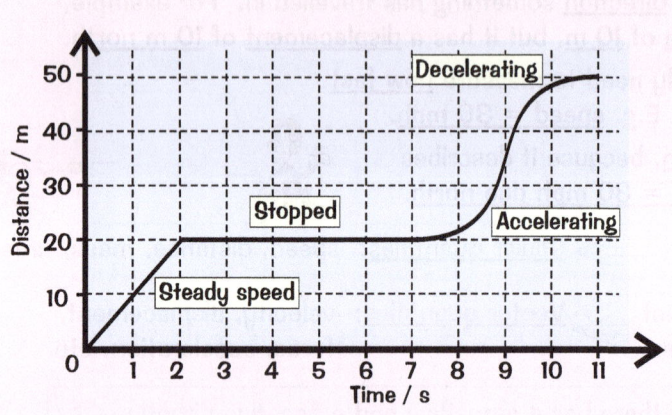

The different parts of a *d-t* graph describe the motion of an object:

- The gradient of the graph is the rate of change of distance — which is the speed.
- Flat sections are where it's stopped.
- A steeper graph means the rate of change of distance is bigger — the object's going faster.
- Curves represent acceleration.
- A steepening curve means it's speeding up (increasing gradient).
- A levelling off curve means it's slowing down (decreasing gradient).

The Speed of an Object can be Found From a Distance-Time Graph

1) The gradient of a distance-time graph at any point is equal to the speed of the object at that time.

2) If the graph is a straight line, the gradient at any point along the line is equal to $\dfrac{\text{change in the vertical}}{\text{change in the horizontal}}$.

> **Example:** In the graph above, the speed at any time between 0 s and 2 s is:
>
> $$\text{Speed} = \text{gradient} = \frac{\text{change in the vertical}}{\text{change in the horizontal}} = \frac{20}{2} = 10\ \text{m/s}$$

3) If the graph is curved, to find the speed at a certain time you need to draw a tangent to the curve at that point, and then find the gradient of the tangent.

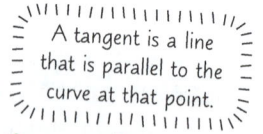

A tangent is a line that is parallel to the curve at that point.

4) You can also calculate the mean (average) speed of an object when it has non-uniform motion (i.e. it's accelerating) by dividing the total distance travelled by the time it takes to travel that distance.

> **Example:** The graph shows the distance-time graph for a bike accelerating for 30 seconds and then travelling at a steady speed for 5 s. The speed of the bike at 25 s can be found by drawing a tangent to the curve (red line) at 25 s and then finding the gradient of the tangent:
>
> $$\text{gradient} = \frac{\text{change in the vertical}}{\text{change in the horizontal}} = \frac{170}{20} = 8.5\ \text{m/s}$$
>
>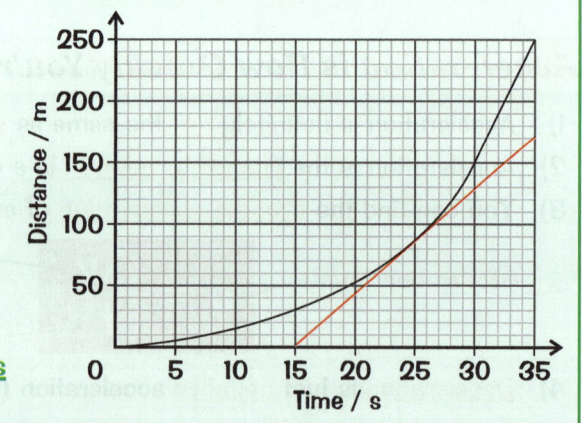
>
> The mean speed of the bike between 0 s and 30 s can also be calculated as:
>
> $$\text{mean speed} = \frac{\text{total distance travelled}}{\text{time taken to travel}} = \frac{150}{30} = 5\ \text{m/s}$$

Understanding motion graphs — it can be a real uphill struggle...

For practice, try sketching *d-t* graphs for different scenarios. Like cycling up a hill or running from a bear.

Q1   Sketch a distance-time graph for an object that initially accelerates, then travels at a constant speed, then decelerates to a stop.

[2 marks]

Velocity-Time Graphs

Huzzah, more graphs. And they're velocity-time graphs too, you lucky thing. Keep an eye out for those negative gradients — they're not too tricky really, it just means the object has a negative acceleration.

Velocity-Time (v-t) Graphs can Be Used to Find Acceleration

- Gradient = acceleration.
- Flat sections represent steady velocity.
- The steeper the graph, the greater the acceleration or deceleration.
- Uphill sections are acceleration.
- Downhill sections are deceleration.
- A curve means changing acceleration.
- The area under any section of the graph is equal to the distance travelled in that time interval.

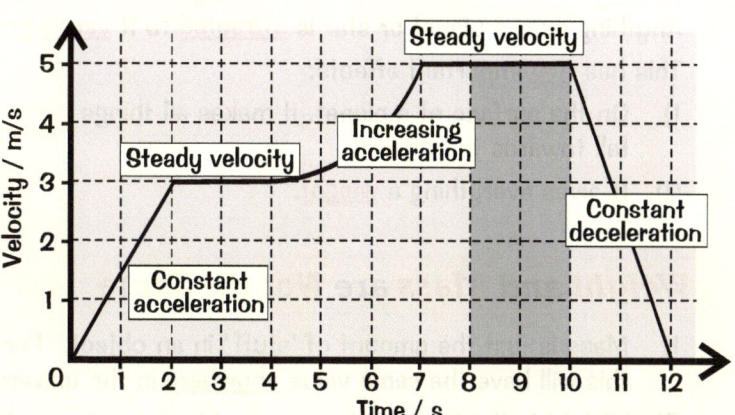

You can find the acceleration, velocity and distance travelled from a velocity-time graph:

1) The acceleration represented between 0 s and 2 s on the graph is:

$$\text{Acceleration} = \text{gradient} = \frac{\text{change in the vertical}}{\text{change in the horizontal}} = \frac{3}{2} = 1.5 \text{ m/s}^2$$

> To find the acceleration at any point on a curved velocity-time graph, you draw a tangent to the curve and then find the gradient of the tangent (see page 91).

2) The velocity at any time is simply found by reading the value off the velocity axis.

3) The distance travelled in any time interval is equal to the area under the graph. For example, the distance travelled between $t = 8$ s and $t = 10$ s is equal to the shaded area, which is 10 m (5 m/s × 2 s).

You can Use the Counting Squares Method To Find the Area Under the Graph

1) If an object has an increasing or decreasing acceleration (or deceleration), the graph is curved. You can estimate the distance travelled from the area under the graph by counting squares.

2) First you need to find out how much distance one square of the graph paper represents. To do this, multiply the width of one square (in seconds) by the height of one square (in metres per second).

3) Then you just multiply this by the number of squares under the graph. If there are squares that are partly under the graph, you can add them together to make whole squares (see below).

The graph below is a velocity-time graph. You can estimate the distance travelled in the first 10 s by counting the number of squares under the graph (shown by the shaded area).

Total number of shaded squares = 32

Distance represented by one square
= width of square × height of square
= 1 s × 0.2 m/s = 0.2 m

So total distance travelled in 10 s
= 32 × 0.2 = 6.4 m

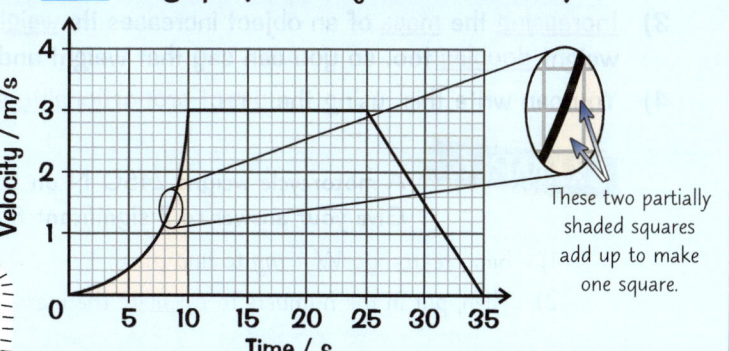

These two partially shaded squares add up to make one square.

> As you go through and count the squares, it helps to put a dot in the square once it's been counted. That way you don't lose track of what's been counted and what hasn't.

The gradient of my revision-time graph is zero...

Remember — the acceleration of an object on a velocity-time graph is the gradient of the curve at that time. And the total distance travelled within a time interval is the area under the graph for that time interval.

Q1   Sketch a velocity-time graph for a car that initially travels at a steady speed and then decelerates constantly to a stop. It is then stationary for a short time before accelerating with increasing acceleration. [3 marks]

Weight and Mass

Now for something a bit more <u>attractive</u> — the force of <u>gravity</u>. Enjoy...

Gravitational Force is the Force of Attraction Between Masses

<u>Gravity</u> attracts <u>all</u> masses, but you only notice it when one of the masses is <u>really really big</u>, e.g. a planet. Anything near a planet or star is <u>attracted</u> to it <u>very strongly</u>.

This has <u>two</u> important effects:

1) On the surface of a planet, it makes all things fall towards the <u>ground</u>.

2) It gives everything a <u>weight</u>.

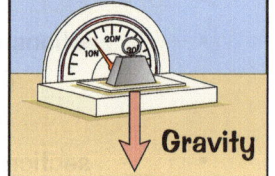

Gravity

Weight and Mass are Not the Same

1) <u>Mass</u> is just the <u>amount of 'stuff'</u> in an object. For any given object this will have the same value <u>anywhere</u> in the universe.

2) <u>Weight</u> is the <u>force</u> acting on an object due to <u>gravity</u> (the <u>pull</u> of the <u>gravitational force</u> on the object). Close to Earth, this <u>force</u> is caused by the <u>gravitational field</u> around the Earth.

3) Gravitational field <u>strength</u> varies with <u>location</u>. It's <u>stronger</u> the <u>closer</u> you are to the mass causing the field, and stronger for <u>larger</u> masses.

4) The <u>weight</u> of an object depends on the <u>strength</u> of the <u>gravitational field</u> at the <u>location</u> of the object. This means that the weight of an object <u>changes</u> with its location.

5) For example, an object has the <u>same</u> mass whether it's on <u>Earth</u> or on the <u>Moon</u> — but its <u>weight</u> will be <u>different</u>. A 1 kg mass will <u>weigh less</u> on the Moon (about 1.6 N) than it does on Earth (about 10 N), simply because the <u>gravitational field strength</u> on the surface of the Moon is <u>less</u>.

6) Weight is a <u>force</u>. It's measured in <u>newtons</u> (N) using a calibrated <u>spring</u> balance (or <u>newtonmeter</u>).

7) <u>Mass</u> is <u>not</u> a force. It's measured in <u>kilograms</u> (kg) with a <u>mass</u> balance.

Mass and Weight are Directly Proportional

1) You can calculate the <u>weight</u> (*W*) of an object if you know its <u>mass</u> (*m*) and the <u>strength</u> of the <u>gravitational field</u> that it is in (*g*):

> weight (N) = mass (kg) × gravitational field strength (N/kg)

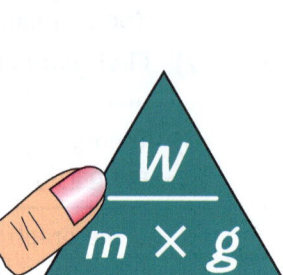

$$\frac{W}{m \times g}$$

2) For Earth, $g \approx 10$ N/kg and for the Moon it's around 1.6 N/kg.

3) <u>Increasing</u> the <u>mass</u> of an object increases its <u>weight</u>. If you <u>double</u> the <u>mass</u>, the weight <u>doubles</u> too, so you can say that weight and mass are <u>directly proportional</u>.

4) You can write this, using the <u>direct proportionality symbol</u>, as $W \propto m$.

EXAMPLE: A motorcycle weighs 2450 N on Earth. Calculate the mass of the motorcycle. Give your answer to 3 significant figures. (g = 10 N/kg)

1) First, <u>rearrange</u> $W = mg$ to find <u>mass</u>.   mass = weight ÷ gravitational field strength

2) Then, put in the numbers to <u>calculate</u> the mass.   mass = 2450 ÷ 10 = 245 kg

I don't think you understand the gravity of this situation...

Remember that weight is a force due to gravity, and that mass is not a force. Weight changes depending on the strength of the gravitational field the object is in, but the object's mass always stays the same.

Q1   Calculate the weight in newtons of a 5 kg mass:
     a) on Earth ($g \approx 10$ N/kg)   b) on the Moon ($g \approx 1.6$ N/kg)   [4 marks]

Resultant Forces

<u>Forces</u> are everywhere, so it only makes sense that you should <u>learn</u> about them. Read on...

Resultant Force is the Overall Force on a Point or Object

1) In most <u>real</u> situations there are at least <u>two forces</u> acting on an object along any direction.

2) The <u>overall</u> effect of the forces decides whether the object <u>accelerates</u>, <u>decelerates</u> or has a <u>steady speed</u>.

3) If a <u>number of forces</u> act at a single point, you can replace them with a <u>single force</u> called the <u>resultant force</u>. The resultant force has the <u>same effect on the motion</u> as the original forces acting altogether.

4) If the forces all act along the <u>same line</u> (they're all parallel and act in the same or the opposite direction), the <u>resultant force</u> is found by just <u>adding</u> or <u>subtracting</u> them.

The diagram on the right shows a <u>ball falling</u>. Weight and air resistance are acting along the <u>same line</u>, so the <u>resultant force</u> acting on the ball = weight − air resistance = 8 − 3 = <u>5 N</u> in the <u>downwards</u> direction.

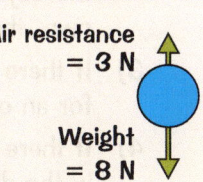
Air resistance = 3 N
Weight = 8 N

EXAMPLE: A skydiver jumps out of a plane. She has a weight of 500 N and, at a certain speed, air resistance acts on her with a force of 50 N. Air resistance acts in the opposite direction to weight. What is the resultant force acting on the skydiver at this speed?

1) The forces are acting in <u>opposite</u> directions so you need to <u>subtract</u> one from the other.

2) Remember to give a <u>direction</u> with your answer.

Resultant force = 500 − 50
= 450 N in the downwards direction.

A Resultant Force of Zero Means all the Forces are Balanced

1) An object with a <u>zero resultant force</u> will either be <u>stationary</u> or moving at a <u>steady speed</u>.

2) The diagram on the right shows an apple sat on a table. The <u>force</u> due to <u>gravity</u> (its <u>weight</u>, see p.200) is acting <u>downwards</u>.

3) The apple isn't moving because there's another force of the <u>same size</u> acting in the <u>opposite direction</u> to <u>balance</u> the weight.

4) This is the <u>normal contact force</u> from the table top pushing <u>up</u> on the apple.

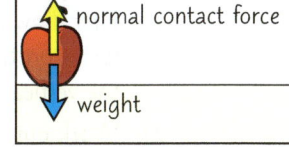
normal contact force
weight

A Non-Zero Resultant Force Means the Forces are Unbalanced

1) If there's a <u>non-zero resultant force</u> on an object, then it will either <u>accelerate</u> or <u>decelerate</u>. This is because the forces are <u>unbalanced</u>.

2) In the example of the <u>car</u> on the right, the <u>thrust</u> is <u>greater</u> than the <u>drag</u>, so the car is <u>accelerating</u>.

3) If the <u>drag</u> was greater than the <u>thrust</u>, the car would <u>decelerate</u>.

4) The <u>normal contact force</u> and the <u>weight</u> acting on the car <u>balance</u> each other (otherwise the car would go <u>flying off</u> or <u>sink through the road</u>).

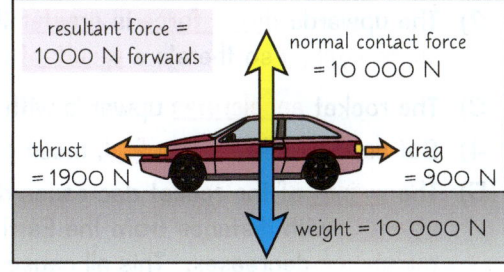
resultant force = 1000 N forwards
normal contact force = 10 000 N
thrust = 1900 N
drag = 900 N
weight = 10 000 N

I really had to force myself not to make a bad joke here...

Always sketch a diagram for resultant force questions. They mean you're less likely to forget any forces.

Q1   A car travelling forwards has a drag force of 500 N acting against it.
What forwards thrust is needed for the car to have a forwards resultant force of 1300 N?   [1 mark]

Newton's First and Second Laws

In the 1660s a guy called <u>Isaac Newton</u> worked out some seriously useful <u>Laws of Motion</u>. Here we go...

Newton's First Law — No Resultant Force Means No Change in Velocity

1) <u>Newton's First Law</u> says that:

> An object will remain <u>at rest</u> or in <u>uniform motion</u> in a straight line unless acted upon by an <u>external resultant force</u>.

Uniform motion in a straight line means there will be no change in velocity (speed or direction).

2) As you saw on p.201, if the <u>resultant force</u> on a <u>stationary</u> object is <u>zero</u>, the object <u>remains stationary</u> — things <u>don't just start moving</u> on their own, there has to be a <u>resultant force</u> to get them started.

3) If there is <u>no resultant force</u> on a <u>moving</u> object it'll just carry on moving at the <u>same velocity</u> — for an object to travel with a <u>uniform</u> (constant) velocity, there must be <u>zero resultant force</u>.

4) If there is a <u>non-zero resultant force</u> (see below), then the object will <u>accelerate</u> in the direction of the force. This <u>acceleration</u> can take <u>five</u> different forms: <u>starting</u>, <u>stopping</u>, <u>speeding up</u>, <u>slowing down</u> and <u>changing direction</u>.

Newton's Second Law — A Non-Zero Resultant Force Causes an Acceleration

<u>Newton's Second Law</u> says:

> resultant force (N) = mass (kg) × acceleration (m/s^2)   or $F = ma$

In other words, the <u>acceleration</u> of a body is <u>directly proportional</u> to the <u>resultant force</u> and <u>inversely proportional</u> to the <u>mass</u>.

If you're doing Higher Tier, you need to be able to state both Newton's First and Second Laws of Motion — you just need to understand these laws for Foundation Tier.

EXAMPLE:

A car of mass 1625 kg has an engine which provides a driving force of 5650 N. The drag force acting on the car is 450 N. Find its acceleration.

1) First draw a <u>diagram</u> to show the horizontal forces on the car (there's no need to show the vertical forces).

5650 N   **450 N**

2) Work out the resultant force.

Resultant force = 5650 − 450 = 5200 N

3) Rearrange $F = ma$ to calculate the acceleration.

$a = F \div m = 5200 \div 1625 = 3.2$ m/s^2

Newton's Second Law can be Used When Mass Isn't Constant

The mass of an object isn't always <u>constant</u>, but you can still apply <u>Newton's Second Law</u> to objects with a <u>changing mass</u>. An example is <u>rockets</u> — they burn lots of fuel to take off, which decreases their <u>mass</u>:

1) Rockets <u>accelerate</u> by burning fuel to create an <u>upwards thrust</u> (see p.204).

2) The upwards <u>thrust force</u> is <u>greater</u> than the <u>downwards forces</u> of <u>weight</u> and <u>air resistance</u> so there's a <u>resultant</u> upwards force on the rocket, F.

3) The rocket <u>accelerates</u> upwards with an acceleration, $a = \dfrac{F}{m}$.

4) But as the rocket <u>burns fuel</u>, mass <u>decreases</u>, so acceleration <u>increases</u>.

5) The <u>weight</u> of the rocket decreases due to decreasing <u>mass</u> and decreasing <u>gravitational field strength</u> with distance from the Earth. The atmosphere gets <u>thinner</u> with distance from the Earth so <u>air resistance</u> decreases. This all causes the <u>resultant upwards force</u>, and so the <u>acceleration</u>, to <u>increase</u>.

6) So for a <u>constant thrust force</u>, a rocket's acceleration <u>increases</u> as it takes off.

7) A rocket travelling through space has <u>no weight</u> or <u>air resistance</u>, but it still <u>loses mass</u> as it uses fuel to accelerate, leading its acceleration to increase for a <u>given thrust</u> force.

Newton's Law of Sunday — a body will remain at rest all day...

Remember, Newton's First Law means that an object at a steady speed doesn't need a resultant force to keep moving.

Q1   Calculate the resultant force acting on a 26 000 kg lorry with an acceleration of 1.5 m/s^2.   [2 marks]

Terminal Speed

Any falling object will eventually reach its <u>terminal speed</u> — this is all to do with resultant forces...

Friction and Drag Will Slow Things Down

1) When an object is <u>moving</u> (or trying to move), <u>friction</u> acts in the <u>opposite</u> direction to movement.

2) <u>Friction</u> makes things <u>slow down and stop</u>, so you need a <u>driving force</u> to keep moving (e.g. thrust).

3) <u>Friction</u> occurs between <u>two</u> surfaces in <u>contact</u> (e.g. tyres and the road).

4) <u>Drag</u> occurs when an object <u>passes</u> through a <u>fluid</u> (a gas or liquid). <u>Air resistance</u> is a type of drag.

5) The most important factor by far in <u>reducing drag</u> in fluids is keeping the shape of the object <u>streamlined</u>. This is where the object is designed to allow fluid to <u>flow easily</u> across it, reducing drag.

6) Parachutes work in the <u>opposite</u> way — they want as much drag as they can get (see below).

Moving Vehicles and Falling Objects Can Reach a Terminal Speed

When objects <u>first set off</u> they have <u>more driving force</u> than <u>friction force</u> (resistance), so they accelerate. But as the <u>speed</u> increases, the resistance <u>increases</u> as well. This gradually <u>reduces</u> the resultant force, and so the <u>acceleration</u> decreases until the <u>friction force</u> is <u>equal</u> to the <u>driving force</u> so the object doesn't accelerate any more. The forces are <u>balanced</u> (there's <u>no resultant force</u>). The object will have reached its maximum speed or <u>terminal speed</u>. An object's terminal speed depends on the <u>driving force</u> and the amount of <u>friction</u>.

1) A <u>skydiver initially accelerates</u> through air as <u>weight > air resistance</u>.

2) But air resistance <u>increases</u> as speed increases until <u>weight = air resistance</u>, and they reach <u>terminal speed</u>.

3) The <u>parachute opens</u> causing air resistance to increase. <u>Weight < air resistance</u>, so they <u>decelerate</u>.

4) As speed <u>decreases</u>, the air resistance also decreases until <u>weight = air resistance</u> — they reach a <u>new lower terminal speed</u>.

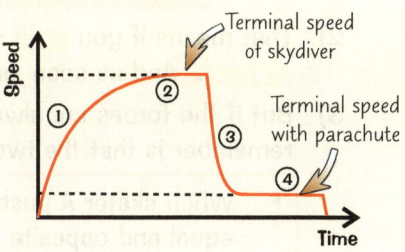

Terminal speed of skydiver

Terminal speed with parachute

You Can Investigate How Terminal Speed Depends on Mass

PRACTICAL

<u>Paper cupcake cases</u> are <u>light</u> and <u>not</u> very <u>streamlined</u>, so they reach a <u>low</u> <u>terminal speed</u> quite <u>quickly</u>. This makes them ideal for <u>investigating</u> terminal speed.

1) Set up a <u>pointer</u> (e.g. a pencil) in a clamp stand on a desk. Use a ruler to measure and record the <u>distance</u> between the <u>pointer</u> and the <u>ground</u> (make sure it's at least 150 cm).

2) Record the <u>mass</u> of a <u>single</u> cupcake case using a mass balance.

3) <u>Drop</u> the cake case from a good distance <u>above the pointer</u> level (e.g. 1 m). This allows the cupcake case to reach its <u>terminal speed</u> before reaching the pointer.

4) Use a <u>stopwatch</u> to record the time it takes to fall between the <u>pointer and the floor</u> — repeat this several times and calculate the <u>mean</u>.

5) Repeat the experiment with <u>different numbers</u> of cupcake cases <u>stacked together</u> to increase the mass, measuring the mass of <u>each stack</u> before you start.

6) You can calculate <u>terminal speed</u> with <u>speed = distance ÷ time</u> and plot a graph of <u>speed</u> against <u>mass</u>.

pointer

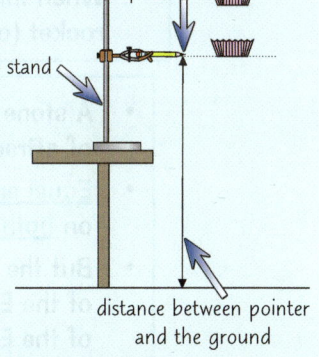
clamp stand

distance between pointer and the ground

Don't let frictional forces slow down your revision...

Make sure you can explain how an object reaches its terminal speed in terms of forces. Then go skydiving.

Q1 Explain why a ball falling from the top of a tall building reaches terminal speed. [3 marks]

Inertia and Newton's Third Law of Motion

Another law eh? Isaac probably wasn't thinking about anyone having to revise them back in the 17th century.

Inertia Explains Why it's Harder to Move a Hammer Than a Feather

1) Inertia is the measure of how difficult it is to change an object's velocity.

2) It is determined by the mass of the object — the larger the mass, the larger the inertia, and the harder it is to change the velocity of the object.

3) Imagine that a bowling ball and a golf ball roll towards you with the same velocity. It would require a larger resultant force to stop the bowling ball than the golf ball in the same time. This is because the bowling ball has a larger mass and a larger inertia.

4) By rearranging the equation for Newton's Second Law (see page 202) you can show that mass is defined as the ratio of the force over acceleration: $\Rightarrow$

$$mass = \frac{force}{acceleration}$$

So a larger mass requires a larger resultant force to accelerate by a certain amount — i.e. it has a larger inertia.

Newton's Third Law — Reaction Forces are Equal and Opposite

1) Newton's Third Law says that:

> If body A exerts a force on body B, then body B exerts an equal and opposite force on body A.

If you're doing Higher Tier, you need to be able to state Newton's Third Law.

2) That means if you push something, say a shopping trolley, the trolley will push back against you, just as hard. And as soon as you stop pushing, so does the trolley. Kinda clever really.

3) But if the forces are always equal, how does anything ever go anywhere? The important thing to remember is that the two forces are acting on different objects. Think about a pair of ice skaters:

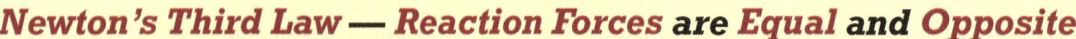

- When skater A pushes on skater B (the 'action' force), she feels an equal and opposite force from skater B's hand (the 'reaction' force).
- Both skaters feel the same sized force, in opposite directions, and so accelerate away from each other.
- Skater A will be accelerated more than skater B, though, because she has a smaller mass, so a smaller inertia — $a = F/m$ (from rearranging Newton's Second Law).

Skater A   Skater B

mass = 55 kg   mass = 65 kg

- When a rocket burns fuel it pushes hot gases out of the bottom of the rocket — the rocket exerts a backwards force on the gas.
- The hot gases exert an equal and opposite force on the rocket.
- When this forwards force (thrust) is bigger than the weight of the rocket (or any other backwards forces), it will accelerate upwards.

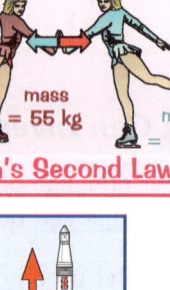

- A stone falls to Earth due to a gravitational force of attraction between the stone and the Earth.
- Equal and opposite forces of attraction act on both the Earth and the stone.
- But the Earth doesn't noticeably move towards the stone because the mass of the Earth is so much bigger than the mass of the stone. The acceleration of the Earth towards the stone is tiny (since $a = F \div m$ and m is large).

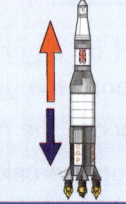

Newton's fourth law — revision must be done with cake...

Mmm... cake. A couple of tricky concepts here — inertia and Newton's Third Law. You can't say I don't spoil you.

Q1   Explain, using Newton's Third Law, how a rocket uses fuel to propel itself upwards.   [2 marks]

Work Done and Energy Conservation

This page is all about <u>work</u>. No, not the kind you're already doing by reading this book...

Work is Done **When a** *Force Moves an Object*

When a <u>FORCE</u> makes an object <u>MOVE</u>, <u>ENERGY IS TRANSFERRED</u> and <u>WORK IS DONE</u>.

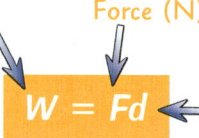
Joules (J) and newton metres (Nm) are equal — you can use either for work done.

1) Whenever something begins to <u>move</u>, or <u>changes</u> how it's moving (e.g. speeds up, slows down or changes direction), something is providing some sort of <u>effort</u> (force) to move it.

2) The <u>formula</u> to calculate the <u>amount of work done</u> (energy transferred) when an object is moved through a distance by a force is:

Work done (J or Nm)   Force (N)   Distance moved in the direction of the force (m)

$$W = Fd$$

3) Whether this energy is <u>transferred usefully</u> (e.g. by <u>lifting a load</u>) or <u>wasted</u> (e.g. dissipated by <u>heating</u> from <u>friction</u>), you still say that '<u>work is done</u>'. '<u>Work done</u>' and '<u>energy transferred</u>' are <u>the same</u>.

Energy is Always Conserved

1) The <u>conservation of energy principle</u> says that energy is <u>always</u> conserved.

A process can only happen if energy before = energy after.

Energy can be transferred usefully, stored or dissipated, but can NEVER be created or destroyed.

2) In situations where there are <u>no frictional forces</u> acting (i.e. no <u>friction</u>, no <u>air resistance</u> etc.), the <u>work done</u> on an object will be <u>equal</u> to the energy transferred usefully.

E.g. a ball being pushed along a smooth horizontal surface: If a force does work to <u>increase</u> the object's <u>velocity</u> (in the direction of the force), <u>energy is transferred</u> to <u>kinetic energy</u>. <u>Without friction</u>, the kinetic energy gained <u>equals</u> the <u>work done</u> by the force.

3) In most processes in the <u>real world</u>, some work must be done <u>against</u> frictional forces, causing some energy to be <u>dissipated</u>, usually through <u>heating</u>.

4) So the <u>useful</u> energy transferred <u>won't equal</u> the <u>work done</u> to cause the energy transfer.

E.g. an object being pushed along a rough horizontal surface: A force <u>does work</u> to <u>increase</u> an object's velocity, and <u>frictional forces</u> act on the object. The <u>kinetic energy</u> gained by the object will be <u>less than</u> the <u>work done</u> by the <u>force</u>. <u>Some</u> energy will be transferred to <u>thermal energy</u>. The <u>work done</u> by the force <u>equals</u> the <u>kinetic energy gained + thermal energy</u>.

5) You can use <u>work done</u> and the <u>kinetic energy gained</u> by an object (or potential energy, see next page) to work out the <u>work done</u> by frictional forces, and so the <u>mean</u> (average) <u>resistive force</u> acting:

EXAMPLE: A person applies a constant force of 10 N to move an object 5 m. The object gains 40 J of kinetic energy. Calculate the mean resistive force acting on the object.

1) Find the <u>work done</u> by the constant pushing force. $W = Fd = 10 \times 5 = 50$ J

2) The work done by <u>friction</u> is equal to the <u>total work done</u> minus the <u>kinetic energy</u> gained. $W = 50 - 40 = 10$ J

3) The <u>mean resistive force</u> is the force causing the work done by <u>friction</u>. $W = Fd$ so $F = \dfrac{W}{d} = \dfrac{10}{5} = 2$ N

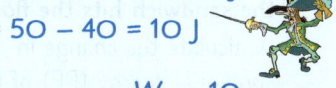

They said joule, Dave.

6) You can use the formula for <u>work done</u> (above) to do <u>energy calculations</u> (see next page).

7) If there is <u>no motion</u> in the <u>direction</u> of the <u>force</u>, no work is done by that force.

- If you push against a wall, the <u>distance moved</u> is <u>zero</u> so <u>no work</u> is done.
- If you carry a box as you walk at a <u>constant speed</u>, no work is done by the lifting force (as there's no up or down motion). The lifting force is at <u>right angles</u> to the motion.

Energy transfers can be a lot of work...

Work done is just energy transferred. Make sure you remember how work done is related to motion and forces.

Q1   A force of 20 N pushes an object 20 cm. Calculate the work done on the object.   [2 marks]

Kinetic and Gravitational Potential Energy

Energy comes in <u>different types</u>. Two important types are <u>kinetic</u> and <u>gravitational potential energy</u>.

An Object at a Height has Gravitational Potential Energy

1) When an object is at a <u>height</u> above the Earth's surface, it will have <u>gravitational potential energy (PE)</u>.

2) When an object is <u>raised</u>, it <u>gains</u> gravitational potential energy.

3) When it is <u>lowered</u>, or <u>falls</u>, the object <u>loses</u> gravitational potential energy.

4) You need to be able to <u>describe</u> the energy transfers in terms of <u>work done</u> when these things happen.

> When an object is <u>lifted above the ground</u>, work is done <u>by the lifting force</u> (against gravity) to move the object. The object gains <u>gravitational potential energy</u>. Assuming there's <u>no friction</u> or <u>air resistance</u>, when the object stops moving, the <u>work done</u> to lift the object will be <u>equal</u> to the <u>gravitational potential energy</u> gained by the object.

5) You can <u>calculate</u> the <u>amount</u> of <u>gravitational potential energy</u> the object has gained using the equation:

$$\text{change in gravitational potential energy} = \text{mass} \times \text{gravitational field strength} \times \text{change in height}$$
$$\text{(J)} \qquad \text{(kg)} \qquad \text{(N/kg)} \qquad \text{(m)}$$

or $PE = mgh$

Higher

A Moving Object has Kinetic Energy

1) When an object is <u>moving</u>, it has <u>kinetic energy (KE)</u>.

2) This <u>energy</u> depends on both the object's <u>mass</u> and <u>velocity</u>.

3) The <u>greater its mass</u> and the <u>faster it's going</u>, the <u>more</u> kinetic energy it has.

4) You need to know how to use the <u>formula</u>:

$$\text{kinetic energy} = 0.5 \times \text{mass} \times \text{(velocity)}^2$$
$$\text{(J)} \qquad\qquad \text{(kg)} \qquad \text{(m/s)}^2$$

or $KE = \tfrac{1}{2}mv^2$

5) You need to be able to use <u>this equation</u> and the one above to <u>calculate</u> energy transfers in a given process or event (e.g. a falling object).

6) Remember, <u>energy is always conserved</u>. So if you <u>assume</u> there are no frictional forces, <u>kinetic energy lost/gained = gravitational potential energy gained/lost</u>.

Higher

EXAMPLE: A seagull is carrying a sandwich. It is flying at a height of 4.0 m above the ground. It drops the sandwich. The sandwich has a mass of 0.2 kg. The gravitational field strength is 10 N/kg. Just before the sandwich hits the floor it has a speed of 8.0 m/s. Calculate the mean resistive force on the sandwich.

1) Calculate the change in <u>gravitational potential energy</u> (PE) of the sandwich.

2) Calculate the final <u>kinetic energy</u> (KE).

3) The <u>difference</u> between the kinetic energy and the gravitational potential energy equals the <u>work done by air resistance</u>.

4) The equation for <u>work done</u> can be used to work out the <u>mean resistive force</u>.

PE = 0.2 × 10 × 4.0
   = 8 J

KE = 0.5 × 0.2 × (8.0)²
   = 6.4 J

work done by air resistance = 8 − 6.4
   = 1.6 J

F = W ÷ d = 1.6 ÷ 4.0
   = 0.4 N

There's potential for a joke here somewhere...

Remember energy is always conserved. If all the PE hasn't been transferred to KE then there are frictional forces.

Q1   Calculate the PE gained by a 0.80 kg ball lifted 1.5 m above the Earth's surface. g = 10 N/kg.   [2 marks]

Q2   A 4.9 kg otter swims with a speed of 2.0 m/s. Calculate the otter's kinetic energy.   [2 marks]

Force and Extension

You can use forces to <u>stretch things</u> too. The fun never ends...

Stretching, Compressing or Bending Transfers Energy

1) When you apply a force to an object you may cause it to <u>stretch</u>, <u>compress</u> or <u>bend</u>.

2) An object has been <u>elastically deformed</u> if it can <u>go back</u> to its <u>original shape</u> and <u>length</u> after the force has been removed.

3) Objects that can be elastically deformed are called <u>elastic objects</u> (e.g. a spring).

4) An object has been <u>inelastically deformed</u> if it <u>doesn't</u> return to its <u>original shape</u> and <u>length</u> after the force has been removed.

5) <u>Work is done</u> when a force stretches or compresses an object and causes energy to be transferred to <u>elastic energy</u>. If it is <u>elastically deformed</u>, <u>ALL</u> this energy is transferred to <u>elastic energy</u> in the object.

Elastic objects —
useful for passing
exams and scaring
small children

Extension is Directly Proportional to Force...

If a spring is supported at the top and then a weight is attached to the bottom, it <u>stretches</u>.

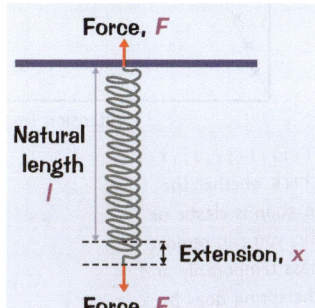

1) The <u>extension</u> of a stretched spring (or other elastic object) is <u>directly proportional</u> to the load or <u>force</u> applied — so $F \propto x$.

2) This is the equation:

Force (N) — $$F = kx$$ — Spring constant (N/m)

Extension (m)

3) The <u>spring constant</u> depends on the <u>material</u> that you are stretching — a <u>stiffer</u> spring has a <u>greater</u> spring constant and <u>extends less</u> for a given force.

4) The equation also works for <u>compression</u> (where x is just the <u>difference</u> between the <u>natural</u> and <u>compressed</u> lengths — the <u>compression</u>).

...but this Stops Working when the Force is Great Enough

There's a <u>limit</u> to the amount of force you can apply to an object for the extension to keep on increasing <u>proportionally</u>.

1) The graph shows <u>force against extension</u> for an elastic object.

2) There is a <u>maximum</u> force above which the graph <u>curves</u>, showing that extension is <u>no longer</u> proportional to force. This is known as the <u>limit of proportionality</u> and is shown on the graph at the point marked P.

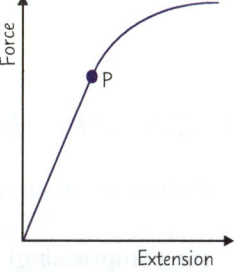

You can Combine k in Parallel or in Series

If a force is applied to <u>more than one</u> spring, you can <u>combine</u> the <u>spring constants</u> of the individual objects to find the <u>overall spring constant</u> of the system. You can then treat the system as <u>one spring</u> with spring constant <u>k</u>. How you combine the spring constants depends on how the springs are <u>arranged</u>:

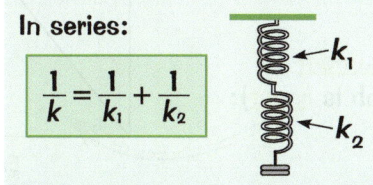

In series:

$$\frac{1}{k} = \frac{1}{k_1} + \frac{1}{k_2}$$

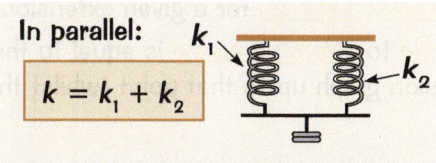

In parallel:

$$k = k_1 + k_2$$

I could make a joke, but I don't want to stretch myself...

That first equation is pretty simple, but that doesn't mean you can skip over it. Have a go at the question below.

Q1   A spring is fixed at one end and a force of 1 N is applied to the other end, causing it to stretch. The spring extends by 2 cm. Calculate the spring constant of the spring.   [2 marks]

Investigating Springs

You can do an easy experiment to see exactly how adding masses to a spring causes it to stretch.

You Can Investigate the Link Between Force and Extension

Set up the apparatus as shown in the diagram. Make sure you have plenty of extra masses, then measure the mass of each (with a mass balance) and calculate its weight (the force applied) using $W = mg$ (p.200).

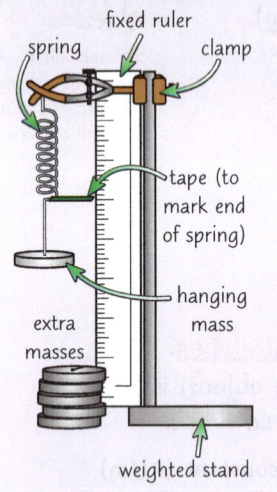

1) Measure the natural length of the spring (when no load is applied) with a millimetre ruler clamped to the stand. Make sure you take the reading at eye level and add a marker (e.g. a thin strip of tape) to the bottom of the spring to make the reading more accurate.

2) Add a mass to the spring and allow it to come to rest. Record the mass and measure the new length of the spring. The extension is the change in length.

3) Repeat this process until you have enough measurements (no fewer than 6).

4) Plot a force-extension graph of your results. It will only start to curve if you exceed the limit of proportionality, but don't worry if yours doesn't (as long as you've got the straight line bit).

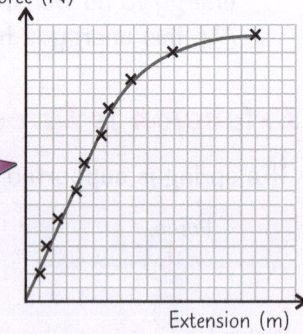

5) When the line of best fit is a straight line it means there is a linear relationship between force and extension (they're directly proportional, see previous page). $F = kx$, so the gradient of the straight line is equal to k, the spring constant.

6) When the line begins to bend, the relationship is now non-linear between force and extension — the spring stretches more for each unit increase in force.

> To check whether the deformation is elastic or inelastic, you can remove each mass temporarily and check the spring goes back to the previous extension.

You Can Find the Work Done for Linear Relationships

1) As long as a spring is not stretched past its limit of proportionality, the work done in stretching (or compressing) a spring can be found using:

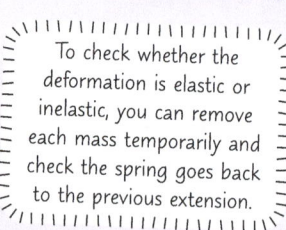

$$W = \frac{1}{2}Fx$$

Work done (J)   Force (N)   Extension (m)

2) For elastic deformation (see previous page) this formula can be used to calculate the spring's elastic energy. It's also the energy transferred to the spring as it's deformed (or transferred by the spring as it returns to its original shape).

3) Below the limit of proportionality, $F = kx$ so $W = \frac{1}{2}Fx = \frac{1}{2}kx^2$. This means that a stiffer spring (with a greater spring constant) stores more elastic energy for a given extension.

4) The work done to stretch a spring is equal to the area under a force-extension graph up to that point (whilst the graph is linear):

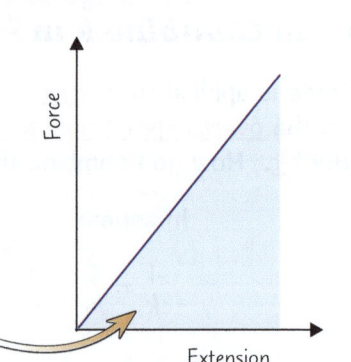

Time to spring into action and learn all this...

Remember that you can only use the gradient to find the spring constant if the graph is linear (a straight line).

Q1   A spring with a spring constant of 40 N/m extends elastically by 20 cm.
Calculate the work done in stretching the spring.   [3 marks]

Improving the Energy Efficiency of Vehicles

Cars are never going to be <u>100% efficient</u>, but there are still lots of ways you can reduce their energy losses.

Vehicles Need to be Energy Efficient

1) <u>Energy</u> in a vehicle can be <u>transferred usefully</u> (e.g. making it move and making all of the accessories work) or it can be <u>wasted</u> (e.g. due to drag).

2) The <u>efficiency</u> of a vehicle depends on the <u>proportion</u> of energy wasted.

3) The <u>lower</u> the <u>energy losses</u>, the <u>higher</u> the efficiency and the <u>less energy</u> is required in total to get the vehicle from place to place and make all of its accessories work.

4) Fuel is <u>expensive</u> and <u>burning</u> it is bad for the <u>environment</u>, so the <u>less</u> you can use to get to your destination, the better.

an ant   a fish-ant   an ant

Vehicle Design is Important for Reducing Energy Losses

Idling losses

Lots of <u>energy is wasted</u> keeping the engine running when the vehicle <u>isn't moving</u> (e.g. in traffic jams or at junctions), especially in urban areas. This results in <u>idling losses</u>. <u>Start-stop</u> technology reduces these energy losses by <u>automatically</u> stopping the vehicle's engine when the car is <u>stationary</u>, and starting it as soon as the <u>driver</u> releases the <u>brake</u> or presses the <u>clutch</u>.

Aerodynamic drag

<u>Drag</u> (p.203) leads to energy losses as the <u>frictional force</u> transfers energy to <u>thermal energy</u>. This effect <u>increases</u> with <u>speed</u>. Drag can be reduced by making a car <u>aerodynamic</u> (<u>streamlined</u>).

- A <u>sports car</u> is designed to allow fluids to flow over it <u>easily</u>, <u>reducing drag</u> and letting it move through air without <u>much effort</u>.

- <u>Normal cars</u> aren't designed to go <u>particularly fast</u> and so their design is <u>less streamlined</u>.

- This means that for a sports car and a normal car of the <u>same mass</u>, the normal car has to use a <u>greater driving force</u> to move at the <u>same speed</u> as a sports car.

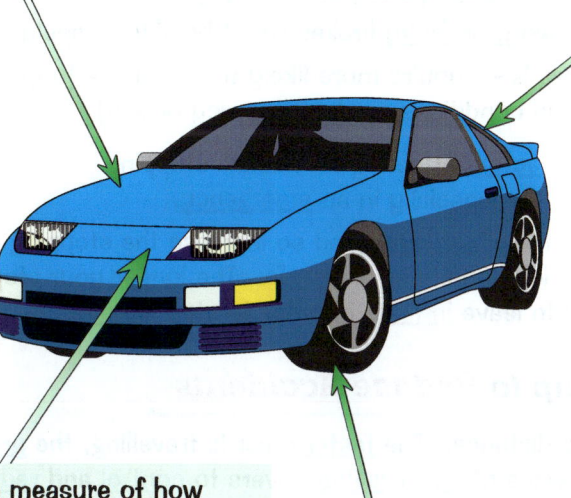

Inertial losses

<u>Inertia</u> (p.204) is a measure of how <u>difficult</u> it is to <u>change</u> an object's <u>velocity</u> — it increases with mass. Adding more mass to a vehicle means <u>more energy</u> is required to change its <u>velocity</u> by the <u>same amount</u>. So more mass leads to more inertial losses. <u>Lightweight materials</u> are used to build cars to <u>reduce</u> these energy losses.

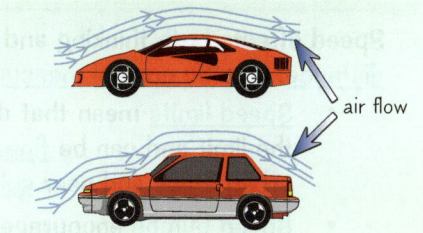

air flow

Rolling Resistance

This is the <u>force</u> that resists the motion of the <u>rolling tyres</u> — leading to energy losses. It can be reduced by having <u>properly inflated</u> tyres and using <u>materials</u> designed to reduce rolling resistance. Rolling resistance also increases with <u>mass</u>, so it can be reduced by using <u>lightweight materials</u>.

I hope this page didn't drag too much...

Now you can use your physics knowledge to explain why your first car needs to be a super streamlined sports car...

Q1   Give one way that the design of a car can reduce energy losses from rolling resistance.   [1 mark]

Stopping Distances

Knowing what affects stopping distances is useful for everyday life, as well as the exam.

Stopping Distance = Thinking Distance + Braking Distance

1) In an emergency (e.g. a hazard ahead in the road), a vehicle driver may perform an emergency stop.

2) This is where maximum force is applied by the brakes in order to stop the vehicle in the shortest possible distance. The longer it takes to perform an emergency stop, the higher the risk of crashing.

3) The distance it takes to stop a vehicle in an emergency (its stopping distance) is the sum of the thinking distance and the braking distance, i.e. stopping distance = thinking distance + braking distance.

The thinking distance is the distance the vehicle travels in the driver's reaction time (the time between noticing the hazard and applying the brakes). Distance = speed × time (p.197) so thinking distance is affected by two main factors:

- Your reaction time — the longer your reaction time, the longer the thinking distance. Reaction time is affected by tiredness, alcohol, drugs and distractions.
- Your speed — the faster you're going, the further you'll travel during your reaction time.

The braking distance is the distance taken to stop once the brakes have been applied. To stop completely, all of the vehicle's kinetic energy has to be transferred to heat by friction in the brakes (i.e KE = work done by the brakes). Since W = Fd (p.205), the distance this takes is equal to work done ÷ force = kinetic energy ÷ braking force. So braking distance is affected by:

- Your speed. Kinetic energy increases with speed (p.206) so the faster you're going, the further it takes to stop.
- The mass of the vehicle. Kinetic energy increases with mass, so a vehicle full of people and luggage won't stop as quickly as an empty one.
- The condition of the brakes — worn or faulty brakes won't be able to apply as big a braking force.
- How good the grip of your tyres is — you're more likely to skid if the tyres are bald (no tread left) or if the road conditions are bad (e.g. icy or wet).

4) You need to be able to describe the factors affecting a vehicle's stopping distance and how this affects safety — especially in an emergency.

5) E.g. icy conditions increase the chance of skidding (and so increase the stopping distance) so driving too close to other cars in icy conditions is unsafe. The longer your stopping distance, the more space you need to leave in front in order to stop safely.

Traffic Control Measures help to Reduce Accidents

Speed affects both thinking and braking distance. The faster a car is travelling, the greater the stopping distance. Traffic control measures are ways of encouraging drivers to control and reduce their speed.

- Speed limits mean that drivers are breaking the law if they drive faster than the limit and can be fined and/or punished. Low speed limits are used in urban areas and near schools, where there will be more pedestrians.

    30

- Speed bumps encourage drivers to slow down because they can damage the vehicle if it's going too fast. They're used in urban areas to help enforce the speed limit.

- Speed cameras catch drivers who are going too fast. They encourage drivers to stay within the speed limit.

- Public awareness campaigns inform drivers about the risks and consequences of driving too fast. They can be on TV or radio, in newspapers, or in the form of road signs.

Stop right there — and learn this page...

Make sure you understand the difference between thinking and braking distance, and the factors affecting them.

Q1   Give one factor that affects braking distance.   [1 mark]

Vehicle Safety Features

You need to know about <u>large stopping forces</u> and how they can be reduced to <u>prevent injuries</u>.

Stopping Over a *Short Distance* can be *Dangerous*

1) When a vehicle comes to a stop, <u>work is done</u> to transfer all of this <u>kinetic energy</u> to <u>other energy types</u>.

2) Since <u>$W = Fd$</u> (p.205), the force required to <u>stop</u> the vehicle <u>depends</u> on the <u>distance</u> over which it's stopping.

3) In the case of an <u>emergency stop</u> or <u>collision</u>, the distance over which the vehicle stops is <u>short</u>.

4) This means that the forces required to stop the vehicle are <u>large</u>.

5) These <u>large forces</u> in accidents are what causes <u>injuries</u>.

Safety Features *Reduce Forces* in Collisions

<u>Safety features</u> in cars are designed to <u>increase the distance</u> over which <u>work is done</u> to bring the vehicle and its passengers to a stop. If the distance is increased then the force on the passenger decreases (**$W = Fd$**), and so the <u>risk of injury is reduced</u>.

Seat Belts

- In vehicles (e.g. cars), the <u>seat belts</u> are designed to <u>stretch</u> slightly when a large force is applied to them.
- This slows passengers down over a <u>longer distance</u> during a crash.
- This means the <u>forces</u> on the passengers during the crash are <u>smaller</u>, so they're <u>less likely</u> to harm the passengers.

Air Bags

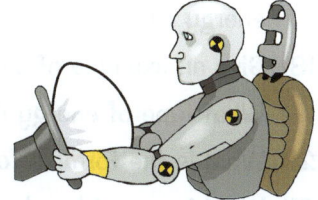

- <u>Air bags</u> in cars inflate rapidly if there's a collision, so the passengers hit the <u>compressible</u> air bag instead of the <u>solid</u> dashboard.
- This increases the <u>distance</u> that the <u>passenger</u> moves whilst <u>work is being done</u> to slow them down, which means the <u>forces</u> on the passenger <u>decrease</u>.

Crumple Zones

- <u>Crumple zones</u> are areas at the front and back of a car which <u>crumple up easily</u> in a collision.
- This increases the distance that the <u>whole car</u> moves whilst work is being done to slow down the car — this reduces the forces on the car <u>and</u> the passengers.

It's enough to put you off learning to drive, isn't it...

So there you go — why not amaze your friends with these fun safety facts next time you're popping a seat belt on? Make sure you can explain how each safety feature helps reduce the risk of passengers getting hurt.

Q1   a) Explain how crumple zones in cars reduce the risk of injury in the event of a collision.   [2 marks]

        b) Name one other car safety feature.   [1 mark]

Revision Questions for Unit 6a

So you've finished <u>Unit 6a</u> — Yay! Now here's a load of questions to see what you've actually learned.

- Try these questions and <u>tick off each one</u> when you <u>get it right</u>.
- When you've done <u>all the questions</u> for a topic and are <u>completely happy</u> with it, tick off the topic.

Distance, Speed, Velocity and Acceleration (p.197-199) ☐

1) What is the difference between a scalar and a vector quantity?
2) What is the equation for acceleration, and what are the units?
3) What does a curved line on a distance-time graph represent?
4) How do you find the speed from a distance-time graph?
5) What does a straight uphill line on a velocity-time graph show?
6) What does the area under a velocity-time graph represent?

Forces and Newton's Laws (p.200-204) ☐

7) What's the difference between weight and mass?
8) What's the equation for calculating the weight of an object from its mass?
9) True or False? Unbalanced forces give a resultant force of zero.
10) Does a non-zero resultant force cause an object to accelerate or stay at a steady speed?
11) State Newton's First law.
12) State Newton's Second law in the form of an equation.
13) Explain why a skydiver's terminal speed decreases when they open their parachute.
14) What is inertia?
15) State Newton's Third law.

Work and Energy (p.205-208) ☐

16) What is the equation for work done?
17) State how the work done to move an object along a horizontal surface is related to the kinetic energy transferred to it in the absence of frictional forces.
18) Give an example of a situation where no work is done by a force on a moving object.
19) What type of energy does a raised object have?
20) What is the formula for kinetic energy?
21) What is meant by elastic deformation?
22) What is the equation linking the applied force and extension of a spring?
23) Draw a typical force-extension graph for a spring being stretched past its limit of proportionality.
24) What is the equation for the work done in stretching a spring?

Vehicles and Safety (p.209-211) ☐

25) Give three methods of energy loss in vehicles, and explain how these energy losses can be reduced by efficient car design.
26) What is meant by thinking distance?
27) Give two factors that affect reaction time.
28) Explain why a vehicle stopping over a short distance is dangerous to passengers inside the vehicle.
29) Name two traffic control measures that encourage drivers to drive at or below the speed limit.
30) Give one safety feature used in a vehicle and describe how it works in terms of forces.

The Solar System

It's time for the really interesting topic — space. There's no better place to start than at our own doorstep...

The *Solar System* has One *Star* — *The Sun*

The Solar System is a planetary system — that's a star and all
the stuff that orbits it (or orbits something that orbits it). It includes:

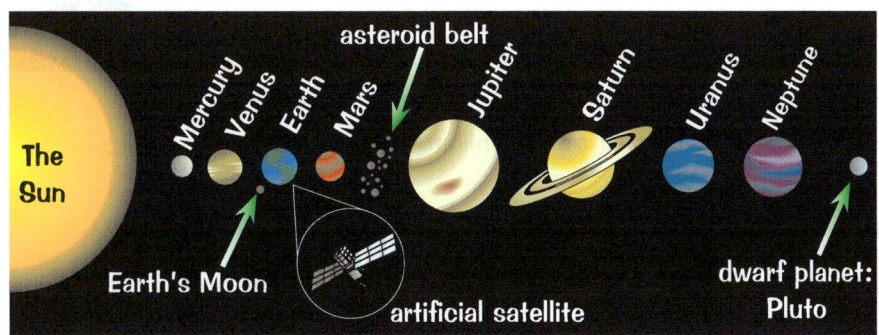

1) The Sun is our star. A star is a hot sphere of gas.

2) Planets are large objects that orbit a star. The eight planets
    in the Solar System are, in order (from the Sun outwards): Mercury,
    Venus, Earth, Mars, Jupiter, Saturn, Uranus and Neptune. The planets
    all orbit in the same plane, and they all have slightly elliptical orbits.

3) The time to complete one orbit increases with distance from the Sun.

4) The inner planets, Mercury, Venus, Earth and Mars, are all terrestrial (rocky) planets.

5) The outer planets, Jupiter, Saturn, Uranus and Neptune, are gaseous giants. They have
    a small rocky core but are mostly made of gases (such as hydrogen and helium).

6) Dwarf planets, like our pal Pluto, are planet-like objects that aren't big enough to be planets.

7) The asteroid belt is made up of asteroids and one dwarf planet, and is between
    Mars and Jupiter. Asteroids are lumps of rock and metal that orbit the Sun.

Moons and *Artificial Satellites* Orbit *Planets*

A satellite is anything that orbits a planet or dwarf planet — these can be natural or artificial (man-made):

1) Moons are natural satellites. Most planets (and some dwarf planets) have moons orbiting
    them. Some of the inner planets have a few moons, and outer planets have many.

2) TV satellites, the International Space Station and the Hubble Space Telescope all orbit the Earth
    and are examples of what we call artificial satellites (they've been put into orbit by humans).

Comets Orbit the Sun in Very *Elliptical Orbits*

1) Comets are balls of rock, dust and ice which orbit the Sun in very
    elongated ellipses, often in different planes from the planets.

2) Comets often have very large orbits that
    can pass far beyond the Solar System.

3) As a comet approaches the Sun, its ice melts, leaving a bright
    tail of gas and debris which can be millions of kilometres long.

Comet in an elliptical orbit (red line).

Happy, Sneezy, Dopey, Grumpy — my favourite dwarf planets...

You need to be able to remember the order of the planets. You could use a handy mnemonic to make it easier.
Here's one I made earlier — Mad Vampires Eat Mangoes And Jump Straight Up Noses (the And is for Asteroids).

Q1   Give one example of a gaseous giant planet.   [1 mark]

Q2   What is an artificial satellite?   [1 mark]

Sizes and Distances in Space

If you thought the Solar System sounded pretty big, you haven't seen anything yet...

The Universe is Made Up of Lots of Galaxies

1) The Universe is a large collection of billions of galaxies.

2) Galaxies are made up of billions of stars (including their planetary systems).

3) Our planetary system is the Solar System (see previous page) — it's one of many billions of planetary systems which form the Milky Way galaxy.

4) The Sun is about halfway along one of the spiral arms of the Milky Way.

5) The observable Universe is just the part of the Universe that we can detect from Earth.

Sizes in the Universe Are Enormous

You need to know the relative sizes of things in the Universe, and be able to put these things in size order:

1) Planets have a diameter of a few thousand to a few hundred thousand kilometres. The diameter of Earth is about 13 000 km.

2) Stars are much bigger than planets — they have diameters from a few hundred thousand km to several billion km.

Planetary systems and galaxies are so big that astronomers use different units of distance such as light years and AU, see below.

3) Planetary systems are bigger than stars as they include all of the objects in orbit around the star too. (The Solar System is thousands of times larger than the Sun.)

4) Galaxies contain billions of stars, so they're much bigger than planetary systems.

Distances in Space are Measured in Light Years

1) All electromagnetic waves (p.120) travel at the speed of light in a vacuum. This speed is about 3.0×10^8 m/s.

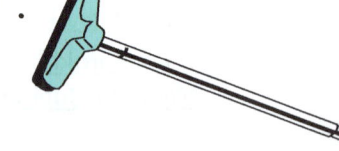

2) The distance that electromagnetic waves travel through a vacuum in one year is called a light year (l-y). So if a star is 5 light years away from Earth, is takes 5 years for light from the star to reach Earth.

3) To convert between light years and metres, first find out the distance in metres that light travels in 1 year using $s = d \div t$ (p.197) — s is the speed of light in m/s, and make sure the time (t) is in seconds.

4) Then multiply this distance by the number of light years.

> **EXAMPLE:** The Andromeda galaxy is the closest galaxy to the Milky Way.
> It is 2.5×10^6 light years away. Calculate this distance in metres.
>
> 1) Rearrange $s = d \div t$ to calculate the distance light travels in 1 year — the number of seconds in one year is 365 days × 24 hours × 60 minutes × 60 seconds.
>
> $d = s \times t = 3.0 \times 10^8 \times (365 \times 24 \times 60 \times 60)$
> $= 9.4608 \times 10^{15}$ m
>
> 2) Multiply this by the number of light years in the question.
>
> $9.4608 \times 10^{15} \times 2.5 \times 10^6 = 2.3652 \times 10^{22}$
> $= 2.4 \times 10^{22}$ m (to 2 s.f.)

5) As well as light years, shorter distances can be measured in light minutes and light seconds. A light minute is the distance that light travels in 1 minute and so on.

6) The astronomical unit (AU) is another unit of measurement used in space. 1 AU is the mean (average) distance from Earth to the Sun.

Phew — all those numbers have made me feel dizzy...

Don't worry, you don't need to remember exact sizes of things in the universe, just how they compare to each other.

Q1   Put the following in size order: a star, a galaxy, a planet, a planetary system.   [1 mark]

Q2   A star is located 4.5 l-ys from Earth. The speed of light is 3.0×10^8 m/s. There are approximately 3.15×10^7 s in a year. Calculate the distance to the star in m.   [2 marks]

The Life Cycle of Stars

The Sun's only _halfway_ through its life but it's already been through a lot...

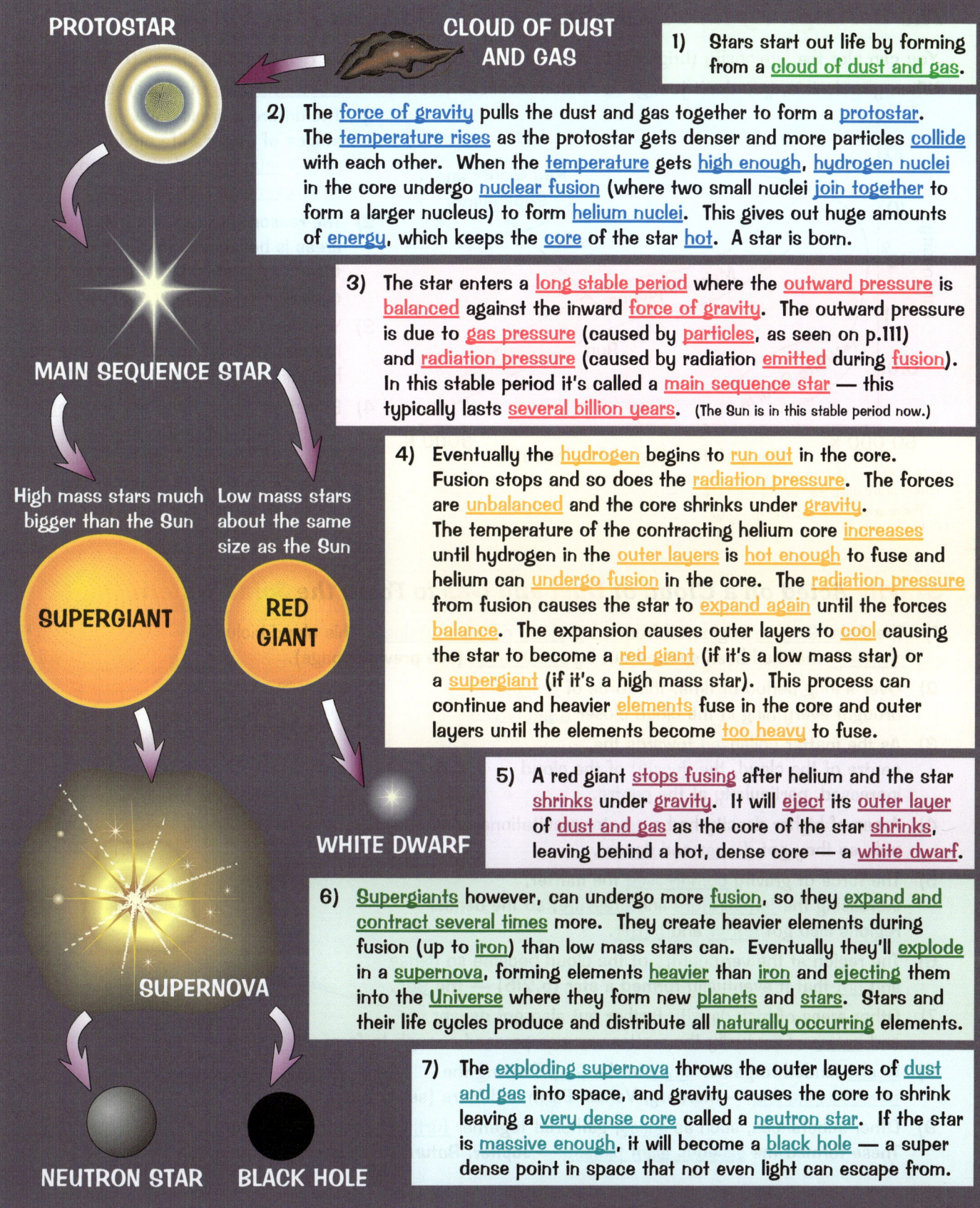

PROTOSTAR

CLOUD OF DUST AND GAS

1) Stars start out life by forming from a cloud of dust and gas.

2) The force of gravity pulls the dust and gas together to form a protostar. The temperature rises as the protostar gets denser and more particles collide with each other. When the temperature gets high enough, hydrogen nuclei in the core undergo nuclear fusion (where two small nuclei join together to form a larger nucleus) to form helium nuclei. This gives out huge amounts of energy, which keeps the core of the star hot. A star is born.

3) The star enters a long stable period where the outward pressure is balanced against the inward force of gravity. The outward pressure is due to gas pressure (caused by particles, as seen on p.111) and radiation pressure (caused by radiation emitted during fusion). In this stable period it's called a main sequence star — this typically lasts several billion years. (The Sun is in this stable period now.)

MAIN SEQUENCE STAR

High mass stars much bigger than the Sun

Low mass stars about the same size as the Sun

4) Eventually the hydrogen begins to run out in the core. Fusion stops and so does the radiation pressure. The forces are unbalanced and the core shrinks under gravity. The temperature of the contracting helium core increases until hydrogen in the outer layers is hot enough to fuse and helium can undergo fusion in the core. The radiation pressure from fusion causes the star to expand again until the forces balance. The expansion causes outer layers to cool causing the star to become a red giant (if it's a low mass star) or a supergiant (if it's a high mass star). This process can continue and heavier elements fuse in the core and outer layers until the elements become too heavy to fuse.

SUPERGIANT

RED GIANT

WHITE DWARF

5) A red giant stops fusing after helium and the star shrinks under gravity. It will eject its outer layer of dust and gas as the core of the star shrinks, leaving behind a hot, dense core — a white dwarf.

6) Supergiants however, can undergo more fusion, so they expand and contract several times more. They create heavier elements during fusion (up to iron) than low mass stars can. Eventually they'll explode in a supernova, forming elements heavier than iron and ejecting them into the Universe where they form new planets and stars. Stars and their life cycles produce and distribute all naturally occurring elements.

SUPERNOVA

7) The exploding supernova throws the outer layers of dust and gas into space, and gravity causes the core to shrink leaving a very dense core called a neutron star. If the star is massive enough, it will become a black hole — a super dense point in space that not even light can escape from.

NEUTRON STAR **BLACK HOLE**

White Dwarf — I thought that was a sitcom from the 90s...

Pretty explosive stuff on this page, but it's important, so don't shrink away from it — just got to learn it I'm afraid.

Q1   Describe how the Sun will move to the next stage of its life cycle.   [4 marks]

The H-R Diagram and the Solar System

Yep, there's <u>more</u> — but it's just one more page and then we're done with <u>space</u>. Woohoo...

The *Hertzsprung-Russell* Diagram Shows Different *Stages* in a *Star's Life*

You can plot the <u>luminosity</u> (brightness) and <u>temperature</u> of a star on a <u>Hertzsprung-Russell</u> (H-R) diagram. When you do this, you don't just get a random collection of stars — <u>different types</u> of star group <u>together</u>.

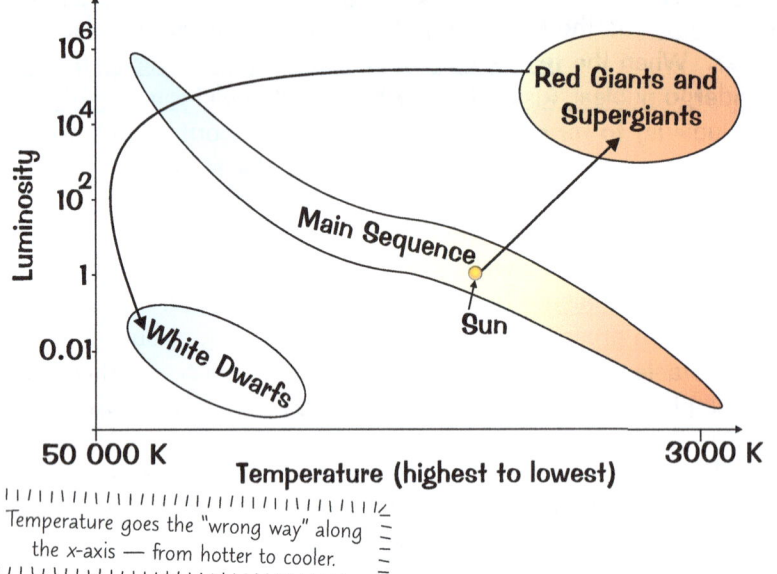

Temperature goes the "wrong way" along the x-axis — from hotter to cooler.

1) The different areas show the main stages of a star's life cycle: the <u>main sequence</u>, <u>red giants</u> and <u>supergiants</u> and <u>white dwarfs</u>.

2) The reason you can see these areas is because stars exist in these <u>stable</u> stages of their life cycle for <u>long periods of time</u>.

3) You don't see <u>unstable</u> phases, like supernovae, on the diagram because they happen too <u>quickly</u>.

4) Based on <u>where</u> the stars are <u>plotted</u> on the diagram, you can <u>predict</u> the <u>star's type</u> and where it's likely to move on the H-R diagram (like we've done with the Sun here).

Gravity Acted on a Cloud of *Dust and Gas* to Form the *Solar System*

1) The <u>Solar System</u> originated from a big <u>cloud of gas and dust</u>. This cloud included <u>elements</u> that had been spewed out by <u>supernovae</u> (see previous page).

2) Over a long period of time, the force of <u>gravity</u> brought everything in the cloud closer <u>together</u>.

3) As the matter <u>collapsed</u> towards the centre of the cloud, the <u>density</u> of the cloud increased, particularly at the <u>centre</u>.

4) Areas of higher density had a <u>greater</u> gravitational pull, so they got <u>denser</u> and <u>denser</u>.

5) The force of gravity <u>compressed</u> the matter, increasing the <u>temperature</u> and <u>pressure</u>, so the denser regions also got <u>hotter</u> and <u>hotter</u>.

6) The region at the very <u>centre</u> of the cloud became so <u>dense</u> and <u>hot</u> that it eventually formed a star (p.215) — the <u>Sun</u>.

7) Other areas of <u>high density</u> further out also got <u>denser</u> and <u>hotter</u>. Eventually the matter was compressed enough to form <u>planets</u>.

8) <u>Rocks</u> tended to gather <u>close</u> to the <u>Sun</u>, forming the <u>terrestrial planets</u> — Mercury, Venus, Earth and Mars (see p.213).

9) Other substances, such as <u>gases</u>, gathered together <u>further away</u> from the Sun. These formed the <u>gaseous giant planets</u> — Jupiter, Saturn, Uranus and Neptune.

If only I could use the H-R diagram to predict my future...

What a page. Remember, you can predict the path a star will take along the Hertzprung-Russell diagram.

Q1 A star with a very low temperature and a very high luminosity is likely to be which type of star? [1 mark]

Q2 Describe the role of gravity in the formation of the Sun and planets in the Solar System. [3 marks]

Isotopes and Radioactive Decay

Understanding what isotopes are is important for learning about radioactive decay. So let's get cracking.

Isotopes are Different Forms of the Same Element

1) Atoms consist of a nucleus (made up of protons and neutrons), surrounded by electrons.

2) The proton (atomic) number (Z) is the number of protons in an atom. The number of protons defines what the element is (e.g. a carbon atom always has 6 protons).

3) Since protons are positively charged and neutrons are neutral, the nucleus of each element has a particular overall positive charge.

4) The nucleon number (A) is the number of protons plus the number of neutrons in an atom — it tells you the mass of the nucleus.

5) You can represent atoms using this notation:

6) Isotopes are atoms of the same element — they have the same number of protons but a different number of neutrons.

Nucleon number — **A**
Proton number — **Z** $\mathbf{X}$ — Chemical symbol

So isotopes have the same proton number, but different nucleon numbers.

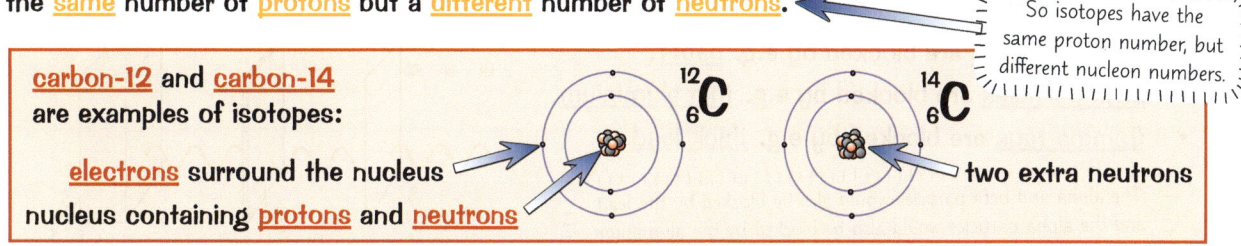

carbon-12 and carbon-14 are examples of isotopes:

$^{12}_{6}C$ $^{14}_{6}C$

electrons surround the nucleus

nucleus containing protons and neutrons

two extra neutrons

7) Most elements have different isotopes, but there are usually only one or two stable ones.

8) The other isotopes tend to be unstable and radioactive, which means they give out nuclear radiation and may decay into other elements.

There are Different Ways that Nuclei can Decay

A nucleus decays because it's unstable. This happens when there is an imbalance between the numbers of protons and neutrons in the nucleus. When a nucleus decays, it can release alpha, beta or gamma radiation.

- An alpha particle (α) is two neutrons and two protons — the same as a helium nucleus. So an alpha particle has a relative mass (p.63) of 4 and a charge of +2.
- Alpha particles are relatively big and heavy and slow moving.

- A beta particle (β) is simply a high energy electron, with virtually no mass and a charge of –1.
- Beta particles move quite fast and are quite small.
- For every beta particle emitted, a neutron turns to a proton in the nucleus.

- After spitting out an alpha or beta particle, the nucleus might need to get rid of some extra energy. It does this by emitting a gamma ray — a type of electromagnetic wave.
- Gamma rays (γ) have no mass and no charge. They are just energy, so they don't change the element of the nucleus that emits them.

You'd beta get stuck into these practice questions...

I'd learn those alpha, beta and gamma decays if I were you. Be extra careful when you talk about alpha decay — make sure you remember to say it's a helium NUCLEUS (not a helium atom, ion, hippopotamus, etc.).

Q1   Iodine is an element used in nuclear medicine in the treatment of thyroid problems.
A common isotope is $^{131}_{53}I$. Why are the nuclei of atoms of this isotope of iodine unstable?   [1 mark]

Radiation Properties and Decay Equations

Time to learn a bit more about some of the <u>types of radiation</u> before putting them in equations. How thrilling.

Different *Types* of Radiation Have Different *Penetrating Powers*

1) When <u>radiation</u> travels through a <u>material</u>, it <u>collides</u> with the material's <u>atoms</u>, which <u>slows it down</u> or <u>stops it</u>. This means the <u>radiation</u> can only <u>penetrate</u> so far into a material before it's <u>absorbed</u>. The <u>range</u> of radiation depends on its <u>type</u> and the <u>material</u> it's travelling through.

> <u>Alpha particles don't get very far</u> before they start hitting atoms — they are the <u>least</u> penetrating.
> <u>Beta particles</u> can travel <u>quite far</u> before hitting an atom.
> <u>Gamma radiation</u> travels a <u>long way</u> before hitting an atom — so it is the <u>most</u> penetrating.

2) <u>Count rate</u> is the <u>number of radioactive particles</u> that reach a <u>detector</u> in a <u>given time</u>. The <u>further</u> the radiation has to travel, the <u>higher</u> the <u>chance</u> it will be <u>absorbed</u> by the material it is travelling through. This means the <u>count rate decreases</u> the <u>further</u> the <u>detector</u> is from a <u>radioactive source</u>.

3) The <u>type</u> and <u>thickness</u> of <u>material</u> needed to stop radiation depends on the radiation's <u>penetrating power</u>.

- <u>Alpha particles</u> are blocked by e.g. <u>paper</u>.
- <u>Beta particles</u> are blocked by e.g. <u>thin aluminium</u>.
- <u>Gamma rays</u> are blocked by e.g. <u>thick lead</u>.

> The alpha and beta particles would also be blocked by the lead, and the alpha particles would also be blocked by the aluminium.

Sheet of paper   Thin aluminium   Thick lead

You Need to be Able to Balance Nuclear Equations

You can write nuclear decays as <u>nuclear equations</u>. You need to be able to <u>balance</u> these equations for <u>alpha</u>, <u>beta</u> and <u>gamma</u> decays by balancing the <u>nucleon number</u> and the <u>proton number</u> on each side.

> If you're doing Foundation Tier, you'll be given a partially complete nuclear equation — you just need to balance the nucleon and proton numbers. If you're doing Higher Tier you might need to write nuclear equations from scratch.

Alpha Radiation

When a nucleus emits an <u>alpha particle</u>:

- The <u>nucleon number decreases by 4</u> — as it <u>loses</u> two protons and two neutrons.
- The <u>proton number decreases by 2</u> — because it has <u>two less</u> protons.

> You can also write an alpha particle as $^{4}_{2}He^{2+}$

$$^{226}_{88}Ra \rightarrow\ ^{222}_{86}Rn +\ ^{4}_{2}\alpha$$

nucleon number:	226	→	222	+ 4 (= 226)
proton number:	88	→	86	+ 2 (= 88)

> In both alpha and beta emissions, a new element will be formed, as the number of protons changes.

Beta Radiation

When a nucleus emits a <u>beta particle</u>, a neutron changes into a proton, so:

- The <u>nucleon number doesn't change</u> — as it has <u>lost</u> a neutron but <u>gained</u> a proton.
- The <u>proton number increases by 1</u> — because it has <u>one more</u> proton.

$$^{14}_{6}C \rightarrow\ ^{14}_{7}N +\ ^{0}_{-1}\beta$$

nucleon number:	14	→	14	+ 0 (= 14)
proton number:	6	→	7	+ (−1) (= 6)

> You can also write the beta particle as $^{0}_{-1}e^{-}$ in equations.

Gamma Radiation

When a nucleus emits a <u>gamma ray</u>:

- The <u>nucleon number</u> and the <u>proton number don't change</u>.
- You might see gamma rays written as γ in <u>balanced equations</u>.

$$^{234}_{91}Pa \rightarrow\ ^{234}_{91}Pa + \gamma$$

My mass number has definitely increased — all these biscuits...

Balancing equations can seem tricky — work through them methodically and you're less likely to make a mistake.

Q1   A uranium (U) atom with 92 protons and 146 neutrons decays into a thorium (Th) atom by emitting an alpha particle. Write a balanced equation to show this decay.   [3 marks]

Half-Life

There's a lot going on in this page. Take this one <u>slowly</u> as it's really important — especially the <u>key equation</u>.

Radioactivity is a Totally Random Process

1) The <u>radiation</u> given out by a sample can be measured with a <u>Geiger-Müller tube and counter</u>. This records the count rate — the number of radiation counts reaching it per second.

2) Radioactive decay is entirely <u>random</u> — you <u>can't predict</u> which nucleus in a sample will decay next.

3) But you <u>can</u> find out the <u>time</u> it takes for the <u>radiation</u> emitted by a source to <u>halve</u> — the <u>half-life</u>.

4) Half-life can be used to find the <u>rate</u> at which a source decays — its <u>ACTIVITY</u>. Activity is measured in <u>becquerels</u>, <u>Bq</u> (1 Bq is <u>1 decay per second</u>).

5) Because it's a <u>totally random process</u>, there are always going to be <u>small variations</u> in count rate.

6) This has knock on effects when doing <u>experiments</u> with radioactive sources. For example, if you're doing an experiment to measure the <u>half-life</u> of a <u>source</u> (see next page), you'll need to measure count rate over a period of time <u>long enough</u> to find <u>several half-lives</u>, and then calculate the <u>mean</u> half-life.

The Activity of a Source Decreases Over Time

1) Each time a radioactive nucleus <u>decays</u> to become a <u>stable nucleus</u> the activity <u>as a whole</u> will <u>decrease</u>. (<u>Older</u> sources emit <u>less</u> radiation.)

2) For <u>some</u> isotopes it takes <u>just a few hours</u> before nearly all the unstable nuclei have <u>decayed</u>, whilst others last for <u>millions of years</u>.

3) The problem with trying to <u>measure</u> this is that <u>the activity never reaches zero</u>, which is why we use <u>half-life</u> to measure how quickly the activity <u>drops off</u>.

4) The <u>half-life</u> is the time taken for the <u>number of radioactive nuclei</u> in an isotope to <u>halve</u>. Half-life can also be the <u>time</u> taken for the <u>activity</u> (and so <u>count rate</u>) to fall to <u>half</u> of its <u>initial value</u>.

5) The activity after <u>one half-life</u> is just the <u>initial activity</u> divided by <u>2</u>. For <u>many</u> half-lives, use this <u>equation</u>:

$$\text{Activity} = \text{initial activity} \div 2^n$$

n is the number of half lives

EXAMPLE:

The initial activity of a radioactive source is 3456 Bq. Calculate the activity after 6 half-lives.

There's been 6 half-lives, so replace 'n' with 6 in the equation. $3456 \div 2^6 = 54$ Bq

Radioactivity can be Really Useful

Radioactive substances are extremely <u>useful</u>. You can use them for all sorts — to diagnose <u>medical problems</u>, <u>sterilise food</u>, and in <u>smoke alarms</u>. You can even use them to <u>date</u> old stuff:

1) The radioactive isotope <u>carbon-14</u> is used in <u>carbon dating</u>.

2) Living plants take in <u>carbon dioxide</u> as part of <u>photosynthesis</u>, including the radioactive isotope carbon-14.

3) When they die, the <u>activity of carbon-14</u> in the plant starts to <u>fall</u>, with a half-life of around 5730 years.

4) Archaeological finds made from <u>once-living material</u> (like wood) can be dated by finding the <u>current amount</u> of carbon-14 in them.

EXAMPLE: A fossil was found to contain 25% of the amount of carbon-14 that a living sample contains. The half-life of carbon-14 is 5730 years. How old is this fossil?

1) Find how many half-lives it takes for the amount of carbon-14 to fall to 25%.

2) Calculate how long this many half-lives takes.

After one half-life, the activity is 100% ÷ 2 = 50%
After two half-lives, the activity will be 50% ÷ 2 = 25%
This fossil has been around for 2 whole half-lives.
The age of the fossil is 2 × 5730 = 10 740 years.

Carbon dating — for all the single atoms out there...

Always double check what a half-life question is asking for — it may want a fraction, ratio or a percentage.

Q1 The activity of a sample is 1000 Bq. Its half-life is 8 days. Calculate the activity after 24 days. [3 marks]

More on Half-Life

All radioactive samples have the same-shaped <u>decay curve</u> — you can plot your own decay curve using a <u>model</u>.

You can *Calculate Half-Lives* Using a *Decay Curve*

1) Any radioactive material has a <u>characteristic</u> half-life — it's the same for <u>any sample</u> of that material.

2) You may be asked to calculate the <u>half-life</u> of a source — this is easy if you have its decay curve.

3) To draw a <u>decay curve</u>, plot <u>time</u> on the x-axis and <u>activity</u> on the y-axis — join the points with a <u>smooth</u> curve of <u>best fit</u>. The shape should always look like the graph below.

4) The <u>time taken</u> for the <u>activity</u> of the source to <u>halve</u> is the <u>half-life</u>.

EXAMPLE: The graph shows the activity of a radioactive source over time. Find the half-life of the source.

1) The <u>initial activity</u> when time = 0 s is 800 Bq.

2) Use the graph to find the time when the activity has halved to <u>400 Bq</u>. This is at t = <u>2 s</u>.

3) So, the half-life is <u>2 s</u>.

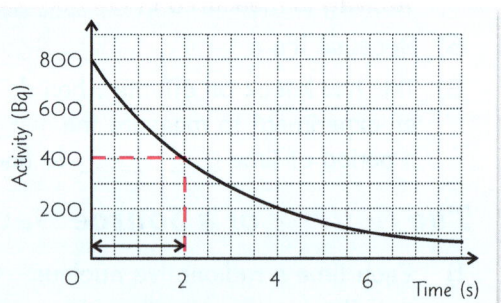

You can *Simulate* Radioactive Decay using *Dice* **PRACTICAL**

Radioactive decay is a <u>random process</u> where there is a <u>constant probability</u> that an <u>unstable nucleus</u> will <u>decay</u>. There are various ways to <u>model</u> this with events that also have a <u>constant probability</u>, e.g. rolling a certain number on a dice or flipping a coin. You can also use a computer program to <u>simulate</u> radioactive decay. Here's a quick <u>experiment</u> to model radioactive decay using dice:

1) You will need a <u>big sample</u> of dice for a good simulation — <u>at least 50</u>.

2) First record the <u>total number</u> of dice. Roll them all and count how many land on 6 — these dice represent the <u>nuclei</u> that have <u>decayed</u>.

3) Remove the '<u>decayed dice</u>' and record the total number of dice <u>remaining</u>. Roll the remaining dice again.

4) Repeat this process until all of the dice have '<u>decayed</u>'. Each roll counts as <u>1 unit of time</u> passing in the sample's <u>life span</u>.

5) <u>Plot a graph</u> of the number of remaining dice each time (i.e. the number of unstable nuclei left in the sample) against the number of rolls (i.e. time). You'll get a graph like this.

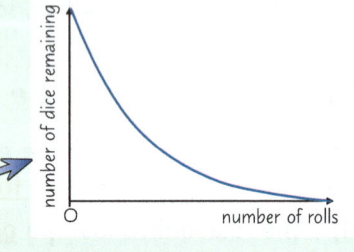

6) You can use the <u>decay curve</u> to calculate the <u>half-life</u> of the model radioactive source in the same way as you did above.

7) This can be repeated by <u>several groups</u> in a class — using <u>more sets of data</u> will make the result for the half-life more <u>reliable</u> and reduce any <u>anomalies</u> and <u>fluctuations</u>.

The half-life of a box of chocolates is about five minutes...

All decay curves look very similar. If yours looks different, then something has probably gone wrong.

Q1 The graph on the right shows a decay curve for a sample of radioactive material.
  a) Use the graph to calculate the half-life of the sample. [2 marks]
  b) Sketch a graph showing what the decay curve would have looked like if the sample had double the half-life. [1 mark]

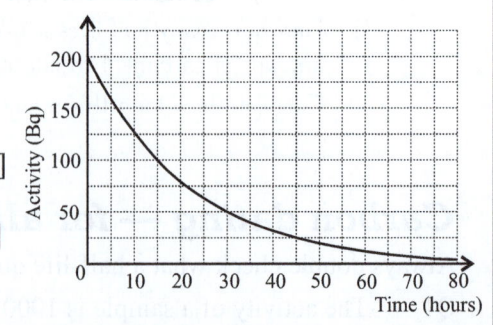

The Dangers of Nuclear Radiation

Time to find out about the hazards of ionising radiation — it damages living cells when it ionises atoms in them.

Ionising Radiation Harms Living Cells

1) Some materials absorb ionising radiation — it can enter living cells and interact with molecules.
2) These interactions cause ionisation (they produce charged particles called ions).
3) Lower doses of ionising radiation damage living cells by causing mutations in the DNA. This can cause the cell to divide uncontrollably — which is cancer.
4) Higher doses tend to kill cells completely, which causes radiation sickness if a lot of cells all get blasted at once.

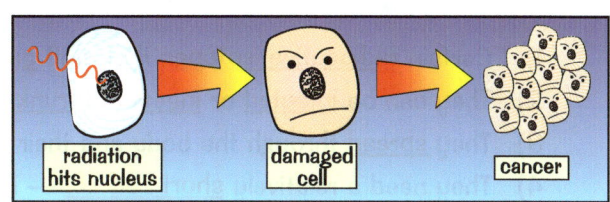

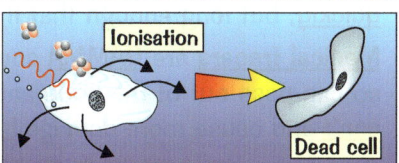

Which Radiation is the Most Dangerous Depends on Where it is

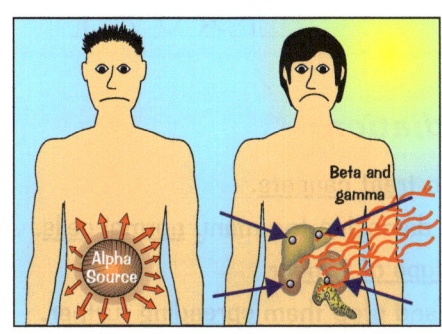

1) OUTSIDE the body, beta and gamma sources are the most dangerous.
2) This is because beta and gamma can still get inside to the delicate organs — they can pass through skin.
3) Alpha is much less dangerous because it can't penetrate the skin.
4) INSIDE the body, an alpha source is the most dangerous because it's the most ionising and it does all of its damage in a very localised area.
5) Beta and gamma sources on the other hand are less dangerous inside the body because they are less ionising, and gamma will mostly pass straight out without doing much damage.

Radioactive Processes have Waste Products

1) Most radioactive waste from nuclear power stations and hospitals is 'low-level' (only slightly radioactive) — things like clothing, syringes, etc. This kind of waste is disposed of in special containers, which are buried in secure landfill sites.
2) High-level waste is the really dangerous stuff — it has a really long half-life (p.219), so it stays highly radioactive for tens of thousands of years, and so has to be treated very carefully.
3) After being cooled in special pools for several years, it's often sealed into glass blocks, which are then sealed in metal canisters. These could then be buried deep underground.
4) However, it's difficult to find suitable places to bury high-level waste.
5) The site has to be geologically stable (e.g. not suffer from earthquakes), since big movements in the rock could disturb the canisters and allow radioactive material to leak out. If this material gets into the groundwater, it could contaminate the soil, plants, rivers, etc., and get into our drinking water.
6) Due to the risks, people usually object to plans to store radioactive waste near their homes.
7) There are other possible methods of disposal, which all have their problems. E.g. radioactive waste can be injected into porous rock deep underground, and in the past several countries have dropped waste onto deep sea beds (this is now banned by international treaties). Disposal in outer space has also been considered, but has been abandoned due to the high risks and cost.

I know some people that are hard to handle. Are they radioactive?

It all comes back to half-life — I told you it was important. When asked about the dangers of a certain type of radiation, think about the half-life — is it so long that it will pose a danger to people or the environment?

Q1 Which radioactive source is most dangerous inside the body? [1 mark]

Q2 Why are beta and gamma radiation more dangerous than alpha radiation outside the body? [1 mark]

Uses of Radiation

Ionising radiation is very dangerous stuff, but used in the right way it can be so useful that it saves lives.

Tracers in Medicine — Short Half-life Gamma Emitters

1) Certain radioactive isotopes that emit gamma radiation are used as tracers in the body.

2) They can be injected or ingested (drunk or eaten) to see how parts of the body, e.g. organs, are working.

3) They spread through the body and their progress is followed from the outside using a radiation detector.

4) They need a relatively short half-life — i.e. a few hours, so that the source becomes relatively safe quite quickly, but long enough that it still emits enough radiation by the time it reaches the correct place.

5) Medical tracers are GAMMA sources. Gamma radiation penetrates tissue, so can pass out of the body and be detected. Alpha and beta radiation can't and cause more damage in the body than gamma radiation.

> E.g. tracers are used to detect cancerous cells in the body.
> Radioactive tracers can be joined to molecules that will be absorbed by the cancerous cells. Then cancerous regions can be detected and seen on a screen.

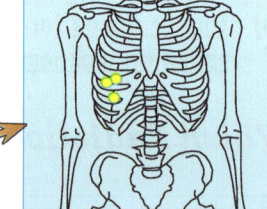

Radiotherapy — the Treatment of Cancer Using Radiation

1) Since high doses of radiation will kill living cells, they can be used to treat cancers.

2) The radiation is directed carefully so it kills the cancer cells without damaging too many normal cells.

3) A specific dosage must be used — this depends on, e.g. the size and type of tumour.

4) Radiation can be used to remove tumours completely or to control and stop them spreading further.

5) However, a fair bit of damage is often done to normal cells, which makes the patient feel very ill.

6) Before ionising radiation is used as part of any medical treatment, both the patient and doctor need to make an informed decision on whether the benefits outweigh the risks.

To treat cancer externally (using gamma rays):

- The gamma rays are focused on the tumour using a wide beam.
- The patient stays still and the beam is rotated round them with the tumour at the centre.
- This minimises the exposure of normal cells to radiation so the damage to healthy tissue is limited.
- The treatment is given in doses with time between for the healthy cells to be repaired or replaced.

Gamma rays focused on tumour
Source rotated outside the body.

To treat cancer internally:

- Implants containing beta-emitters are placed next to or inside the tumour. The beta particles damage the cells in the tumour, but have a short enough range that the damage to healthy tissue is limited.
- An implant with a long half-life should be removed once the cancerous cells have been killed to stop the radiation killing healthy cells. If the half-life is short enough, the implant can be left in.
- Alpha-emitters can be injected into a tumour. Alpha particles are strongly ionising, so they do lots of damage to the cancer cells. But as they have a short range, damage to normal tissue is limited.

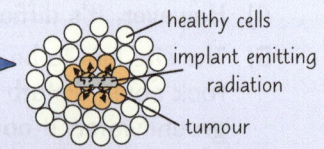
healthy cells
implant emitting radiation
tumour

All we hear is... Radiotherapy...

Try making lists of when and why the different types of radiation are used in medicine to see what you've learnt.

Q1   Technetium-99m is a gamma emitter with a half-life of 6 hours. It is the most common radioactive isotope used as a tracer. Explain why technetium-99m is used for this purpose.   [2 marks]

Q2   Describe how gamma radiation is used to treat cancerous tumours.   [2 marks]

Background Radiation

Where you live affects how much radiation you are exposed to — you need to know where it comes from.

Background Radiation is Present at All Times

1) Background radiation is the low-level radiation that is present all the time, wherever you go. It can be natural or artificial (man-made):

- Naturally occurring unstable isotopes in the air, in food, in building materials and in the rocks under our feet produce natural background radiation.
- Plants absorb radioactive isotopes from the soil and they are passed up the food chain.
- Radiation from space, which is known as cosmic rays, contributes to natural background radiation. These come mostly from the Sun and are absorbed by the Earth's atmosphere. Background radiation due to cosmic rays increases with altitude, because the atmosphere gets thinner as altitude increases.

- Medical X-rays in hospitals produce the most artificial background radiation.
- Nuclear power stations release a small amount of man-made radioactive material into the environment. Accidents at nuclear power plants can lead to a high level of background radiation.
- Nuclear bombs have also released artificial radioactive isotopes into the environment.

2) Everyone gets a small dose of radiation from background radiation. Radiation dose is a measure of the damage that radiation will cause to the body.

3) Dose depends on the type and amount of radiation you've been exposed to. The higher the radiation dose, the more at risk you are of developing long-term effects like cancer.

4) Different sources of radiation have different doses, for example medical X-rays of different parts of the body lead to different doses:

mSv (milli-sieverts) are the units for radiation dose — you don't need to remember these.

A CT scan is a just type of X-ray.

Type of X-ray	Dose (mSv)
Chest X-ray	0.014
CT head scan	1.4
CT spine scan	10

Radon is a Common Source of Natural Background Radiation

1) Radioactive radon gas is produced by certain underground rocks, especially granite.

2) Nearly half of the UK's background radiation comes from radon.

3) The level of radon in a particular area depends on the type of rock in that area.

4) Radon gas tends to get trapped inside people's houses and is linked to lung cancer.

5) As the ground is the main source of radon gas, householders can protect themselves against it by installing special types of flooring.

6) Ventilation is also important to prevent radon gas from building up inside.

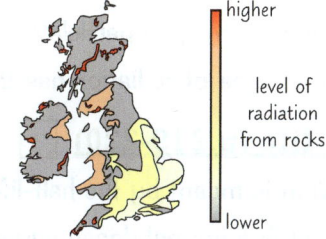

higher

level of radiation from rocks

lower

Don't Ignore Background Radiation when Doing Experiments

1) When doing an experiment, you need to take background radiation into account.

2) If you're measuring the activity of a source and forget to take background radiation into account, the activity of the source will be recorded as higher than it actually is.

3) To allow for background radiation, just measure the average background radiation count rate over a long enough time. Then subtract this from the count rate you measure from a radioactive source.

You mustn't forget about background radiation...

Make sure you know the difference between natural and artificial sources, cover up this page and make a list of a few natural sources and a few artificial ones. It might seem obvious but they can be really easy to get mixed up.

Q1   Explain the reason for the variation in the level of radon gas present across the UK.   [2 marks]

Revision Questions for Unit 6b

Well, that wraps up Unit 6b — let's see if any of that's sunk in. Give these questions a go and see.

- Try these questions and tick off each one when you get it right.
- When you've done all the questions for a topic and are completely happy with it, tick off the topic.

The Solar System (p.213) ☐

1) Explain the difference between a terrestrial planet and a gas giant. ☐
2) What's the order of the planets in the Solar System from the Sun outwards? ☐
3) What is a satellite? ☐
4) Describe the shape of a comet's orbit. ☐

Sizes and Distances in Space (p.214) ☐

5) What is a galaxy? ☐
6) Which is bigger — the Milky Way or the Solar System? ☐
7) What is a light year? ☐
8) Give one unit, other than the light year, used for measuring distances in space. ☐

The Life Cycle of Stars and the Solar System (p.215-216) ☐

9) What is a main sequence star? ☐
10) What is the force of gravity balanced against when a star is in its stable period? ☐
11) What is the final stage in the life cycle of a low mass star? ☐
12) What does the Hertzsprung-Russell diagram show? ☐
13) What force turned dust and gas into the early Solar System? ☐

Isotopes and Radioactive Decay (p.217-218) ☑

14) What do Z and A mean in terms of atomic structure? ☐
15) Isotopes have:
    a) The same number of what?   b) A different number of what? ☐
16) What is an alpha particle? ☐
17) What type of radiation has the greatest penetrating power. Alpha, beta or gamma? ☐

Half-life (p.219-220) ☑

18) What is meant by the half-life of a radioactive sample? ☐
19) Sketch a normal decay curve — don't forget to label the axes. ☐
20) Explain how you can model radioactive decay using dice,
    and how you can calculate the half-life of the model source. ☐

Dangers and Uses of Radiation (p.221-222) ☑

21) Which radioactive sources are the most dangerous when outside of your body? ☐
22) How is low-level waste from nuclear power plants disposed of? ☐
23) What type of radiation is used to treat cancer externally? ☐

Background Radiation (p.223) ☑

24) Give two sources of natural background radiation. ☑
25) Give an example of a source of artificial background radiation. ☑
26) Is radon a solid, a liquid or a gas? ☑

Measuring Techniques

Safety specs out and lab coats on, it's time to find out about the skills you'll need in experiments. Finally time to look like a real scientist... hurrah! But you also need to know about this stuff in your exams... boooo...

Mass Should Be Measured Using a Balance

1) To measure mass, start by putting the container you're measuring the substance into on the balance.

2) Set the balance to exactly zero and then start adding your substance.

3) It's no good carefully measuring out your substance if it's not all transferred to your reaction vessel — the volume in the reaction vessel won't be the same as your measurement. Here are a couple of methods you can use to make sure that none gets left in your weighing container...

> • If you're dissolving a mass of a solid in a solvent to make a solution, you could wash any remaining solid into the new container using the solvent. This way you know that all the solid you weighed has been transferred.
>
> • You could set the balance to zero before you put your weighing container on the balance. Then reweigh the weighing container after you've transferred the substance. Use the difference in mass to work out exactly how much substance you've transferred.

Different Ways to Measure Liquids

There are a few methods you might use to measure the volume of a liquid. Whichever method you use, always read the volume from the bottom of the meniscus (the curved upper surface of the liquid) when it's at eye level.

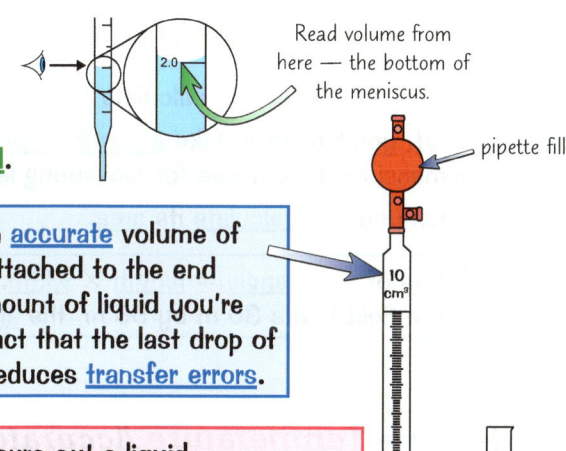

Read volume from here — the bottom of the meniscus.

pipette filler

> Pipettes are long, narrow tubes that are used to suck up an accurate volume of liquid and transfer it to another container. A pipette filler attached to the end of the pipette is used so that you can safely control the amount of liquid you're drawing up. Pipettes are often calibrated to allow for the fact that the last drop of liquid stays in the pipette when the liquid is ejected. This reduces transfer errors.

> Measuring cylinders are the most common way to measure out a liquid. They come in all different sizes. Make sure you choose one that's the right size for the measurement you want to make. It's no good using a huge 1000 cm³ cylinder to measure out 2 cm³ of a liquid — the graduations will be too big, and you'll end up with massive errors. It'd be much better to use one that measures up to 10 cm³.

If you only want a couple of drops of liquid, and don't need it to be accurately measured, you can use a dropping pipette to transfer it. For example, this is how you'd add a couple of drops of indicator into a mixture.

Gas Syringes Measure Gas Volumes

1) Gases can be measured with a gas syringe. They should be measured at room temperature and pressure as the volume of a gas changes with temperature and pressure. You should also use a gas syringe that's the right size for the measurement you're making. Before you use the syringe, you should make sure it's completely sealed and that the plunger moves smoothly.

2) Alternatively, you can use an upturned measuring cylinder filled with water. The gas will displace the water so you can read the volume off the scale — see page 229.

3) Another method to measure the amount of gas is to count the bubbles produced during a reaction (see p.40). This method is less accurate, but will give you relative amounts of gas to compare results.

4) When you're measuring a gas, you need to make sure that the equipment is set up so that none of the gas can escape, otherwise your results won't be accurate.

Measuring Techniques

Measure *Most Lengths* with a *Ruler*

1) In most cases a bog-standard centimetre ruler can be used to measure length. It depends on what you're measuring though — metre rulers are handy for large distances, while micrometers are used for measuring tiny things like the diameter of a wire.

2) The ruler should always be parallel to what you want to measure.

3) If you're dealing with something where it's tricky to measure just one accurately (e.g. water ripples), you can measure the length of ten of them and then divide to find the length of one.

4) If you're taking multiple measurements of the same object (e.g. to measure changes in length) then make sure you always measure from the same point on the object. It can help to draw or stick small markers onto the object to line up your ruler against.

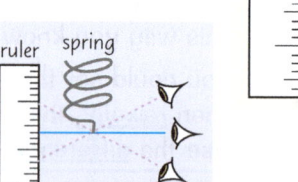

5) Make sure the ruler and the object are always at eye level when you take a reading. This stops parallax affecting your results.

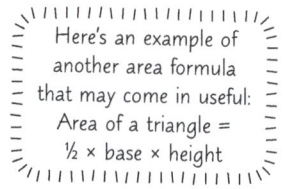

> Parallax is where a measurement appears to change based on where you're looking from. The blue line is the measurement taken when the spring is at eye level. It shows the correct length of the spring.

Use *Lengths* to Calculate *Area*

Sometimes you'll need to calculate the area of something. If you need to, here's how:

1) First, you'll need to take accurate measurements of its dimensions (see above for measuring lengths).

2) Then you can calculate its area.

> Area of a rectangle = length × width. So, if you're measuring the area of a field that's 30 m by 55 m, the area would be 30 × 55 = 1650 m².

> Here's an example of another area formula that may come in useful:
> Area of a triangle = ½ × base × height

Measure *Temperature* Accurately

You can use a thermometer to measure the temperature of a substance:

1) Make sure the bulb of your thermometer is completely submerged in any substance you're measuring.

2) If you're taking an initial reading, you should wait for the temperature to stabilise first.

3) Read your measurement off the scale on a thermometer at eye level to make sure it's correct.

Use a *Measuring Cylinder* to find the *Volume* of an *Irregular Solid*

1) If you've got an irregular shaped solid, you can't use side lengths to find its volume.

2) Instead, you can find its volume by completely submerging it in a measuring cylinder of water.

> If it's a regular shaped solid then just calculate the volume by measuring its dimensions (e.g. use width × height × length for a cuboid).

3) Put a set volume of water in a measuring cylinder, and then put the object in.

4) Record the new volume of water in the measuring cylinder.

5) Subtract the original volume from this. This'll give you the volume of the solid object. Nifty or what...

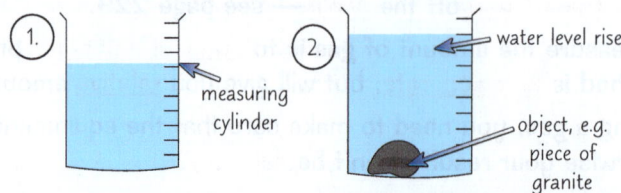

1. measuring cylinder
2. water level rises — object, e.g. piece of granite

Measuring Techniques

You May Have to Measure the *Time Taken* for a Change

1) You should use a <u>stopwatch</u> to <u>time</u> experiments.
   These measure to the nearest <u>0.1 s</u> or <u>0.01 s</u>, so are <u>sensitive</u>.

2) Always make sure you <u>start</u> and <u>stop</u> the stopwatch at exactly the right time. Or alternatively, set an <u>alarm</u> on the stopwatch so you know exactly when to stop an experiment or take a reading.

3) You might be able to use a <u>light gate</u> instead (p.231). This will <u>reduce the errors</u> in your experiment.

4) Think about how much to <u>round</u> your results. E.g. if you're measuring the time taken for a <u>colour change</u>, it's hard to judge the exact moment of the change, so you might just record to the <u>nearest second</u>.

Measure *pH* to Find Out How *Acidic* or *Alkaline* a Solution is

You need to be able to decide the best method for measuring pH, depending on what your experiment is.

1) <u>Indicators</u> are dyes that <u>change colour</u> depending on whether they're in an <u>acid</u> or an <u>alkali</u>.
   You use them by adding a couple of drops of the indicator to the solution you're interested in.

2) <u>Universal indicator</u> is a <u>mixture</u> of indicators that changes colour <u>gradually</u> as pH changes. It doesn't show a <u>sudden</u> colour change. It's useful for <u>estimating</u> the pH of a solution based on its colour.

3) Indicators can be soaked into <u>paper</u> and strips of this paper can be used for testing pH.
   If you use a dropping pipette to spot a small amount of a solution onto some indicator paper, it will <u>change colour</u> depending on the pH of the solution.

> <u>Litmus paper</u> turns <u>red</u> in acidic conditions and <u>blue</u> in basic conditions.
> <u>Universal indicator paper</u> can be used to <u>estimate</u> the pH based on its colour.

4) Indicator paper is useful when you <u>don't</u> want to change the colour of <u>all</u> of the substance, or if the substance is <u>already</u> coloured so might <u>obscure</u> the colour of the indicator.
   You can also hold a piece of <u>damp indicator paper</u> in a <u>gas sample</u> to test its pH.

5) <u>pH probes</u> are attached to pH meters which have a <u>digital display</u> that gives a <u>numerical</u> value for the pH of a solution. They're used to give an <u>accurate value</u> of pH.

Data Loggers can be Used to Take Continuous Samples

1) <u>Continuous sampling</u> is when <u>lots of samples</u> are taken at <u>regular intervals</u> over a particular time period.

2) Taking lots of samples means you can see what is happening <u>during the experiment</u>, not just the outcome of it.

3) Using a <u>data logger</u> connected to a computer is an <u>example</u> of continuous sampling.
   If you're going to use a data logger in one of your experiments, you'll need to:

   - Decide <u>what</u> you are <u>measuring</u> and <u>what type</u> of <u>data logger</u> you will need, e.g. temperature, pH.

   - Connect an <u>external sensor</u> to the data logger if you need to.

   - Decide <u>how often</u> you want the data logger to take readings depending on the <u>length of the process</u> that you are measuring.

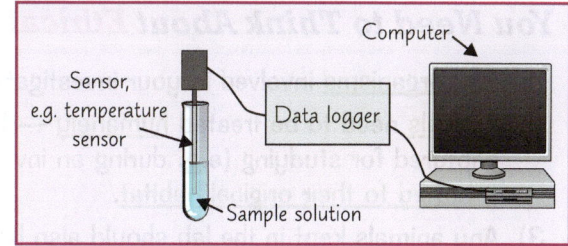

4) You can use the computer to <u>view the data</u> and to <u>process</u> it (draw graphs, calculate a mean, etc.).

5) Using a data logger to take measurements can improve the <u>accuracy</u> of your results because you can take a <u>large sample size</u>.

Experimentus apparatus...

Wizardry won't help you here, unfortunately. Most of this'll be pretty familiar to you by now, but make sure you know these techniques inside out so they're second nature when it comes to any practicals.

Safety and Ethics

Before you start any experiment, you need to know what safety precautions you should be taking. And they depend on your method, your equipment, and the chemicals you're using.

Make Sure You're Working Safely in the Lab

1) Make sure that you're wearing sensible clothing when you're in the lab (e.g. open shoes won't protect your feet from spillages). When you're doing an experiment, you should wear a lab coat to protect your skin and clothing. Depending on the experiment, you may need to also wear safety goggles and gloves.

2) You also need to be aware of general safety in the lab, e.g. keep anything flammable away from lit Bunsen burners, don't directly touch any hot equipment, handle glassware carefully so it doesn't break, etc.

3) You should follow any instructions that your teacher gives you carefully. But here are some basic principles for dealing with chemicals and equipment...

Be Careful When You're Using Chemicals...

1) The chemicals you're using may be hazardous — for example, they might be flammable (catch fire easily), or they might irritate or burn your skin if it comes into contact with them.

2) Make sure you're working in an area that's well ventilated and if you're doing an experiment that might produce nasty gases (such as chlorine), you should carry out the experiment in a fume hood so that the gas can't escape out into the room you're working in.

3) Never directly touch any chemicals (even if you're wearing gloves). Use a spatula to transfer solids between containers. Carefully pour liquids between containers, using a funnel to avoid spillages.

4) Be careful when you're mixing chemicals, as a reaction might occur. If you're diluting a liquid, add the concentrated substance to the water (not the other way around) or the mixture could get very hot.

...and Equipment

1) Stop masses and equipment falling by using clamp stands. Make sure masses are of a sensible weight so they don't break the equipment they're used with.

2) When heating materials, make sure to let them cool before moving them, or wear insulated gloves while handling them. If you're using an immersion heater to heat liquids, you should always let it dry out in air, just in case any liquid has leaked inside the heater.

3) When working with electronics, make sure you use a low enough voltage and current to prevent wires overheating (and potentially melting) and avoid damage to components, like blowing a filament bulb.

You Need to Think About Ethical Issues In Your Experiments

1) Any organisms involved in your investigations need to be treated safely and ethically.

2) Animals need to be treated humanely — they should be handled carefully and any wild animals captured for studying (e.g. during an investigation of the distribution of an organism) should be returned to their original habitat.

3) Any animals kept in the lab should also be cared for in a humane way, e.g. they should not be kept in overcrowded conditions.

4) If you are carrying out an experiment involving other students (e.g. investigating the effect of caffeine on reaction time), they should not be forced to participate against their will or feel pressured to take part.

Safety first...

I know — lab safety isn't the most exciting topic. But it's mega important. Not only will it stop you from blowing your eyebrows off, it'll help you pick up more marks in the exam. And that IS worth getting excited about...

Setting Up Experiments

Setting up the equipment for an experiment correctly is <u>important</u>. <u>Drawing</u> it neatly can come in handy too...

To Collect *Gases*, the System Needs to be *Sealed*

1) There are times when you might want to <u>collect</u> the gas produced by a reaction. For example, to investigate the <u>rate</u> of reaction.

2) The most accurate way to measure the volume of a gas that's been produced is to collect it in a <u>gas syringe</u> (see page 225).

3) You could also collect it by <u>displacing water</u> from a measuring cylinder. Here's how you do it...

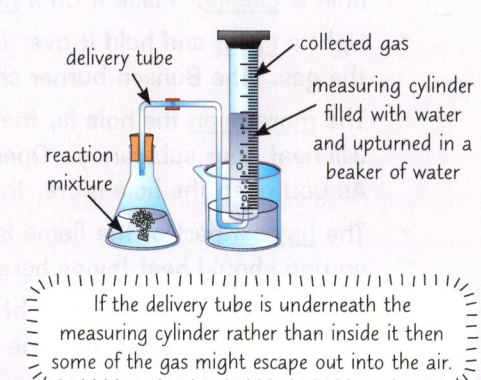

- Fill a <u>measuring cylinder</u> with <u>water</u>, and carefully place it <u>upside down</u> in a container of water. Record the <u>initial level</u> of the water in the measuring cylinder.

- Position a <u>delivery tube</u> coming <u>from</u> the reaction vessel so that it's <u>inside</u> the measuring cylinder, pointing upwards. Any gas that's produced will pass <u>through</u> the delivery tube and <u>into</u> the <u>measuring cylinder</u>. As the gas enters the measuring cylinder, the <u>water</u> is <u>pushed out</u>.

- Record the <u>level of water</u> in the measuring cylinder and use this value, along with your <u>initial value</u>, to calculate the <u>volume</u> of gas produced.

If the delivery tube is underneath the measuring cylinder rather than inside it then some of the gas might escape out into the air.

4) This method is <u>less accurate</u> than using a gas syringe to measure the volume of gas produced. This is because some gases can <u>dissolve</u> in water, so less gas ends up in the measuring cylinder than is <u>actually produced</u>.

5) If you just want to <u>collect</u> a sample to test (and don't need to measure a volume), you can collect it over water, as above, using a <u>test tube</u>. Once the test tube is full of gas, you can stopper it and store the gas for later.

Remember — when you're measuring a gas, your equipment has to be sealed or some gas could escape and your results wouldn't be accurate.

Make Sure You Can *Draw Diagrams* of Your Equipment

1) When you're writing out a <u>method</u> for your experiment, it's always a good idea to draw a <u>labelled diagram</u> showing how your apparatus will be <u>set up</u>.

2) The easiest way to do this is to use a scientific drawing, where each piece of apparatus is drawn as if you're looking at its <u>cross-section</u>. You can simplify a Bunsen burner though. For example:

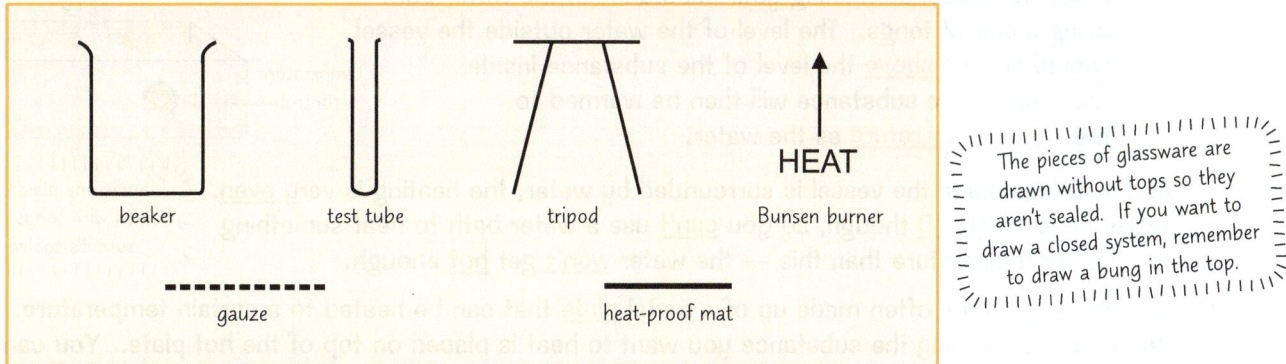

The pieces of glassware are drawn without tops so they aren't sealed. If you want to draw a closed system, remember to draw a bung in the top.

Science exams — they're a set-up...

It may seem like science exams are a devious ploy by the creatures of darkness to set you up for misery and heartache... and maybe they are. But whether they are or not, you need to know each of the experimental set-ups on these pages. It'll be worth it in the end, when you ace the exam and smite the evil ones with your top grades...

Heating Substances

Heating a reaction isn't as simple as wrapping it up in a lumpy wool jumper and a stripy scarf.
There's more than one way to do it, and you need to be able to decide on the best, and the safest, method.

Bunsen Burners Have a Naked Flame

Bunsen burners are good for heating things quickly. You can easily adjust how strongly
they're heating. But you need to be careful not to use them if you're heating flammable
compounds as the flame means the substance would be at risk of catching fire.

Here's how to use a Bunsen burner...

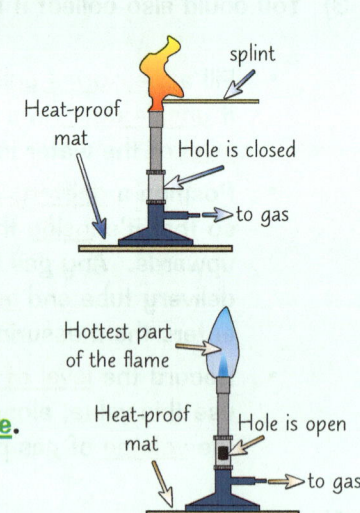

splint

Heat-proof mat

Hole is closed

to gas

Hottest part of the flame

Heat-proof mat

Hole is open

to gas

- Connect the Bunsen burner to a gas tap, and check that the hole is closed. Place it on a heat-proof mat.
- Light a splint and hold it over the Bunsen burner. Now, turn on the gas. The Bunsen burner should light with a yellow flame.
- The more open the hole is, the more strongly the Bunsen burner will heat your substance. Open the hole to the amount you want. As you open the hole more, the flame should turn more blue.
- The hottest part of the flame is just above the blue cone, so you should heat things here.
- If your Bunsen burner is alight but not heating anything, make sure you close the hole so that the flame becomes yellow and clearly visible.
- If you're heating something so that the container (e.g. a test tube) is in the flame, you should hold the vessel at the top, furthest away from the substance (and so the flame) using a pair of tongs.
- If you're heating something over the flame (e.g. an evaporating dish), you should put a tripod and gauze over the Bunsen burner before you light it, and place the vessel on this.

The Temperature of Water Baths and Electric Heaters Can Be Set

1) A water bath is a container filled with water that can be heated to a specific temperature. A simple water bath can be made by heating a beaker of water over a Bunsen burner and monitoring the temperature with a thermometer. However, it is difficult to keep the temperature of the water constant.

2) An electric water bath will monitor and adjust the temperature for you. Here's how you use one:

rubber duck (optional)

reaction vessel

temperature control

- Set the temperature on the water bath, and allow the water to heat up.
- Place the vessel containing your substance in the water bath using a pair of tongs. The level of the water outside the vessel should be just above the level of the substance inside the vessel. The substance will then be warmed to the same temperature as the water.

As the substance in the vessel is surrounded by water, the heating is very even. Water boils at 100 °C though, so you can't use a water bath to heat something to a higher temperature than this — the water won't get hot enough.

Handle any glassware you've heated with tongs until you're sure it's cooled down.

3) Electric heaters are often made up of a metal plate that can be heated to a certain temperature. The vessel containing the substance you want to heat is placed on top of the hot plate. You can heat substances to higher temperatures than you can in a water bath but, as the vessel is only heated from below, you'll usually have to stir the substance inside to make sure it's heated evenly.

A bath and an electric heater — how I spend my January nights...

You know, I used to have a science teacher who'd play power ballads when the Bunsen burners were alight and sway at the front of the class like he was at a gig. You think I made that up, but it's true.

Working with Electronics

Electrical devices are used in a bunch of experiments, so make sure you know how to use them.

You Have to Interpret Circuit Diagrams

Before you get cracking on an experiment involving any kind of electrical devices, you have to plan and build your circuit using a circuit diagram. Make sure you know all of the circuit symbols on page 95 so you're not stumped before you've even started.

There Are a Couple of Ways to Measure Potential Difference and Current

Voltmeters Measure Potential Difference

1) If you're using an analogue voltmeter, choose the voltmeter with the most appropriate unit (e.g. V or mV). If you're using a digital voltmeter, you'll most likely be able to switch between them.

2) Connect the voltmeter in parallel (p.99) across the component you want to test. The wires that come with a voltmeter are usually red (positive) and black (negative). These go into the red and black coloured ports on the voltmeter. Funnily enough.

3) Then simply read the potential difference from the scale (or from the screen if it's digital).

Ammeters Measure Current

1) Just like with voltmeters, choose the ammeter with the most appropriate unit.

2) Connect the ammeter in series (p.98) with the component you want to test, making sure they're both on the same branch. Again, they usually have red and black ports to show you where to connect your wires.

3) Read off the current shown on the scale or by the screen.

Turn your circuit off between readings to prevent wires overheating and affecting your results.

Multimeters Measure Both

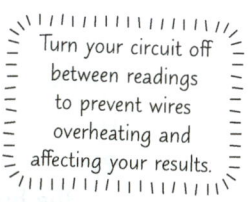

1) Instead of having a separate ammeter and voltmeter, many circuits use multimeters. These are devices that measure a range of properties — usually potential difference, current and resistance.

2) If you want to find potential difference, make sure the red wire is plugged into the port that has a 'V' (for volts).

3) To find the current, use the port labelled 'A' or 'mA' (for amps).

4) The dial on the multimeter should then be turned to the relevant section, e.g. to 'A' to measure current in amps. The screen will display the value you're measuring.

Light Gates Measure Speed and Acceleration

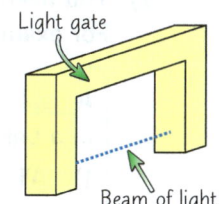

Light gate

Beam of light

1) A light gate sends a beam of light from one side of the gate to a detector on the other side. When something passes through the gate, the beam of light is interrupted. The light gate then measures how long the beam was undetected.

2) To find the speed of an object, connect the light gate to a computer. Measure the length of the object and input this using the software. It will then automatically calculate the speed of the object as it passes through the beam.

3) To measure acceleration, use an object that interrupts the signal twice in a short period of time, e.g. a piece of card with a gap cut into the middle.

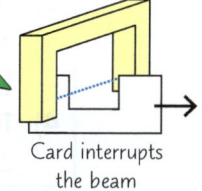

Card interrupts the beam

4) The light gate measures the speed for each section of the object and uses this to calculate its acceleration. This can then be read from the computer screen.

A light gate is better than a heavy one...

After finishing this page, you should be able to take on any electrical experiment that they throw at you... ouch.

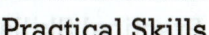

Sampling

I love <u>samples</u>... especially when I'm a bit <u>peckish</u> in the supermarket and they're handing out <u>free cheese</u>. Unfortunately, this page isn't about those samples. It's a lot more useful than that...

Sampling Should be Random

1) When you're investigating a population, it's generally <u>not possible</u> to study <u>every single organism</u> in the population. This means that you need to take <u>samples</u> of the population you're interested in.

2) The sample data will be used to <u>draw conclusions</u> about the <u>whole</u> population, so it's important that it <u>accurately</u> represents the <u>whole population</u>.

3) To make sure a sample represents the population, it should be <u>random</u>.

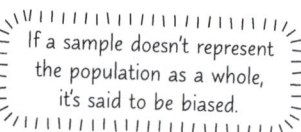
If a sample doesn't represent the population as a whole, it's said to be biased.

Organisms Should Be Sampled At Random Sites in an Area

1) If you're interested in the <u>distribution</u> of an organism in an area, or its <u>population size</u>, you can take population samples in the area you're interested in using <u>quadrats</u> or <u>transects</u> (see pages 128-129).

2) If you only take samples from <u>one part</u> of the area, your results will be <u>biased</u> — they may not give an <u>accurate representation</u> of the <u>whole area</u>.

3) To make sure that your sampling isn't biased, you need to use a method of <u>choosing sampling sites</u> in which every site has an <u>equal chance</u> of being chosen. For example:

If you're looking at plant species in a field...

1) <u>Divide</u> the field into a <u>grid</u>.

2) <u>Label the grid</u> along the bottom and up the side with numbers.

3) Use a <u>random number generator</u> (on a computer or calculator) to select coordinates, e.g. (2,6).

4) Take your samples at these coordinates.

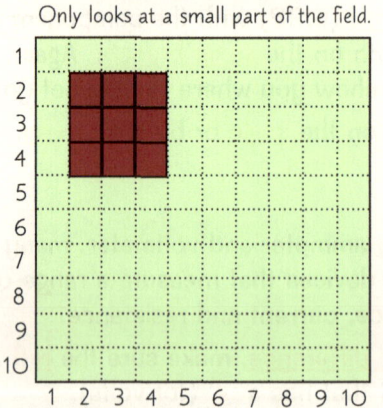
Non-random sampling
Only looks at a small part of the field.

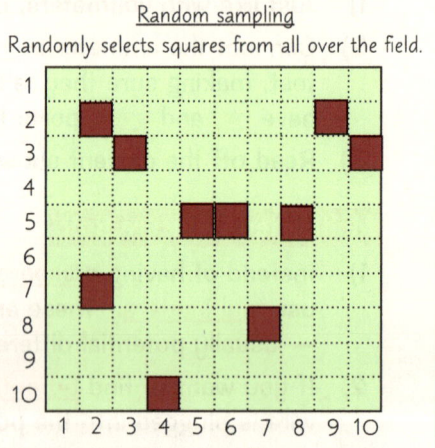
Random sampling
Randomly selects squares from all over the field.

Health Data Should be Taken from Randomly Selected People

1) As mentioned above, it's not practical (or even possible) to study an <u>entire human population</u>.

2) You need to use <u>random sampling</u> to choose members of the population you're interested in. For example:

A <u>health professional</u> is investigating <u>how many</u> people diagnosed with <u>type 2 diabetes</u> in a particular country <u>also</u> have <u>heart disease</u>:

1) All the people who have been diagnosed with type 2 diabetes in the country of interest are identified by <u>hospital records</u>. In total, there are <u>270 196</u> people.

2) These people are assigned a <u>number</u> between 1 and 270 196.

3) A <u>random number generator</u> is used to choose the sample group (e.g. it selects the individuals #72 063, #11 822, #193 123, etc.)

4) The <u>proportion</u> of people in the <u>sample</u> that have heart disease can be used to <u>estimate</u> the <u>total number</u> of people with type 2 diabetes that also have heart disease.

'Eeny, meeny, miny, moe' just doesn't cut it any more...

Sampling is an important part of an investigation. It needs to be done randomly, or the data won't be worth much.

Comparing Results

Being able to compare your results is really important. Here are some ways you might do it. I spoil you.

Percentage Change Allows you to Compare Results

1) When investigating the change in a variable, you may want to compare results that didn't have the same initial value. For example, you may want to compare the change in mass of potato cylinders left in different concentrations of sugar solution that had different initial masses (see page 18).

2) One way to do this is to calculate the percentage change. You work it out like this:

$$\text{percentage (\%) change} = \frac{\text{final value} - \text{original value}}{\text{original value}} \times 100$$

EXAMPLE: A student is investigating the effect of the concentration of sugar solution on potato cells.

She records the mass of potato cylinders before and after placing them in sugar solutions of different concentrations. The table on the right shows some of her results.

Which potato cylinder had the largest percentage change?

Potato cylinder	Concentration (mol/dm³)	Mass at start (g)	Mass at end (g)
1	0.0	7.5	8.7
2	1.0	8.0	6.8

1) Stick each set of results into the equation:

$$\% \text{ change} = \frac{\text{final value} - \text{original value}}{\text{original value}} \times 100$$

1. $\frac{8.7 - 7.5}{7.5} \times 100 = 16\%$ — The mass at the start is the original value. The mass at the end is the final value.

2. $\frac{6.8 - 8.0}{8.0} \times 100 = -15\%$ — Here, the mass has decreased so the percentage change is negative.

2) Compare the results. **16% is greater than 15%, so the potato cylinder in the 0.0 mol/dm³ sugar solution had the largest percentage change.**

Percentiles Tell you Where in Your Data Set a Data Point Lies

1) Percentiles are useful if you want to compare the value of one data point to the rest of your data.

2) To find a percentile, you rank your data from smallest to largest, then divide it into one hundred equal chunks. Each chunk is one percentile.

3) This means that each percentile represents one percent of the data, and so the value of a percentile tells you what percentage of the data has a value lower than the data points in that percentile.

> E.g. Mike the Meerkat is in the 90th percentile for height in his gang. This means that 90% of the gang are shorter than Mike.

4) Percentiles can be used to give a more realistic idea of the spread of data than the range (see p.7) — by finding the range between the 10th and 90th percentiles in a data set (the middle 80% of the data), you can look at the spread of the data while ignoring any outlying results.

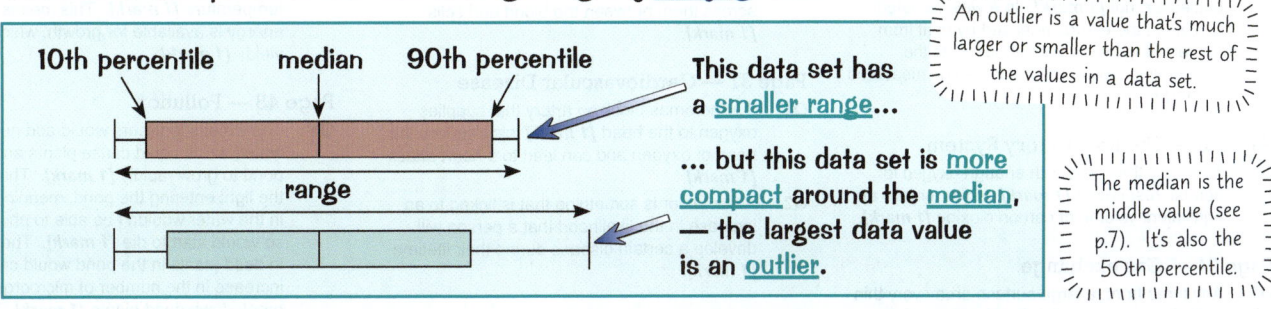

An outlier is a value that's much larger or smaller than the rest of the values in a data set.

This data set has a smaller range...

... but this data set is more compact around the median, — the largest data value is an outlier.

The median is the middle value (see p.7). It's also the 50th percentile.

Percentage change in how much I love maths after this page — 0%

Aaaand that's the end of Practical Skills, folks. Go forth, and science like you've never scienced before...

Answers

Unit 1a — Cells and Respiration

Page 12 — Cells
Q1 Cell wall *[1 mark]*. Vacuole *[1 mark]*. Chloroplasts *[1 mark]*.

Page 13 — Microscopy
Q1 real size = image size ÷ magnification
= 7.5 mm ÷ 100
= 0.075 mm *[1 mark]*
0.075 × 1000 = 75 µm *[1 mark]*

Page 14 — More Microscopy
Q1 To highlight objects within the sample by adding colour to them / in order to see objects in more detail *[1 mark]*.

Page 15 — Cell Organisation
Q1 That it is made up of different tissues *[1 mark]* that work together to perform a particular function *[1 mark]*.

Page 16 — Cell Membranes and Diffusion
Q1 The net movement of particles from an area of higher concentration to an area of lower concentration / the net movement of particles down their concentration gradient *[1 mark]*.

Page 17 — Osmosis and Active Transport
Q1 E.g. active transport is the movement of particles across a membrane against a concentration gradient, whereas diffusion is the movement of particles down a concentration gradient *[1 mark]*. Active transport uses ATP but diffusion does not *[1 mark]*.

Page 18 — Investigating Osmosis
Q1 percentage change $= \dfrac{11.4 - 13.3}{13.3} \times 100$
−0.142...
= −14.3%
[2 marks for correct answer, 1 mark for correct answer without minus sign]

Page 19 — Enzymes
Q1 The enzyme's active site changes shape *[1 mark]* and the enzyme denatures *[1 mark]*.

Page 20 — Investigating Enzyme Activity
Q1 $1 \div 65 = 0.015... \ s^{-1} = 0.02 \ s^{-1}$ to 1 s.f.
[2 marks for the correct answer to 1 s.f., otherwise 1 mark for 0.015... s^{-1}]

Page 21 — Respiration
Q1 glucose + oxygen → carbon dioxide + water
[1 mark for correct reactants, 1 mark for correct products]

Page 22 — Investigating Respiration
Q1 a) A flask with boiled/dead beans *[1 mark]*.
b) Vacuum flasks are well-insulated, but plastic bottles are not *[1 mark]*. In a well-insulated container, the energy released by heat from the respiring beans will not be lost to the surrounding environment and can be measured *[1 mark]*.

Page 23 — The Respiratory System
Q1 To supply their cells with enough oxygen for aerobic respiration *[1 mark]* and to remove an equivalent volume of carbon dioxide *[1 mark]*.

Page 24 — Gas exchange
Q1 Any three from: a large surface area / very thin walls / a moist lining for dissolving gases / a good blood supply. *[1 mark for each]*

Page 25 — Smoking
Q1 Chemicals in cigarette smoke paralyse cilia in the throat *[1 mark]*. This prevents mucus, and any bacteria trapped in it, from being effectively removed *[1 mark]*. This makes it more likely that bacteria will enter the respiratory system and cause an infection *[1 mark]*.

Unit 1b — Digestion and Circulation

Page 27 — Digestion
Q1 Bile is alkaline, so it neutralises the stomach acid and makes conditions in the small intestine alkaline *[1 mark]*. The enzymes of the small intestine work best in these alkaline conditions *[1 mark]*. It also emulsifies fats/breaks down fats into tiny droplets *[1 mark]*. This gives a bigger surface area of fat for the enzyme lipase to work on, making digestion faster *[1 mark]*.

Page 28 — Testing for Biological Molecules
Q1 Proteins are present *[1 mark]*.

Page 29 — The Digestive System
Q1 Any two from: e.g. stomach / pancreas / small intestine *[1 mark for each]*.

Page 30 — More on the Digestive System
Q1 E.g. villi increase the surface area of the small intestine *[1 mark]* and have a good blood supply which maintains a glucose diffusion gradient *[1 mark]*.

Page 31 — Diet
Q1 Any one from: e.g. they may need to eat more protein to support increased muscle development / for repair of muscle tissue *[1 mark]*.

Page 32 — Food and Health
Q1 E.g. type 2 diabetes, obesity, tooth decay *[1 mark for each correct answer]*

Page 33 — Energy in Food
Q1 To get a more accurate result / so heat isn't lost from the water to the surroundings *[1 mark]*.

Page 34 — Circulatory System — Blood
Q1 They help the blood to clot at a wound *[1 mark]*.
Q2 haemoglobin *[1 mark]*

Page 35 — Circulatory System — Heart
Q1 They supply oxygenated blood to the heart/ cardiac muscle *[1 mark]*.

Page 36 — Circulatory System — Blood Vessels
Q1 Valves keep the blood flowing in the right direction / prevent backflow of blood *[1 mark]*.
Q2 It increases the rate of diffusion of substances across them between the blood and cells *[1 mark]*.

Page 37 — Cardiovascular Disease
Q1 If artheromas block an artery that supplies oxygen to the heart *[1 mark]* this deprives the heart of oxygen and can lead to a heart attack *[1 mark]*.
Q2 A risk factor is something that is linked to an increase in the likelihood that a person will develop a certain disease during their lifetime *[1 mark]*.

Unit 1c — Photosynthesis, Ecosystems and the Environment

Page 39 — Photosynthesis
Q1 Plants produce glucose during photosynthesis. Some of this glucose is stored as starch *[1 mark]*. If you perform the starch test on a leaf grown without CO_2, the leaf will not turn blue-black *[1 mark]*, which means that there is no starch present in the leaf *[1 mark]*. As no starch has been made in the leaf grown without CO_2, it shows that CO_2 is needed for plants to photosynthesise *[1 mark]*.

Page 40 — Investigating the Rate of Photosynthesis
Q1 Plants release oxygen into the atmosphere when they photosynthesise *[1 mark]*, therefore the more a plant photosynthesises, the more oxygen it produces *[1 mark]*.

Pages 41-42 — Limiting Factors of Photosynthesis
Q1 The rate of photosynthesis increases with increasing light intensity *[1 mark]* up to a point at which the rate levels off *[1 mark]*.
Q2 a) CO_2 concentration *[1 mark]*
b) light intensity *[1 mark]*

Page 43 — Food Chains and Food Webs
Q1 They break down the remains of organisms and waste products *[1 mark]*.

Page 44 — Pyramids of Biomass and Numbers
Q1 B, because the bar for the producer is smaller than for the first stage consumer *[1 mark]* and just one tree/large plant may feed many consumers *[1 mark]*.

Page 45 — Energy Transfer
Q1 Any two from: e.g. respiration / in waste materials / in uneaten parts of organisms *[1 mark for each correct answer, up to 2 marks]*

Page 46 — Humans and Wildlife
Q1 E.g. an increasing amount of sewage/toxic chemicals from industry and agriculture may pollute water sources *[1 mark]*, affecting organisms which rely on the water for survival *[1 mark]*. / Building new housing/quarrying/ farming can lead to habitat destruction *[1 mark]*, which reduces the amount of land and resources for wildlife *[1 mark]*.

Page 47 — Intensive Farming
Q1 Limiting the movement of animals and keeping them in a temperature-controlled environment *[1 mark]* means the animals use less energy moving around and controlling their own body temperature *[1 mark]*. This means that more energy is available for growth, which increases yields *[1 mark]*.

Page 48 — Pollution
Q1 The excess fertilisers would add nutrients to the water, which could cause plants and algae in the pond to grow rapidly *[1 mark]*. This would block the light entering the pond, meaning that plants in the water wouldn't be able to photosynthesise, so would start to die *[1 mark]*. The increase in dead plants in the pond would cause an increase in the number of microorganisms that break down dead plants *[1 mark]*. The increase in the number of microorganisms would mean that more dissolved oxygen was used up in the water, so the oxygen concentration of the water would decrease *[1 mark]*.

Answers

Page 49 — Indicator Species
Q1 The presence of lichen indicates the air is clean *[1 mark]* because the lichen needs clean air / air with a low level of sulfur dioxide to grow *[1 mark]*.

Unit 2a — The Nature of Substances and Chemical Reactions

Page 51 — Elements, Compounds and Mixtures
Q1 a) compound *[1 mark]*
b) element *[1 mark]*
c) mixture *[1 mark]*

Page 52 — Separating Mixtures
Q1 evaporation *[1 mark]*
Q2 The solution is heated so that the part of the solution with the lowest boiling point evaporates first *[1 mark]*. The vapour is then cooled, condensed and collected *[1 mark]*. The rest of the solution is left behind in the flask *[1 mark]*.

Page 53 — Chromatography
Q1 $R_f = 2 \div 6$
$= 0.33 = 0.3$ *[1 mark]*

Page 54 — Chemical Formulae
Q1 12 *[1 mark]*

Page 55 — Chemical Equations
Q1 $2Fe + 3Cl_2 \rightarrow 2FeCl_3$ *[1 mark]*
Q2 a) water $\rightarrow$ hydrogen + oxygen *[1 mark]*
b) $2H_2O \rightarrow 2H_2 + O_2$
[1 mark for correct reactants and products, 1 mark for a correctly balanced equation]

Page 56 — Chemical Reactions
Q1 E.g. colour change / temperature change / effervescence *[1 mark]*.

Page 57 — Relative Formula Mass
Q1 a) A_r of H = 1 and A_r of O = 16
M_r of $H_2O = (2 \times 1) + 16 = 18$ *[1 mark]*
b) A_r of Li = 7, A_r of O = 16 and A_r of H = 1
So M_r of LiOH = 7 + 16 + 1 = 24 *[1 mark]*
c) A_r of H = 1, A_r of S = 32 and A_r of O = 16
M_r of $H_2SO_4 = (2 \times 1) + 32 + (4 \times 16) = 98$ *[1 mark]*
Q2 A_r of K = 39, A_r of O = 16 and A_r of H = 1
M_r of KOH = 39 + 16 + 1 = 56 *[1 mark]*
$\frac{39}{56} \times 100 = 70\%$ (2 s.f.) *[1 mark]*

Page 58 — The Mole
Q1 M_r of $H_2O = 16 + (2 \times 1) = 18$ *[1 mark]*
number of moles = mass $\div M_r$
number of moles = 90 g $\div$ 18 = 5 moles *[1 mark]*
Q2 M_r of $Na_2SO_4 = (23 \times 2) + 32 + (16 \times 4) = 142$ *[1 mark]*
mass = number of moles $\times M_r$
mass = 0.20 $\times$ 142 = 28 g (to 2 s.f.) *[1 mark]*

Page 59 — Calculating Masses in Reactions
Q1 a) M_r(KBr) = 39 + 80 = 119
M_r(Br_2) = 80 $\times$ 2 = 160 *[1 mark]*
moles of KBr = mass $\div M_r$ = 23.8 $\div$ 119
= 0.200 moles *[1 mark]*
From the equation, 2 moles of KBr react to produce 1 mole of Br_2. So 0.200 moles of KBr will produce (0.200 $\div$ 2) = 0.100 moles of Br_2 *[1 mark]*.
So mass of Br_2 = moles $\times M_r$ = 0.100 $\times$ 160
= 16.0 g *[1 mark]*
b) Percentage yield = actual yield $\div$ theoretical yield $\times$ 100 = 12.4 g $\div$ 16.0 g $\times$ 100 *[1 mark]*
= 77.5% *[1 mark]*

Page 60 — Calculating Formulae from Reacting Masses
Q1 moles of sulfur = 40.0 $\div$ 32 = 1.25
moles of oxygen = 60.0 $\div$ 16 = 3.75 *[1 mark]*
Divide by the smallest number (1.25):
sulfur = 1.25 $\div$ 1.25 = 1
oxygen = 3.75 $\div$ 1.25 = 3
Ratio of S : O = 1 : 3
So simplest formula = SO_3 *[1 mark]*
Q2 mass of oxygen = 45.6 − 13.9 = 31.7 g *[1 mark]*
moles = mass $\div M_r$
moles of oxygen = 31.7 $\div$ 16 = 1.98125
moles of nitrogen = 13.9 $\div$ 14 = 0.99... *[1 mark]*
Divide by the smallest number (0.99...).
oxygen = 1.98125 $\div$ 0.99... = 2
nitrogen = 0.99... $\div$ 0.99... = 1
Ratio of O : N = 2 : 1.
So simplest formula = NO_2 *[1 mark]*

Page 61 — Calculating Formulae from Reacting Masses
Q1 Heat a crucible until it's red hot, leave it to cool, and then weigh it, along with its lid *[1 mark]*. Add a sample of the metal that you're investigating and reweigh the crucible, lid and contents *[1 mark]*. Heat the crucible strongly for around 10 minutes, with the lid on but leaving a small gap for oxygen to get in *[1 mark]*. Allow the crucible to cool and reweigh the crucible, lid and contents *[1 mark]*.

Unit 2b — Atomic Structure and the Periodic Table

Page 63 — The Atom
Q1 electrons = 19 *[1 mark]*,
protons = 19 *[1 mark]*,
neutrons = 39 − 19 = 20 *[1 mark]*

Page 64 — Ions, Isotopes and Relative Atomic Mass
Q1 a) Bromine-79: 35 protons, 35 electrons and (79 − 35 =) 44 neutrons *[1 mark]*.
Bromine-81: 35 protons, 35 electrons and (81 − 35 =) 46 neutrons *[1 mark]*.
b) 35 + 1 = 36 electrons *[1 mark]*

Page 65 — The Periodic Table
Q1 2 *[1 mark]*
Q2 Both chlorine and bromine have the same number of electrons in their outer shell *[1 mark]*.
You know this because they're both in the same group.
Q3 E.g. potassium forms 1+ ions because it's in the same group as sodium / has the same number of electrons in its outer shell, so will react in a similar way *[1 mark]*.

Page 66 — Electron Shells
Q1 2.8.3 or
[1 mark]
Q2 Group 2 *[1 mark]*
Period 4 *[1 mark]*

Page 67 — Group 1 — The Alkali Metals
Q1 Reactivity increases down Group 1 *[1 mark]*. As you go down the group, the outer electron is further away from the nucleus *[1 mark]*. This means the attraction between the nucleus and the electron decreases, so the electron is more easily removed. *[1 mark]*.

Page 68 — Reactions of the Alkali Metals
Q1 lithium *[1 mark]*
Q2 $2Na + 2H_2O \rightarrow 2NaOH + H_2$ *[1 mark for correct reactants and products, 1 mark for correctly balanced equation.]*

Page 69 — Group 7 — The Halogens
Q1 Bromine would be a solid at this temperature *[1 mark]*. The melting points of the halogens increase as you go down the group, so at the melting point of chlorine, bromine would still be solid *[1 mark]*.

Page 70 — Reactions of the Halogens
Q1 $2Na + I_2 \rightarrow 2NaI$
[1 mark for correct reactants and products, 1 mark for correctly balanced equation]
Q2 $2Fe + 3Cl_2 \rightarrow 2FeCl_3$
[1 mark for correct reactants and products, 1 mark for correctly balanced equation]

Page 71 — Halogen Displacement Reactions
Q1 Bromine water *[1 mark]*.

Page 72 — Group 0 — The Noble Gases
Q1 They have a full outer shell of electrons. *[1 mark]*

Page 73 — Tests for Ions and Hydrogen
Q1 Barium *[1 mark]*

Unit 2c — Water and the Earth

Page 75 — Water Treatment
Q1 A sedimentation process is used which involves larger particles settling at the bottom of the water tank due to gravity *[1 mark]*. The water is then filtered through gravel and sand to filter out smaller solid objects *[1 mark]*. Finally, chlorine gas is bubbled through the water to kill harmful bacteria *[1 mark]*.

Page 76 — Distillation and Desalination
Q1 Distillation requires a lot of energy to heat the sea water. *[1 mark]*

Page 77 — Solubility Curves
Q1 The ability of a substance to dissolve in a solvent *[1 mark]*.
Q2 46 g per 100 g of water *[1 mark]*.

Page 78 — Investigating Solubility
Q1 E.g. weigh out an excess of the solid and add it to a boiling tube containing a known volume of water to make a saturated solution *[1 mark]*. Stir the solution and place the boiling tube in a water bath set to 40 °C for 5 minutes *[1 mark]*. Filter out the excess solid using filter paper *[1 mark]*. Dry and weigh the excess solid that was removed from the solution *[1 mark]*. To find the solubility of the solid in g per 100 g of water, you would then divide the mass of solid dissolved in the solution by the mass of water and multiply by 100 *[1 mark]*.

Page 79 — Water Hardness
Q1 The columns contain sodium ions attached to a resin *[1 mark]*. When water runs through the column, the calcium or magnesium ions in the water are exchanged for sodium ions, making the water soft *[1 mark]*.

Page 80 — Measuring Water Hardness
Q1 Add soap solution 1 cm³ at a time to set volumes of the three water samples *[1 mark]* and shake for 5 seconds each time until a lasting lather is formed *[1 mark]*. Boil the water samples and repeat the experiment *[1 mark]*. Distilled water will need the least soap to form a lasting lather, and will do so before and after boiling *[1 mark]*. Temporary hard water will need lots of soap to give a good lather before boiling but much less after boiling *[1 mark]*. Permanent hard water will need lots of soap to give a lather before and after boiling *[1 mark]*.

Answers

Page 81 — The Earth's Structure
Q1 Iron *[1 mark]*

Page 82 — Plate Tectonics
Q1 E.g. matching layers in the rocks on different continents / fossils of very similar plants and animals found on different continents / jigsaw like fit of some continents (Africa and South America) *[1 mark]*

Page 83 — Plate Boundaries
Q1 Constructive plate boundaries are found where two plates are moving away from each other *[1 mark]*. Magma (molten rock) rises from the mantle to fill the gap and cools, creating new crust *[1 mark]*.

Page 84 — The Atmosphere
Q1 Green plants evolved and removed CO_2 from the atmosphere through photosynthesis *[1 mark]*. Some of the early CO_2 dissolved into the oceans *[1 mark]*. Much of the remaining CO_2 got locked up in fossil fuels and sedimentary rocks *[1 mark]*.

Page 85 — Greenhouse Gases and Climate Change
Q1 E.g. flooding due to rising sea levels/increased rainfall in some areas / droughts due to hotter, drier weather in some areas *[1 mark]*.

Page 86 — Reducing Pollution and Tests for Gases
Q1 E.g. the company could invest in a scheme to offset the carbon dioxide they emit / use carbon capture and storage and storage to capture the carbon dioxide before it's released into the atmosphere / plan how to reduce its emissions in future by reducing energy usage or using renewable energy *[1 mark]*.
Q2 Any two from e.g. causes lakes to become acidic and harm aquatic life / kills trees (and other plants) / damages limestone buildings / corrodes metal structures faster *[2 marks]*.

Unit 2d — Rate of Chemical Change

Page 88 — Reaction Rates
Q1 E.g. put a conical flask on a mass balance and add your reactants *[1 mark]*. As gas is produced from the reaction, measure how quickly the reading on the balance drops until the balance stops changing *[1 mark]*. Plot the results in a graph of change in mass against time *[1 mark]*.
Q2 E.g. it gives more accurate results *[1 mark]*.

Page 89 — Rate Experiments Involving Gases
Q1 E.g. place a measured volume of hydrochloric acid of a known concentration in a conical flask. Add a known mass of calcium carbonate in the form of marble chips *[1 mark]*. Use a gas syringe to take readings of the volume of gas produced at regular time intervals *[1 mark]*. Repeat the experiment with the same volume and concentration of acid and the same mass of calcium carbonate but increase the surface area by crunching the marble chips up *[1 mark]*.

Page 90 — Rate Experiments Involving Precipitation
Q1 The time taken would decrease *[1 mark]*.

Page 91 — Calculating Rates
Q1 E.g.

E.g. Change in y = 23 − 11 = 12
Change in x = 45 − 5 = 40
Gradient = 12 ÷ 40 = 0.30 cm³/s
[1 mark for a rate between 0.25 cm³/s and 0.40 cm³/s]

Page 92 — Factors Affecting Rate of Reaction
Q1 The energy transferred during a collision *[1 mark]* and the collision frequency *[1 mark]*.
Q2 Breaking a solid into smaller pieces will increase the surface area to volume ratio *[1 mark]*. This means that particles of the other reactant will have more area to work on *[1 mark]*. This increases the frequency of collisions and speeds up the rate of reaction *[1 mark]*.

Page 93 — More Factors Affecting Rate of Reaction
Q1 A catalyst is a substance which increases the rate of reaction *[1 mark]*, without being chemically changed or used up *[1 mark]*.
Q2 The manganese dioxide is not chemically changed or used up so only a tiny amount is needed to catalyse a large quantity of reactant *[1 mark]*.
Q3 In industrial processes there may be impurities present *[1 mark]*, which cause catalysts to lose their activity and work less effectively over time *[1 mark]*.

Unit 3a — Electric Circuits

Page 95 — Circuits — The Basics
Q1

[1 mark]
Q2 $I = V ÷ R$ so $R = V ÷ I$ *[1 mark]*
$= 4.25 ÷ 0.25$ *[1 mark]*
$= 17 Ω$ *[1 mark]*

Page 96 — Investigating *I-V* Characteristics
Q1 E.g.

[1 mark for a complete circuit with a power supply, variable resistor and filament lamp in series, 1 mark for a voltmeter connected in parallel across the filament lamp and 1 mark for an ammeter connected in series with the filament lamp]

Page 97 — Circuit Devices
Q1 As light intensity increases, the resistance decreases / as light intensity decreases, the resistance increases. *[1 mark]*

Page 98 — Series and Parallel Circuits
Q1 $3.6 ÷ 3 = 1.2$ V *[1 mark]*

Page 99 — More on Series and Parallel Circuits
Q1 Current is split between parallel branches:
$I = V ÷ R = 6 ÷ 8$ *[1 mark]*
$= 0.75$ A *[1 mark]*

Page 100 — Energy and Power in Circuits
Q1 $11 × 60 = 660$ seconds *[1 mark]*
energy transferred = power × time
$= 1.5 × 10^3 × 660$
$= 990\,000$ J *[1 mark]*
Q2 power = current² × resistance, so
current = $\sqrt{\text{power} ÷ \text{resistance}}$ *[1 mark]*
$= \sqrt{375 ÷ 15}$ *[1 mark]*
$= 5$ A *[1 mark]*
Q3 power = voltage × current
current = power ÷ voltage *[1 mark]*
$= 8.5 ÷ 2.5$ *[1 mark]*
$= 3.4$ A *[1 mark]*

Page 101 — Current and Mains Supply
Q1 In an alternating current (a.c.) supply, the current is constantly changing direction *[1 mark]*. In a direct current (d.c.) supply, the current always travels in the same direction *[1 mark]*.
Q2 E.g.

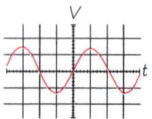

[1 mark for correct shape of graph]

Page 102 — The Ring Main
Q1 Each wire has less current flowing through it so thinner wires can be used. This saves money as less metal is used *[1 mark]*.

Page 103 — Fuses and Circuit Breakers
Q1 $I = V ÷ R$
$= 230 ÷ 25$ *[1 mark]*
$= 9.2$ A *[1 mark]*
A 13 A fuse should be used in the kettle *[1 mark]*.

Unit 3b — Energy

Page 105 — Efficiency and Sankey Diagrams
Q1 a) Convert W to kW by dividing by 1000:
$750 ÷ 1000 = 0.75$ kW
units of energy = power × time
$= 0.75$ W × 2 hours *[1 mark]*
$= 1.5$ kWh *[1 mark]*
b) Total number of units used
$= 10 × 1.5$ kWh $= 15$ kWh *[1 mark]*
cost = units of energy × cost per unit
$= 15 × 0.14$ *[1 mark]*
$= £2.10 / 210$p (units needed) *[1 mark]*

Page 106 — Energy Resources
Q1 Any two from: e.g. coal, oil, gas, nuclear *[1 mark each, 2 marks in total]*

Page 107 — Renewable Energy Resources
Q1 Advantage: e.g. no pollution *[1 mark]*
Disadvantage: e.g. can't work continuously as wind is not always consistent. *[1 mark]*

Page 108 — More Renewable Energy Resources
Q1 E.g. it disturbs the seabed / it disturbs the habitats of marine animals *[1 mark]*

Answers

Page 109 — Using Energy Resources

Q1 E.g. Electric cars are typically more expensive to buy than petrol cars *[1 mark]*. / Electric cars typically have a shorter range than petrol cars *[1 mark]*. / Electric cars take longer to refuel than petrol cars *[1 mark]*. / There are fewer different models of electric cars to choose from than petrol cars *[1 mark]*.

Page 110 — The National Grid

Q1 If the electricity was transmitted at a high current this would cause the power lines to heat up more *[1 mark]*. This causes more energy to be lost as thermal energy to the surroundings *[1 mark]*.

Page 111 — Density and Matter

Q1 Density = mass ÷ volume
178 ÷ 20 = 8.9 g/cm³
119 ÷ 14 = 8.5 g/cm³ (to 2 s.f.)
93 ÷ 10 = 9.3 g/cm³ *[1 mark]*
Mean density = (8.9 + 8.5 + 9.3) ÷ 3 *[1 mark]*
= 8.9 g/cm³ *[1 mark]*

Page 112 — Energy Transfer and Conduction

Q1 When an object is heated, the particles in the object gain kinetic energy and vibrate faster *[1 mark]*. These particles collide with neighbouring particles and transfer kinetic energy to them, increasing the kinetic energy of the neighbouring particles *[1 mark]*.

Page 113 — Investigating Energy Transfer by Heating

Q1 The student could attach material A and material B to the end of a thermometer *[1 mark]*. The student could then clamp the materials at the same distance away from a heat lamp, making sure that only the material (and not the thermometer) is illuminated by the heat lamp *[1 mark]*. The student could record the initial temperatures on the two thermometers and record the temperature on the thermometers after 10 minutes of the heat lamp being switched on *[1 mark]*. The material that is the better absorber of heat is the one attached to the thermometer that has gone up more *[1 mark]*.

Page 114 — Reducing Unwanted Energy Transfers

Q1 a) Cavity wall insulation:
payback time = installation cost ÷ annual saving
= 700 ÷ 200
= 3.5 years *[1 mark]*
Draught-proofing:
payback time = 150 ÷ 25
= 6 years *[1 mark]*
b) Cavity wall insulation *[1 mark]*

Page 115 — Evaluating Energy Costs

Q1 A scheme in which homeowners are paid for energy they produce and use from renewable energy resources *[1 mark]*.

Unit 3c — Waves

Page 117 — Wave Basics

Q1 a) E.g. an electromagnetic wave / a water wave *[1 mark]*
b) E.g. a sound wave *[1 mark]*

Page 118 — Wave Speed

Q1 $\lambda = 20$ cm = 0.2 m
$v = \lambda f$ so $f = v \div \lambda$
= 340 ÷ 0.2 *[1 mark]*
= 1700 Hz / 1.7 kHz *[1 mark]*

Page 119 — Reflection and Refraction

Q1 The frequency of the wave cannot change *[1 mark]*. Because $v = \lambda f$, the wavelength must decrease if the speed decreases *[1 mark]*.

Page 120 — Electromagnetic Waves

Q1 E.g. Damaged/destroyed cells / gene mutation / cancer *[1 mark]*.
Q2 X-rays, visible light, microwaves *[1 mark]*.

Page 121 — Uses of Electromagnetic Waves

Q1 A geostationary satellite remains in the same position above the Earth at all times, so it can remain in continuous contact/communication with a base station *[1 mark]*.

Page 122 — More Uses of Electromagnetic Waves

Q1 Any from: e.g. creating X-ray images to look at bones / cancer treatment / producing X-ray images of bags at airports *[1 mark each, 2 marks in total]*.
Q2 Any from: e.g. sterilising hospital equipment / tanning lamps *[1 mark]*.

Unit 4a — Classifying Organisms and Biodiversity

Page 124 — Classification

Q1 *Castor [1 mark]*

Page 125 — Adaptations

Q1 a) A behavioural adaptation *[1 mark]*.
b) E.g. it has flippers *[1 mark]* so it can swim for food *[1 mark]*. / A thick layer of fat *[1 mark]* so it retains heat *[1 mark]*. / A small surface area compared to its volume *[1 mark]* so it retains heat *[1 mark]*.

Page 126 — Factors Affecting Population Size

Q1 Any two from: e.g. competition / pollutants / number of predators / disease *[2 marks — 1 mark for each]*.

Page 127 — Biodiversity

Q1 Any three from: e.g. seed banks conserve biodiversity by storing seeds from a wide variety of plant species. / Sperm banks conserve biodiversity by storing sperm from endangered species. / Captive breeding programmes increase the number of individuals of a species. / National parks/SSSIs keep specific areas safe for wildlife, preventing hunting and habitat destruction. / The Convention on Internal Trade in Endangered species helps to protect endangered species through trade restrictions. / Local biodiversity action plans protect and restore biological systems through conservation. *[3 marks — 1 mark for each]*.

Page 128 — Investigating Ecosystems

Q1 0.75 × 4 = 3 buttercups per m² *[1 mark]*
3 × 1200 = 3600 buttercups in total *[1 mark]*

Page 129 — More on Investigating Ecosystems

Q1 E.g. they could mark out a line across the field, from the hedgerow to the middle *[1 mark]*. Then they could set out several quadrats along the line at regular intervals *[1 mark]*, and count all of the dandelions within each quadrat *[1 mark]*.

Page 130 — Biological Control and Invasive Species

Q1 E.g. invasive species may grow faster than native species / they may poison native species *[1 mark]*. This could upset the natural ecosystem by reducing biodiversity *[1 mark]*. Invasive species may out-compete native species *[1 mark]*. This could mean that native species are less able to find food/shelter, leading to a decrease in population size *[1 mark]*.

Unit 4b — Inheritance, Variation and Evolution

Page 132 — Chromosomes and Mitosis

Q1 Mitosis is when a cell reproduces itself by dividing to form two identical offspring *[1 mark]*.

Page 133 — Meiosis

Q1 two *[1 mark]*

Page 134 — Stem cells

Q1 The process by which a cell becomes specialised for its job/function *[1 mark]*.

Page 135 — DNA

Q1 A and T *[1 mark]*
C and G *[1 mark]*

Page 136 — Genetic Profiling

Q1 E.g. the DNA fragments are separated by size, using gel electrophoresis *[1 mark]*. Small fragments travel faster than big fragments, so they get further through the gel *[1 mark]*.

Page 137 — Sex Determination

Q1 XX *[1 mark]*
Q2 Male *[1 mark]*

Page 138 — Inheritance

Q1 Your genotype is the combination of alleles you have *[1 mark]*. Your phenotype is the characteristics you have *[1 mark]*.

Page 139 — Genetic Modification

Q1 Any two from: transplanted genes may get out into the environment. / Genetically modified crops could adversely affect food chains/human health. / Changing an organism's genes might create unforeseen problems that would be passed on to future generations. / Growing genetically modified crops might reduce farmland biodiversity *[2 marks]*.

Page 140 — Variation

Q1 Differences between members of the same species *[1 mark]* that have been caused by the environment/conditions something lives in *[1 mark]*.

Page 141 — More On Variation

Q1 Continuous variation is when the individuals in a population vary within a range *[1 mark]*. Discontinuous variation is when there are two or more distinct categories *[1 mark]*.

Page 142 — Asexual and Sexual Reproduction

Q1 There are two parents, so the offspring contain a mixture of their parents' genes *[1 mark]*. This mixture of genetic information produces variation *[1 mark]*.

Page 143 — Mutations

Q1 A mutation is a random change in an organism's DNA *[1 mark]*.
Q2 Ionising radiation *[1 mark]*

Answers

Page 144 — Cystic Fibrosis
Q1 Ff and ff *[1 mark]*

Page 145 — Natural Selection
Q1 Some of the musk oxen may have had an allele which gave them thicker fur *[1 mark]*. These oxen would have been more likely to survive and reproduce *[1 mark]* and so pass on the allele for thicker fur *[1 mark]*. This process of natural selection may have continued over many generations, until all the musk oxen had thick fur *[1 mark]*.

Page 146 — More on Natural Selection
Q1 Wallace provided evidence for natural selection *[1 mark]* and worked with Darwin to develop the theory *[1 mark]*.

Page 147 — Evidence for Evolution
Q1 Antibiotic-resistant bacteria are better adapted to their environment *[1 mark]* and as a result become more common in the population over time *[1 mark]*.

Page 148 — The Human Genome
Q1 A person's genes can be used to help predict what diseases they're most at risk of developing *[1 mark]*. This means that they could be given lifestyle and diet advice to help prevent them from getting the diseases *[1 mark]*.

Unit 4c — Nervous and Hormonal Control

Page 150 — The Nervous system
Q1 242 + 256 + 253 + 249 + 235
= 1235 *[1 mark]*
1235 ÷ 5 = 247 ms *[1 mark]*

Page 151 — Reflexes
Q1 Impulses are sent from receptors in his hand along a sensory neurone to the CNS *[1 mark]*. The impulse is transferred across a synapse to a relay neurone *[1 mark]*. It is then transferred across another synapse to a motor neurone *[1 mark]* and travels along the motor neurone to the effector (a muscle in his arm) *[1 mark]*.

Page 152 — Homeostasis
Q1 So that all the metabolic reactions that are vital for keeping you alive can continue to work at an appropriate rate *[1 mark]*.
Q2 receptor (cell) *[1 mark]*

Page 153 — Temperature Regulation
Q1 Less blood flows near the surface of the skin *[1 mark]* because blood vessels near the surface constrict (vasoconstriction) *[1 mark]*.

Page 154 — Controlling Blood Sugar Level and Diabetes
Q1 In type 1 diabetes, the person doesn't produce insulin *[1 mark]*, whereas in type 2 diabetes, the person still produces insulin but they are resistant to it/don't respond properly to it / don't produce enough of it *[1 mark]*.

Page 155 — Lifestyle Choices
Q1 The food a person chooses to eat can result in obesity *[1 mark]*. It is thought that obesity can directly cause type 2 diabetes *[1 mark]*.

Unit 4d — Disease

Page 157 — Pathogens
Q1 Any three from: e.g. in water / by aerosol / by contact / in body fluids / by insects / in food *[1 mark for each correct answer, up to 3 marks]*.

Page 158 — Fighting Disease
Q1 Blood clots seal cuts to the skin which would otherwise allow micro-organisms to enter the body *[1 mark]*. This reduces the number of pathogens that can infect the body and cause disease *[1 mark]*.

Page 159 — Vaccinations
Q1 They produce antibodies *[1 mark]* that attack the specific antigens present in the vaccine *[1 mark]*.

Page 160 — Antibiotics
Q1 Many antibiotics are being overused *[1 mark]*, which has caused antibiotic-resistant strains of bacteria to become more common *[1 mark]*. This means that many antibiotics are less effective at killing the bacteria that cause bacterial infections *[1 mark]*.

Page 161 — Developing New Drugs
Q1 For: e.g. at the moment, it's the safest way to make sure that a drug isn't dangerous before it's given to humans. *[1 mark]*
Against: e.g. experiments can cause animals pain and distress. / Some people think that animals are so different from humans that testing drugs on them is pointless. *[1 mark]*

Unit 5a — Bonding, Structure and Properties

Page 163 — Metallic Bonding
Q1 Copper is a good electrical conductor *[1 mark]* as it contains delocalised electrons which are able to carry an electrical charge *[1 mark]*.
Q2 Magnesium is made up of Mg^{2+} ions and sodium is made up of Na^+ ions *[1 mark]*. The greater number of delocalised electrons in magnesium means the electrostatic forces of attraction are stronger *[1 mark]* and so they need more energy to be broken *[1 mark]*.

Page 164 — Ionic Bonding
Q1 A calcium atom loses two electron to form a Ca^{2+} ion *[1 mark]*. Each fluorine atom gains an electron to form a F^- ion *[1 mark]*. The oppositely charged ions are attracted to each other by electrostatic attraction *[1 mark]*.
Q2

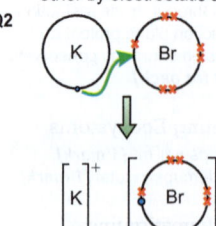

[1 mark for showing electron transferred from potassium to bromine, 1 mark for correct outer shell electron configurations (with or without inner shells), 1 mark for correct charges on ions]

Page 165 — Ionic Compounds
Q1 A lot of energy is needed to break the strong ionic bonds / electrostatic forces of attraction *[1 mark]*.

Page 166 — Simple Molecules
Q1

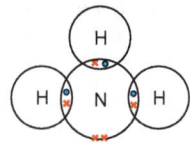

[1 mark for correct diagram (with or without inner shells)]

Page 167 — Giant Covalent Structures and Fullerenes
Q1 Each carbon atom in graphite forms three covalent bonds and has one electron that is delocalised and can carry charge *[1 mark]*. Each carbon atom in diamond forms four covalent bonds and so diamond has no delocalised electrons, meaning it cannot carry charge *[1 mark]*.

Page 168 — Nanoparticles
Q1 E.g. sun cream *[1 mark]*

Page 169 — Smart Materials
Q1 Heat both samples / place both samples in hot water *[1 mark]*. The shape memory alloy will return to its original shape *[1 mark]*.

Unit 5b — Acids, Bases and Salts

Page 171 — Acids and Bases
Q1 orange *[1 mark]*
Q2 alkaline *[1 mark]*

Page 172 — Acid and Alkali Strength
Q1 hydroxide ions / OH^- *[1 mark]*
Q2 A strong acid ionises/dissociates almost completely in water *[1 mark]*. A weak acid only ionises/dissociates partially in water *[1 mark]*.

Page 173 — Reactions of Acids
Q1 $2HCl + CaCO_3 \rightarrow CaCl_2 + H_2O + CO_2$
[1 mark for correct reactants and products, 1 mark for a correctly balanced equation]

Page 174 — Making Salts
Q1 E.g. add copper carbonate to acid in a flask until all the acid has been neutralised. At this point, no more copper carbonate will react and it will sink to the bottom of the flask *[1 mark]*. Filter out the excess solid using filter paper *[1 mark]*. Evaporate off some of the water from the salt solution and leave it until salt crystals form and filter off the crystals and leave them to dry / leave the solution to evaporate over a few days and allow crystals to form *[1 mark]*.

Unit 5c — Metals, Extraction and Energy

Page 176 — Metal Ores and The Reactivity Series
Q1 Tin is less reactive than carbon *[1 mark]* so you could extract tin from its ore by reducing it with carbon *[1 mark]*.
Q2 E.g. $2ZnO + C \rightarrow 2Zn + CO_2$
[1 mark for correct reactants and products, 1 mark for balanced equation]

Page 177 — Extracting Iron
Q1 $3CO + Fe_2O_3 \rightarrow 3CO_2 + 2Fe$ *[1 mark]*

Answers

Page 178 — Metal Displacement Reactions
Q1 Silver would not displace iron from iron(II) chloride solution, because it's below iron in the reactivity series/less reactive than iron *[1 mark]*.

Page 179 — Electrolysis
Q1 a) chlorine gas/Cl_2 *[1 mark]*
b) sodium atoms/Na *[1 mark]*

Page 180 — Uses of Metals
Q1 E.g. car bodies / bridges / cutlery *[1 mark]*

Page 181 — Transition Metals
Q1 E.g. Haber process / ammonia production and iron *[1 mark]*.
Q2 The iron(II) chloride will be green *[1 mark]* and the iron(III) chloride will be brown *[1 mark]*.

Page 182 — Sustainability of Metal Extraction
Q1 Advantage: building the plant near to a town means that workers can travel easily from their homes *[1 mark]*. Disadvantage: the plant might create noise/air pollution/a loss of the natural landscape so local residents might oppose the build *[1 mark]*.

Page 183 — Endothermic and Exothermic Reactions
Q1 The products are at a higher energy than the reactants so the reaction must be endothermic *[1 mark]*. This means the reaction mixture must have decreased in temperature *[1 mark]*.

Page 184 — Bond Energies
Q1 Energy required to break original bonds:
$(1 \times N{\equiv}N) + (3 \times H{-}H)$
$= 941 + (3 \times 436) = 941 + 1308$
$= 2249$ kJ/mol *[1 mark]*
Energy released by forming new bonds:
$(6 \times N{-}H)$
$= 6 \times 391 = 2346$ kJ/mol *[1 mark]*
Overall energy change:
$= 2249 - 2346 = -97$ kJ/mol *[1 mark]*

Unit 5d — Crude Oil, Fuels and Carbon Compounds

Page 186 — Fractional Distillation of Crude Oil
Q1 It suggests that the hydrocarbons in petrol have lower boiling points than those in diesel *[1 mark]*.

Page 187 — Crude Oil and Cracking
Q1 C_3H_6 *[1 mark]*

Page 188 — Hydrocarbons
Q1 Dodecane molecules are much bigger/longer than methane molecules *[1 mark]* and so there are more/stronger intermolecular forces between dodecane molecules than between methane molecules *[1 mark]*.

Page 189 — Burning Fuels
Q1 A fire needs fuel, oxygen and heat to burn *[1 mark]*. Putting a blanket over the fire blocks oxygen from getting to it, and so the fire cannot keep burning *[1 mark]*.

Page 190 — Measuring Energy Changes
Q1 Energy released per gram of fuel
$$= \frac{100 \ \square \ 18.7 \ \square 4.2}{0.2} \ \textit{[1 mark]}$$
$= 39\ 270$ J *[1 mark]*
$= 40$ kJ (2 s.f.) *[1 mark]*

Page 191 — Alkanes
Q1 C_8H_{18} *[1 mark]*

Page 192 — Alkenes
Q1
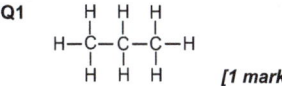
[1 mark]

Page 193 — Addition Polymers
Q1 Propene has a double covalent bond which can open up to join to other monomers *[1 mark]*. Propane is saturated so cannot form any more bonds *[1 mark]*.

Page 194 — Uses of Plastics
Q1 Any two from: e.g. it has a high melting point. / It is almost completely unreactive. / It has a very slippery surface. *[2 marks]*

Page 195 — Disposing of Polymers
Q1 E.g. if not controlled, toxic gases can be released from burning plastics / carbon dioxide is released when plastics are burned which contributes to global warming *[2 marks]*.
Q2 Polymers are made from crude oil *[1 mark]*. Crude oil is a finite resource *[1 mark]* so the more of it we use up, the more expensive it will become and this will increase the price of polymer products *[1 mark]*.

Unit 6a — Forces and Motion

Page 197 — Speed, Velocity, and Acceleration
Q1 First convert minutes into seconds:
$2.0 \times 60 = 120$ s
Then substitute this into the equation for speed:
$\text{speed} = \frac{\text{distance}}{\text{time}} = \frac{660}{120}$ *[1 mark]*
$= 5.5$ m/s *[1 mark]*
Q2 $a = \Delta v \div t$
$= 10.0 \div 3.5$ *[1 mark]*
$= 2.857...$
$= 2.9$ m/s^2 (to 2 s.f.) *[1 mark]*

Page 198 — Distance-Time Graphs
Q1 E.g.
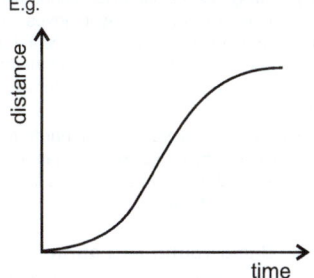
[1 mark for a continuous line that initially curves upwards, and which curves downwards at the end until it becomes horizontal. 1 mark for a straight middle section.]

Page 199 — Velocity-Time Graphs
Q1 E.g.
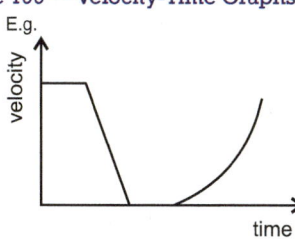
[1 mark for line which is initially horizontal, then bends to give a straight line with a negative gradient, continuing until it meets the time axis. 1 mark for showing the line then continuing horizontally along the time axis, and 1 mark for then showing the line curving upwards.]

Page 200 — Weight and Mass
Q1 a) $W = mg = 5 \times 10$ *[1 mark]*
$= 50$ N *[1 mark]*
b) $W = 5 \times 1.6$ *[1 mark]*
$= 8$ N *[1 mark]*

Page 201 — Resultant Forces
Q1 thrust $- 500 = 1300$
thrust $= 1300 + 500$
$= 1800$ N *[1 mark]*

Page 202 — Newton's First and Second Laws
Q1 $F = ma$
$= 26\ 000 \times 1.5$ *[1 mark]*
$= 39\ 000$ N *[1 mark]*

Page 203 — Terminal Speed
Q1 As the ball starts to fall, it accelerates towards the Earth due to the force of gravity *[1 mark]*. Air resistance increases with speed, so eventually the air resistance will be equal to the weight of the ball and the resultant force on the ball will be zero *[1 mark]*. The object cannot go any faster — this is its terminal speed *[1 mark]*.

Page 204 — Inertia and Newton's Laws of Motion
Q1 The rocket exerts a backwards force on the hot gases from the burning fuel *[1 mark]* and, due to Newton's Third Law, the hot gases exert an equal but opposite upwards force on the rocket, accelerating it upwards. *[1 mark]*

Page 205 — Work Done and Energy Conservation
Q1 20 cm = 0.2 m
$W = Fd$
$= 20 \times 0.2$ *[1 mark]*
$= 4$ J *[1 mark]*

Page 206 — Kinetic and Gravitational Potential Energy
Q1 $PE = mgh$
$= 0.80 \times 10 \times 1.5$ *[1 mark]* $= 12$ J *[1 mark]*
Q2 kinetic energy $= 0.5 \times \text{mass} \times \text{velocity}^2$
$= 0.5 \times 4.9 \times 2.0^2$ *[1 mark]*
$= 9.8$ J *[1 mark]*

Page 207 — Force and Extension
Q1 2 cm = 0.02 m
$k = F \div x$
$= 1 \div 0.02$ *[1 mark]*
$= 50$ N/m *[1 mark]*

Page 208 — Investigating Springs
Q1 20 cm = 0.2 m
$F = k \times x$
$= 40 \times 0.2 = 8$ N *[1 mark]*
$W = \frac{1}{2} \times F \times x$
$= \frac{1}{2} \times 8 \times 0.2$ *[1 mark]*
$= 0.8$ J *[1 mark]*

Answers

Page 209 — Improving the Energy Efficiency of Vehicles

Q1 E.g. properly inflated tyres / the right size tyre / materials designed to reduce rolling resistance / lightweight car design. *[1 mark]*

Page 210 — Stopping Distances

Q1 E.g. the vehicle's speed / the mass of the vehicle / condition of the brakes / the grip of the tyres / road conditions. *[1 mark]*

Page 211 — Vehicle Safety Features

Q1 a) Crumple zones crumple easily, increasing the distance over which the vehicle (and passengers) come to a stop *[1 mark]*. This reduces the force on the passengers *[1 mark]*.

b) E.g. air bags / seat belts *[1 mark]*

Unit 6b — Space Physics and Radioactivity

Page 213 — The Solar System

Q1 Jupiter / Saturn / Uranus / Neptune *[1 mark]*
Q2 An object that has been placed into orbit around a planet (or dwarf planet) by humans. *[1 mark]*

Page 214 — Sizes and Distances in Space

Q1 In increasing size order:
a planet, a star, a planetary system, a galaxy *[1 mark]*.

Q2 1 light year is the distance light travels in 1 year, calculate 1 light year in metres:
speed = distance ÷ time
so distance = speed × time
$$= 3.0 \times 10^8 \times 3.15 \times 10^7$$
$$= 9.45 \times 10^{15} \text{ m } \textbf{\textit{[1 mark]}}$$
The star is 4.5 light years away,
total distance $= 4.5 \times 9.45 \times 10^{15}$ m
$$= 4.2525 \times 10^{16} \text{ m}$$
$$= 4.3 \times 10^{16} \text{ m (to 2 s.f.) } \textbf{\textit{[1 mark]}}$$

Page 215 — The Life Cycle of Stars

Q1 E.g. when the Sun runs out of hydrogen to fuse *[1 mark]*, the radiation pressure will be smaller than the gravitational force *[1 mark]*. The core of the Sun will contract until helium can fuse in the core *[1 mark]*. The fusion causes radiation pressure to be greater than the gravitational force. So, the outer layers will expand and cool and the Sun will become a red giant *[1 mark]*.

Page 216 — The H-R Diagram and the Solar System

Q1 Red giant / supergiant *[1 mark]*
Q2 A cloud of dust and gas, including elements ejected from supernovae *[1 mark]* was attracted together by gravity, causing the density of some areas to increase *[1 mark]*. The force of gravity eventually compressed parts of the dust cloud to enough to form the Sun and the planets *[1 mark]*.

Page 217 — Isotopes and Radioactive Decay

Q1 There is an imbalance between the number of protons and neutrons. *[1 mark]*

Page 218 — Radiation Properties and Decay Equations

Q1 $$^{238}_{92}\text{U} \longrightarrow ^{234}_{90}\text{Th} + ^{4}_{2}\alpha$$

[1 mark for the correct nucleon number of uranium, 1 mark for a correct alpha particle symbol and nucleon and proton numbers and 1 mark for the correct nucleon number for thorium]

Page 219 — Half-life

Q1 24 days = 3 half-lives *[1 mark]*
activity = 1000 ÷ 2^3 *[1 mark]*
= 125 Bq
= 130 Bq (to 2 s.f.) *[1 mark]*

Page 220 — More on Half-life

Q1 a) The initial activity of the sample is 200 Bq, after 1 half-life this will have fallen to:
200 ÷ 2 = 100 Bq
Draw a line on the graph from 100 Bq on the y-axis, along to the curve, and then down to the x-axis:

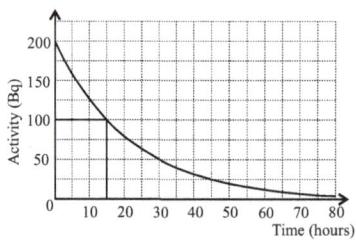

[1 mark for correct method to find the time taken for the activity to halve]
The time taken for the activity to halve
= 15 hours *[1 mark]*.

b)

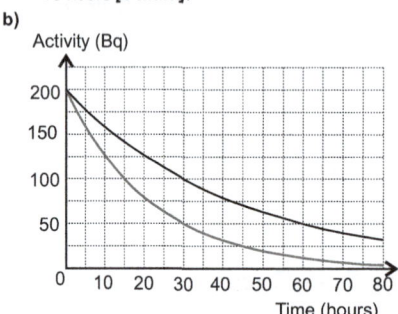

[1 mark for correct graph]

Page 221 — The Dangers of Nuclear Radiation

Q1 Alpha *[1 mark]*.
Q2 Beta and gamma radiation are penetrative enough to get inside the body from outside, and so can reach organs *[1 mark]*.

Page 222 — Uses of Radiation

Q1 Technetium-99 emits gamma radiation which can be detected outside the body / does not cause too much damages as it passes out the body *[1 mark]*. Its half-life is long enough for it to continue to emit radiation as it moves around the body and gets to the correct place in the patient's body / reasonably short so that the patient does not remain radioactive for too long *[1 mark]*.

Q2 Gamma rays are directed at a tumour from outside of the body *[1 mark]*. The gamma rays penetrate the patient's body and kill the cancerous cells *[1 mark]*.

Page 223 — Background Radiation

Q1 Radon gas is produced by certain types of rocks such as granite *[1 mark]*. The type of rock varies across the UK *[1 mark]*.

The Periodic Table

Periods

Relative atomic mass →

Atomic number →

Group 1	Group 2										Group 3	Group 4	Group 5	Group 6	Group 7	Group 0
1							**1** **H** Hydrogen 1									**4** **He** Helium 2
2	7 **Li** Lithium 3	9 **Be** Beryllium 4									11 **B** Boron 5	12 **C** Carbon 6	14 **N** Nitrogen 7	16 **O** Oxygen 8	19 **F** Fluorine 9	20 **Ne** Neon 10
3	23 **Na** Sodium 11	24 **Mg** Magnesium 12									27 **Al** Aluminium 13	28 **Si** Silicon 14	31 **P** Phosphorus 15	32 **S** Sulfur 16	35.5 **Cl** Chlorine 17	40 **Ar** Argon 18

Period 4																
39 **K** Potassium 19	40 **Ca** Calcium 20	45 **Sc** Scandium 21	48 **Ti** Titanium 22	51 **V** Vanadium 23	52 **Cr** Chromium 24	55 **Mn** Manganese 25	56 **Fe** Iron 26	59 **Co** Cobalt 27	59 **Ni** Nickel 28	63.5 **Cu** Copper 29	65 **Zn** Zinc 30	70 **Ga** Gallium 31	73 **Ge** Germanium 32	75 **As** Arsenic 33	79 **Se** Selenium 34	80 **Br** Bromine 35 / 84 **Kr** Krypton 36

Period 5:
85 **Rb** Rubidium 37, 88 **Sr** Strontium 38, 89 **Y** Yttrium 39, 91 **Zr** Zirconium 40, 93 **Nb** Niobium 41, 96 **Mo** Molybdenum 42, 98 **Tc** Technetium 43, 101 **Ru** Ruthenium 44, 103 **Rh** Rhodium 45, 106 **Pd** Palladium 46, 108 **Ag** Silver 47, 112 **Cd** Cadmium 48, 115 **In** Indium 49, 119 **Sn** Tin 50, 122 **Sb** Antimony 51, 128 **Te** Tellurium 52, 127 **I** Iodine 53, 131 **Xe** Xenon 54

Period 6:
133 **Cs** Caesium 55, 137 **Ba** Barium 56, 139 **La** Lanthanum 57, 178 **Hf** Hafnium 72, 181 **Ta** Tantalum 73, 184 **W** Tungsten 74, 186 **Re** Rhenium 75, 190 **Os** Osmium 76, 192 **Ir** Iridium 77, 195 **Pt** Platinum 78, 197 **Au** Gold 79, 201 **Hg** Mercury 80, 204 **Tl** Thallium 81, 207 **Pb** Lead 82, 209 **Bi** Bismuth 83, 209 **Po** Polonium 84, 210 **At** Astatine 85, 222 **Rn** Radon 86

Period 7:
223 **Fr** Francium 87, 226 **Ra** Radium 88, 227 **Ac** Actinium 89, 261 **Rf** Rutherfordium 104, 262 **Db** Dubnium 105, 266 **Sg** Seaborgium 106, 264 **Bh** Bohrium 107, 277 **Hs** Hassium 108, 268 **Mt** Meitnerium 109, 271 **Ds** Darmstadtium 110, 272 **Rg** Roentgenium 111

Formula Triangles

It's pretty important to learn how to put any formula into a triangle. There are two easy rules:

1) If the formula is "$A = B \times C$" then A goes on the top and $B \times C$ goes on the bottom.

2) If the formula is "$A = B \div C$" then B must go on the top (because that's the only way it'll give "B divided by something") — and so pretty obviously A and C must go on the bottom.

Two Examples:

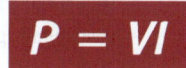

turns into:

$$P = VI$$

$$I = V \div R$$

turns into:

How to use them: Cover up the thing you want to find and write down what's left showing.

EXAMPLE: To find V from the first one, cover up V and you get $\frac{P}{I}$ left showing, so "$V = \frac{P}{I}$".

Using Formulas — the Three Rules:

1) Find a formula which contains the thing you want to find together with the other things which you've got values for. Convert that formula into a formula triangle.

2) Think very carefully about all the units, then stick the numbers in.

3) Work out the answer and check that it is sensible.

Index

Index

Index